H-L·Kahn
Stanford 1977

PEKING POLITICS,
1918-1923

MICHIGAN STUDIES ON CHINA
*Published for the Center for Chinese Studies
of the University of Michigan*

北京政治

PEKING POLITICS,

1918-1923

*Factionalism and the Failure
of Constitutionalism*

BY ANDREW J. NATHAN

虹橋書店

Rainbow-Bridge Book Co.

中華民國六十六年 三 月十六日第一版
內政部登記證內版臺業字第〇〇四六號
發 行 人：孫 國 仁
住 址：臺北市峨眉街107號
發 行 所：虹 橋 書 店
發行所地址：臺北市峨眉街107號
印 刷 所：合興彩色印刷有限公司
印刷所地址：台北市大理街130巷2弄1號

To Sharon

CONTENTS

vii

TABLES AND FIGURES

TABLES

FIGURES

ACKNOWLEDGMENTS

It is a pleasure and a shock to see how long and venerable is the list of teachers, colleagues, friends, and institutions with whom this project brought me into profitable association. The seed was planted as early as my first undergraduate year at Harvard by John K. Fairbank's lectures; his guidance and stimulation from then on were a nurturing medium. As the study grew into a dissertation, it was stimulated by the friendship and intellectual lucidity of Ezra F. Vogel and shaped by the supervision and suggestions of Benjamin I. Schwartz and Samuel P. Huntington.

As an itinerant researcher, I was generously received by scholars and librarians. In Taiwan, Ho Lieh patiently shared his deep understanding of modern China. Chang P'eng-yuan bestowed the intellectual excitement of frequent discussions. Professor Kuo T'ing-i, then Director of the Institute of Modern History of the Academia Sinica, allowed access to his superb manuscript chronology of republican China. I am also grateful to Kuo Cheng-chao, Liu Feng-han, Shen Yun-lung, and Wang Erh-min of the Institute; to Wu Chien-hsiung, who helped with the compilation of biographical material; and to the staff of the Kuomintang Party History Archives in Taichung, who made available important materials.

In Japan, I worked mainly at the Tōyō Bunko, where Professor Ichiko Chūzō was generous with advice and introductions. Yamamoto Masayuki taught me to read the Japanese of the Taishō era. Thanks also for research guidance to John T. Ma of the Hoover Institution, T. K. Tong of the East Asian Library of Columbia University, Eugene Wu of the Harvard-Yenching Library, and the staff of the Public Record Office in London. Valuable comments and criticisms on sections of the dissertation came from Ellen Frost, Charles W. Hayford, Roy Hofheinz, Jr., John Houston, Carl F. Nathan, Evelyn Sakakida Rawski, Thomas G. Rawski, Robert H. Silin, Mi Chu Wiens, and Edwin A. Winckler.

After the dissertation came the equally important task of rethinking and rewriting. In an informal seminar on republican China at the Center for Chinese Studies of the University of Michigan, I received thoughtful and unstinting criticisms from Ch'i Hsi-sheng, Joseph W. Esherick, Albert Feuerwerker, Rhoads Murphey, Andrea Solomon, Ronald Suleski, and Ernest P. Young. At the East Asian Institute of Columbia University, sections of the manuscript received critical readings from Dorothy Borg, Richard C. Bush, Donald W. Klein, Steven I. Levine, Kenneth Lieberthal, C. Martin Wilbur, and David C. Wilson. Thomas A. Metzger made valuable comments on Chapter I. Sharon G. Nathan helped clarify the factionalism model presented in Chapter II. Anonymous readers for the *Journal of Asian Studies* and the University of California Press provided useful comments. The late Maeve Southgate wrestled with the problem of a title. Mervyn Adams Seldon skillfully edited the final manuscript. I wish also to draw attention to the names of those acknowledged in my *China Quarterly* article, "A Factionalism Model for CCP Politics," part of which reappears in Chapter II. I am grateful to the Columbia University Press for permission to base the map in this volume on the map, "China in the Warlord Era," in O. Edmund Clubb, *Twentieth Century China* (New York, 1964); to Professor Clubb for lending me the original copy of that map; and to Henry H. Wiggins and Lee Chong of the Press for helping arrange for revisions of the original.

In addition to the University of Michigan Center for Chinese Studies, this research received financial support from the National Defense Education Act fellowship program, the Foreign Area Fellowship Program, the Columbia University Council on the Social Sciences, the East Asian Institute of Columbia University, and the Guggenheim Foundation. Neither they nor my intellectual abettors can be held responsible for the study's errors and shortcomings, except that without their help these would never have come to be sufficiently mixed with nonerrors and nonshortcomings to see the light of day.

A NOTE ON CURRENCY

The average 1920 exchange rate at Shanghai in customs taels (an arbitrary standard used only in customs transactions) for the currencies mentioned in this book was as follows:

One customs tael = English £0 6s 9.5d
= U.S. $1.24
= Japanese ¥ 2.38
= Mex. $1.58 or 1.58 Chinese yuan
= Shanghai taels 1.1140

The rates varied from month to month and year to year; in 1920, the exchange value of the customs tael was relatively high.

Mexican dollars, American trade dollars, and other foreign dollars, all standing for the same intrinsic value, were brought into China from the mid-nineteenth century on. In the late Ch'ing, provincial mints began to issue dollars, taking the Mexican dollar as the standard of value. The various Chinese dollars (yuan) such as the Peiyang dollar (Tientsin), Ta-Ch'ing dollar (Tientsin), Szechwan dollar, Fengtien dollar, Kiangsu dollar, Sun Yat-sen dollar (Nanking), Li Yuan-hung dollar (Wuchang), and Yuan Shih-k'ai dollar (Tientsin) were exchanged at a premium or discount depending upon distance from the place of issue and other factors, while the Mexican dollar remained at par everywhere. From 1914 on, national government accounts and Chinese banking accounts were legally required to be expressed in yuan. Commercial transactions were often expressed in taels (of which there were many kinds). Most foreign obligations of the Chinese Government were contracted in foreign currencies. Unless otherwise specified, figures are given in U.S. dollars.

Sources: *The China Year Book 1921–2*, pp. 286–88; *The China Year Book 1924–5*, p. 699; A.W. Fervin, *Chinese Currency and Finance* (Washington, D.C., 1919), pp. 11–13.

CHRONOLOGY

Note: Information in Peking heads of state column is complete; in others, it is selective. Unless otherwise noted, the head of state in Peking held the title of president.

Head of State in Peking	Prime Minister in Peking	Head of State in Canton	Major Events
Yuan Shih-k'ai (provisional president); March 10, 1912–October 10, 1913 (president); October 10, 1913– June 6, 1916			
Li Yuan-hung; June 7, 1916–July 2, 1917			Chang Hsun restoration; July 1–12, 1917
Feng Kuo-chang; August 1, 1917– October 10, 1918		Sun Yat-sen (marshal of military government); September 1, 1917– May 4, 1918	
Hsu Shih-ch'ang; October 10, 1918– June 2, 1922	Ch'ien Neng-hsun; October 10, 1918– June 13, 1919		
	Kung Hsin-chan; June 13–September 24, 1919	Ts'en Ch'un-hsuan et al. (directors of military government); May 20, 1918–June 3, 1920	Incident of May 4, 1919

Head of State in Peking	Prime Minister in Peking	Head of State in Canton	Major Events
	Chin Yun-p'eng; September 24, 1919–May 14, 1920		Anfu-Chihli war; July 14–19, 1920
	Chou Tzu-ch'i; April 9–June 12, 1922	Sun Yat-sen (extraordinary president); May 5, 1921–June 16, 1922 (expelled)	First Chihli-Fengtien war; April 28–May 5, 1922
Li Yuan-hung; June 11, 1922–June 13, 1923	Yen Hui-ch'ing; June 11–August 5, 1922		
	T'ang Shao-i (did not take office)		
	Wang Ch'ung-hui ("able men cabinet"); September 19–November 29, 1922		
	Wang Ta-hsieh; November 29–December 11, 1922		
	Wang Cheng-t'ing; December 11, 1922–January 4, 1923		
Kao Ling-wei (regency cabinet); June 14–October 10, 1923	Chang Shao-tseng; January 4–June 6, 1923	Sun Yat-sen (marshal); March 1, 1923–March 12, 1925	
Ts'ao K'un; October 10, 1923–November 3, 1924			
Huang Fu (regency cabinet); November 2–23, 1924			Second Chihli-Fengtien war October 13–23, 1924

Head of State
in Peking

Tuan Ch'i-jui (pro-
visional chief execu-
tive); November 24,
1924–April 20, 1926

Yen Hui-ch'ing, Tu
Hsi-kuei, Welling-
ton Koo (regency
cabinets); May 13,
1926–June 17, 1927

Chang Tso-lin
(marshal); June 18,
1927–June 3, 1928

Sources: Liu Shou-lin, *Hsin-hai i-hou shih-ch'i nien chih-kuan nien-piao* (Peking, 1966), pp.
4–5, 230–31; Kao Yin-tsu, *Chung-hua min-kuo ta-shih chi* (Taipei, 1957).

ABBREVIATIONS

AHKC	Nan-hai yin-tzu, *An-fu huo-kuo chi*
APSR	*The American Political Science Review*
ATTA	Lai-chiang cho-wu, *An-fu ta-tsui an*
CQ	*The China Quarterly*
CWCY	Ta yin-chü-shih, *Cheng-wen chi-yao*
F.O.	Great Britain, Foreign Office Archives
GJMK	Gaimushō jōhōbu, *Gendai Shina jimmeikan*
GSK	Hatano Ken'ichi, comp., *Gendai Shina no kiroku*
HSC	Fei Hsing-chien, *Hsu Shih-ch'ang*
LSINP	Ts'en Hsueh-lü, *San-shui Liang Yen-sun hsien-sheng nien-p'u*
MJTC	Yang Chia-lo, *Min-kuo ming-jen t'u-chien*
NCH	*The North-China Herald and Supreme Court and Consular Gazette*
NPIHWH	Chu Ch'i-ch'ien, comp., *Nan-Pei i-ho wen-hsien*
PYCF	T'ao Chü-yin, *Pei-yang chün-fa t'ung-chih shih-ch'i shih-hua*
SKJ	*Shina kinyū jijō*
"SSG"	Tokō Fumio, "Shina seitō no genkyō"
STSP	*Shun-t'ien shih-pao*
TTMJ	Fei Hsing-chien, *Tang-tai ming-jen hsiao-chuan*
Who's Who	*Who's Who in China: Biographies of Chinese Leaders*, Fifth Edition

OUTER MONGOLIA

HEILUNGKIANG

°Tsitsihar

°Urga

Harbin

KIRIN

Kirin

MANCHURIA

SINKIANG

Urumchi°

CHAHAR
SPECIAL
REGION

JEHOL
SPECIAL
REGION

FENGTIEN

Shenyang°

SUIYUAN SPECIAL
REGION Suiyuan°

Kalgan°

Chengtehfu°

Paotow°

Peking°

°Dairen
Port Arthur

KANSU

Taiyuanfu°

Tientsin°

CHIHLI

KOREA

Sining°

TSINGHAI

Lanchowfu°

SHENSI

SHANSI

°Tsinan

SHANTUNG

°Tsingtao

Kaifeng°

Chengchow°

KIANGSU

TIBET

SZECHWAN
SPECIAL BORDER
DISTRICT

Sianfu°

HONAN

ANHWEI

°Nanking

Shanghai°

Lhasa°

Kangting°

SZECHWAN

Chengtu°

HUPEH

Hankow°

Anking°

CHEKIANG

NEPAL

Chungking°

Yochow°

Nanchang°

KIANGSI

Foochow°

BHUTAN

Changsha°

HUNAN

FUKIEN

KWEICHOW

Kweichow°

Amoy°

Yunnanfu°

KWANGSI

KWANGTUNG

YUNNAN

Nanning°

Canton°

Swatow°

FORMOSA
(TO JAPAN, 1895)

INTRODUCTION

On January 1, 1912, the world's oldest, most populous empire bowed to the tide of history and became a republic. Since the American revolution, one nation after another had adopted a constitution, often with remarkable regenerative results—Japan was the most impressive recent example. "The future of China is like building a railroad," Sun Yat-sen had pointed out. "Should we use the first locomotive ever invented or today's improved and most efficient one?"[1] Many Chinese expected the new China, with its up-to-date governmental machinery, to drive straight for national wealth and power.

Sixteen years later the dream was rubble. The republic had shrunk to a fig-leaf marshal's government run by Chang Tso-lin. Years of warlord devastation had ruined the agriculture and disrupted the trade of North China, and a major famine was imminent. The Kuomintang was poised to complete national reunification under its own auspices, bringing a merciful end to an experiment that had dragged on too long.

The republic's failure was a formative disappointment for twentieth-century Chinese politicians. In its matrix, the radical alternatives of authoritarianism and revolution were conceived. In 1923, Sun Yat-sen justified the Kuomintang's turn toward Leninist-style party organization by pointing out that persistent effort had "not enable[d] us to attain the aim of the revolution. That is, although military force had succeeded [in overthrowing the Manchus, Yuan Shih-k'ai and, in 1922, Hsu Shih-ch'ang], the revolution still had not been accomplished, because our Party still lacked power."[2] And Mao Tse-tung told Edgar Snow that warlord suppression of a student demonstration in Changsha in 1920 made

---

1. Cited in Michael Gasster, *Chinese Intellectuals and the Revolution of 1911: The Birth of Modern Chinese Radicalism* (Seattle, 1969), p. 138. Quotation slightly altered.

2. Ssu-yü Teng and John K. Fairbank, *China's Response to the West: A Documentary Survey, 1839–1923* (Cambridge, Mass., 1961), p. 265.

him "more and more convinced that only mass political power, secured through mass action, could guarantee the realization of dynamic reforms."[3]

The Chinese had "taken for granted," as Liang Ch'i-ch'ao perceptively commented in 1922, that if only foreign political organizations and forms could be introduced into China, "myriads of other problems would be solved."[4] Instead, in Sun Yat-sen's words, "The course of the revolution might be compared to that of a rock rolling down a mountainside leaving destruction in its wake and incapable of being checked until it came to rest on level ground."[5]

What went wrong? This book attempts to contribute to an understanding of that question by examining the workings of the Peking political system, showing how the informal political rules of factionalism undermined the formal political system of constitutionalism. This is not an attempt to explain why, in terms of larger economic, social, or cultural variables, a stable republic could not survive in China. It is an investigation rather of *how* constitutionalism failed, of the political processes that occurred under the early republic, and of how they undermined the new institutions in which such great hopes were placed. It is the story of how politicians who believed in constitutionalism were driven to destroy it by the short-term tactical requirements of their chosen political game.

An obvious purpose of such a study is to throw light into what is still perhaps the darkest corner of twentieth-century Chinese history. This book makes a beginning at sorting out the facts of a complex but fascinating period. Further, the warlord era has special importance because it formed later political leaders' image of the kind of chaos that could engulf China in the absence of strong political organizations. It is against the fear of backsliding into this type of politics that Chiang Kai-shek, Mao Tse-tung, and others have struggled to build a new political order.

Chinese political traits are illuminated when we study this, the most disorderly period in the history of modern China. Of course, Chinese political styles differ over time, class and region (although we would be hard put today to say concretely how), but any political culture reveals a great deal of itself when formal institutions decay and informal alignments and tactics come to the fore. Factionalism, the use of personal connections, the deployment of secrecy and rumor, the handling of timing and surprise, are subsidiary and perhaps underappreciated themes when the bureaucracy is strong; in the present case, they thrust themselves to the fore.

Finally, on the most abstract level, this book is intended as a contribution to the organizational analysis of political behavior. Factions are treated here as one

3. Edgar Snow, *Red Star Over China* (New York, 1961), p. 155.
4. Teng and Fairbank, *China's Response*, p. 271.
5. F.O. 228/3001, Despatch 19A, Jamieson to Peking, March 1923.

kind of political conflict structure. Just as the incentive and communications structures of a political party can be analyzed to reveal the constraints they place on cadres' behavior, just as the technological and ideological structures of an army can be probed to show what types of warfare they enable soldiers to fight—so factions can be described structurally, and their typical modes of conflict can be explained in organizational terms. This is the burden of Chapter II, which discusses factionalism as a general phenomenon as well as describing the particular shapes taken by early republican factions. (Concrete historical factions are described in the Appendix.)

If Chapter II's model helps light a way among the complexities of the case-study chapters, they in turn are meant to flesh out the meaning of the theoretical discussion. The two cases I have selected were key episodes in the decline of the constitutionalist faith in face of factional realities. The Anfu Parliament period, 1918–20—treated in chapters IV and V—saw the first full-scale effort to renew the republic with a fresh parliament and president in the aftermath of Yuan Shih-k'ai's and Chang Hsun's attempts to restore the empire. Under vigorous presidential initiative, it seemed possible that peace would be made with the dissident South, enabling China to seize at Paris the fruits of its entry on the side of the Allies into World War I. Instead, North-South talks collapsed, the Paris peace conference humiliated China, and the factional kaleidoscope turned to civil war. In 1922–23, as described in chapters VI and VII, the political public suspended its increasing cynicism to give the republic a last chance; the constitutional fabric torn by civil war was repaired with the restoration of the former president; and a cabinet of talents was appointed. But the problem of succession to the presidency gave rise to a bitter factional struggle that resulted in the decisive alienation of most Chinese from the constitutionalist faith.

Before we can investigate the failure of constitutionalism, we must understand the dream. Especially since constitutionalist beliefs have waned in the West where they started, it requires some effort of imagination to understand how sophisticated politicians could have believed in a constitution's power to save China. This is the problem discussed in the first chapter.

I

CONSTITUTIONALISM AND ITS FAILURE

In 1898, K'ang Yu-wei memorialized the Kuang-hsu Emperor, "I have heard that the strength of nations both east and west is due to the establishment of constitutions and the opening of national assemblies . . . . Can these nations be anything but strong when their rulers and the millions of their people are united in a single body?"[1] In 1906, the imperial edict ordering preparations for the adoption of a constitutional system of government argued in the same vein, "That other countries are wealthy and strong is primarily due to the adoption of a constitution, by which all the people are united in one body and in constant communication, sane and sound opinions are extensively sought after and adopted, powers are well divided and well defined, and financial matters and legislation are discussed and decided upon by the people."[2]

This belief in a constitution's efficacy to make China strong remained vital even as disappointments mounted after the formation of the republic. After Yuan Shih-k'ai's death in 1916, President Li Yuan-hung proclaimed, "The parliament must be summoned quickly to decide on the constitution, in order that the will of the people may be followed and the foundations of the nation consolidated"; and *The Chinese Social and Political Science Review* stated, "We believe that an early promulgation of the constitution is absolutely necessary to the consolidation of the national foundations. . . . The formal enactment of the organic law will go a long way in dispelling from the mind of the people the vague apprehension over a recurrence of political disturbance, in forestalling political adventurers from indulging in extravagant and unwarranted ambi-

1. Quoted in Richard C. Howard, "The Concept of Parliamentary Government in 19th Century China: A Preliminary Survey," unpublished paper delivered to University Seminar on Modern East Asia—China and Japan, Columbia University, New York, January 9, 1963, p. 21.

2. Quoted in Joshua Mingchien Bau, *Modern Democracy in China* (Shanghai, 1923), p. 7.

tions, and in setting up a standard whereby the people can learn to conduct themselves in their social, civil, and political relations."[3] Even as late as January 1926, with the republic a virtual corpse, one prominent educator-diplomat felt sufficient optimism to propose a constitutional panacea:

Let a small body of men of unimpeachable character and integrity be elected or appointed to form a Council of Elder Statesmen according to the fashion of Japan. . . . It is their duty to encourage or impeach all Government policies fearlessly and in the interest of the people. As their combined opinion will be respected by the whole nation, even cabinet ministers or military leaders will eventually have to take their counsels to heart. . . . China provided with such a national conscience, the President, the Cabinet Ministers, the Provincial Tuchuns or Civil Governors will be able to concentrate the authority of the Central Government and nationalize the finances of the country without much difficulty.[4]

Not that the republic's difficulties were ever unrecognized. Chang Hsun's 1917 restoration of the Hsuan-t'ung Emperor, the subsequent emergence of a rival Canton government, the Anfu-Chihli war of 1920, the first and second Chihli-Fengtien wars of 1922 and 1924—these episodes but punctuated a ceaseless series of military and civilian conflicts. As chaos deepened, however, politicians and intellectuals diagnosed causes and prescribed cures in constitutional terms.

According to one persistent idea, all problems could be solved if the original 1913 parliament, dissolved by Yuan in 1914 and again in 1917 in the course of the Chang Hsun restoration, could be recalled to finish writing a permanent constitution. (China during most of this period was governed under the Provisional Constitution of 1912). Once promulgated, the permanent constitution would set republican government on the right course. Finally put into effect in 1922, this proposal proved incapable of saving the republic.[5]

Another diagnosis, that of the federalists, argued that national disunity and military dominance of government were due to excessive centralization and that

3. Li Chien-nung, *The Political History of China, 1840–1928*, trans. Ssu-yu Teng and Jeremy Ingalls (Princeton, N.J., 1956), p. 356; "Editorial Notes," *The Chinese Social and Political Science Review* 1, no. 4 (December 1916): 1–2. The Chinese Social and Political Science Association was a group of Western-oriented Chinese and Westerners in China.

4. Y. S. Tsao, "The Cause of Democracy in China," *The Chinese Social and Political Science Review* 10, no. 1 (January 1926): 84, italics removed. Mr. Tsao (Ts'ao Yun-hsiang), holder of a Yale B.A. and a Harvard M.B.A. degree, was president of Tsinghua University and had formerly served in the Chinese diplomatic service; see *Who's Who in China: Biographies of Chinese Leaders*, 5th ed. (Shanghai, 1936; reprinted [Hongkong, 1968?], p. 234 (hereafter abbreviated *Who's Who*).

5. See Chapters VI–VII. Despite its failure, this idea persisted even after 1924; for example, the agitation of the old parliament M.P.'s for that body's recall in 1924–25, as reported in Hatano Ken'ichi, comp., *Gendai Shina no kiroku*, November 1924 and subsequent months (hereafter abbreviated *GSK*).

the condition could be cured by adopting a federal form of government that would grant more power to the provinces. A provincial constitution on federalist lines was adopted in Hunan in 1922, but the movement did not spread.[6] A third line argued that since the constitution was supposed to have been produced by parliament, and parliament's legal status had become confused, a national conference of all major political and military figures should be convened to cut the Gordian knot, agree on a constitution, and set the republic back on the right track. This idea was finally realized in the form of the Reconstruction Conference (*Shan-hou hui-i*) of 1925,[7] which, however, failed to arrest the accelerating slide into disorder.

Constitutionalist pipe dreams and protestations were greeted skeptically even by some contemporaries. "The Republic was never more than a sham," wrote one foreign observer; it was a comic opera in which "we see the most sedate and law-abiding people in the world temporarily swept with a fever for boyish adventures."[8] A distinguished Chinese political scientist called the republic a "farce," noting that "no fixed principles and no unchanging loyalties marked the factions."[9] A popular history of the republic, the *Min-kuo yen-i* [Romance of the republic], cynically assimilated the political struggles of the period to the genre of strategems played in popular novels by power-seeking rivals constrained only by the fertility of their imaginations.[10]

Contemporaries' skepticism is reinforced for late twentieth-century students by a growing body of social-science scholarship which rejects the former Western faith in constitutional engineering as the road to stable democratic government and looks instead to economic, social and cultural variables to explain political phenomena.[11] We now hold that "a republic cannot be

6. Li Chien-nung, *Political History*, pp. 403–404.

7. For examples of the conference idea, see Wu P'ei-fu's Lushan conference proposal, described in Li Chien-nung, *Political History*, p. 420; Liang Shih-i's conference proposal of 1922, in F.O. 228/2994, "Memorandum", by Mr. Mayers, Peking, February 9, 1922; Sun Yat-sen's concept of a citizen's convention (*kuo-min hui-i*) in late 1924 and early 1925, covered in *Ko-ming wen-hsien* 10 (1955) and *GSK*, January 1925, and following months. There are many sources for the study of the 1925 Reconstruction Conference (a study not undertaken here). Columbia University's East Asian Library has a set of the *Shan-hou hui-i kung-pao* (Reconstruction Conference gazette). Ko Kung-chen, *Chung-kuo pao-hsueh shih* (Taipei, 1964), p. 254, shows a sample of the *Shan-hou hui-i jih-k'an* (Daily publication of the Reconstruction Conference), of which copies may survive somewhere. Extensive coverage is given to the conference in *GSK*.

8. Upton Close (pseud. of Josef Washington Hall), *In the Land of the Laughing Buddha: The Adventures of an American Barbarian in China* (New York, 1924), pp. xii, xvi.

9. Ch'ien Tuan-sheng, *The Government and Politics of China, 1912–1949* (Stanford, Calif., 1970), pp. 61, 76.

10. Ts'ai Tung-fan, *Min-kuo t'ung-su yen-i* (Shanghai, 1936).

11. See, for reviews of the literature, Harry Eckstein, "Introduction: Constitutional

achieved merely by enacting republican constitutions and laws."[12] How could the early republican leaders have failed to wake up to this fact as mishap piled upon disaster? As Lyon Sharman puts it, "Our perception of the impracticality of [the republic's] policies has been so sharpened that is it difficult to credit even the leaders with the optimism that their words and actions so clearly expressed."[13]

But we will understand the republic ill if we content ourselves with analysis by ridicule. "The wrangles [over constitutions] might be unreal, but they nevertheless absorbed the interest of the literati-official class."[14] Politicians might often wield the language of constitutionalism for ulterior purposes, but it must been have a politically meaningful language to be worth using at all. If the republic commanded the loyalty of an ever-decreasing cadre of politicians and intellectuals, still those who continued for seventeen years to try to make it work did so on the basis of a true constitutionalist faith, whose sources and meaning to its proponents we must try to understand.

Social Sources

Only a small proportion of the 400 million Chinese around 1920 knew or cared anything about constitutionalism, and of these a still smaller group was so placed as to be able to attempt to put the belief into practice. The interests and outlooks of the political elite go some way to explain the appeal of the constitutionalist faith.[15]

Engineering and the Problem of Viable Representative Government," in Harry Eckstein and David E. Apter, eds., *Comparative Politics: A Reader* (New York, 1963), pp. 97–104; and Harry Eckstein, *Division and Cohesion in a Democracy: A Study of Norway* (Princeton, N.J., 1966), pp. 20–32, 269–87. Of course, this body of scholarship does not establish irrefutably that constitutional engineering cannot create stable government, but at the least it shows that the constitutionalist faith is not self-evidently true, but is an ideology requiring analysis. See Chapter III for a brief discussion of ways in which the republican constitution did affect politics.

12. Ch'ien Tuan-sheng, *Government and Politics*, p. 61.

13. Lyon Sharman, *Sun Yat-sen: His Life and Its Meaning; A Critical Biography* (Stanford, Calf., 1968), p. 140.

14. Ch'ien Tuan-sheng, *Government and Politics*, p. 74.

15. This section makes a first approximation at understanding constitutionalism in the early republic through what Clifford Geertz calls the "interest theory" of ideology, while the next section looks at the ideology as a system of meaning. Cf. Clifford Geertz, "Ideology as a Cultural System," in David E. Apter, ed., *Ideology and Discontent* (New York, 1964), pp. 47–76.

It is not easy to decide what analytical language to use in parsing the social composition of the early republican political elite. Traditional terminology for social levels is outdated for the 1920s; Western terms are forced. Broad terminology does not distinguish sufficiently

THE BUREAUCRATS

The most influential portion of the national political elite was in a broad sense bureaucrats—"members—actual, would-be, or recently laid off—of the military and civilian bureaucracy."[16] If Yuan Shih-k'ai can be called the "father of the warlords," it is equally true that the late Ch'ing bureaucracy fathered the early republican government as a whole. A military man or administrator who was in his forties during the warlord era had almost certainly passed the first ten or fifteen years of his professional career as a Ch'ing bureaucrat. As Sun Yat-sen is quoted as telling a British diplomat in 1923, "the premature outbreak at Wuchang . . . and the ensuing unlooked for adherence to Republican principles on the part of the whole nation, upset all calculations. Methods of Government had at once to be extemporized, and human instruments of Government on the spot immediately to be utilized. The upshot ha[s] been the concentration of power in the hands of officials of the old regime."[17]

On this occasion, Sun went on to say that "the professed republicanism" of the bureaucrats "was a mere cloak for personal ambition,"[18] but here he missed the point that constitutional republicanism, as it was then understood, was entirely consonant with the central values of the "new-style" bureaucrats who had become dominant in Peking by 1911. To the new-style bureaucrats, constitutionalism spelled modernization along Western lines, and, although the overthrow of the Manchu court was not something most of them actively favored, they did not balk at it so long as it implied no challenge to their administrative predominance. This predominance they had won in the course of the late Ch'ing reforms—reforms that achieved a considerable modernization of government through the establishment of new technically specialized institutions, including the New Army, with its foreign advisors, technical training for officers, and advanced weapons and medical techniques; the Ministry of Posts

---

among the upper social groups, while narrow terminology disguises intraelite connections. Analysis of elite social composition in terms of fathers' backgrounds is inappropriate in view of the rapidity of social change; categories based upon relations to the means of production ignore the complexity of elite members' careers. Terminology must be suited to purpose, and since the goal here is to relate political ideology to elite interests and outlooks, I have adopted a rough-and-ready set of categories, based essentially on occupation and style of life, which seem to illuminate the shared interests perceived by elite members. The generalizations offered in this section are tentative ones based primarily upon an impressionistic summary of the many politicans' biographies used for this study.

16. Fred W. Riggs, *Thailand: The Modernization of a Bureaucratic Polity* (Honolulu, 1966), p. 149. This broad definition permits us to speak about a social group rather than the incumbents of a set of organizational roles.

17. F.O. 228/3001, Despatch 19A, Jamieson to Peking, March 1923.

18. *Ibid.*

and Communications, which ran steamship lines, railways, telegraph and postal services, and a bank; and the ministries of Foreign Affairs, Interior, and Education. The new government organs had outdistanced the old central organs in power and importance so that, by the fall of the Ch'ing, the most powerful bureaucratic positions in the central government were held by officials whose .commitment to modernization was to prove stronger than their loyalty to the dynasty.[19]

The key to this sea-change in bureaucratic loyalties lay in the requirement of new kinds of institutions for new kinds of men. The staffs of the new, semi-modern late Ch'ing institutions commanded a far greater degree of specialized training and technical expertise than the bureaucrats of the tradition. Some were specialists in railway administration, finance, banking, communications, police administration, education, and the like. Others were experts in foreign ways: the foreign affairs technocrats whose command of foreign languages and customs suited them for the specific and increasingly important task of liaison with foreigners. Still others had special expertise in the area of military organization and leadership: for example, Yuan Shih-k'ai, who rose in the bureaucracy by virtue of military "merit" despite his lack of the usual examination degrees, or Chang Tso-lin, who proved his military abilities in the role of a bandit before being recruited, with his whole force, as a battalion commander. By and large, they were technocrats and active modernizers.[20] Their overriding goal was a strong China, their models the Western nations and Japan, where constitutions and national power seemed conspicuously linked.

On closer inspection one discerns three "generations" among the late Ch'ing specialist bureaucrats who became leaders of the republic.[21] Each generation's members regarded one another as being at roughly the same level of seniority,

19. See, e.g., Meribeth E. Cameron, *The Reform Movement in China, 1898–1912* (New York, 1963); John K. Fairbank, Edwin O. Reischauer, and Albert M. Craig, *East Asia: The Modern Transformation* (Boston, 1965), pp. 619–25.

20. The specialist bureaucrats of the late Ch'ing had predecessors throughout the history of Chinese bureaucracy and were especially anticipated by such mid-nineteenth-century figures as Hsu Chi-yü, a foreign affairs specialist of the Tsungli Yamen, or Tso Tsung-t'ang, a military official of poor peasant background. What is new in the last decade of the Ch'ing is the numerical and political florescence of these types and the increasingly modern and foreign technical content of their specializations.

21. These three generations included most of the major politicians of the era. A few born before 1860—Wu T'ing-fang (1846), Hsu Shih-ch'ang (1858), Wang Ta-hsieh (1858), Li Ting-hsin (1859)—were active in republican politics, but most surviving members of their generations, like Chao Erh-hsun (1842) and Chang Chien (1852), played only occasional roles as prestigious elders (*yuan-lao*) in republican politics. On the other hand, politicians born after 1890 were too young during the early republic to play prominent roles. Chang Hsueh-liang (1890) was an exception.

and each generation held distinctive political views that were formed by characteristic educational and career experiences.[22]

Men born in the 1860s belonged to the generation of the immediate followers of Yuan Shih-k'ai (born 1859). Tutoring in the Confucian classics in preparation for government examinations remained the normal education for this generation. Holders of the *chin-shih* degree who were born in the 1860s and later became prominent republican era politicians included, for example, Tung K'ang (1866) and Ch'ien Neng-hsun (1868). Yet the educational experience of some of the most prominent members of the generation included a degree of technical, foreign or new-style education. Chang I-lin (1864) and Liang Shih-i (1869) not only won traditional examination degrees but also passed a special public administration examination given in the late Ch'ing. Wang Chan-yuan (1860), Wang Shih-chen (1861) and Ts'ao K'un (1862) were among the earliest officers to graduate from the Peiyang Military Academy in Tientsin, which gave specialized military education. A few military officers not only studied in China but went abroad for further study: these included Tuan Ch'i-jui (1864), Li Yuan-hung (1866), and Chang Shao-tseng (1869). There were other types of specialized study for this generation, too: Chou Tzu-ch'i (1868) was a graduate of the Canton and Peking foreign language institutes. A few members of this generation, such as T'ang Shao-i (1860), even took the bulk of their higher education abroad.

These men were not made instant constitutionalists by their exposure to the new learning; constitutionalism was something most of them came to reluctantly after the disappointments of defeat by Japan in 1895 and the Boxer fiasco of 1900, or accepted as a fait accompli in 1911. Their commitment to the constitutional republic always remained imperfect (their generation provided the main support for the Ch'ing-restoration schemes that were discussed and occasionally tried), and their leadership of it was autocratic and personalistic. The new-style education had come to them too late in life—usually after a traditional period of home training in the classics, and, except for the few who studied overseas, without the added impact of an unsettling change of environment—and they had passed too long a time in the service of the Ch'ing to be anything but ambivalent republicans. But in the end, the commitment to mod-

22. Unless otherwise noted, the biographical information in the following paragraphs comes from the appropriate entries of the following sources: Gaimushō jōhōbu, *Gendai Shina jimmeikan* (Tokyo, 1924 and 1928), and *Gendai Chūka minkoku Manshū(tei)koku jim-meikan* (Tokyo, 1932 and 1937), hereafter abbreviated as *GJMK*, 1924; *GJMK*, 1928; *GJMK*, 1932; and *GJMK*, 1937 respectively; and Yang Chia-lo, *Min-kuo ming-jen t'u-chien* (Nanking, 1937) (hereafter abbreviated as *MJTC*). See further footnotes in subsequent chapters and appendix. Birthdates are given in parentheses; they must be regarded as approximate since sources often disagree on the exact year.

ernization and the fact that the republic left them in, if anything, enhanced positions of power, was sufficient to win their acquiescence in the experiment.

In the generation of the 1870s, the experience of new-style education became more common. Kung Hsin-chan (1871), for example, studied at the foreign languages school in Nanking; Wu P'ei-fu (187_) was a graduate of the Peiyang Military Academy. Another common pattern for this generation was to pass the *chü-jen* examination, then enter the bureaucracy, picking up special skills during subsequent assignments. Such *chü-jen* included P'an Fu (1870), Chu Ch'i-ch'ien (1871), Chang Kuo-kan (1872), Chang Hu (1875), and Wang K'o-min (1878), all experts in the area of finance. The pure classical education also remained in style: a prominent *chin-shih* of the 1870s generation was Hsiung Hsi-ling (1870). Overseas education, while still fairly unusual, continued to grow in importance: Ch'en Chin-t'ao (1870) studied at Yale University, Ts'ao Ju-lin (1875) at Waseda University, Yen Hui-ch'ing (1877) at the University of Virginia, Wang I-t'ang (1878) at Hōsei University.

As with the earlier generation, the new learning, if it came at all, came relatively late in the lives of the generation of the 1870s. Many of them had been sufficiently tutored at home in the classics to pass the examinations for returned students and enter the bureaucracy at high levels.[23] New-style education, if taken within China, retained a high traditional content, especially with regard to fundamental social and political values.[24] Students who went abroad tended to be from wealthy families with stakes in the status quo. For all these reasons, the 1870s cohort shared the fundamental political conservatism of their seniors. On the other hand, their greater exposure to both the technical and the political cultures of Japan and the West gave them greater facility in operating a republican form of government and providing administrative leadership in fields like railway administration, finance, and foreign relations. The generation was a generous supplier of cabinet ministers to early republican governments.

For the generation of the 1880s, pure classical education was no longer a realistic option. Those who began their training with classical study aimed at the examinations had to shift course when examinations based on the classical curriculum were abolished in 1905.[25] Young men of this generation who aspired

23. See Y. C. Wang, *Chinese Intellectuals and the West, 1872–1949* (Chapel Hill, N.C., 1966), pp. 79, 86–87. Ts'ao Ju-lin, Wang I-t'ang, Yen Hui-ch'ing, and Ch'en Chin-t'ao were all returned-student *chin-shih*.

24. This remained so as late as the Kuomintang period. See Allen Bernard Linden, "Politics and Higher Education in China: The Kuomintang and the University Community, 1927–1937" (Ph.D. diss., Columbia University, 1969), pp. 113, 182, 236–37.

25. For examples, see the biographies of Huang Fu in Howard L. Boorman and Richard C. Howard, eds., *Biographical Dictionary of Modern China* (New York, 1967–1971), 2: 188; and Chao Hsi-en in *Who's Who*, p. 19.

to government service had to prepare themselves either through new-style domestic education or by study overseas, or both. New-style domestic education must have been the path chosen by the majority of students, for example Yeh Kung-ch'o (1880) and Li Ssu-hao (1880), but one has the impression that among those who were to become especially prominent, overseas education was the more common experience. Examples of members of this generation who studied abroad before taking up careers in the bureaucracy are Hsu Shu-cheng (born 1880, graduate of Japanese Officers' Academy), Huang Fu (1880, Japanese Military Survey Academy), Ch'ien Yung-ming (1885, Kobe Commercial College), Chia Shih-i (1886, Meiji University), Chang Ying-hua (1886, Victoria University, England), Wellington Koo (1887, Columbia University) and Lo Wen-kan (1888, Oxford University).

The vast majority of students from this generation who studied abroad went to Japan. The Chinese student population in Japan exploded from about 100 students in 1900 to about 13,000 in the period around 1905. Some graduated from Japanese universities; others attended special schools established for Chinese students.[26] Transplanted to a student community in a foreign country with other students from all over China and from various age groups, they were thrown together as individuals and as members of the Chinese nation. At the same time, they were exposed to ideas of individualism, equality and freedom. There was a tendency to reject Chinese traditions, aggressively to copy Japanese and Western customs and fashions, and to adopt the view that "nothing Chinese was good and everything Western was worth emulating."[27]

Between the generation of the 1870s and that of the 1880s there was thus a major divide in elite political culture. It was the latter generation that contributed the senior leadership of the May Fourth Movement and provided the eldest major age cohort of Chinese Communist party leaders.[28] Of course, those whose career choice was to enter the Ch'ing bureaucracy under the tutelage and patronage of elder bureaucrats were not so radical as their to-be-Communist contemporaries. Over the chasm of a half century, their political style strikes us as sharing more of the assumptions of their elders than those of their radical contemporaries. But because they understood better and were more

26. Chi Ping-feng, Ch'ing-mo ko-ming yü chün-hsien ti lun-cheng (Nankang, 1966), pp. 154–55; Sanetō Keishū, Chūgokujin Nihon ryūgakushi (Tokyo, 1960), pp. 137–40.

27. Y. C. Wang, Chinese Intellectuals, p. 147; Sanetō, Chūgokujin, pp. 195–96. Such a rejection of Chinese ways, of course, was in many cases temporary, followed by a reaffirmation of Chinese values.

28. On May Fourth, see Chow Tse-tsung, The May Fourth Movement: Intellectual Revolution in Modern China (Stanford, Calif., 1967), esp. Chapter I and Appendix A. On the CCP, see Donald W. Klein and Anne B. Clark, Biographic Dictionary of Chinese Communism, 1921–1965 (Cambridge, Mass., 1971), 2: 1043.

committed than their seniors to the values underlying the republican ideal, they became the major in-house critics of the republic's failings. If the 1880s cohort shared with that of the 1860s an ambivalence about the republic, in their case it came not from a feeling that the republic might be going too far but from a frequent sense that it did not go far enough.

PROFESSIONALS AND POLITICIANS

The second major component of the early Republican national political elite consisted of the new professional and quasi-professional strata of educators, lawyers, engineers, journalists, modern businessmen and bankers. The emergence of such strata was a natural concomitant of the increasing complexity of late Ch'ing society. Banks, newspapers, modern colleges, courts and other specialized institutions demanded staff with professional qualifications, and new-style and overseas education provided individuals trained to fill the new roles. The late Ch'ing reforms gave a special impetus to the modernizing trend by translating and promulgating foreign laws that required the establishment of professional associations (fa-t'uan)—chambers of commerce, lawyers' associations, bankers' associations—for self-regulation of the infant professions. Because the fa-t'uan were charged with quasi-governmental functions, the professions, unlike such other middle class groups as students and small businessmen, came to be regarded as sectors of the elite with legitimate voices in public affairs.

The origins of fa-t'uan lay in a series of laws that the government promulgated between about 1903 and 1915, which required certain professions to organize themselves in "associations established by law," and charged them with a range of quasi-governmental functions. In 1903, regulations were published which provided for the establishment of chambers of commerce (shang-wu hui) in the various commercial centers and ordered that "in addition to the duties discharged by the chambers of commerce in foreign countries, they be responsible for unifying the protection of industry, fiscal policy, regulation of prices, and the accounts of enterprises; managing registration of enterprises, copyrights, patents, and licenses; and settling commercial disputes."[29] Under regulations promulgated in 1912, lawyers' associations (lü-shih hui), to which every practicing lawyer was obliged to belong, were charged with "maintaining the morality of the legal profession, and . . . determin[ing] the scale of fees and costs." An association had the right to recommend to the procurator of the local court that a member be expelled from the bar for offending association rules.[30]

29. Kōjima Shōtarō, *Shina saikin daiji nempyō* (Tokyo, 1942), p. 291. See also John Stewart Burgess, *The Guilds of Peking* (Taipei, 1966), p. 228.
30. *The China Year Book 1919–20*, pp. 696–97; Kōjima Shōtarō, *Daiji nempyō*, p. 340.

Bankers' associations (*yin-hang kung-hui*) were established in each banking center under a government order of August 1915.[31] While the government did not require journalists to form professional associations, it did backhandedly recognize their professional and political status by promulgating a series of laws setting qualifications for, and requiring the registration of, editors, writers, publishers and printers, and setting limits on what could be printed. The quasi-official role of the press was also institutionalized in the subsidies which most newspapers received from government organs or political groups. National and local journalists' associations were formed, in part to handle relations between the press and the government.[32]

The political role of the *fa-t'uan* was even greater than suggested by their legal duties. At times of disorder and stress, they often exercised additional political functions, such as raising troops and keeping order (chambers of commerce) and imposing fiscal policies on the government (bankers' associations).[33] They worked closely with government ministries in their areas of interest to define and carry out policy.[34] Chambers of commerce often served as the representatives of local communities in dealing with warlords, sometimes raising money to bribe warlords not to enter their cities. From time to time, chambers of commerce and other *fa-t'uan* issued public telegrams calling for civil peace or supporting certain stands on foreign relations, fiscal policy, and the like.[35] And when politicians or warlords issued public telegrams (*t'ung-tien*),

31. Kōjima Shōtarō, *Daiji nempyō*, p. 415. Although the order was published in 1915, bankers' associations in Shanghai and Peking were not formed until 1918. *Ibid.*, p. 444.

32. Ko Kung-chen, *Pao-hsueh shih*, pp. 372, 395, 409–47; Roswell S. Britton, *The Chinese Periodical Press, 1800–1912* (Taipei, 1966), p. 128.

33. On chambers of commerce, see John Fincher, "Political Provincialism and the National Revolution," in Mary Clabaugh Wright, ed., *China in Revolution: The First Phase, 1900–1913* (New Haven, Conn., 1968), p. 216; Burgess, *Guilds*, p. 221; Marie-Claire Bergère, "The Role of the Bourgeoisie," in Wright, ed., *China in Revolution*, pp. 249, 268; Albert Feuerwerker, *China's Early Industrialization: Sheng Hsuan-huai (1844–1916) and Mandarin Enterprise* (Cambridge, Mass., 1958), p. 71. On bankers' associations, see *Shina kin'yū jijō* (Tokyo, 1925), p. 729 (hereafter abbreviated *SKJ*); F.O. 371/6650, F1188/1188/10, Enclosure in Peking Despatch 70: "Memorandum by Mr. A. Rose, Commercial Secretary to the British Legation, respecting the Financial Situation in China," February 8, 1921, confidential print. See also discussion of banks in Chapter III.

34. See citations on bankers' associations in preceding footnote. Also see newspaper reports on the September 1924 National Industrial Conference in Peking: *Ching pao* 1924.9.2 in *GSK* 1924.9.17–27 and elsewhere. Also see report of the tenth annual meeting of the National Association of Education Associations: *I-shih pao* 1924.10.3 in *GSK* 1924.10. 275–78.

35. For examples from the period covered in this study, see Lai-chiang cho-wu, *An-fu ta-tsui an* (Peking, 1920), *chüan* 3, pp. 1–32 (hereafter abbreviated *ATTA*); also see, in F.O. 228/2990, the translation of a telegram from the Shanghai Chamber of Commerce to the ministers of Great Britain, the United States of America, France, and Japan, May 30, 1921.

the equivalent of today's press conference or policy statement, the addressees always included not only the "high civil and military officials of the provinces" but the "various professional associations" (*ko fa-t'uan*) as well.

The new professional strata, in short, enjoyed a relationship of formal and informal cooperation with the national government analogous to that traditionally enjoyed by the gentry. Indeed, to some degree they gradually replaced local landholding elites as the major recruitment pool and "public opinion" backdrop for twentieth-century Chinese national governments. The traditional examination system had demarcated the "gentry" as a monolithic national ruling class, which fused landed and commercial wealth, scholarship and office-holding, and whose members shuttled continuously between local and national political arenas. After the abolition of the classics-based examinations in 1905, wealth and status could best be translated into a national career through new-style or foreign education. But such education produced professionals and quasi-professionals, urbanites less likely to return for extended stays in the local community as landholders, local capitalists, and local influentials. At the same time, the increasing autonomy of local power centers, ultimately taking the form of warlordism, ended the ability of the center to control the appointment of most local officials or to validate local elites. National and local levels were increasingly distinct, the former dominated by specialist bureaucrats and professionals and the latter still to some extent the bailiwick of traditional landholders. In this way, the professionalization of the national elite went hand-in-hand with the growing alienation of the national political level from the rural hinterland. While arriviste landholding and military elites rivaled the old gentry on the local level, the professional strata succeeded to its position at the national level.

Because the new professional strata were so easily seen as a reincarnation of the gentry—educationally qualified to serve in government, literate and wealthy, most of them from gentry family backgrounds—the dominant bureaucrats were able to make a painless conceptual transition from the tradition of gentry participation in government to the potentially revolutionary idea of a "public opinion" of the urban professional classes. Less wealthy and educated sectors of the newly emerging urban "middle" classes—small and medium merchants, artisans, students—were rigorously excluded from the elite's conception of the legitimate public. Thus, although the early republican political elite was new in content—Confucian generalists had been replaced by specialists and professionals—it was not new in form: a bureaucracy and small surrounding public were knit together by common educational experiences and career qualifications but excluded participation not only by the masses but even by the other middle strata of society. The only innovation in the shape of political society was in the increased isolation of the central political arena from the nation as a whole.

Like the traditional gentry, the new professionals were able to participate in politics not only as members of organizations but also as individuals. Many of the 5,105 lawyers who achieved certification in China between 1912 and 1917[36] played prominent roles in republican politics: examples in the present study include Chu Shen,[37] minister of justice from 1918 to 1920, and Yao Chen,[38] an Anfu Club (*An-fu chü-le-pu*) leader. The role of big businessmen in politics is illustrated by the career of Pien Yin-ch'ang, a prominent Tientsin millionaire who was chairman of the National Chamber of Commerce, a member of the House from Chihli in the 1918–20 parliament, and a member of the Anfu Club. Pien's political connections were useful from a business standpoint (during his tenure in parliament, he steered through the ministries of Finance and Agriculture and Commerce the formalities for establishing the National Commercial Bank [*Ch'uan-kuo shang-yeh yin-hang*] for which he raised capital among various merchant colleagues[39]), and his Chamber of Commerce position was useful for his political activities (on May 17, 1918, the National Chamber of Commerce issued a public telegram implicitly laying the blame for national disunity on the rebel southwestern provinces[40]). K'ang Shih-to was an example of a prominent journalist in politics. According to a biographer, "In 1909, newspapers were beginning to develop in Peking . . . and K'ang became a hanger-on of several leading editors. Rushing between the National Assembly, the Board of Laws, and the Administrative Court, he sought news from fellow natives of Chihli. It was with K'ang that the Peking newspapers began the practice of openly seeking news. . . . Using his status as a reporter, he became familiar with many officials and politicians, and rapidly became more self-assertive."[41] K'ang was an Anfu Club leader in the 1918–20 parliament. Professional bankers often served as members of parliament or government officials. Examples in this study include Chou Tso-min, Feng Keng-kuang, Wang Yu-ling, and Wu Ting-ch'ang.

Among the new professionals, one type played a particularly prominent role in republican politics—the professional politician, that type of professional who, in Max Weber's definition, lives both "for" and "off" politics.[42] Men like

36. *T'ung-chi yueh-k'an* 3 (September 15, 1918), pp. 32–35.

37. *MJTC, chüan* 8, p. 32; *ATTA, chüan* 2, pp. 10–11; *GJMK*, 1932, pp. 150–51.

38. *GJMK*, 1924, p. 581; *GJMK*, 1937, p. 497; *ATTA, chüan* 2, p. 17.

39. *GJMK*, 1932, p. 330; *The China Year Book 1926–7*, p. 1191; Nan-hai yin-tzu, *An-fu huo-kuo chi* (n.p., 1920), 1:58 (hereafter abbreviated *AHKC*); *STSP* 1918.9.5.2.

40. Ta yin-chü-shih, *Cheng-wen chi-yao* (in special issue no. 1 of *Chin-tai shih tzu-liao*, Peking, 1962), p. 416 (hereafter abbreviated *CWCY*).

41. *ATTA, chüan* 2, pp. 19–20.

42. Max Weber, "Politics as a Vocation," *From Max Weber: Essays in Sociology*, translated and edited by H. H. Gerth and C. Wright Mills (New York, 1958), p. 84. The distinctions developed here among specialized bureaucrats, professional politicians, and other professionals are not hard and fast. Some careers, e.g., those of Chang Chien, Liang Ch'i-ch'ao and Ts'ai Yuan-p'ei, combined elements of all three.

Liang Ch'i-ch'ao and Sun Yat-sen, knocking at the door of government, finding it barred, and finding in the West and Japan alternate models for ways to influence the national polity, were late nineteenth-century pioneers and harbingers. From about 1900 on, the Tokyo Chinese student community proved a fruitful recruiting ground. Here students were exposed to notions of constitutionalism, nationalism and revolution, and to living examples of professional party men and revolutionaries, and some of them chose to forego bureaucratic careers to imitate these new patterns of political action. They chose between Liang's path of agitation and propaganda for establishment of a constitution under the Ch'ing and Sun's program of secret organization for a revolution to establish a republic.

The door on which the young political professionals were knocking was partially opened by the regime itself, pursuing its program of reform. The convening of the provincial assemblies in 1909 and of the National Assembly in 1910 provided an opportunity for many politicians to pursue their careers within the establishment. The typical late Ch'ing provincial assemblyman was young (average age, 41), wealthy, of gentry class origin; one-third had received new-style or overseas education.[43] Although these assemblies, like those in the republic, included bureaucrats, professionals, businessmen, landholders, and the like, it was the professional politicians who dominated and set the tone.[44]

The fact that the professional politicians had not served in the bureaucracy tended to relegate them permanently to peripheral positions in early republican politics. The pinnacles of power in the republic could be scaled only by bureaucrats and ex-bureaucrats. Few cabinet ministers and no presidents (with the brief exception of Sun Yat-sen) were professional politicians in our sense. Between parliamentary sessions, the politicians were forced to play the roles of intermediaries, brokers, and allies of the major bureaucratic factions. Their highest glory was reached when parliament was in session and the struggle to expand its powers could be pursued. In this struggle, the professional politicians, like their opposite numbers, the party politicians of Taishō Japan, often engaged in disruptive, obstructionist tactics and in blatant political opportunism. A contemporary writer described and criticized this behavior in the following terms:

As soon as you M.P.'s came to Peking in 1912, you started playing with party funds, scheming and plotting . . . joining as many as two or three parties each! Later, you demanded money to elect the president, money to elect the vice-president, money to confirm the cabinet—you even required money to declare war on a foreign country!

43. Chang P'eng-yuan, "Ch'ing-chi tz'u-i-chü i-yuan ti hsuan-chü chi ch'i ch'u-shen chih fen-hsi," *Ssu yü yen* 5, no. 6 (March 1968): 1439–42. Also see P'eng-yuan Chang, "The Constitutionalists," in Wright, ed., *China in Revolution*, pp. 149–53.

44. Cf. Cameron, *Reform Movement*, p. 122; also see Chang P'eng-yuan, "Ch'ing-chi tz'u-i-chü," p. 1442.

After Yuan Shih-k'ai dissolved parliament, you gentlemen served as officials or advisors until parliament was restored, upon .which you returned to serving as M.P.'s. After [the dissolution of parliament in] 1917 it was even worse: one day, you would run down to Kwangtung to serve as M.P.'s in the extraordinary session [convened by Sun Yat-sen]: the next, run back to Peking to serve as special appointees on the Economic Investigation Bureau (*Ching-chi tiao-ch'a chü*) [appointed by Sun's enemies]. Several of you served as special advisors in the Yuan Shih-k'ai period and as Anfu clique M.P.'s in the Tuan Ch'i-jui period, were elected after the Anfu-Chihli war to the "New-New Parliament" (*Hsin-hsin kuo-hui*) [which never met], and now [that the original parliament has been recalled once again], with the qualification of having been elected ten years ago, you come to serve as "elders of the sixth Imperial reign" [persons who have transferred their loyalty to a series of new masters].[45]

In addition to suggesting the length to which the parliamentarians would go in seeking to expand their precarious political toehold, the quotation also suggests how seats in parliament came to be considered almost as prebends, analogous to official appointments in old China.[46] Just as the republican notion of "public" was treated as an extension of the traditional concept of "gentry," so the office of "representative" in the republic was seen bifocally as "representative" and "office," with the latter perspective, defined by tradition, remaining dominant.[47] If the traditional *hsien* magistrate had made a living by attaching part of the revenue of his office, which consisted partly of fees for the performance of official duties, so the republican M.P. made a living by accepting gratuities (*chin-t'ieh*) for the performance of such official duties as voting on presidential and cabinet appointments and even on declarations of war. Such behavior persisted although more and more seen as corrupt, as contradictory standards were applied by simultaneous traditional and Western frameworks to a newly emerging role.

Intellectual Sources

Late Ch'ing modernization, we have argued, produced a new political elite dominated by new-style bureaucrats and professionals, including professional politicians. Constitutionalism served the interests of these groups because it offered each a legitimate political role without opening the political arena to the groups below them. (It was secondary whether the constitution should be monarchical or republican; the bureaucrats' lukewarm preference for the former

45. Ts'ung Yen, "Ch'ung-kao chiu kuo-hui i-yuan," *Nu-li chou-pao* 9 (July 2, 1922), p. 3.
46. For the idea of prebendalism in China, see Max Weber, *The Religion of China: Confucianism and Taoism*, trans. and ed. by Hans H. Gerth (Glencoe, Ill., 1951), p. 56 and *passim*.
47. Cf. Fincher, "Political Provincialism," p. 208, and P'eng-yuan Chang, "Constitutionalists," p. 147, note 12.

bowed before the politicians' insistent campaign for the latter.) Furthermore, a constitutional regime was consistent with the new-style elite's modernizing values and Western orientation. This point must now be examined more closely.

Granted that the notion of saving China through adoption of a constitution was consistent with the interests and training of members of this elite, what precisely did constitutional republicanism mean to them? Of course, not every early republican political figure accepted the constitutional faith, nor did those who did so accept it with equal commitment. But constitutionalism, as subsequent chapters will repeatedly illustrate, was the dominant set of assumptions to which the defense of political action had to be referred. That some may have appealed to constitutionalism half-heartedly or cynically does not alter the fact that it made sufficient sense to enough people in Peking in the years around 1920 to serve as the touchstone of political discussion. In what way did such an idea make intellectual sense?[48]

"The trust which men repose in the power of words engrossed on parchment to keep a government in order,"[49] although rooted in Greece and Rome, swept all before it in the West from about the time of Montesquieu's *The Spirit of Laws* (1748) and the American revolution (1776). The "floodgates of constitutional change" were opened, and the next century and a half saw scores of constitutions adopted throughout Europe and the Americas, and then Asia.[50] At the time of the early republic, the Chinese consulted with western experts, who confirmed the importance of a properly drafted constitution for nation-building. "The political troubles with which the Chinese have . . . been afflicted," wrote W. W. Willoughby, professor of political science at Johns Hopkins and for years a constitutional advisor to the Chinese government, "have been due not so much to a general lack of capacity to maintain a self-governing or representative scheme of political control as that they have been attempting to govern themselves under an essentially defective constitution."[51]

An earlier consultant, Frank J. Goodnow, Eaton Professor of Public Law and

48. This section by no means constitutes a study of the theories and positions taken in constitutional discussion in China over the years. Such a study would be of considerable interest and the materials are abundant, but the purpose here is only to sketch some common themes that underlay the vitality of the constitutional notion as such.

49. Walton H. Hamilton, "Constitutionalism," in Edwin R. A. Seligman, ed., *Encyclopedia of the Social Sciences* (New York, 1931), 4: 255.

50. John A. Hawgood, *Modern Constitutions Since 1787* (London, 1939), p. 4; Carl J. Friedrich, "Constitutions and Constitutionalism," in David L. Sills, ed., *International Encyclopedia of the Social Sciences*, (New York, 1968), 3: 323; Hamilton, "Constitutionalism," p. 255.

51. W. W. Willoughby, *Constitutional Government in China: Present Conditions and Prospects* (Washington, D.C., 1922), p. 33.

Municipal Science at Columbia University, returning in disillusionment to the United States when the draft constitution he had prepared was not adopted, had remarked, "The Chinese wanted me to teach them politics. But I was not a politician. I was just interested in the scientific and theoretical side of administrative law."[52] This was a pregnant distinction. "It is by no means accidental," Karl Loewenstein notes, "that the climate for the birth of the written constitution was the eighteenth century, fascinated not only by what were believed to be the imperatives of natural law but also by the application of the laws of nature to social dynamics. The science of mechanics was transferred to the science of government."[53] Western constitutional thinkers assumed that constitutions could be "engineered" to put predictable human forces in a balance that would be self-regulating. There could, therefore, be a "science" of politics, which specialized in such constitutional engineering. How to achieve the obedience of political actors to the written rules—the problem of legitimacy—was not recognized as a problem in this science. "We look in vain for any theory of political education, of political leadership, or, until recently, of social consensus."[54] As with Willoughby, the answer to the failure of constitutions was better engineering.

This view, dominant in Western political science until after World War II[55], fell on fertile Chinese intellectual soil. The sheer prestige and self-confidence of the West, the desire in some Chinese circles to achieve world acceptance by

52. *Baltimore News*, 1928.1.16 (made available to me by Professor Y. C. Wang). More than most of his contemporaries, Goodnow stressed the adaptation of constitutional provisions to social and cultural realities (a belief that helped get him into the position of backing Yuan Shih-k'ai's ill-fated attempt to restore the emperorship; see Noel Pugach, "Embarrassed Monarchist: Frank J. Goodnow and Constitutional Development in China, 1913–1915," *Pacific Historical Review* 42, no. 4 (November 1973: 499–517). But he shared the key assumption that a constitution properly adapted to variations in the human material could serve as a blueprint for political stability. For example, his Peking University lectures (published as *Principles of Constitutional Government* [New York, 1916]) affirm briefly that the constitution does not necessarily tell how the political game is really played but move immediately to detailed descriptions of the constitutional systems of various countries, reprinting in an appendix the American, French, German, Belgian, and Japanese constitutions.

53. Karl Loewenstein, "Reflections on the Value of Constitutions in Our Revolutionary Age," in Eckstein and Apter, eds., *Comparative Politics*, p. 150.

54. Sheldon S. Wolin, *Politics and Vision: Continuity and Innovation in Western Political Thought* (Boston, 1960), p. 390.

55. See further Harry Eckstein, "A Perspective on Comparative Politics, Past and Present," in Eckstein and Apter, eds., *Comparative Politics*, pp. 3–32; Albert Somit and Joseph Tanenhaus, *The Development of American Political Science: From Burgess to Behavioralism* (Boston, 1967), pp. 68–69. For a book as recent as 1963, which stresses constitutional engineering, see C. F. Strong, *A History of Modern Political Constitutions* (New York, 1964).

becoming more like the Western nations, and the evident success of constitutional regimes in becoming world powers, were only the more obvious motives for imitation. There was also the vogue of scientism in Chinese thought—the belief in the efficacy of a mechanistic version of modern science to solve human problems. Just as part of the attraction of "scientific" Marxism in both the West and China was its claimed linkage with the nature-mastering powers of science, so modern "political science" laid claim to the same secondhand charisma. Like Marxism a few years later, constitutionalism seemed to link what Ch'en Tu-hsiu was to call Mr. Te (democracy) and Mr. Sai (science) by providing for democracy to be scientifically engineered.[56]

Even more fundamentally, the faith in constitutions fell in with a deep-seated Chinese belief in the dominant role of the conscious mind in the process of action. Confucius had traced the ordering of the state to the ordering of the mind: "The ancients who wished to illustrate illustrious virtue throughout the empire, first ordered well their own States. Wishing to order well their States, they first regulated their families. Wishing to regulate their families, they first cultivated their persons. Wishing to cultivate their persons, they first rectified their hearts. Wishing to rectify their hearts, they first sought to be sincere in their thoughts."[57] Mao Tse-tung has frequently expressed the same idea: "Whether one is correct or not in the ideological and political line determines everything. With a correct Party line, we will have everything. If we do not have people, we will get them; if we do not have guns, we will get them; if we do not have political power, we will get it. However, if the political line is not correct, we will lose everything we have. The line is the key link; once the key link is grasped, every problem will be solved."[58] Sun Yat-sen formulated the belief most succinctly: "Whatever can be known can certainly be carried out."[59] The common thread is the notion that if the conscious mind can be set straight as to how to do a thing, the actual doing of it will be relatively unproblematical. Correlatively, if a thing is being done wrong, the solution lies in correcting the conscious thoughts of the doer.[60]

56. Cf. D. W. Y. Kwok, *Scientism in Chinese Thought, 1900–1950* (New Haven, 1965).

57. *The Great Learning*, paragraph 4, as translated by James Legge, *The Chinese Classics: With a Translation, Critical and Exegetical Notes, Prolegomena, and Copious Indexes* (London, 1861), 1:221–22.

58. "Document of the Central Committee of the Chinese Communist Party, *Chung-fa* (1972) No. 12", in *Issues and Studies* 8, no. 12 (September 1972): 65.

59. Quoted in Teng and Fairbank, *China's Response*, p. 264.

60. Cf. Robert and Ai-li S. Chin, *Psychological Research in Communist China, 1949–1966* (Cambridge, Mass., 1969), esp. pp. 13–15, 76–82, 87–91; David S. Nivison, "The Problem of 'Knowledge' and 'Action' in Chinese Thought Since Wang Yang-ming," in Arthur F. Wright, ed., *Studies in Chinese Thought* (Chicago, 1967), pp. 112–45; Donald J. Munro,

Such a belief can lead in quite a different direction from constitutionalism—it can lead to the authoritarianism that says that rules and regulations are powerless to enforce good government in the absence of indoctrination or "thought reform,"[61] and such that indoctrination makes constitutions superfluous. Indeed, one might argue that this is the more consistent deduction from such a "voluntarist" position; certainly, it is the one more frequently arrived at in Chinese history, by both Confucianists and Maoists. Yet the voluntarist assumption was also capable of being turned to a defense of constitutionalism. As Sun Yat-sen says, "A race is an aggregation of human beings; a human being is ruled by the mind; and the nation and the government are the manifestations of the psychology of a group. Therefore the foundation of a nation is first based on the working of the mind."[62] Let the provisions of the constitution be regarded as the thing "known" by the conscious national mind, and there is no reason a constitutional republic should not work. If it fails, the reason must be either imperfect mastery of and commitment to its principles, or flaws in the constitutional instrument itself.

Thus, early republican politicians endlessly debated the adaptation of constitutional provisions to Chinese conditions and searched constantly for that fixed institutional order suited to command the national mind. What they did not debate was the assumption that a set of correct governmental procedures for China was discoverable and that once known those procedures would almost magically solve China's problems—the assumption, in short, that effort to solve China's problems could profitably be invested in debating alternative constitutional provisions.[63] In the midst of upheaval, the search for the proper constitution was carried out in the public prints, in parliament, and in a succession of councils and conventions. The call for some kind of constitutional restoration or revision was the typical riposte to deepening chaos, and it flowed from the belief that if the nation were "sincere in its thoughts," the state would become "well ordered."

But if consistency with the voluntarist tradition helped make constitutionalism plausible, its expected contribution to national wealth and power made it positively attractive. From the self-strengtheners of the 1860s to Mao Tse-tung, modern Chinese leaders have sought to transform China to make it strong. First,

"The Malleability of Man in Chinese Marxism," *The China Quarterly*, no. 48 (October–December 1971) pp. 609–40 (hereafter abbreviated *CQ*).

61. Nivison, "The Problem of 'Knowledge' and 'Action'," p. 141.

62. Teng and Fairbank, *China's Response*, p. 264.

63. On the strand of traditional belief, which argued that the state must be founded on some fixed, unchanging order, and on the related "euphoric idea that good government is easy if the ruler will simply adopt the right policies," see Thomas A. Metzger, *The Internal Organization of Ch'ing Bureaucracy: Legal, Normative, and Communication Aspects* (Cambridge, Mass., 1973), pp. 28–42, 74–80.

technology, then educational institutions, then political institutions, and finally social institutions have been transformed by successive generations of leaders seeking national power to throw off the yoke of imperialism. The adoption of a republican constitution was one step in this process. As noted, a constitution seemed conducive to national strength simply because the strong nations had constitutions; the Japanese experience in particular seemed to show how quickly a constitution could produce strength. But there was more than an empirical correlation in the republican leaders' belief in the strengthening effect of constitutions; there was also an analysis of the reasons for this effect.

Constitutionalism had achieved its late eighteenth-century political importance in the West in the context of the struggle for power between aristocracies and monarchs.[64] For kings (e.g., Gustavus III of Sweden), promulgation of a constitution was a way of seizing power from an aristocratic diet. By extending individual "rights" beyond the aristocracy to the masses, the monarch dissolved the special rights of the aristocracy into the general rights of the people, at the same time gaining popular support for the regime. For aristocracies (e.g., the French *parlements*), a constitution was a way of limiting the monarch's power with such notions as the legal basis of authority, individual rights, and representation. With the monarch's powers defined and limited, the aristocracy could play a larger role.

Although seeking opposite goals, the two sides shared a common ground of controversy. Arguments on either side were couched in terms of the same philosophical problem: on individualistic assumptions, what can justify authority? As Hobbes put it, what is "the final cause, end, or design of men, who naturally love liberty . . . , in the introduction of that restraint upon themselves, in which we see them live in commonwealth"?[65] Or, in Rousseau's phrase, "Man is born free, and everywhere he is in chains . . . . What can render [this] legitimate?"[66] In constituting the state, the theoretical source of obedience and citizen commitment lay in the solution of the paradox between the individual's interest in selfish freedom and his need for government. The solution, for Hobbes, Locke, Rousseau and others, was to prove a (more or less limited) identity of interests between the individual and the state.

This solution caught the eye of early twentieth-century Chinese thinkers. The original problem—justifying authority—was not a Chinese philosophical problem; the Chinese lacked the individualistic assumptions that made it prob-

---

64. The analysis here follows R. R. Palmer, *The Age of the Democratic Revolution, A Political History of Europe and America: The Challenge* (Princeton, N.J., 1959).

65. Thomas Hobbes, *Leviathan, or the Matter, Forme and Power of a Commonwealth, Ecclesiastical and Civil* (New York, 1962), p. 129 (Chapter 17).

66. Jean-Jacques Rousseau, *The Social Contract, or Principles of Political Right* in Frederick Watkins, trans. and ed., *Rousseau: Political Writings* (Edinburgh, 1953), pp. 3–4 (Chapter 10).

lematic. But the Chinese did have a problem to which the solution seemed appropriate: how to release the innate energy of the community and turn it into a source of national strength.[67] To Chinese eyes, the constitutionalist connection between the individual's interests and those of the state was seen as a device capable of arousing the people to greater effort and creativity on behalf of national goals. The trouble with old China, many modern Chinese thinkers have believed, was the passivity and narrow selfishness of the people. In a modern state, on the other hand, because the people rule, they devote themselves wholeheartedly to the nation. When there are "ten thousand eyes with one sight, ten thousand hands and feet with only one mind, ten thousand ears with one hearing, ten thousand powers with only one purpose of life; then the state is established ten-thousandfold strong. . . . When mind touches mind, when power is linked to power, cog to cog, strand around strand, and ten thousand roads meet in one center, this will be a state."[68] The theme of constitution as energizer, although initially found on the monarchist side of the European debate, was eventually developed to its highest point in the West by Rousseau, who showed in *The Social Contract* how constitutionalist assumptions could conduce to strengthening the national community and its "general will." In this sense, the 1906 imperial edict cited at the beginning of this chapter ("That other countries are wealthy and strong is primarily due to the adoption of a constitution, by which all the people are united in one body and in constant communication") was in the Rousseauian tradition.[69]

The Chinese were particularly equipped to perceive and develop this aspect of constitutional thought because of its resonances with what Paul Cohen has called "the Mencian view of power."[70] Throughout Mencius is the powerful image of the people flocking to the benevolent ruler.

"If there were a single ruler," Mencius told King Hsiang, "who did not delight in slaughter, he could unite the whole world."

"And who would side with him?" the king asked.

"Everyone in the world. Your majesty knows how in the seventh and eighth months the new grain becomes parched. But soon the clouds roll up, heavy rain falls, and the young plants shoot up in lusty growth. When this is so, it is as if nothing could hold them

67. This discussion draws heavily on Hao Chang's brilliant *Liang Ch'i-ch'ao and Intellectual Transition in China, 1890–1907* (Cambridge, Mass., 1971).

68. *Ibid.*, p. 100, quoting Liang Ch'i-ch'ao. See generally Chang's chapters 4 and 6.

69. That this Rousseauian, communitarian theme is also a key assumption of Maoist thinking is pointed out in Benjamin I. Schwartz, "The Reign of Virtue: Some Broad Perspectives on Leader and Party in the Cultural Revolution," in John Wilson Lewis, ed., *Party Leadership and Revolutionary Power in China* (Cambridge, England, 1970), pp. 149–69.

70. Paul A. Cohen, "Wang T'ao's Perspective on a Changing World," in Albert Feuerwerker, Rhoads Murphey, and Mary C. Wright, eds., *Approaches to Modern Chinese History* (Berkeley, Calif., 1967), p. 160.

back. Today among those that are the shepherds of men there is not in the whole world one who does not delight in slaughter. Should such a one arise, then all people on earth would look towards him with outstretched necks. If he were indeed such a one, the people would come to him as water flows downward, in a flood that none could hold back."[71]

The Mencian notion is that, in Cohen's paraphrase, "just policies and causes command popular support," and "a ruler with popular support is invincible."[72] Constitutionalism could be seen as such a just policy. The popular support it would command would, on the Rousseauian assumptions of its supporters, provide the key to wealth and power for China.

Constitutionalism, in short, achieved intellectual plausibility as a device to save China when it was interpreted in the light of deeply rooted assumptions available in the Chinese tradition. Once a proper constitution was written and promulgated, it could be willed to succeed. Because it would be a correct constitution, it would achieve popular support. Because it would involve the people, it would tap wells of popular commitment. China would be invincible. The scientific claims of Western experts and the successful experiments in the West and Japan provided any proof needed that this solution would succeed.

The Problem of Failure

The irony of China's constitutional experiment was that the country imported a Western ideology founded on individualism and conflict because of its presumed ability to overcome individualism and conflict. In the twelve years after the death of Yuan Shih-k'ai the young republic saw ten heads of state, forty-five cabinets, five legislatures, and seven constitutions or basic laws—not counting the rival heads of state, cabinets, parliaments, and constitutions in Canton.[73] Instead of uniting state and citizen in a new consensus, constitutionalism

71. Arthur Waley, *Three Ways of Thought in Ancient China* (New York, n.d.), p. 91.

72. Cohen, "Wang T'ao," p. 160. Cohen points out the obvious relevance to Mao.

73. The figure for heads of state is compiled from data provided by the Oral History Project of the Institute of Modern History, Academia Sinica, Taipei, Taiwan. It includes four presidents, one chief executive (Tuan Ch'i-jui), one marshal (Chang Tso-lin), and four regent cabinets. The figure for cabinets is obtained from Ch'en Hsi-chang, *Pei-yang ts'ang-sang shih-hua* (Tainan, 1967), vol. 2, appendix 2, pp. 504–509. The five legislatures include two sessions of the old parliament, one of the Anfu parliament, the Provisional National Council of 1917–18 and the Provisional National Council of 1925. The seven constitutions are the Provisional Constitution as interpreted from 1916 to 1917, the Provisional Constitution as interpreted from 1917 to 1922, the Provisional Constitution as interpreted from 1922 to 1923, the Ts'ao K'un constitution of 1923–24, the Regulations of the Executive Government, 1924–26, the Provisional Constitution as interpreted from 1926 to 1927, and the regulations of the Marshal's government, 1927–28.

provided a medium for amplifying dissension and disorder. Where was the flaw in the Chinese logic? What missing element would make a constitution work?

To ask this is to raise questions so complex and ramified that they have never been answered adequately for the politics of any country: what social, economic, psychological, and cultural conditions are needed for particular patterns of government to function?[74] Modern social science at least knows how little it knows about this set of questions. In China's twentieth-century search for national strength based on political unity and consensus, the constitutionalist solution was undermined by many factors whose separate effects we are still unable to weigh. A sullen, desperate peasantry; a fragmented military scattered over a vast, poorly integrated national landscape; a hierarchical, authoritarian, and personalistic elite political culture—these were some of the refractory blocks with which the new China had to be built. The belief that a certain kind of normative political order imposed at the top could bring all these elemen:s into line was clearly, in retrospect, mistaken. But more revolutionary solutions were suggested neither by foreign precedent nor by elite self-interest—not, that is, until the bankruptcy of the republic became inescapably clear. Meanwhile, the only cure for constitutionalist chaos was felt to be more constitutionalism. But repeated doses of constitutionalism had no mitigating effect upon the real, and destructive, dynamic of politics—factionalism.

74. This is the general theoretical issue lying behind such specific formulations as "What are the conditions for 'stable democracy'?" "What are the causes of revolution?" and "What are the effects of modernization on politics?" Each question has recently produced a large but inconclusive literature.

II

FACTIONALISM AND POLITICAL RECRUITMENT

"Old China," as Lyon Sharman points out, "was governed by a vast outreaching network of officials organized upon the strict principle of graded subordination. . . . None of these individuals ruled in collaboration with equals; each was a highly individualized trustee of power stationed at a particular post. . . . By the revolution of 1911, the huge nation that is China was required to transform itself by the mere writing of a constitution from a close-knit hierarchy of individual officials to a federation of popularly elected provincial legislatures, each with its attendant executive and judiciary," the whole headed by a president, cabinet, and parliament at Peking.[1]

The transformation did not work. "Chinese in all walks of life understand what it is to be trusted with authority, and what it is to be subordinated to authority. But to be thrown into equality-groups with no one in authority and no one subordinated calls for a radical change of their whole sense of human relationships."[2] Rather than make such a change, bureaucrats and politicians

1. Sharman, *Sun Yat-sen*, pp. 353, 356.
2. Sharman, *Sun Yat-sen*, p. 363. Sharman's argument points to the contribution that the political culture approach makes to understanding factionalism in China—roughly, that the hierarchical and authority-"dependent" Chinese culture makes factions a particularly comfortable form of organization. This does not mean, however, that factionalism is a peculiarly Chinese phenomenon. Almost all other cultures seem to contain elements that make factionalism possible. Comparative study might show that Chinese factions are more frequent, politically more central, more stable and persistent, or more hierarchical than factions in some other cultures. Three works that discuss Chinese political and organizational culture in ways that are particularly relevant to the factionalism problem are Lucian W. Pye, *The Spirit of Chinese Politics: A Psychocultural Study of the Authority Crisis in Political Development* (Cambridge, Mass., 1968); Robert Henry Silin, "Management in Large-Scale Taiwanese Industrial Enterprises" (Ph.D. diss., Harvard University, 1970); and Richard H. Solomon, *Mao's Revolution and the Chinese Political Culture* (Berkeley, Calif., 1971).

fell back informally on familiar hierarchical forms of cooperation. Instead of "equality groups," they organized themselves in personal followings, each centered on a particular leader and composed of his individually recruited, personally loyal followers. It was as if the removal of the dynasty had initiated an unravelling of the great skein of hierarchical relationships that had been the old Chinese bureaucracy. It now broke down into its smallest constituent informal units of cooperation. Parties, parliaments, cabinets, clubs, bureaucracies—all seemed to degenerate into the lowest common organizational denominator in their real functioning, even while maintaining their respective organizational facades.

This factional form of organization gave rise in turn to what Sharman calls "disintegrative behavior"—"processes of disintegration that frustrate group functioning." As she describes the process:

A group is nucleating about some project which shows promise of success. Those who wish the project ill or those who covet it for themselves attack it with criticism, severely, often violently, insisting that the organization of the nucleus is wrong, or arguing for drastic modification of its purposes and objectives, or for the removal of this or that person from the group . . . . [The group] disintegrates before such an attack. The result is that a fresh nucleus must be formed, and it is subjected to a similar attack, and in turn disintegrates . . . . and China wonders why there is chaos![3]

Why might leaders who were committed to constitutionalism and to making China strong repeatedly resort to such disintegrative behavior in cabinets, parliaments, and political parties?[4] The argument developed here is that in a political arena, like the early republican national government, organized primarily by factions, leaders' constructive long-term goals are subordinated to the immediate tactical demands of conflict, in such a way as to produce a kind of disintegrative behavior profoundly subversive of a constitutional system.[5]

3. Sharman, Sun Yat-sen, pp. 360, 362, 367.

4. If it were only the politicians of the early republic who were guilty of such behavior, one might dispose of this question by discrediting their motives. But when Kuomintang, CCP, and other twentieth-century Chinese leaders seem to have been dogged by the same organizational problems, it is more difficult to argue that their commitment to the goal of a strong China was only a slogan. On the KMT, see, inter alia, Sharman, Sun Yat-sen; Hung-mao Tien, Government and Politics in Kuomintang China, 1927–1937 (Stanford, Calif., 1972); Lloyd E. Eastman, "China's Abortive Revolution: China Under Nationalist Rule, 1927–1937," manuscript of a forthcoming book, n.d. On the CCP, see Andrew J. Nathan, · "A Factionalism Model for CCP Politics," CQ no. 53 (January-March 1973), pp. 52–66.

5. The argument in the following three sections of this chapter was first presented in Nathan, "A Factionalism Model," pp. 34–52. It is couched at the level of abstract "model-building" in order to demonstrate the strictly structural nature of the argument. I am trying to show which aspects of early republican political behavior can be explained in terms of factionalism alone, before proceeding to a discussion of the specific historical setting and its

Factions Defined

Let us begin with a kind of human behavior found in all societies—the "clientelist tie."[6] A clientelist tie is a nonascriptive two-person relationship founded on exchange, in which well-understood rights and obligations are established between the two parties. The earmarks of a clientelist tie are as follows:

1. It is a relationship between two people.

2. It is a relationship especially selected for cultivation by the members from their total social networks.

3. It is cultivated essentially by the constant exchange of gifts or services (this does not imply that the subjective content of the relationship is cynical or unfriendly: the contrary is normally the case).

4. Since the exchange involves the provision by each partner of goods or services the other wants, the parties to the tie are dissimilar; very often they are unequal in status, wealth or power.

5. The tie sets up well-understood, although seldom explicit, rights and obligations between the partners.

6. It can be abrogated by either member.

7. It is not exclusive; either member is free to establish other simultaneous ties (so long as they do not involve contradictory obligations).

Such ties include patron–client relations, godfather–parent relations, some types of trader–customer relations, and so forth. Corporate ties, such as lineage relations, comembership in an association, or comembership in a group of blood brothers exceeding two in number, are not clientelist ties, although shared corporate membership often provides an initial contact which leads to the establishment of clientelist ties as defined here.

The clientelist tie must be clearly distinguished from two other kinds of

---

effect on conflict behavior. Furthermore, insofar as structural constraints explain behavior, they can be applied to settings other than early republican China; an abstract model is thus more useful for comparative work than a case study in which various elements of explanation are not clearly distinguished.

6. In recent years, studies of the political and other functions of clientelist ties have proliferated. Terminology varies ("dyadic contract," "dyadic alliance," "patronage tie," "patron–client tie," and so on), but there is little question that various authors are referring to the same quite clearly defined phenomenon. Among the many discussions of clientelist ties or their political uses are George M. Foster, "The Dyadic Contract: a Model for the Social Structure of a Mexican Peasant Village," in Jack M. Potter, May N. Diaz, and George M. Foster, eds., *Peasant Society: A Reader* (Boston, 1967), pp. 213–30; James C. Scott, "Patron–Client Politics and Political Change in Southeast Asia," *American Political Science Review* 66, no. 1 (March 1972): 91–113 (hereafter abbreviated *APSR*); and Carl H. Landé, "Networks and Groups in Southeast Asia: Some Observations on the Group Theory of Politics," *APSR* 67, no. 1 (March 1973): 103–27.

relationship with which it is readily confused, the power relationship and the (generic) exchange relationship. To take the second problem first, the clientelist tie is founded on exchange. But, according to Peter M. Blau, all social processes except those that are irrational or non–goal-oriented or expressive—in other words, all social processes in which people interact with other people in order to elicit behavior instrumental to some goal—can profitably be analyzed in terms of exchange.[7] And, according to Marshall Sahlins, any kind of reciprocity, including the "negative reciprocity" of an eye for an eye, can be usefully classified as exchange.[8] Blau and Sahlins are persuasive on the utility of their respective analytical systems, but it is essential to be clear that the clientelist tie as defined here is an exchange relationship of a limited and specific kind. Embedded in different cultures, it takes somewhat different forms and is more or less explicitly recognized, spelled out, legitimated, and reinforced. But, in any case, it is relatively stable and persistent, involves well-understood rights and obligations, and is purposely cultivated by the participants. If nearly all of social life is to be regarded as exchange, then clientelist ties should be regarded as a special, quasi-contractual subtype of exchange relationship.

At the other extreme, the clientelist tie must be distinguished from the power relationship of "imperative coordination."[9] If for some reason the subordinate has no real choice but obedience, the consequences for political behavior of the superior-subordinate relationship will be quite different from what they would be if the real possibility of abrogating the tie existed. Since the consequences are so different, the distinction is analytically necessary. It may be objected that, in many cases, the right of abrogation formally exists but in fact cannot be exercised, as in the relationship between landlord and tenant on some Latin American haciendas, or between lord and vassal in feudal Europe. These relationships, I would argue, should be regarded as relationships of imperative coordination rather than as clientelistic relations. Of course it is often difficult to tell the difference. There is a grey area, e.g., as the hold of the landlord begins to weaken but before it is effectively challenged by that of a local political machine. The analytic boundary lies somewhere within that grey area.

Clientelist ties in a given society articulate to form complex networks that serve many functions, including social insurance,[10] trade,[11] and the mobiliza-

7. Peter M. Blau, *Exchange and Power in Social Life* (New York, 1964), p. 5 and *passim*.

8. Marshall D. Sahlins, "On the Sociology of Primitive Exchange," in Michael Banton, ed., *The Relevance of Models for Social Anthropology* (London, 1965), p. 144 and *passim*.

9. Max Weber, *The Theory of Social and Economic Organization*, trans. by A. M. Henderson and Talcott Parsons (New York, 1964), pp. 152–53.

10. Cf. Foster, "Dyadic Contract."

11. For suggestive studies of clientelist ties in operation in nonpolitical contexts, see,

tion and wielding of influence (i.e., political conflict). I am concerned here with the latter function. What happens when political conflict is organized primarily through clientelist ties rather than through formal organizations, corporate lineage units, or mass or class movements? I would argue that there are three possibilities.

First, the individual seeking to engage in political conflict may do so by cashing in on his personal ties in order to operate as a power broker, without directly and explicitly involving his partners in any common or sustained endeavor. Examples include influence-peddling by lawyers who specialize in arranging access to particular bureaucracies, mediation of political disputes by middlemen, and the bridging of government/village gaps by local "linkage figures."[12] The second possibility, which occurs in a setting of genuine electoral competition, has been called the "clientelist party," "vertical group", or "machine"—a mass political organization that buys electoral support with particularistic rewards distributed through a leader-follower network of clientelist ties.[13]

The third possibility occurs in an oligarchic or relatively small-scale setting when an individual leader mobilizes some portion of his network of primary,

---

among others, James N. Anderson, "Buy-and-Sell and Economic Personalism: Foundations for Philippine Entrepreneurship," *Asian Survey* 9, no.9 (September 1969): 641–68; Mary R. Hollnsteiner, "Social Structure and Power in a Philippine Municipality," in Potter, *et al.*, eds., *Peasant Society: A Reader*, pp. 200–212; Sidney W. Mintz, "Pratik: Haitian Personal Economic Relationships," *ibid.*, pp. 98–110; and Robert H. Silin, "Marketing and Credit in a Hong Kong Wholesale Market," in W. E. Willmott, ed., *Economic Organization in Chinese Society* (Stanford, Calif., 1972), pp. 327–52.

12. See, for example, Karl D. Jackson, "Communication and National Integration in Sundanese Villages: Implications for Communications Strategy," paper prepared for presentation at a meeting of the Indonesia Seminar, Southeast Asia Development Advisory Group, New York City, March 30–April 1, 1972; Martin and Susan Tolchin, *To the Victor . . . Political Patronage from the Clubhouse to the White House* (New York, 1972); William Foote Whyte, *Street Corner Society: The Social Structure of an Italian Slum*, enl. ed. (Chicago, 1955), pt. 2.

13. Distinctions can probably fruitfully be made between "clientelist parties," defined as integrating all levels of the political system through clientelist ties, and "machines," defined as operating strictly on the local level. Among the major theoretically-oriented studies of such organizations are James C. Scott, *Comparative Political Corruption* (Englewood Cliffs, N.J., 1972), chapters 6–9; and John Duncan Powell, "Peasant Society and Clientelist Politics," *APSR* 64, no.2 (June 1970): 411–25. For case studies of political systems organized by clientelist parties, see Robert H. Dix, *Colombia: The Political Dimensions of Change* (New Haven, Conn., 1967), esp. Chapters 8 and 9; Keith R. Legg, *Politics in Modern Greece* (Stanford, Calif., 1969), esp. Chapters 6–8; Myron Weiner, *Party Building in a New Nation: The Indian National Congress* (Chicago, 1967); and William Foote Whyte, *Street Corner Society*, esp. Chapter 6. I am grateful to Michael Bucuvalas and Pedro Cabán for bringing Legg and Dix to my attention.

secondary, tertiary ties, and so on[14] for the purpose of engaging in politics. A machine or clientelist party consists of a great many layers of personnel, but this third type of clientelist political structure consists of only one or a few layers.[15] I call such a structure—one mobilized on the basis of clientelist ties to engage in politics and consisting of a few, rather than a great many, layers of personnel— a faction.[16] Such configurations include what may be called simple or complex factions and may control from within or without one or more "support structures" or power bases, such as clubs, parties, mobs, newspapers, banks, ministries, armies, and the like (see Figure 1). What all these configurations share in common is the one-to-one, rather than corporate, pattern of relationships between leaders (or subleaders) and followers. Structurally, the faction is articulated through one or more nodes, and it is recruited and coordinated on the basis of the personal exchange relationships I have called clientelist ties.[17]

Structural Characteristics of Factions

Because it is based upon personal exchange ties rather than authority relations,

14. For ways of conceptualizing a network from the standpoint of an individual ego, see J. A. Barnes, "Networks and Political Process," in Marc J. Swartz, ed., *Local-Level Politics: Social and Cultural Perspectives* (Chicago, 1968), pp. 107–30; and Adrian C. Mayer, "The Significance of Quasi-Groups in the Study of Complex Societies," in Michael Banton, ed., *The Social Anthropology of Complex Societies* (London, 1966), pp. 97–122.

15. It seems unnecessary to specify an exact size boundary between factions and machines since the difference between the two is so large. The difference, of course, is not just one of size; as a consequence of their different sizes and different degrees of selectivity in recruitment, as well as of the different natures of their respective arenas, machines and factions behave in thoroughly distinguishable ways.

16. This conception of a faction is similar to that offered by Ralph Nicholas, "Factions: a Comparative Analysis," in Michael Banton, ed., *Political Systems and the Distribution of Power* (London, 1965), pp. 27–29, and to Landé's concept of the "dyadic following" in his "Networks and Groups." Let me stress that I have defined "faction" in a technical sense. By faction I do not mean an "organized opinion group" (cf. Franz Schurmann, *Ideology and Organization in Communist China* [Berkeley, Calif., 1966], p. 56), contending warlords, or Red Guards. Nor should the word faction as used here be regarded as a translation of the Chinese terms *p'ai, hsi, tang,* or *hui*. Whether any of these things can be called a faction by the present definition can only be determined upon close structural analysis. Although restrictive, the definition advanced here seems to fit a wide range of configurations found in political systems and subsystems, including governments, parties, bureaucracies, parliaments, courts, and villages in a number of different geographical areas and historical periods. Some examples are cited in Andrew James Nathan, "Factionalism in Early Republican China: The Politics of the Peking Government" (Ph.d. diss., Harvard University, 1970), pp. 372–85.

17. Each structural characteristic discussed below is not necessarily unique to factions (for example, guerrilla bands may be equally flexible, and for some of the same reasons), but none of them is universal and the combination of characteristics is distinctive.

Figure 1. Some Factional Configurations

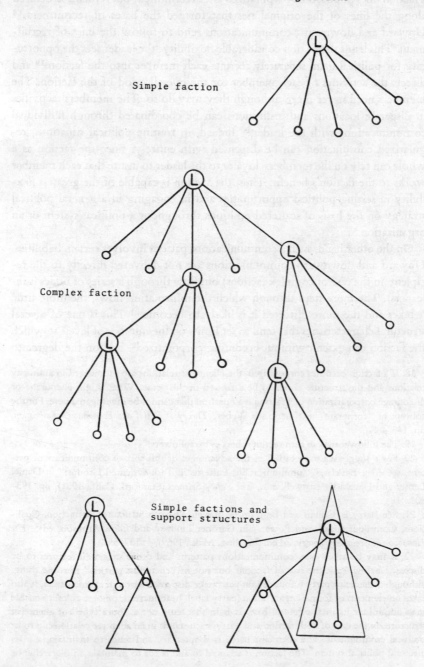

Simple faction

Complex faction

Simple factions and
support structures

a faction does not become corporatized after recruitment but remains structured along the lines of the original ties that formed the bases of recruitment.[18] Upward and downward communications tend to follow the lines of recruitment. This lends the faction considerable flexibility: the leader sees the opportunity for political gain, separately recruits each member into the faction,[19] and directs the activities of each member for the overall good of the faction. The members need never meet, although they may do so. The members' activities in disparate locations and institutions can be coordinated through individual communications with the leader.[20] Indeed, in routine political situations, regularized coordination can be dispensed with entirely, since the faction as a whole can rely on the members' loyalty to the leader to insure that each member works to the faction's benefit. Thus, the faction is capable of the greatest flexibility in seizing political opportunities and in engaging in a general political strategy on the basis of scattered positions throughout a political system or an organization.

On the other hand, such a communications pattern involves certain liabilities. Upward and downward communications are not delivered directly to the recipient (in the case of complex factions) but flow through a series of nodes (subleaders). The more steps through which the information flows, the more time it takes and the more distorted it is likely to become.[21] This is one of several structural characteristics that tend to set limits on the number of levels to which the faction can extend without becoming corporatized[22] and on the degree to

18. If a faction becomes corporatized, the clientelist relations are submerged in authority relations and the structure ceases to be a faction in this sense. What might encourage or discourage corporatization of a faction is a question that cannot be investigated here. For the concept of "corporate" used here, see Weber, *Theory of Social and Economic Organization*, pp. 145–48.

19. The follower may in turn recruit others as his followers.

20. For a suggestive exploration of the advantages of this sort of communications pattern, see Alex Bavelas, "Communications Patterns in Task-Oriented Groups," in Daniel Lerner and Harold D. Lasswell, eds., *The Policy Sciences* (Stanford, Calif., 1951), pp. 193–202.

21. See Barry E. Collins and Bertram H. Raven, "Group Structure: Attraction, Coalitions, Communications, and Power," in Gardner Lindzey and Elliot Aronson, eds., *The Handbook of Social Psychology*, 2d ed. (Reading, Mass., 1969), 4: 137–55.

22. It may be asked why communications patterns and other structural features to be discussed below limit the size of factions but not of "clientelist parties." For one thing, although a clientelist party is founded on patronage dispensed through clientelist ties, it also takes on elements of formal organization (party label, headquarters, officers, rules) to enable it to administer its mass electoral base. It is in this sense not a "pure type" of clientelist structure. In the case of both faction and party, each stands in an adaptive relationship to its political environment. The clientelist party is adapted to, and tends to maintain, a mass electoral political system. The faction is adapted to and tends to maintain an oligarchic or

which large factions can engage in finely coordinated activities. The faction, in short, is highly flexible but self-limiting in its extensiveness.

Since it is founded upon exchange relationships, a faction depends for its growth and continuity upon the ability of the leader to secure and distribute rewards to his followers. It tends to expand and contract with success or failure and may even be dissolved when removed from power. But the leader can always reconstitute it when he regains the capability to reward the members. The faction is thus capable of intermittent but persistent functioning. It takes form out of the broader network of clientelist ties in response to an opportunity for political gain, and when it becomes necessary to retire from politics, as during the dominance of the political arena by an enemy, it can become relatively dormant. Its political activities temporarily cease, especially if the members have scattered, or the activities may continue at a low level of occasional contact with other opposition groups to scheme for a return to power. When the enemy is overthrown, the faction may return to full activity unchanged in form and flexibility.

It also follows that a faction cannot survive its leader. The members may continue in political activity after the leader's death or retirement; several members may associate for a time and continue to be known by the original name of the faction. Members may also join other factions as temporary allies, or they may seek to found their own faction. But since the set of clientelist ties on which it is founded forms a unique configuration centered on the leader, the faction can never be taken over as a whole by a successor. The unique combination of personnel and strategic political positions held by the faction cannot be completely reconstructed once the leader is lost.

The more extended the complex faction becomes, the greater the number of subordinate leaders it contains and the farther removed they are from the primary leader. The leader of each simple faction within the complex faction is primarily responsible to his own followers for political spoils. This responsibility may come into contradiction with the loyalty he owes his own leader, who is pursuing the interests of a different set of persons. This creates the tendency for the leaders of lower segments to betray the interests of the faction as a whole in order to secure greater rewards for the segments they lead, which are capable of operating as distinct factions if they free themselves from the larger faction.[23]

Because of this tendency toward breakdown, complex factions are most

---

small-scale system. Thus, although I argue here that certain elements of factional structure limit factional size, I could just as well build the argument in reverse: a political setting that involves relatively few people makes it possible for people to organize in ways that would not be suited to mass-participation settings and large-scale organizations.

23. Cf. the "size principle" as enunciated by William H. Riker, *The Theory of Political Coalitions* (New Haven, Conn., 1962), pp. 32–33.

likely to develop, and are likely to develop to the largest size, within bureaucratic formal organizations. First, in formal organizations, the personal loyalty of faction leaders at lower levels to leaders at higher levels is reinforced by hierarchical authority patterns. Second, the faction benefits from the intraorganizational communications network in coordinating its activities. Third, the effort to gain control of the organization or to influence its policies requires the cooperation of the subleaders at the various levels and tends to bring their interests into harmony. In short, the hierarchy and established communications and authority flow of the existing organization provide a kind of trellis upon which the complex faction is able to extend its own informal, personal loyalties and relations.

There is a tendency for vertical cleavages to develop within the complex faction, running up to the level directly under the highest leader. Vertical cleavages also develop at each lower level, but remain latent as long as they are submerged within the greater rivalry between the two major segments. (Because the struggle is for access to and influence over the leader, cleavages tend to be limited to two.) The conflict between the two major entities within a faction is kept under tight rein by the faction leader. After his retirement or death, however, the two entities become two new complex factions.

Internal cleavage tends to be increased by the fruits of victory. First, the path to victory inevitably involves reaching opportunistic alliances with factional leaders who are incorporated as allies within the faction but are not reliable. Second, the increased scale and numerical force of the growing faction enhances the tendency mentioned earlier for divergent interests to emerge among subleaders and subfactions. Even if loyalty prevents an open revolt against the leader, it permits political clashes and struggles among his subordinates. Third, if the faction comes near to or achieves victory in a conflict arena as a whole, the unifying factor of a common enemy ceases to exist, while divisive factors, such as struggle over spoils and efforts by smaller, enemy factions to buy over component units, increase in salience. Fourth, the growth of the faction tends to deprive the leader of direct control over component units, weakens his position vis-à-vis subordinates, and thus hastens his political retirement and the consequent open split of the faction. In short, division and decline is the almost inevitable result of success. The only way to avoid such disintegration is to refuse to expand beyond the borders of an internally unified, and easily defended, factional base.

Finally, it follows from all the above that the faction is limited in the amount and kinds of power it can generate and wield. A faction is limited in size, follower commitment, and stability by the principles of its own organization. Certain other types of conflict structure, for example highly organized political parties or armies, can, by virtue of their complex, functionally specialized organization, their clear boundaries, and their high degree of control over participants, engage in feats of mobilization, indoctrination, and coordination that are beyond the capacities of factions.[24] A faction, of course, is limited in power only so long as it remains a faction; there is nothing inherent in the existence of a faction to prevent the members, if they need more power, from organizing in some other way. However, people often do not organize in another way, but in factions. Why they choose to do so, and what conditions may cause them to shift to another form of organization, are important questions beyond the scope of this model.

Characteristics of Factional Politics

For the sake of simplicity, I limit the following discussion to an ideal-typical political system that is organized primarily by factions. Factions will behave differently when they are competing against structures that are not factions (for example, clans or political parties), but the easiest case to deal with is the "pure case" of an all-factional system. What modes of conflict will be typical of factions operating in an environment consisting primarily of rival factions?[25]

A first set of propositions is based upon the power limitations typical of factions. Factions enjoy less power capability than formal organizations because of the limitations on their extent, coordination, and control of followers implied by their basis in the clientelist tie, their one-to-one communications structure, and their tendency toward breakdown. Consequently, the several factions in a given factional arena will tend, over time, to enjoy relative power equality; for no faction will be able to achieve and maintain overwhelmingly superior power. One faction may for the moment enjoy somewhat greater power than rival factions, but this power will not be so much greater that the victorious faction is capable of expunging its rivals and assuring permanent dominance.[26] This is the more so because the flexibility of the weaker factions and their capability for intermittent functioning enhance their ability to evade and survive repression. A faction engaging in conflict with other factions must therefore operate on the assumption that it will not be able decisively and finally to eliminate its rivals. The faction that holds power today can expect to be out of power

24. Cf. Amitai Etzioni, *Modern Organizations* (Englewood Cliffs, N.J., 1964), *passim*.

25. As was the case with the structural characteristics of factions, the claim is not made that the modes of conflict characteristic of factions are each unique to factional systems, merely that none of them is universal to all political systems and that the combination of all of them is found only in factional systems.

26. A major reason for differences in the power of factions is the differing power of their support structures (regional and/or institutional power bases). But opposing power bases cannot be entirely eliminated, nor, given the tendency of large, victorious factions to split, can they be taken over.

and vulnerable tomorrow. Politicians in a factional system are "condemned to live together."[27] This enables us to posit that the following modes of conflict will be typical of factional systems.

1. Since the impulse to crush one's rivals decisively is stymied by the limited nature of power, a code of civility circumscribes the nature of political conflict.[28] Factions relatively seldom kill, jail, or even confiscate the property of their opponents within the system (the killing and jailing of persons felt to present a threat to the system is another matter: see point 12). Indeed, factional systems require punctiliously polite face-to-face conduct between politicians. As Nathan Leites has written with respect to the French National Assembly of the Third and Fourth republics, "the vicissitudes of political life exacerbate one's feelings, but it is imperative that rage be channelled into entirely appropriate expressions so as not to endanger one's career."[29]

2. Since factions are incapable of building sufficient power to rid the political system of rival factions, they have little incentive to try to do so. For any given faction, the most important and usually most immediate concern is to protect its base of power while opposing accretions of power by rival factions; initiatives to increase its own power and position are of secondary importance. Defensive political strategies therefore predominate over political initiatives in frequency and importance.

3. When a faction does take a political initiative (which it does only on those rare occasions when it feels that its power base is secure and its rivals are relatively off balance), it relies upon secret preparation and surprise offensive. This minimizes the ability of rivals to prepare defensive moves in advance and enables the aggressive faction, until such defensive moves stop its progress, to gain more ground than would otherwise be the case.

4. In the face of such an initiative, the defensive orientation of the other factions in the system tends to encourage them to unite against the initiative. Thus, factional political systems tend to block the emergence of strong leaders. The strong leader constitutes a threat to the other factions' opportunities for power, and they band together long enough to topple him from power. (In many political systems, governmental instability results. In France under the Third and Fourth republics, for example, where the government was dependent for its office upon an alignment of parliamentary factions, the very fact that a

27. Nathan Leites, *On the Game of Politics in France* (Stanford, Calif., 1959), pp. 23, 45.

28. Cf. F. G. Bailey, "Parapolitical Systems," in Swartz, ed., *Local-Level Politics*, p. 282; Bernard Gallin, "Political Factionalism and its Impact on Chinese Village School Organization in Taiwan," *ibid.*, p. 390; and Melford E. Spiro, "Factionalsim and Politics in Village Burma," *ibid.*, pp. 410–12.

29. Leites, *On the Game*, p. 117.

politician was able to organize a cabinet set in motion the jealousy and opposition that soon led to its fall. Where the titular government leader is suprafactional and enjoys little power, however, the formal governmental leadership of a factional system may remain stable for long periods.)

5. Since the political life of a factional system consists of occasional initiatives by constituent factions, followed by defensive alliances against the initiator, any given faction is obliged to enter into a series of constantly shifting defensive alliances. Factional alliances cannot remain stable. Today's enemy may have to be tomorrow's ally.

6. It is therefore impossible for factions to make ideological agreement a primary condition for alliance with other factions. As argued below, factions operate within a broad ideological consensus (point 13) while exaggerating the small differences that remain among them (point 10). The struggle for office and influence is unremitting, immediate, and never decisively resolved. In order to stay in the game, factions must often cooperate with those with whom they have recently disagreed. Although factional alignments do not cross major ideological boundaries, within those boundaries, they are not determined by doctrinal differences.[30]

7. When decisions (resolutions of conflict, policy decisions) are made by the factional system as a whole, they are made by consensus among the factions. To attempt to take action without first achieving such a consensus would take the ruling coalition beyond the limits of its power: the decision could never be enforced. Furthermore, the effort to enforce a decision would hasten the formation of an opposition coalition to topple the ruling group from power. Decision by consensus also has the advantage that action is taken in the company of one's rivals, so that responsibility cannot be pinned on any single faction.[31]

8. A typical cycle of consensus formation and decline characterizes factional systems. It begins with a political crisis. As the factions contemplate the crisis, "the limits of what every party (or every clique or individual) may be capable of attaining" become clear to all, and after a lapse of time the crisis becomes "ripe." "Imperious necessity . . . make[s] the . . . groups disregard their

30. In the Chinese context, for example, factional alignments did not cross the ideological boundaries between the late Ch'ing conservatives on the one hand and the constitutionalists and revolutionaries on the other, or between the Kuomintang and the CCP. But within each major ideological current, factional alignments were not (how could they be?) determined by pure, *a priori* ideological compatibilities. Ideological stands were developed and revised in the course of politics. For a case study of the process by which ideological standpoint becomes defined in the course of political conflict, as rivals force one another to delineate and clarify their positions, see Benjamin I. Schwartz, *Chinese Communism and the Rise of Mao* (Cambridge, Mass., 1952).

31. Cf. Leites, *On the Game*, pp. 48–49.

positions of principle," which had blocked consensus, and action becomes possible.[32]

As a result of the consensus among the factions on the need for action, a faction or factional alliance achieves office and receives a mandate to act. The victorious faction takes culturally appropriate actions to test and solidify the support the other factions have been obliged to give it. The leader may refuse to take office until the other factions have publicly committed themselves to him; he may try to associate the leaders of other factions in the action he proposes to take; he may allow, or encourage, the crisis to worsen. Ultimately, however, he acts.

The third phase is the decline of the factional consensus. The actions taken by the faction in power inevitably have implications for the relative strength of all the factions in the system. While the actions carry the system through the crisis that had produced the consensus, they benefit some factions—usually the one in power and its allies—more than others. The other factions act to block the effort of the leading faction to strengthen itself, and the factional consensus deteriorates. The factions return to mutual squabbling.

The period of factional conflict often lasts a long while as the factions maneuver for political resources, alliances, and a favorable moment and pretext for precipitating a new crisis. Eventually a faction feels it is in a good position to take a political initiative, to precipitate a test of strength with its major opponent. In many factional systems, this takes the form of asking the most obstructive opposition factions to form a government in the expectation that they will fail.[33] Whatever its form, the test of strength initiates a new crisis which begins another cycle.

A second set of propositions is based upon the fact that factions consist of a series of clientelist ties. The resources with which the faction carries out political conflict are not corporate, shared resources, but the personal resources of the individual members—their personal prestige, official positions, and their own further clientelist ties.

9. To weaken their rivals, factions try to discredit opposition faction members, dislodge them from their posts, and buy away their allies. Such efforts lead to a politics of personality in which rumor, character assassination, bribery, and deception are used. Passions of jealousy and revenge are aroused, opportunism and corruption are fostered, and urgent short-term political goals require the compromise of principles. These, in short, are the "comic opera" politics or "pure politics" so characteristic of factional systems.[34]

10. A further characteristic of factional political conflict may be called doc-

32. *Ibid.*, Chapter 4, esp. pp. 97–98.

33. Cf. *ibid.*, pp. 82–83.

34. Cf. James L. Payne, *Patterns of Conflict in Colombia* (New Haven, Conn., 1968), pp. 3–24. Payne attempts to explain factionalism in Colombian politics on the basis of the preva-

trinalism, i.e., the couching of factional struggle for power in terms of abstract issues of ideology, honor, and face.[35] Factions adopt rigid and minutely defined ideological positions, exaggerate small differences on abstract questions, and stress the purity of their own motives. Yet the issues that arouse such fierce and elaborate debate appear upon close examination to be those with strategic im- -plications for factional power.[36] Although the real distance between factions in ideology and program is small (points 12 and 13), and although no faction is likely to be able to carry out an innovative political program, grand policies and sweeping programs are articulated and debated, with small points attracting the most passionate and lengthy discussion.

Such debate serves several purposes. First, it distinguishes one faction from another,[37] providing a rationale for continued struggle among such otherwise similar entities. Second, it provides an opportunity to discredit other politicians and to justify oneself on abstract or ideological grounds. Third, the broad programs often include inconspicuous provisions of true strategic political importance. The struggle, which is couched in abstract terms, is really over the advantages of a policy to one side or the other.

A third set of propositions concerns the size and shape of the factional system as a whole and the way it relates to its political environment.

11. Any factional arena is composed of a rather small number of factions. When a great many factions interact in an arena, they find it in their interests to amalgamate, in order to defend against other factions doing the same thing. The incentives to amalgamate cease to be stronger than those to engage in conflict only when the total number of factions has been reduced to the point where most constituent factions enjoy enough strength to launch political initiatives and defend themselves, and when further amalgamation would simply bring in more followers to share the rewards of the faction without decisively affecting its ability to survive. It is doubtful that more than a score or two of factions can exist in a given factional system or arena. (The limitations on the number of members in a faction, and on the number of factions in a system, form a logical circle with the initial assumption of an oligarchic or small-scale arena.)

12. I have already stated that the members of the small factional elite act

---

lence of "status," rather than "program," incentives among Colombian politicians. However, if my model is correct, factionalism can occur in the presence of either type of incentive. Politicians in factional systems will tend to act as if they were motivated by status incentives because of the importance of personal prestige and personal connections as political resources in factional systems. It is immaterial to the model how high-minded the ultimate motives for conflict are.

35. Cf. Leites, *On the Game*, pp. 7–34.

36. Cf. Payne, *Patterns of Conflict*, pp. 249–50.

37. Myron Weiner, *Party Politics in India: The Development of a Multi-Party System* (Princeton, N.J., 1957), pp. 237–40. See also Lewis A. Coser, *The Functions of Social Conflict* (New York, 1964), pp. 33–38.

within a code of civility that limits the severity of the sanctions they employ and under tactical constraints that require alliances with former enemies and opposition to former allies.[38] This closely knit elite is further united by one overriding shared interest: that the resources over which they are struggling should be allocated among themselves and in accordance with the rules of conflict they are following, rather than to some force from outsde the system which pays no attention to those rules and whose victory would end the political existence of the factions. The result is a sharp difference between the modes of intraelite conflict described in points 1 through 10 and the drastic steps that may be taken by the united factional elite to resist external enemies or to destroy counterelites who challenge the legitimacy of the factional system.[39] When, for example, foreign conquest, rebellion, or a military coup threatens to overthrow a factional regime, the factions unite behind a suitable leader long enough to preserve the system, before returning to politics as usual.[40] If the threat to the system comes from within, from a factional leader attempting to break the rules, the efforts of the other factions are directed toward defeating that attempt and reestablishing the stability of the system.

13. Within the factional elite, it is taboo to question the principle of legitimacy upon which the factions base their claim to a role in the larger society. Thus, for example, a factional parliament, regime, or party may play the role, in the larger society, of a central or local government, on the basis of a constitutional or charismatic claim to legitimacy. No matter how much the vicissitudes of struggle oblige the factions to trample in fact upon constitutional principles, or to disobey in fact their symbolic leader, these must never be openly questioned or flouted since that would encourage other forces in the larger society to "throw the rascals out."[41] Thus, politicians in factional systems com-

38. On the unifying effects of conflict, see further Coser, *Functions, passim;* and George Simmel, *Conflict and The Web of Group-Affiliations,* trans. by Kurt H. Wolff and Reinhard Bendix (New York, 1955), pp. 13-123.

39. The same distinction holds if the group of factions is itself the counterelite and its enemies are the ruling elite.

40. Of course, they do not always succeed in preserving the regime. If the social context of the regime has been changing so that, e.g., new problems demand solutions or new groups demand access to the system, immobilism (see below) may prevent the regime from responding successfully. The consequent loss of legitimacy may make the regime an easy target for a strong rival. An example is the crumbling of the Peking government before the Kuomintang advance in 1928.

The Clemenceau and Poincaré ministries in France are well-known instances of resistance by a factional system to external threat. See Philip M. Williams, *Crisis and Compromise: Politics in the Fourth Republic* (Garden City, N.Y., 1966), p. 11.

41. Cf. Simmel, *Conflict,* p. 41.

pete in expressions of fealty to the constitution or leader and rationalize every action and every position in terms of their fidelity to it or him. Care is taken to ensure the constitutional or charismatic continuity of the regime.

14. Issues that arise within the elite are resolved only slowly and with difficulty. The consensus necessary for action is difficult to achieve because every decision is more advantageous to some factions than to others. Only the cycle of crisis and consensus brings action, but it is short-term action to meet the immediate emergency and may in any case be followed by contradictory decisions after the next cycle of conflict. The resulting failure of policy to move clearly in any one direction is what was called, in the French Third and Fourth republics, *immobilisme*.

15. The immobilism of factional systems, the lack of extreme sanctions employed in their struggles, and their tendency to defend their existence against rival elites or external threats mean that they are in a certain sense extremely stable. It does not seem to be true, as some observers have suggested, that factional systems have an inherent tendency to break down.[42] In the absence of pressures from outside the system (in which I include those from social forces within the society), no force within the factional system is capable of amassing enough power to overthrow it. Thus, only continued factionalism can be predicted for a system that is already factional.

A factional system tends to preserve itself; yet at the same time, if it is a constitutional system, it eats away at its own legitimacy with every cycle of conflict. The politics of personality, the defeat of all constructive projects, the repeated collapse of governments, all run radically counter to the political ideals likely to be embodied in any constitution—those of stable government, regulated conflict based on debate over issues, and government capability to take constructive initiatives. If no constitutional government fully achieves such ideals, none is likely to deviate further from them than a factional regime. The consequence is likely to be that, although the factional system is internally stable, it alienates the social support upon which it is based and eventually bows to a counterelite that promises more effective rule. Such seems to have been the fate of the early republic, whose urban, professional base of support turned almost unanimously in the mid and late 1920s to the Kuomintang to reconstruct China.

42. Bernard J. Siegel and Alan R. Beals, "Pervasive Factionalism," *American Anthropologist* 62, no. 3 (June, 1960), pp. 394–417. For a critique, see Nicholas, "Factions," pp. 56–57. There will, of course, be other causes acting upon a factional system, which also affect the outcome. Personal, cultural, and technical resources for more complex organizations may be present to a greater or lesser degree; so may leaders' political vision and the will to move beyond the factional form of organization; and so may the challenge of changing social conditions.

Early Republican Factions

The organizational roster of the early republic was a long and rich one, in-cluding parties, clubs, military units, banks, schools, guilds, chambers of commerce, lawyers' associations, learned societies, student and peasant move-ments, bandit bands, and philanthropic and religious institutions. In the na-tional-level arena, focused on Peking, the most prominent organizations were political parties and clubs, military units, banks, and, at one remove, the *fa-t'uan* whose voices represented public opinion. But this apparent organizational rich-ness masked actual poverty: in the national arena, factional alignments were the dominant ones whenever major political issues came to a head. Banks and parties, clubs and armies became in crises pawns in a game whose rules were essentially factional.

In keeping with the predominance of bureaucrats in early republican govern-ment, the most powerful factions were those that emerged out of the new late Ch'ing reform institutions, both civilian and military.[43] Late Ch'ing army-builders like Yuan Shih-k'ai had reinforced the formal hierarchical authority of their military units with clientelist ties, which bound their leading sub-ordinates to them personally; these subordinates had done the same with their underlings.[44] Clientelist ties also grew up among officers who shared such experiences as late Ch'ing border pacification efforts or teaching or study at the Yunnan Military Academy.[45] As institutions weakened in the early republic, these personal ties became more and more important within the military hierarchy. Each military faction leader was supported by his personal followers and his followers' followers, placed at subordinate levels of the army. (There were also, of course, officers at all levels who did not belong to factions.) Each high officer was, at the same time, surrounded by a group of civilian politicians and advisors who helped him draft letters and telegrams and deal with local affairs in the area where he was stationed. The military units that such officers commanded, although nominally part of the Chinese army, became in fact personal military forces, organized along a combination of legal-rational and personalistic lines, loyal to their commander alone, and assuring him territorial control over the area where he was stationed. Thus, seen as whole, a single mili-

43. See Appendix for profiles of seven concrete historical factions.
44. Stephen R. MacKinnon has argued that the Peiyang Army was not a "personal army," but even he seems forced to concede a large element of clientelist loyalty in the relations of top officers to Yuan Shih-k'ai; "The Peiyang Army, Yüan Shih-k'ai, and the Origins of Modern Chinese Warlordism," *Journal of Asian Studies* 32, no.3 (May 1973): 405–23.
45. Wen Kung-chih, *Tsui-chin san-shih nien Chung-kuo chün-shih shih* (Taipei, 1962), *pien* 2, pp. 372–73.

tary faction was extremely complex and led by a series of steps from the central leader to various territorial forces and local politicians.[46]

The history of the civil wars in early republican China can be understood to some extent as the progressive splintering of the late Ch'ing military along the vertical cleavages within its component factions. As the older leaders died or retired, younger leaders emerged at the head of military factions of their own, which they built up to massive sizes before these in turn suffered splits.

The tendency of complex factions to break down was countered in the case of the military not only by the "trellis effect" of the formal hierarchy and by the personal loyalties of subordinates to superiors but also by the military advantages to be gained for the faction as a whole from cooperation against enemy factions. On the other hand, military factions also had special features that tended to increase the pressures to break down. First, the path to military victory inevitably involved forming opportunistic alliances with powerful local commanders whose defeat in battle would be costly. These allies were unreliable. Second, the increased territorial scale and numerical force of the rising faction led to the emergence of divergent geopolitical interests on the part of the component military forces and their commanders. Even if loyalty prevented an open revolt against the leader, it permitted political clashes and struggles (although not usually wars while the leader was still active) among his subordinates. Third, if the faction achieved military victory in North China as a whole, the unifying factor of a common enemy ceased to exist, while divisive factors, such as struggle over spoils and efforts by smaller, enemy factions to buy over military units, increased in salience. Fourth, the growth of the faction always tended to deprive the leader of direct control over military units and thus hastened his political retirement and the consequent open split within the faction. Beginning as local warlords directly controlling troops and territory, figures like Feng Kuo-chang and Ts'ao K'un ended up handing troops and territory to subordinates and taking up high political posts in Peking. Tenure in such posts was insecure and soon led to political retirement. The only way to avoid such disintegration was to refuse to expand beyond the borders of an internally unified and easily defended territorial base,[47] such as Manchuria or Shansi: Chang Tso-lin and Yen Hsi-shan are examples of warlords who fol-

46. Two studies of warlords are Donald G. Gillin, *Warlord: Yen Hsi-shan and Shansi Province, 1911–1949* (Princeton, N.J., 1967); and James E. Sheridan, *Chinese Warlord: The Career of Feng Yü-hsiang* (Stanford, Calif., 1966).

47. C. Martin Wilbur, "Military Separatism and the Process of Reunification under the Nationalist Regime, 1922–1937," in Ping-ti Ho and Tang Tsou, eds., *China in Crisis* 1, book 1 (Chicago, 1968): 205–9, discusses geographical areas of China in terms of their qualities as territorial bases.

lowed this strategy for long periods. (Chang, however, ultimately responded defensively to a power vacuum in Peking by allowing himself to be drawn into a general North China battle, and this situation can be regarded as one cause of the Kuo Sung-ling rebellion of 1925, which nearly toppled him from power.)

On the civilian side, bureaucratic factions occurred within the boundaries of such late Ch'ing and early republican organizations as ministries and banks. Bureaucratic factions extended their vertical skein of clientelist ties from the top leader down through junior leaders and into all the management levels and many of the branches of the organization. The typical pattern was for a leader to recruit young men into the organization and patronize their careers. In return, the followers offered support in struggles over the policy or personnel of the bureaucracy.

Unlike military factions, bureaucratic factions shared a broad commonality of interests with the institutions within which they operated. The resource for which bureaucratic factions competed was control over the bureaucracy. In struggling for positions, funds, and policy influence, the factions wished to influence and control the institution but not to break it up—in contrast to military factions, which were willing to force open breaks in the military hierarchy in order to gain control over the key resource of territory. Since the special features that enhanced the splitting tendency in military factions were not present in bureaucratic factions, they tended to function for long periods without splitting. If the leader was forced out of the organization (as was, for example, Liang Shih-i from the Ministry of Communications), he often retained considerable influence within it by virtue of his former leadership of the faction and his recruitment and patronage of many of the executives of the organization. But cleavages did develop within factions, and, with the death or retirement of the leader, struggle often broke out among the successor factions for control of the organization.

The early republic also saw the development of a number of major bureaucrat and ex-bureaucrat factions, which enjoyed multiple institutional power bases. Such factions had members scattered in important posts in a variety of ministries, political parties, armies, banks and other organizations. Since the faction members were highly influential in their respective organizations, their factions enjoyed extensive possibilities for power despite their limited size. Thus, the Communications Clique built a commanding position in the world of Chinese finance; Tuan Ch'i-jui's faction was able to wield the predominant military power in China in 1916–20.

The leader's role in such a faction was often complicated by a form of competition and hostility among followers analogous to fraternal rivalry. Maurice Freedman has written that in China "the fraternal relationship was one of competition, and potentially of a fierce kind. Order was kept among brothers by the presence of an effective father."[48] Similarly, it was not unusual in Chinese factions for some of the followers of a given leader to regard one another with dislike and to compete rather than cooperate in serving the leader. When the faction had various support structures at its disposal, these structures might be found working to some extent at cross-purposes. Of course, such a situation could be reversed by the leader's personal intervention with the competing subordinates and would never occur in situations where the leader was coordinating activities from the first. But the leader of a large faction often refrained from an active coordinating role and let his followers take their own initiatives in the context of a broad strategy he had framed. When this led to conflict, as it did for example between Chin Yun-p'eng and Hsu Shu-cheng in 1920, the leader (Tuan Ch'i-jui) stepped in to resolve the disagreement. Such conflict within a faction was normal, if stressful. It did not lead to the faction's breakup, since the followers all remained loyal to the leader. Conflict also declined when the welfare of the entire faction was threatened by outside enemies.

Partly because of the obscurity of most of their members, the factions of professional politicians present the greatest difficulties for structural analysis. Although based in parliament, the professional politicians supplemented their uncertain parliamentary livings with journalism, teaching, and advisory posts— often sincures—in business or government. Groups perceptible within parliament often represented merely the most visible portion of a network of factional alliances whose leadership nodes were outside parliament, and strategies and alignments pursued within parliament often reflected the political or ideological alliances struck up by *eminences grises* outside that body. Because the professional politicians were politically weaker than the bureaucrats—often observing key political struggles helplessly from outside—they were less intimately bound up in the dynamics of factional politics and were more frequently able to honor ideology-based alliances, to which they were in any case more inclined than were the technocratically-oriented bureaucrats.

Political Recruitment and "Connections"

Who was recruited into a particular faction? In republican China, as elsewhere, accidental meetings, personal compatibility, the leader's need for a follower with particular skills, and the potential follower's desire to become involved in politics, all played a role in determining the shape of political alignments. Equally, however, in republican China as elsewhere, one politician was more likely to recruit another if the two shared some relationship or bond that created a

---

48. Maurice Freedman, *Chinese Lineage and Society: Fukien and Kwangtung* (London, 1966), p. 46. Freedman says sources of this hostility included jealousy over the estate and the power struggle among the sons' wives.

presumption that they could trust one another. What that bond might be is defined differently by each culture: in early republican China, most politicians had a clear mental map of society in terms of "connections" (*kuan-hsi*)—particularistic dyadic relations, either actual or potential.[49] Such connections defined relationships within which relatively high levels of trust were expected, and they therefore laid down lines along which recruitment was most likely to occur. In this sense, clientelist ties and factions were not the most fundamental structural component of republican politics; beneath them lay the murky and complex networks of connections out of which most clientelist relationships and factions were mobilized. Knowledge of connections often enables us to understand why particular factions were composed as they were, when there is no obvious explanation based on interest, ideology, or personality.

Connections were rooted in the conception of the social order (*chi-kang*) not as a class structure or hierarchy of status groups but as a web of defined role relations such as father-son, ruler-minister, husband-wife, and teacher-student. Each set of two defined roles—that is, each type of connection—was specified by name and involved a distinct set of appropriate mutual behaviors, rights and duties. The rules of conduct for the various fixed social roles were known collectively as *li*.[50] A basic principle underlying the *li* was respect for seniority, actual or imputed. The greatest respect was due to grandparents, somewhat less to parents, and less still to older siblings. Nonfamily ties were assimilated into the same pattern: one's teacher, whatever his actual age, was considered on a level equal to a parent; one's colleagues were treated as siblings. The concept of seniority stressed generation and status rather than exact age. Status differences within the same generation were given the trappings of seniority differences by having the higher status person take the role of elder brother. The "junior" person in each relationship owed loyalty, obedience, and respect to the "senior." The senior owed protection and assistance in advancement to the younger.

No one knew personally all those with whom he had some connection. But when one met a person with whom one had a connection, cooperation was facilitated in a number of ways. First, the connection eased social intercourse by establishing which of the two persons was to be treated as the senior or superior

49. For the role of connections in modern Taiwan and Hongkong commercial behavior, see Donald R. DeGlopper, "Doing Business in Lukang," in W. E. Willmott, ed., *Economic Organization in Chinese Society* (Stanford, Calif., 1972), pp. 297–326; and Robert H. Silin, "Marketing and Credit," pp. 327–52. See further Talcott Parsons, *The Social System* (New York, 1951), pp. 195–98, for a discussion of "the particularistic achievement pattern" as exemplified by premodern Chinese society.

50. Cf. Benjamin Schwartz, "On Attitudes Toward Law in China," in Jerome Alan Cohen, *The Criminal Process in the People's Republic of China, 1949–1963: An Introduction* (Cambridge, Mass., 1968), p. 63.

in status and which as the junior or inferior. Second, it rendered the behavior of the members of the dyad toward each other predictable, both with regard to social formalities such as who should sit where, and with regard to potentially politically critical questions such as what one person had a right to ask of the other. Third, predictability and ease of social intercourse contributed to the establishment of trust. Fourth, most fundamentally, trust was established by the obligation that the connection established to offer one another aid and support and not to betray one another. As Lucian Pye has pointed out, "when some political actor is not a clear friend, that is, he does not fit comfortably into the system of role relationships explicity recognized, then the Chinese tend to suspect that he is a potential enemy."[51]

A number of factors modified and complicated the way in which connections worked. First, some connections involved greater and more solemn obligations than others. Duty owed to a fellow provincial or fellow student could not be compared to the duty owed to a father or teacher. Second, within each broad type of connection there were infinite shadings of importance and degrees of emotional commitment. Thus, coming from the same province and coming from the same county would both be classed as a locality (t'ung-hsiang) tie, but the first was of less importance than the second. (Because of such shadings, a typology of Chinese connections might well include several to several dozen categories.) Third, the emotional content of a relationship varied with factors other than the nature of the formal connection between two persons. All former students of the same master shared the same tie, but some students might become more intimate than others in the course of their shared experience.[52] Fourth, the significance of a connection varied with the number of persons sharing it who were present at a given time and place. The significance of the locality connection among Cantonese was far greater in Peking than it was in Canton.

Furthermore, where close connections were lacking, more far-fetched ones could be imputed to provide a common ground for two persons who were forced by circumstance into association (la-shang kuan-hsi). Satiric examples are provided by the Ch'ing novel, The Scholars:

"Just now I saw a list of successful candidates. Your patron, Mr. Tang, was a pupil of my grandfather; so I feel very close to you."

51. Pye, Spirit, p. 79.
52. Kenneth E. Folsom, Friends, Guests, and Colleagues: The Mu-fu System in the Late Ch'ing Period (Berkeley, Calif., 1968), in discussing connections, uses the word friendship to denote connections (e.g., p. 16) and also to denote warm, close, personal relationships (e.g., p. 17). This leads to the difficulty of having to distinguish between "friendship" and "real friends" (p. 19). To avoid this confusion. I prefer to use the term "connections" for the socially defined role sets, and "friendship" to describe a type of content of a relationship.

"Mr. Chu is the grandson of the Prefect Chu of Nanchang," put in Lovely Yu. "My father served as an examiner in Nanchang. So Mr. Chu and I are related."[53]

Or, an example from real life:

As for connections based on locality [chi-i], Mr. Han is from Sungtzu hsien and I am from Chienli; so prior to the abolition of fu we were fellow-locals of Chingchou fu. As for connections based on fellow studentship (yu-i), both Mr. Han and myself at different times studied under the present Senator Chang Chih-pen, so we are fellow alumni. As for our present occupations, Mr. Han is military representative of the Hupei Army, while I am military representative of western Hunan, so we are in the same line of work. Thus private feeling dictates we should be close to one another just as political alliance requires us to cooperate.[54]

The practice of searching one another's backgrounds for some connection to serve as a basis for a relationship indicates the importance of connections for establishing trust and the difficulty of proceeding politically without them. Far-fetched connections, however, did little more than smooth the path for polite social intercourse. They did not really establish the same set of obligations and the same degree of trust as were established by primary connections.

Connections, in short, were by no means a straitjacket for political activity. A politician's birthright included some connections, and others could be cultivated. Both inherited and cultivated connections were but structural factors that facilitated and increased the probability of recruitment by directing the paths along which recruitment tended to proceed. Of nine types of late Ch'ing/early republican connections identified by a simple analytic typology, three (lineage, family friendship of former generations, locality) were ascriptive; four (teacher-student, bureaucratic superior-subordinate, bureaucratic colleagues, schoolmate) were established early in a young man's career by virtue of a combination of circumstance and choice; and two (inlaws, sworn brotherhood) were established entirely on the participants' initiative. (Letters assigned to the nine types of connections and two other relationships below are keyed to figures in the Appendix.)

A. Lineage connections (ch'in-shu kuan-hsi).[55] Two members of the same blood line had an obligation of mutual support and a basis of trust. Freedman points out that such connections theoretically extended as far as all persons sharing a surname. Clans defined by genealogies were more restricted but nonetheless often extremely extensive; actual clan organizations were still more

53. Quoted in Folsom, Friends, Guests, p. 21.
54. Chiang Yü-sheng, "Hu-fa cheng-yen (hsuan-lu)," in I-chiu i-chiu nien Nan-Pei i-ho tzu-liao, special issue no. 1 of Chin-tai shih tzu-liao (Peking, 1962), p. 364.
55. See Feng Han-chi, The Chinese Kinship System (Cambridge, Mass., 1948), for an extensive list of kinship terminology.

restricted and "local lineages . . . living in one settlement or a tight cluster of settlements" were yet smaller. Thus, "the ties of clanship may be almost devoid of significance" in one case and in another may "be used for genealogical reference and for forming . . . alliances."[56]

Chinese culture had developed to a high level of articulation the ideals that were supposed to inform the father-son and brother-brother relationships—the stern, fair authority of the father, the filial piety of the son, the mutual aid and mutual respect of the older and younger brother—and these ideals were the effective patterns for all the other types of connection.[57] For example, the teacher-student and bureaucratic superior-subordinate relationships were assimilated to the father-son pattern; the bureaucratic colleagues, schoolmate, and sworn brother relationships were modeled on the brother-brother ideal. But although the Chinese ideal of family ties served as the model for all connections, in reality, family connections were usually less politically important than other ties. Father-son, brother-brother and cousin-cousin connections occasionally played a role in recruitment to politically important posts, but, as Pye has pointed out, "nepotism usually took the form of granting sinecures" rather than politically sensitive posts to members of one's family.[58] Politicians preferred to fill sensitive positions with able persons, whether relatives or not.

B. Family friendship of former generations (shih-i kuan-hsi, shih-chiao kuan-hsi). This connection linked members of the same generation of two families because of the close friendship of the fathers or grandfathers of the two families; the term also applies to the connection between a man and his friend's son. A famous example is the initial connection between Tseng Kuo-fan and Li Hung-chang: "Li Hung-chang's relationship with Tseng Kuo-fan was based on his being the son of one of Tseng's classmates."[59]

C. Locality connection (t'ung-hsiang kuan-hsi). Persons coming from the same locality or region were considered to have a basis for trust. Region was an important part of one's identity: the county of birth commonly appeared along with the inhabitant's name on doorplates and was used in newspapers and correspondence as an honorific given name for prominent figures (thus Yuan Hsiang-ch'eng was Yuan Shih-k'ai of Hsiangch'eng County; Li Huang-p'i was Li Yuan-hung of Huangp'i County; Tuan Ho-fei was Tuan Ch'i-jui of

---

56. Freedman, *Chinese Lineage*, pp. 20–31.

57. Cf. Folsom, *Friends, Guests*, p. 5.

58. Lucian W. Pye, *Warlord Politics: Conflict and Coalition in the Modernization of Republican China* (New York, 1971), p. 46. Pye cites Wu P'ei-fu's brother, who was appointed director of the Peking Zoo, and relatives of Tuan Ch'i-jui, who got posts in the Peking Municipal Light and Power Company.

59. Folsom, *Friends, Guests*, p. 78. Also see Lien-sheng Yang, "The Concept of *Pao* as a Basis for Social Relations in China," in John K. Fairbank, ed., *Chinese Thought and Institutions* (Chicago, 1957), pp. 292, 302.

Hofei City). In culturally and linguistically fragmented China, persons from the same locality literally spoke the same language.

Like the other types of connection, locality connections were open to varying definitions and might hold greater or lesser significance depending upon several variables. For one thing, the geographical unit subjectively defined as significant varied from locality to locality. Wu P'ei-fu, who was from P'englai, a not particularly well-known county in Shantung, surrounded himself with fellow provincials without regard to the county of their origin; but Tuan Ch'i-jui, who came from the famous and prosperous town of Hofei, did not feel an equally close connection to people from other sections of Anhwei. (The relative local chauvinism of various localities was probably connected with their size and influence, the degree to which the province was geographically and linguistically split, and so forth). Secondly, the distance from home and the relative plenitude or paucity of co-locals played a role in defining the significance of locality connections. Persons from Kwangtung Province would tend to regard one another as co-locals in Peking, where Kwangtungese were relatively few; while in Canton locality connections would be restricted to Kwangtungese from the same *hsien* or village. Third, significant locality connections might crosscut political boundaries to take account of geographic, economic, or linguistic regions. Thus, Liang Shih-i of western Kwangtung had a locality connection with Kuan Mien-chün of eastern Kwangsi.[60] Fourth, of course, the preference of the given leader would affect the importance of locality connections in recruitment to the particular faction.

D. Teacher-student connection (*shih-sheng kuan-hsi*). The duty of a student to his teacher was a solemn and lifelong one, comparable to a man's duty to his parents and involving certain rites and respect. The teacher, for his part, was expected to advance the student's career. In addition to his actual teachers, a man had this connection with those who tested him for the civil service examinations.[61]

E. Bureaucratic superior-subordinate connection (*liao-shu kuan-hsi*). This was the connection between a bureaucrat and the superiors under whom he worked at various stages in his career. The mutual rights and duties involved were similar to those in the teacher-student connection. Like the teacher-student connection, the bureaucratic superior-subordinate connection typically involved members of two different generations and was modeled on the father-son relationship. The bureaucratic superior-subordinate tie tended to be established by virtue of the accidents of assignment within the bureaucracy rather than by choice. It might or might not become a close personal relationship, but in any

---

60. Ts'en Hsueh-lü, *San-shui Liang Yen-sun hsien-sheng nien-p'u*, 2 vols. (Taipei, 1962), 1:18 (hereafter abbreviated *LSINP*).

61. Cf. Yang, "Concept of *Pao*," p. 304.

case it required respect toward superiors and former superiors. The connection took on added significance if a patron-client tie was also established.

The bureaucratic superior-subordinate connection, reinforced by patronage ties, guaranteed that a high official who served for a considerable period in a government organ would retain important influence in that body after he left the post. This was even more the case when the official's tenure coincided with a period of expansion of the bureau, so that he presided over the recruitment and early careers of many young officials; after leaving office, such a high official would leave behind a body of subordinates and clients who remained personally tied to him. Since the late Ch'ing was a period of expanding new bureaucratic organs, the bureaucratic superior-subordinate connection played an important role in late Ch'ing and early republican politics. An example is the continued influence throughout the early republican period of Liang Shih-i and other Communication Clique members in the Ministry of Communications and various banks and railways.

F. Schoolmate connection (*t'ung-hsueh kuan-hsi*). Fellow alumni shared a basis of trust. Traditionally, the men who passed a given examination (e.g., the *chü-jen* or *chin-shih* examination) at the same sitting were considered schoolmates. The solemnity of the relationship was especially strong in the case of the *chin-shih* degree. The schoolmate connection was assimilated to the model of brother-brother relations, but was often a closer and more intimate relationship than that between brothers. "Since classmate relationship was customarily regarded as almost an extension of kinship and often obliged classmates to stand by and help one another, class lists all stress the 'fraternal' element. . . . members of the class called each other 'brothers,' and this particular kinship extension often passed on to the next generation"[62] (cf. family friendship of former generations, above). The tie was reinforced by the common obligation to the same teacher or examiner. A given teacher's students (*men-sheng, men-hsia, men ti-tzu*) often joined to publish the teacher's chronological biography (*nien-p'u*) or official papers.

When students began to attend new-style and overseas schools, the traditional schoolmate connections were replaced by two new forms that went under the same name: graduates of the same school were considered schoolmates, and students who had gone abroad to the same country in the same year or "period" (*ch'i*) were also considered schoolmates. In these new forms, the schoolmate connection became less solemn; often, schoolmates did not know one another. The new-style schoolmate connection was more significant if the number of Chinese graduates of the school in question was fairly small, as in the case of Keiō University in Japan, if the number of students going to

62. Ping-ti Ho, *The Ladder of Success in Imperial China: Aspects of Social Mobility, 1368–1911* (New York, 1964), p. 99.

the country in question that year was small (as in the earlier years of Chinese study in Japan); or if the people involved actually knew one another during student days. Despite the shifts in form, the schoolmate connection remained in China, as in many other societies, an important basis of political recruitment.

G. Connection between bureaucratic colleagues (*t'ung-liao kuan-hsi*). Just as the teacher-student connection has its bureaucratic analogue in the bureaucratic superior-subordinate connection, so the schoolmate connection is paralleled by that between bureaucratic colleagues. Whatever the content of the personal relationship, it was felt that colleagues in the same office or enterprise, particularly those who worked under the same superior, owed one another certain types of friendly behavior and mutual support. An important example is the "Peiyang Clique," a broad set of military and civilian officials centered on those who had worked directly under Yuan Shih-k'ai in the training of his Newly-Founded Army at Hsiaochan.

H. Inlaw tie (*yin-ch'in kuan-hsi*). In a society where arranged marriage was the norm, inlaw connections were naturally important, because marriages were arranged with an eye to their advantages in politics or business. Polygyny made it possible to utilize marriage in this way more freely.[63] Marriages often formalized alliances already made for political cooperation, thus giving social sanction and structural reinforcement to relationships which might originally have been opportunistic and where the participants wanted the assurance that the inlaw connection provided.

I. Sworn brotherhood (*chieh-pai hsiung-ti kuan-hsi*). Like the inlaw relationship, sworn brotherhood lent structural reinforcement to an alliance, or to a personal relationship, by establishing a connection with all the obligations and cultural sanctions involved.

The absence of any of the nine connections by no means precluded political cooperation. Indeed, the able bureaucrat or politician was always on the lookout for promising younger men with whom to establish patronage ties (marked J in the Appendix). We are told that Tseng Kuo-fan "kept systematic lists of able men and encouraged them by writing to them, paying them visits, and lecturing them."[64] Commenting on Feng Kuo-chang's failure in this regard, a republican politician noted, "Feng's relations with others were based on nothing more than mutual cooperation for mutual benefit. As a consequence, there were few who were personally loyal to him. His power was thus far from comparable to that of Tuan Ch'i-jui in the solidity and depth of its foundation."[65] The

---

63. I am indebted to Ernest P. Young for pointing this out.

64. Mary Clabaugh Wright, *The Last Stand of Chinese Conservatism: The T'ung-Chih Restoration, 1862–1874*, 2d printing (New York, 1966), p. 78.

65. *Shun-t'ien shih-pao* 1919.12.31.2 (hereafter abbreviated *STSP*).

presence of connections was helpful but not essential in initiating patronage relationships.

Outside of the bureaucracy, within the late Ch'ing student, intellectual and politician communities in Tokyo and Shanghai, there also grew up master-disciple relationships based on ideological affinity (marked K in the Appendix). Examples are provided by Liang Ch'i-ch'ao and the younger men who worked with him as propagandists and editors for the constitutionalist cause and by Sun Yat-sen and his closest revolutionist followers. Discipleship ties were more heavily based on intellectual agreement than were clientelist ties, so the groups formed on the basis of such ties were somewhat deviant from the pure type of faction outlined earlier in the chapter. Yet even the beginning of these relationships was eased by the existence of connections (school or locality connections, for instance, brought many disciples within the orbits of their respective masters). And the master-disciple tie among these modern-minded intellectuals became closely assimilated to the old-fashioned teacher-student tie (the terms for teacher and master, and student and disciple, are not distinguished in Chinese). The disciple in principle accepted the master's intellectual leadership and owed him personal loyalty. If, in practice, he moved beyond the master's ideological position, it was difficult for him directly to contradict or criticize the master and it was only with reluctance that he would publish his deviant viewpoint.[66] In this way, early republican ideology-based groupings, among both ex-constitutionalists and ex-revolutionaries, were infused with many of the diffuse, personalistic, and particularistic norms of leader-follower relations governing the less ideological bureaucratic factions that dominated the political scene.

Selection of faction members was not the only area of political recruitment in which connections played a facilitating role. For one thing, alliances between factions or between an individual and a factional leader often occurred along lines laid down by the network of connections. Since the motivation for such alliances was essentially opportunistic, and the alliance was only valid as long as it served the interests of both parties, the need for a preexisting basis of trust was less critical than in the case of factional recruitment. However, such a connection was still to be preferred; its existence meant that the ally's behavior was to some extent predictable; personal relations occurred within a stereotyped mold, solving problems of precedence and deference, smoothing social contacts, and providing greater safety from betrayal.

66. Liang Ch'i-ch'ao's relations with K'ang Yu-wei exemplify these restrictions on disciples. Cf. Joseph R. Levenson, *Liang Ch'i-ch'ao and the Mind of Modern China* (Cambridge, Mass., 1953), pp. 59, 92–96; Chi Ping-feng, *Ch'ing-mo ko-ming yü chün-hsien ti lun-cheng*, pp. 62, 81.

The more powerful the leader, the fewer the persons on his own level with whom he could choose to ally. For example, when there were three leading military factions (a common situation in North China during the early republic), a given leader had only two choices for high-level allies. Even if he had a connection with one of the two, it might be impossible to make it the deciding factor. The field of choice might also be limited by the institutional structure within which the alliance had to be carried out. For example, factions in parliament had to choose their intraparliamentary allies from a limited number of factions and individuals who were also in this body. To retain flexibility, parliamentary factions could not restrict themselves to the network of connections. Yet, even in these situations, the existence of a connection enhanced the probability of alliance formation. In any case, rigidly limited fields of alliance potential were the exception rather than the rule in the early republic. Although the prominent warlord might have a choice of only two other major warlord factions to ally with, he had a wide choice of lower-level factions throughout the political system; the parliamentary faction was restricted in its choice of allies within parliament but had a wide range of choices for extraparliamentary allies.

Connections also influenced the choice of negotiators. The crucial role in negotiations was often played by intermediaries or emissaries, who had to be trusted by both sides. The existence of a connection to both sides was therefore a desirable qualification, and negotiators were usually chosen from among persons whose position in the network put them in connection with all parties to the negotiations. Of course, the negotiators also needed other qualities: prominence, seniority, political skill, and so forth.

A third area of recruitment affected by connections was the allocation of posts. When one faction was clearly dominant with regard to a particular post, a member or ally of that faction got the job. But in balance-of-power situations, where the incumbent had to be on good terms with both sides, a candidate with good connections in both camps was chosen. Similarly, if the faction with the power to make the appointment was not the same as the one in whose territory the appointment occurred, a mutually acceptable person might be sought in order to avoid an open break.

Finally, connections affected the formation of elite subgroups. If it were possible to map all the connections among the members of the early republican elite, one would be able to discern "clusters"—"sets of persons whose links with one another are comparatively dense."[67] One cluster might consist of all politicians from a certain province; another of all the students of a certain teacher. By arbitrarily raising the threshold of density defining a cluster, we might dis-

67. Barnes, "Networks," p. 118. Barnes explores the possibility of dealing with this concept mathematically, but since our data are inadequate to map all connections, we can only use the concept heuristically.

cover a cluster of politicians from a certain province who also worked in the same bureaucratic organization, or a teacher's cluster of students who also shared locality and bureaucratic ties. At a fairly low threshold of density, the boundaries of certain very extensive clusters of connections defined cleavages that became the basis of successive progovernment or opposition groupings in the national political elite. The major cleavage was between the "Peiyang" portion of the elite, which dominated the Peking government, and the relatively excluded Canton-based opposition.

The Peiyang group consisted primarily of bureaucrats who had made their late Ch'ing careers under the aegis of Yuan Shih-k'ai or his lieutenants. Central figures in this popularly-termed "Peiyang Clique" included Hsu Shih-ch'ang, Tuan Ch'i-jui, Liang Shih-i, and Ts'ao K'un. The Peiyang group was thickly laced with regional, inlaw, bureaucratic superior-subordinate, bureaucratic colleague, and teacher-student connections as well as with patron-client ties. Less than two years after the 1911 revolution, the Peiyang bureaucrats emerged in control of the government and most of the provinces. Although extensive, the Peiyang group excluded many bureaucrats and most politicians. Within the bureaucracy, non-Peiyang figures included warlords, especially numerous in the South, who had not been involved in Yuan's Newly-Founded or Peiyang armies (e.g., T'ang Chi-yao, Lu Jung-t'ing), and bureaucrats who had not been involved in, or who had even opposed, Yuan's undertakings (e.g., Ts'en Ch'un-hsuan). Outside the bureaucracy, few educators, professionals, businessmen or professional politicians enjoyed close Peiyang links.

It is difficult to discern any common tie among the members of the persistent opposition group that provided the core support for the rival Canton governments of 1916[68] and 1917–22 except exclusion from the dominant Peiyang cluster of connections. Former bureaucrats, former bandits, and modern young Japanese-educated politicians were part of it. The Research, Political Study, and various Kuo-min tang parliamentary factions, the Kwangsi, Yunnan, and various Kwangtung-based warlord factions, and parts of the navy participated. With some exceptions, including Sun Yat-sen, most members of this intraelite opposition differed little from the progovernment sectors of the elite with respect to social background or political culture. Nor did they display a consistent ideological or principled objection to the Peking government, for, although they often couched their opposition in such terms, they repeatedly proved willing to cooperate with Peking and to participate in Peking politics when the opportunity arose (1912–13, 1916–17, 1922–24, and, in some cases, 1924–26). Although a few members of the Canton opposition enjoyed very dense ties with

68. The 1916 military government was actually located at Chaoch'ing, Kwangtung. Its anti-Yuan platform was eventually accepted by many of Yuan's followers who could not stomach his imperial ambitions.

the Peiyang bureaucrats and still joined the opposition (T'ang Shao-i, Wu T'ing-fang), by and large, the major shared characteristic of opposition members seems to have been exclusion from the Peiyang group.

At a somewhat higher threshold of density, there were smaller clusters of connections within the progovernment and opposition sectors of the elite. Within the Peiyang portion of the elite, for example, there was a cluster of locality, patron-client, and bureaucratic ties loosely known as the Anhwei Clique and another loosely known as the Chihli Clique; even whle struggling against the Canton opposition in 1918–1920, these two clusters broke from one another and fought for the control of the government (the structure of these groups is further discussed in the Appendix). Each cluster was later to fragment further. As republican political history unfolded, clusters and cleavages in the network of connections thus became the basis for new government or opposition formations.

Connections, Factions, and the Failure of Constitutionalism

Lyon Sharman's diagnosis seems apt: "A people habituated by ages of tradition to individualized administration in governmental affairs was not able to take up quickly a form of government whose proper functioning depends upon the smooth cooperation of groups of men brought together on a basis of equality."[69] The bureaucrats who inherited the Chinese government from the Ch'ing and to a lesser degree their junior partners, the professionals and politicians, conceived of society as composed of hierarchical, particularistic pairs of roles—connections. On the basis of these, one could develop a network of clientelist relationships and a supplementary set of more transitory alliances; from here, one could build to the organizational level of factions, which were often rather complex and were supported by the resources of banks, newspapers, military units, and the like. Beyond this, however, to cooperate on a nonhierarchical basis and to do so with all comers, friends or strangers, proved difficult for these generations of Chinese leaders. In the absence of a dynastic focus of loyalty, the orderly conduct of politics would have required just this sort of cooperation. The majority of republican leaders came to constitutionalism with optimism and a desire that it should work. But as issues arose, factions semeed the most accessible form of political group to those who wished to influence political outcomes. Organization in factions led inexorably to the "disintegrative behavior" that could not be resisted despite repeated attempts to overcome it by improving or reaffirming the constitutional order.

69. Sharman, *Sun Yat-sen*, p. 357.

III

THE SETTING OF CONFLICT:
The Peking Government, 1916–28

Each factional system adopts the contours, the language, and the techniques of its institutional arena, be it a village, legislature, bureaucracy, or royal court. Republican political tactics can be fully understood only in the context of the formal and informal institutional structure of the Peking government.

Peking's Role and the Support of the Powers

It was commonly remarked of the Peking government that its writ did not run beyond the city walls. While not literally true, the statement accurately reflected the government's lack of political muscle. Orders emanating from Peking were obeyed only when it suited local commanders and officials to do so. The functions of the central government during the warlord era were in fact not primarily those of political decision-making and administration. Rather, the Peking government was itself an object of political conflict, a source of political "goods." Government organs functioned less as administrative "output" institutions than as valuable resources for the conduct of political struggle.

Peking, first of all, held the key to a limited type of legitimacy in Chinese politics. Although lacking the broader legitimacy to resolve political disputes and issue binding administrative and legislative decisions, Peking was universally recognized until 1927 as the legitimate capital of a unitary China. Unity (t'ung-i) was an emotionally powerful slogan in politics. A warlord could justify his struggle for territory by declaring that he was fighting to unify the country. To each aspiring unifier of China, control of Peking was a necessary goal. Whoever controlled Peking was by definition closest to unifying the country. Even when independence from Peking was openly declared, as by the southern provinces in 1917, it was never in order to establish a separate country but merely constituted a refusal to deal with the current administration in Peking.

The government also enjoyed a not wholly illusory power to make appointments. Although military control was the basis of warlord regimes, legitimation through appointments conferred by Peking was valued and sought for high-level provincial posts. Particularly in the provinces over which wars were fought because of geopolitical position or a succession crisis, appointment from Peking was a valuable resource for either defender or attacker, lending his cause legitimacy and permitting him to brand his opponent as a rebel or bandit. Many local wars began with the appointment by Peking of one warlord to a post in territory controlled by another: the attacking warlord had postponed his advance until he could manage to get an appointment to justify it.

A second good to which Peking held the key was foreign recognition. The powers insisted upon recognizing only one government of China, at Peking, and they held rigidly to the view that only this central government could conduct foreign relations, conclude foreign loans, negotiate over the status of treaty ports and railways, and the like.[1] The roots of this position lay in the peace treaties, oral agreements, and railway construction contracts the powers had concluded with China in the nineteenth and early twentieth centuries. Although the traditional Chinese state was highly decentralized, the powers had behaved in a fashion consistent with the centralized Western view of the state and had signed all their agreements with Peking. With the post-1916 decay in the power of the Peking government, defense of their treaty position involved the powers in supporting the central government against the provinces.

One way in which this support for the Peking government was expressed was in the physical protection the presence of the legations afforded Peking. Ever mindful of the humiliating and costly Boxer intervention and aware that any violation of the protocols of 1901, which were aimed against the recurrence of a threat to the legations, would lead to another intervention, all but a few warlords took care not to make Peking a battlefield in the wars in its vicinity. With remarkable restraint, the changeover from one warlord to another in Peking was almost always carried out peacefully, with interim control exercised by a civilian committee of public safety. Military forces in the city were kept to a minimum. The Peking-Tientsin Railway, protected under the protocols, was seldom interfered with, even when crucial battles occurred along its line.

An even more important form of indirect foreign support for the Peking government was the foreign role in protecting the customs and salt revenues for the central government. In the case of customs, the provinces had originally

1. Even in 1926–28, the period of most extreme fragmentation, when the powers did not recognize the Chang Tso-lin government in Peking, they carried on business with it on a de facto basis, taking the position that they recognized a state, China, with its capital at Peking, but did not at the moment recognize any head of state or any government of China. See, e.g., F.O. 371/11663, F5628/10/10, Strang, "The Question of the Recognition of the Southern Government," December 12, 1926, confidential print, pp. 1–2.

enjoyed 60 percent of customs revenues, but in the years 1894–1901 a series of foreign loans culminating in the Boxer Indemnities were secured on these revenues, so that by 1901 the whole revenue was committed for the service of the obligations of the central government to foreign powers and businesses. In 1912, to protect these foreign obligations against the possibility of default through seizure of the revenues by the rebel provinces, the powers persuaded the central government to agree to extend the role of the Maritime Customs Administration. Until then, the administration had merely supervised the collection of revenue without handling it; now, it would actually collect the revenues, which for the first time would be lodged in foreign treaty port banks under the trusteeship of the diplomatic corps.[2]

In 1917, this new arrangement proved to have unintended implications when, due to the international rise in the price of silver and other factors not anticipated in 1912, the customs revenue began to show a surplus over what was needed to service the foreign obligations secured on it. This surplus was handled under the old arrangements and was therefore in effect collected for the sole benefit of the central government to the detriment of the provinces' traditional call upon customs revenues. The authority of the diplomatic corps now protected not only the rights of foreign creditors but the interests of whoever happened to be in control in Peking. "In its essentials," wrote the British Foreign Office in late 1925, "this means that customs revenues collected all over China reach the hands of the Peking government only because the foreign powers have been prepared to use force against any Chinese official attempting to prevent their doing so."[3] Thus, for example, the Canton government threatened five times to seize the customs revenues collected at Canton and each time was prevented by an international show of gunboats.[4] The revenue collected at Canton was preserved for the benefit of Peking.

2. F.O. 371/11648, F360/8/10, Lampson, "Memorandum Respecting the Control of the Chinese Maritime Customs Funds by the Diplomatic Body at Peking," March 31, 1921, brought up to date by Pratt, January 27, 1926, confidential print, pp. 1–5, 16–20. See also Stanley F. Wright, *The Collection and Disposal of the Maritime and Native Customs Revenue Since the Revolution of 1911. With an Account of the Loan Services Administered by the Inspector General of Customs*, 2d ed. (Taipei, 1966), pp. 2–8; F.O. 371/11648, F558/8/10, Wellesley, "Memorandum on British Policy in China," February 9, 1926, confidential print, pp. 10–11.

3. F.O. 371/10925, F6117/2/10, Telegram 381, [Chamberlain] to Macleay, London, December 31, 1925, p. 2. In preparing for the Tariff Conference, British diplomats had begun to realize for the first time the implications of what they had been doing for eight years.

4. F.O. 371/11648, F558/8/10, Wellesley, "Memorandum on British Policy in China," Feburary 9, 1926, confidential print, p. 12. The five occasions were in 1918, 1919, 1920, 1921 and 1923. The same thing nearly happened again in 1924. The implicit foreign threat also prevented seizures of revenues by Chang Tso-lin in 1922 and 1924 and by Wu P'ei-fu in 1925 at Hankow, although no gunboats were actually used in these instances.

The Salt Revenue Administration presented a similar case. Salt revenues had traditionally been collected by the provincial authorities, and some portion, never amounting to more than 13 million taels, was remitted to the center. The Reorganization Loan Agreement of April 26, 1913, however, committed all of the salt revenue to the service of a loan contracted by the central government and provided for the reorganization of the salt administration with the participation of foreign experts and a foreign associate chief inspector to implement Peking's control of salt revenue collection. Because the increasingly valuable customs revenue began to bear the service of the Reorganization Loan in 1914, there was from that year a surplus of salt revenue over what was required for the service of obligations secured upon it. But instead of releasing this surplus to the provincial authorities, the salt administration under the 1913 agreement released it to the central government.

The legal and political status of the salt revenues, however, differed in several respects from that of the customs. The diplomatic corps had no formal trusteeship over the salt revenues; the highest foreign officer in the Salt Revenue Administration was subordinate to a Chinese chief inspector; the annual service of foreign obligations secured on the salt revenue was such a small portion of the total revenue that seizure of even substantial portions of the revenue by local warlords did not threaten foreign interests enough to justify the use of gunboats.[5] Furthermore, salt revenue was collected all over China, instead of in the treaty ports, and entirely from Chinese instead of partly from foreigners. For all these reasons, mounting warlord seizures of salt revenues went unchallenged by the powers. But the basic impact of the foreign presence was the same as with customs revenue. Revenues that the Peking government in its weakness could not have obtained for itself were obtained for it as a consequence of China's relations with the foreign powers.

Nor were these the only implications of foreign recognition of Peking. The financial and treaty interests of the powers in treaty ports and railways located within the territory of the warlords, combined with the foreign insistence on dealing formally with only one center of power, further enhanced the role of Peking. In the case of treaty ports, the lucrative post of treaty port superintendent (shang-p'u tu-pan) could only be allocated with the cooperation of Peking, for the incumbent would not otherwise be recognized by the powers. This was also the case with the financially valuable post of railway superintendent, since the powers were large-scale creditors of most of the railways, having built them, lent money to them, and supplied them with materials and railway cars on credit. Although there is no denying the frequent interference by warlords

5. F.O. 371/11675, F1539/255/10, Pratt, "Memorandum on Salt Administration," March 27, 1926, confidential print, pp. 1–11; F.O. 371/11675, F415/255/10, Pratt, minute, February 8, 1926; same file, minute by Lampson, February 10, 1926.

in the railways, ranging from seizing and holding rolling stock for future military use to attaching most of the net revenue, the foreign interest in the railways was a cause of warlord caution and discouraged outright seizure of control.[6] The fiction, and some of the reality, of central government control over the railways was thus preserved.[7]

A final consequence of foreign recognition of Peking was the necessity imposed upon local warlords to involve the Ministry of Foreign Affairs in the settlement of many of their problems with foreign powers and individuals. Although the foreign consuls dealt informally with local authorities, the powers —particularly the British, whose China interests were greatest—insisted that treaties and settlements be formalized through Peking. The specter haunting British policy-makers was that excessive dealing with local authorities would lead to "the absence of any central body whom we could hold even nominally responsible for the carrying out of China's treaty and loan obligations."[8]

A last area in which Peking was a valuable political resource was that of

6. Thus, for example, in 1923, in the aftermath of the so-called Lincheng outrage in which a number of foreign passengers were kidnapped from the Pukow-Tientsin express at Lincheng by brigands, Britain submitted proposals to the diplomatic corps for the policing of trunk railway lines by police under foreign officers and for additional foreign control over management and accounting of railways in order to assure payment of the police force. The Peking government moved to forestall the idea by mandating on September 2 regulations for a reorganized railway police force under central government control. See F.O. 371/ 9189, 9190, 9191, 9192, 9193, passim. An interesting aspect of this controversy is the role played in blocking the foreign proposal by the Communications Clique. The Peking Daily News, owned by Communications Clique members Chou Tzu-ch'i and Yeh Kung-ch'o and subsidized by several government ministries including Communications and Foreign Affairs, led the press attack on the proposals. See F.O. 371/9192, F3114/22/10, Despatch 524, Macleay to Curzon, Peking, September 13, 1923. For the earlier history of the railway unification issue, see LSINP, 2: 11 ff.

7. For example, the directors of major railways and most of the technical personnel of railways were appointed by the central government, although often enough the director appointed was a nominee of the local warlord. Central coordination was maintained on rates and other practices (see The China Year Book 1926-7, p. 270). The seizure of funds by warlords was usually limited to profits so that foreign obligations could continue to be met, although this restraint decreased toward the end of the period.

8. F.O. 371/9182, F2987/12/10, Despatch 476, Macleay to Curzon, Peking, August 18, 1923, confidential print, p. 3. From time to time, more adventurous souls proposed that a Chinese central government was not essential to British interests because consuls were already dealing directly with local officials, but policy continued to insist on one central, responsible authority that could at least receive protests even if it could do nothing about their causes. Cf. F.O. 371/7985, F2675/59/10, Telegram 268, Clive to F.O., Peking, August 16, 1923, p. 2. For an extended case study showing the important role of the Foreign Affairs Ministry in international relations affecting even regional warlord interests, see Leong Sowtheng, "China and Soviet Russia: Their Diplomatic Relations, 1917-1924" (unpublished ms., Canberra, 1972), esp. p. 432.

finance. The fact that the ruler of Peking was the recipient of the customs and salt surpluses has already been mentioned. An even more important source of revenue in the early years of the warlord period was loans. The customs and salt revenues served as securities on which to raise both foreign and domestic loans. Even when these were pledged and pledged again, Peking remained a favorable base for concluding unsecured loans because its position as the internationally and domestically recognized government of China meant that its obligations would have to be respected by subsequent governments in order to preserve their credit. Control of Peking thus helped substantially to supplement the income a military faction gained from control of territory: although Peking was supposed to support all central divisions of the Chinese Army, in fact, only members of the controlling factions received their stipends from the Ministry of War; central divisions controlled by members of enemy factions usually saw their pay go into arrears.

In short, the role of Peking in the warlord system was far more important than its inability to enforce its writ over any significant portion of the country would suggest. "It may be wondered why such powerful people as [the warlords] have not swept aside the Peking Government and usurped their positions and their functions," observed the British Secret Intelligence Service. "To this it may be replied that the Government of Peking is recognized to be a necessity— possibly an unfortunate necessity—by most Chinese because it is through its medium that the connection with foreign powers is kept up, and it is to this Government that all communications with China from outside are made. Further . . . it is to the Peking Government that the Chinese Maritime Customs and, to a lesser extent, the Salt Gabelle pay in the money collected by them. . . ."[9] Peking, as a source of the goods of legitimacy, foreign recognition and funds, was a political resource necessary for any warlord with major pretensions.

Nor should it be thought that because Peking lacked the power to rule, its politicians were merely puppets of the warlords. The Peking politicians had a good deal of bargaining power and tactical leeway and many opportunities to play off warlords aginst one another. Since the direct use of warlord force within Peking would harm its legitimacy, bring into question foreign recognition, and indeed quite possibly call down foreign intervention to the disadvantage of the warlord responsible, the civilians and their institutions enjoyed considerable autonomy. Especially on the frequent occasions when Peking found itself in an analogue of an international situation, dealing with a number of virtually independent warlord powers in a rough balance of power, there was considerable scope for Peking politics to influence events in China as a whole.

9. F.O. 371/7996, F109/84/10, Secret Intelligence Service, "China. The Political Situation," January 3, 1922, pp. 3–4.

Structure of the Peking Government

For most of the warlord period, the Peking government operated on the basis of the Provisional Constitution (*Lin-shih yueh-fa*)[10] promulgated in 1912. Except for the interlude of Yuan Shih-k'ai's Constitutional Compact (1914–16), the Provisional Constitution remained in force until the promulgation of a new constitution under Ts'ao K'un in October 1923.[11] The Ts'ao K'un constitution was in turn replaced by the Regulations of the Chinese Republican Provisional Government (*Chung-hua min-kuo lin-shih cheng-fu chih*) in 1924.[12] These gave way in 1926 to a series of regency cabinets and in 1927 to the Mandate on the Organization of the Marshal's Government.[13]

The major institutions of government under the Provisional Constitution were president, cabinet, and parliament.[14] Their constant struggle for power was a major theme in the history of the Peking government. The constitutional provisions concerning their functions were ambiguous enough to permit the balance to shift with the realities of power. Constitutional law experts justly criticized this ambiguity, an unintended consequence of provisions designed by the framers to prevent a strong presidency, as conducive to cabinet-president and parliament-executive conflicts.[15] Yuan Shih-k'ai early defeated the intention to lodge predominant influence in the cabinet, reducing its role to that of countersigning his decisions, and he dissolved parliament when it became an obstacle to his plans. The first presidency of Li Yuan-hung (1916–17) saw an inconclusive struggle between Li and Prime Minister Tuan Ch'i-jui, and between Tuan and the parliament, in which the power of the presidency declined. The institutional conflict was resumed minus parliament when Feng Kuo-chang succeeded Li as president in 1917. Feng and Tuan fought to a virtual standoff.

10. The discussion of the Provisional Constitution is based on Franklin W. Houn, *Central Government of China, 1912–1928: An Institutional Study* (Madison, Wisc., 1957), pp. 21–82; Yang Yu-chiung, *Chin-tai Chung-kuo li-fa shih*, rev. ed. (Taipei, 1966), pp. 91–97; Sih-gung Cheng, *Modern China: A Political Study* (Oxford, 1919), pp. 47–120; Joshua Mingchien Bau, *Modern Democracy in China* (Shanghai, 1923); and W. W. Willoughby, *Constitutional Government*. For its text, see, among others, Wang Shih-chieh and Ch'ien Tuan-sheng, *Pi-chiao hsien-fa* (Shanghai, 1938), 2: 252–57.

11. An English translation of the text can be found in Ch'ien Tuan-sheng, *Government and Politics*, pp. 436–46.

12. Text in Sun Yao, comp., *Chung-hua min-kuo shih-liao* (Taipei, 1967), p. 539.

13. "Mandate on the Organization of the Ta-yuan-shuai Government, June 18th, 1927," *Public Documents Supplement of the Chinese Social and Political Science Review* 11, no. 1 (January 1927): 133–34.

14. The courts played virtually no political role. See Houn, *Central Government*, pp. 71–74.

15. See, for example, Willoughby, *Constitutional Government*, pp. 33–42; Bau, *Modern Democracy*, pp. 93–106.

Under Feng's successor, Hsu Shih-ch'ang, the presidency became relatively weak, while cabinet and parliament struggled for power, with the cabinet eventually holding the upper hand. Such battles continued in subsequent presidencies.

The basic presidential functions were ceremonial and symbolic. The president, like the emperor before him, promulgated laws with the phrase "it is so ordered" (tz'u-ling). He appointed officials and conferred decorations. The presidents took upon themselves the responsibility for the multitude of disorders that swept China and admitted that these were due to their own moral shortcomings. Whether a president could parlay the prestige of his office into a role of real power and influence depended upon the incumbent.

Despite the effort of the authors of the Provisional Constitution to upgrade its importance, the cabinet as a body played a passive, merely formal role, ratifying decisions made elsewhere. The real significance of cabinet membership lay in the power derived from control of the ministries. Since the ministerial positions were a prime goal of factional conflict, the cabinet usually contained representatives of each of the major factions supporting the government. Decisions had to be made through negotiation among the factions involved and not simply by agreement within the cabinet. Thus, the cabinet as such could only handle relatively simple or factionally noncontroversial questions.

The prime minister, as distinct from the cabinet, however, could carve a powerful role for himself. Although the Provisional Constitution did not spell out specific prime ministerial powers beyond that of heading the cabinet in its task of "assisting" the president in the functions of administration, the prime ministership became the most important post in the politics of factional struggle. The incumbent of the presidency could not be changed easily and frequently enough to mirror the changes in actual power among factions, so presidents such as Li Yuan-hung and Hsu Shih-ch'ang, who did not control major factions, had less real political power than their prime ministers. The prime minister was able to capitalize on factional support to exercise political power: a dominant parliamentary or military faction would put foward a prime minister from its own ranks; or if there was a balance of power among various military and parliamentary factions, a prime minister acceptable to all parties would be found.

Custom prescribed that in selecting a cabinet the prime minister first be named by the president and approved by parliament, and that the other ministers then be chosen by the prime minister and their names submitted to parliament for approval. The process naturally involved negotiations with parliamentary, military, and financial factions over allocation of the seats in the cabinet. Certain features of the ministries were relevant to these negotiations.[16]

First, there were four relatively nonpolitical cabinet posts. Two of these were usually allocated with an eye to the cooperation of the personnel over whom the ministers had authority: the minister of foreign affairs was chosen from within the foreign affairs technocracy and the minister of the navy from among a small group of senior naval officers. From 1912 to 1928, a period that saw forty-five cabinets, only nine men served as minister of the navy and nineteen as minister of foreign affairs (some serving more than once). The political element was muted in the choice of the ministers of navy and foreign affairs because these two ministries were not useful as political resources. The Ministry of Foreign Affairs carried out China's foreign policy virtually independently of the factional rivalries in Peking, since the factions agreed in viewing foreign relations as essentially a technical problem in which all Chinese shared the same interests. (Politically significant loans from foreign countries to Chinese politicians were not concluded through the Ministry of Foreign Affairs but through other offices such as the Ministry of Communications or War or various subcabinet agencies.) The post of minister of the navy carried little power. The tiny navy was but a peripheral element in China's military balance of power, and in any case the various factions within the navy followed their own political strategies without regard to the views of the minister.

The other two nonpolitical cabinet posts, the ministries of Justice and Education, were often filled with an eye to increasing the prestige of government in legal and educational circles. It was customary to appoint a distinguished lawyer to the justice post and an educator or writer as minister of education. Although starved of funds, these two ministries appear to have formed the only consistent exceptions to the rule that Peking's writ did not run beyond its walls, for there is some evidence that, while the administration of justice and education was largely carried out by local officials and gentry, their efforts were often guided by Peking's modernizing standards and regulations.[17]

The five remaining cabinet posts were valuable political resources, control of which was an object of factional struggle. The minister of war was able to allocate large sums of money to militarists allied with his faction whenever the conclusion of a large loan or the release of the salt surplus put money into the hands of the government. His ministry also bestowed promotions in rank and assignments to provincial military commands, with which a warlord's control over territory could be either confirmed or threatened.

16. Ministry organization and duties are described in Cheng, *Modern China*, pp. 75–87; and Udaka Yasushi, *Genkō Shina gyōsei* (Shanghai, 1926), pp. 114–231.

17. This is the implication in F.O. 371/12401, F1619/2/10, minute by Pratt, February 21, 1927. See also *The China Year Book 1926–7*, pp. 407–10, 753–62.

The Ministry of the Interior was important because it was in charge of parliamentary elections. Contention for its control was especially heated when a parliamentary election was in the offing. Other politically valuable duties of the ministry were the control of the Peking city administration and police and the right to register and regulate newspapers. Its duties in public health, famine relief, and local administration were neglected.[18]

The Ministry of Agriculture and Commerce was politically valuable because of its right to approve charters for the foundation of new businesses and banks. The granting of such charters, including trade monopolies or the right to issue bank notes, was a valuable form of patronage and source of income for the faction controlling the ministry.

The Ministry of Finance was a valuable resource because of its control over taxation (which became less important as tax receipts declined) and its right to issue and administer domestic bonds and treasury notes.[19] The minister and his cronies were in a position to profit from fluctuations in currency and bond values on the market because of inside knowledge.[20] The Ministry of Finance also had the right to appoint one director to each of the eighteen major provincial banks that were classified as official banks.[21]

The Ministry of Communications was a great source of funds for the faction of the incumbent, since it handled receipts from railways, and from telegraph, postal, and shipping services and was able to conclude loans with foreign governments and businesses. More than any other ministry, Communications controlled property of real value, from which a steady income was realized. Although the revenues were often seized by local warlords, the powers helped to some extent to protect the ministry's stake in them. To a unique degree, the Ministry of Communications was subject to influence from a single faction, the Communications Clique. Although the post of minister several times fell into the hands of other factions, the personnel makeup of the ministry remained relatively impervious to outside influence. Most of the staff had been recruited under leaders of the Communications Clique during the late Ch'ing, and because of their technical expertise they proved impossible to replace on a wholesale basis over the relatively short periods of time available to rival factions.

The third major branch of government was of course parliament. Parliament's legislative role was relatively unimportant. Most rules pertaining to government organization and policy were promulgated in the form of ad-

18. Ministry of Interior responsibilities are described in Juan Hsiang *et. al., Ti-i-hui Chung-kuo nien-chien* (Shanghai, 1924), pp. 199–200. On Peking city administration, see *Ching-tu shih-cheng hui-lan* (Peking, 1919).

19. Juan Hsiang, *Nien-chien*, pp. 201–203.

20. *SKJ*, pp. 540–41.

21. Juan Hsiang, *Nien-chien*, pp. 201–203.

ministrative regulations by the president. The major legislative duty of parliament was to write a constitution to replace the Provisional Constitution, a process that took until 1923. In addition, parliament supervised the administration by exercising such powers as electing the president, passing the budget, passing on bond issues, and concurring with the president in making war, peace, and treaties. The powers used most frequently and to best effect were those of ratifying the appointment of cabinet officials and of interpellating, investigating, and impeaching them. These powers were used to extract concessions and bribes from the administration. To some extent, the obstructive role of parliament in China, as in other countries with new republican systems, was aimed at gaining greater powers for a new institution whose role was not well defined by the constitution or tradition. But the obstructive role of the Chinese parliament was also an outcome of factional struggle within it for perquisites such as cabinet posts and financial support from the government. Only in rare instances was it possible to build a relatively enduring parliamentary coalition, like the Anfu Club, large enough to enable parliament to take decisive action. More commonly, even when the interests of parliament as an institution were not served by an obstructive role, such a role was inevitable because of the inability of its many small factions to cooperate. Instead of helping to increase the role of parliament, obstructionism in the end contributed to its decline, since it was unable to pass laws, enforce its supervision of the budget, or bargain effectively with the cabinet. For long periods, government was carried on with no parliament in session, and the convening of a new one was postponed beyond the lawful period, because parliament was simply not necessary for the conduct of government.

The Flavor of Peking Politics

The pace of affairs in Peking was leisurely, and few important decisions were made. There were periods of several months at a time when little of political significance occurred, and there were much longer periods when nothing occurred except political infighting. Even during periods of relatively intense political activity, such as those selected for scrutiny in this study, there were stretches when the political struggle seemed to hang fire as Peking waited for the turn of events elsewhere in the country. Thanks to the backwardness of China's transport and communications, most political crises developed slowly. As in all factional systems, crises could be resolved only by negotiation and waiting—waiting either for an opportunity to precipitate a showdown or for a balance of forces to emerge.

The Peking government was in any case a relatively small operation. The budgets occasionally submitted to parliament showed a yearly expenditure in the neighborhood of 500 or 600 million Mexican dollars.[22] But these figures bore no relation to reality. They were based on the fiction that the government received the funds it was supposed to from the provinces and financially supported the activities of the armed forces all over the country. A rare glimpse into the actual expenses of the Peking government is afforded by a "List of Administrative Expenditure[s] of the Central Government" submitted by the Ministry of Finance in January 1926 to the diplomatic corps in support of a request for an extension of the customs surtax. The list shows that the Peking government was spending on the order of Mex. $52 million a year, including about $14 million on the Peking city police and gendarmery, $33 million on other government organs, and $4 million on education.[23] Even with such a small governmental establishment, the government was heavily in debt to its employees.

The leisurely Peking routine was enlivened by feverish gossip, speculation, and rumormongering. The subtle, ceremonious politicians of Peking took intense pleasure in drama and innuendo, in well-executed maneuvers, in adroitly concealed meanings. The more Machiavellian the tactics of one's opponent, the more pleasurable it was to be able to see beneath the surface to his real goals. Peking was a highly literate small world where style—political, literary, personal—was highly valued.

Reliable intelligence was essential in such an atmosphere. It was important to hear all the rumors but not to be misled. Independent newspapers, such as the *Shun-t'ien shih-pao*—a major source for this study—were avidly read both for outport news and for Peking political intelligence.[24] But the highly unreliable political press was also closely followed. Peking in about 1920 had seventy-seven daily newspapers,[25] and almost all of these were "subsidized by political

22. *The China Year Book 1926–7*, p. 438, and Chia Shih-i, *Min-kuo ts'ai-cheng shih, hsu-pien* (Taipei, 1962), pien 1, pp. 38–46. The exact figures were as follows: Mex. $642,236,876 (1913 budget), Mex. $351,024,030 (1914 budget), Mex. $471,519,436 (1916 budget), Mex. $472,838,584 (second 1916 budget), Mex. $495,762,888 (1919 budget), Mex. $634,361,-957 (1925 budget).

23. F.O. 371/11684, F1015/1001/10, Despatch 55, Macleay to Chamberlain, Peking, January 21, 1926, confidential print, enclosures 1 and 2. In 1918, when the government had more income, expenditure was running about Mex. $15 million a month, of which $12 million was devoted to military expenses. F.O. 371/3188, 162953 (f88573), Despatch 353, Jordan to Balfour, Peking, July 25, 1918, confidential print, p. 2.

24. The *Shun-t'ien shih-pao* was a Japanese-owned and -managed Chinese-language newspaper with a high reputation for reliability (see Roswell S. Britton, *Periodical Press*, pp. 124–25, and other sources cited in note 27 below). Its importance to Peking politicians can be gauged by the fact that the retired official who was the author of *Cheng-wen chi-yao* refers more frequently to it in his diary than to any other newspaper. See *CWCY*, pp. 376–494.

25. *The China Year Book 1921–2*, pp. 99–104.

parties, government departments, statesmen in office and out, and any kind of individual who wants to have his trumpet blown in public."[26] Nothing was easier than the production of a daily newspaper. There was no need for printing machinery or reporters. One room, an editor, a "boy" and someone willing to be registered as publisher were all that were required. Copy could be had cheaply from the many news services or could be reprinted from the larger papers. Printing of 1,000 issues a day cost only Mex. $200 monthly. Circulation of 500 copies, together with the subsidy from the sheet's political sponsor, was adequate to insure survival.[27] The function of the subsidized press in Peking politics was to add its own politically inspired news and rumors to the turbulent stream of political intelligence.

Corruption was endemic in the Peking government. Nepotism in the allocation of jobs, bribery of members of parliament, wholesale creation of sinecures, pocketing by military officers of 30–40 percent of the money allocated to their units for salaries, and by civilian officials of the money that passed through their hands, and speculation in government securities by banks whose boards of directors included high government officials were by all accounts common phenomena in a list that could be extended indefinitely. All prominent public officials were wealthy men, and most were even richer when they left office.

Disapproval of political pocket-lining by the more modern elements in the treaty ports and on the better newspapers was not always matched by a sense of shame on the part of the peculating officials, who were more traditional in their thinking. The forms of corruption had been pioneered in the traditional bureaucracy and were not the invention of the republic. However, they seem to have reached new levels of quantity, blatancy, and frequency. Political and judicial institutions were too weak to fight the politicians' tendencies to enrich themselves: there was simply no one to set a limit and to punish offenders. Furthermore, in the absence of a consensus on policy or of institutionalized

26. *The North-China Herald and Supreme Court and Consular Gazette*, hereafter abbreviated *NCH*, 1918.6.13.84 (year-month-date-page).

27. Britton, *Periodical Press*, pp. 121–32; "Shina ni okeru shimbun hattatsu shikō," *Pekin Mantetsu geppō* 1, no. 3 (July 15, 1924): 31–36. Five papers are cited as having circulations around 100,000: *Shun-t'ien shih-pao, I-shih pao*, and *Ch'en pao* of Peking, and *Hsin-wen pao* and *Shang pao* of Shanghai. Other sources give different circulation estimates (the newspapers did not publish circulation figures). The most bullish, attributing circulations of 200,000 to the *Hsin-wen pao, Shang pao* and *Shen pao*, and circulations in the range of 150,000 to 170,000 to the *I-shih pao, Ch'en pao, Ching pao* and *Shun-t'ien shih-pao*, is Kaji Ryūichi, "Shina ni okeru shimbun hattatsu shōshi," *Keizai shiryō* 13, no. 3 (March 20, 1927): 50–51. At the other extreme, the British Foreign Office's *A Guide to the Press of Asia*, 2d ed. (London, 1925), vol. 3, *China*, attributes only 60,000 circulation to the *Shen pao*, which it identifies as the biggest newspaper, and 4,000 to 6,000 to the *Ch'en pao, Ching pao* and *I-shih pao*. It gives no figure for the *Shun-t'ien shih-pao*.

channels for reaching policy decisions and enforcing compliance, corruption became a convenient means of uniting various groups around decisions: it served as a basis of compromise, decision-making, and the enforcement of decisions. Indeed, there might be no better basis on which to make a decision than the sum one could get from it personally.

Corruption of the parliament was even more blatant than that of the bureaucracy. Parliament was low in the hierarchy of real power among governmental institutions, but thanks to its prestige and its constitutional right to approve cabinet and some other official appointments, its concurrence was useful to those who did hold real power. It naturally became a target of manipulation, and since the members proved willing to sell their votes, the purchase of votes became the major feature of parliament-administration relations. In view of the M.P.'s loud espousal of modern democratic values, parliamentary bribetaking was more shocking to the public than was the traditional-style bribetaking of bureauorats.

Surprisingly, republican corruption did not take the form of a "spoils system" in which government posts were systematically reallocated with each change of administration. The republic began by simply keeping on the same bureaucrats in the same posts that they had staffed in the Ch'ing. Subsequent changes were glacially slow, except at the "political level" of minister, vice-minister, chief of staff, cabinet secretary, and the like.

Several factors militated against cleaning out and restaffing the bureaucracy at each change of cabinet. One was the technical qualifications required by many of the posts in ministries like Foreign Affairs, Communications, and Finance and the scarcity of persons qualified to do the jobs. To replace qualified personnel with novices would cause a financial loss to the faction running the ministry, since it would hinder the successful operation of the ministry's routine business. Therefore, in many republican ministries, the technical personnel originally recruited and trained in the Ch'ing tended to become an independent constituency that had to be coopted by the government and could not be freely tampered with. Another consideration was that the term of office of a minister was not fixed and was in many cases expected to be short. The replacement of the personnel of a ministry was a time-consuming process, and it was necessary to make one's profit more quickly and less arduously. In any case, there were rules protecting the tenure of the officials within the ministries, and if a clumsy, wholesale effort was made to fire them, they could and did sue.[28]

Comparison of successive issues of a monthly list of high Chinese government officials covering the period from August 1924 to November 1926, during

28. Civil service regulations may be found in various issues of *Chih-yuan lu*. Suits for unjustified termination of governmental employment were sometimes brought before the Supreme Court (*Ta-li yuan*).

which there were two major changes in the control of government and many minor ones, shows a slow turnover in even high-level positions.[29] In general, the following rules seem to have applied:

1. Replacement of high-level personnel did not occur with each change of government but only with a major change in the factions dominating the government, and then often at a leisurely pace taking several months.

2. While the posts of minister and vice-minister were generally political, there are many cases of relatively stable tenure as vice-minister through several changes of cabinet, especially when the cabinet changes occurred under the aegis of one major faction and when the ministry had a higher technical than political content. At the next level down, that of section heads (k'o-chang and ssu-chang) the incumbents were normally secure.[30]

3. The posts with the greatest technical content were generally the most stable of the higher posts. Posts on the basis of which money could be made (railway superintendent, head of the Domestic Bond Bureau, and so on) were the least stable.

The surprising fact is that the major subcabinet posts in the Chinese governmental bureaucracy in the chaotic years of the early republic were more stable than comparable posts are today in the American bureaucracy, where "political" appointments extend to a lower level. The imperial bureaucratic tradition of job security was hardly touched behind the facade of chaos. Political revenge seldom took the form of firing a man from his post. Although nepotism and sinecures were common, they were effected by creating new posts and adding

29. *Shina shokuin hyō,* 2, nos. 5–8, 3, nos. 1–5, 4, nos. 1–2 (August, September, November, and December 1924; February, April, July, September, and October 1925; and February and November 1926), *passim.* Now that a nearly complete set of the *Chih-yuan lu* has been made available by the Center for Chinese Research Materials in Washington, D.C., and Liu Shou-lin's list of officials for the republic has become available in reprint form, it will be possible to test these hypotheses and more complicated ones more carefully. (Liu's book was published in China in 1966 but did not become known to researchers outside China until 1974, when a Japanese publisher reprinted it; Liu Shou-lin, *Hsin-hai i-hou shih-ch'i nien chih-kuan nien-piao* ([Kyoto?][1974?]). Work on a similar list was under way in Taiwan when Liu's book became available; for the first part of the Taiwan project see Chang P'eng-yuan and Shen Huai-yü, "Min-kuo chih-kuan nien-piao ch'u-kao," in *Chin-tai shih yen-chiu so chi-k'an,* vol. 3, pt. 2 [December 1972], 122 pp. The Chang-Shen list differs from Liu's in more systematically including acting incumbents of posts and the dates of appointment to, assumption of, and departure from posts. The Liu list is more inclusive chronologically and in terms of organizations covered.)

30. See *Pei-ching kuan-liao tsui-e shih* ([Peking?], 1922) 1:2–4, for a description of the increase in power of the *k'o-changs* and *ssu-changs* in the Ministry of Interior as ministers came and went. Sun Hung-i reportedly was unable to fire two *ssu-changs* he wanted to get rid of when he was minister of the interior. By the time Kao Ling-wei was minister, the power of the *ssu-changs* was so great they could disobey the minister's direct orders without fear.

useless personnel rather than by replacing the incumbents of working positions. Appointment as an "advisor" or member of a special commission was a common form of sinecure.

Even in the higher reaches of the military and civilian bureaucracy, recruitment was strongly influenced by the phenomenon of cooptation.[31] Local militarists were appointed governors of provinces; prominent bankers were appointed ministers of finance or given other financial posts; men with prestige in educational or judicial circles were appointed ministers of education or justice. The government ratified and tried to make use of the existing system of power; it was too weak to do otherwise. Government was dependent upon the means of administration privately controlled by the coopted parties for the nominal extension of its authority into a locality or a sphere of activity.

The principle of cooptation particularly affected the appointment of higher officials in the financial sphere. If the prime minister intended to raise a loan from the domestic banks, he selected as minister of finance or director of the Currency Reform Bureau (Pi-chih chü) someone with great prestige in the banking community; if he wanted a loan from the Americans, he chose an official with good relations with the American legation and American banks; to raise a Japanese loan, he used a returned student from Japan. A slightly different twist was given to the cooptation phenomenon in the case of the more technocratic ministries where, as we have seen, in order to get the cooperation of the ministry staff, high officials were appointed because of seniority and their following within the ministry career staff; sometimes even the minister of communications was chosen in this way.

The cooptative nature of recruitment in the Peking government, which flowed from the weakness of government institutions, in turn contributed to the inability of the political system to absorb new groups like the students who became mobilized during the May Fourth Movement. Relying upon independently powerful social forces for its power, the government became subject to the interests of the forces it had coopted. While the entrance of new groups into the system would have been beneficial to the government as such, it was unable to pursue its interests when they conflicted with those of the coopted social groups. The government was thus reduced to a representative of the forces that supported it.

Government Finance and the Role of the New-Style Banks

The Peking government had an insatiable appetite for funds. The need for money was not limited to what was required to run the administration in Pek-

---

31. This phenomenon and its consequences have been described by Vernon K. Dibble, "The Organization of Traditional Authority: English County Government, 1558 to 1640," in James G. March, ed., Handbook of Organizations (Chicago, 1965), pp. 879–909.

ing. There were large projects of army-building afoot in the provinces, with the warlords deluging the government with demands for funds. Official peculation was capable of consuming almost any quantity of money. Parliamentary factions depended for their growth and well-being on sums leaked from government coffers. Government money, in short, was an object of political struggle, and its provenance and distribution were hotly political issues.

Not surprisingly in these circumstances, the Peking government, instead of satisfying the endless demands upon its resources, became increasingly impecunious. The regime was fiscally healthiest in the years of Yuan Shih-k'ai's rule (1912–16). During several of these years, the Peking government commanded even more revenue from the provinces than it had done under the Ch'ing. It also concluded several foreign loans, most of them adequately secured. First steps were made in exploiting domestic sources of capital. After Yuan's death, however, the breakdown of central government control over revenues began and increasing reliance was placed on foreign loans. Huge sums were borrowed for political purposes, resulting first in heavy pledging of future salt and customs revenues and eventually in destruction of the government's credit with foreign lenders. Money was spent as it came in, on military costs and on lining officials' pockets, while arrears for troop support owed to military commanders, for the salaries of officials, and for general administrative expenses piled up to an estimated Mex. $90 million.[32] "The present administration," lamented British Minister Sir John Jordan in 1918, "is pursuing a veritable rake's progress; each party is ready to sacrifice the general good for its individual aims, to pledge national assets and revenues in return for immediate party funds, and to forget the responsibilities of Government in a hasty effort to collect funds before loss of office."[33]

By about 1920, the Peking government was deeply and irreparably in debt. A statement provided by the Ministry of Finance showed a total unsecured debt, domestic and foreign, of Mex. $299 million as of September 30, 1921. But this figure included only sums actually borrowed in cash by the Ministry of Finance. According to Inspector General of Customs Sir Francis Aglen, if one added to this "the indebtedness of the various Ministries . . . , [including] salaries in arrear, bills unpaid and small loans contracted independently of the Ministry of Finance . . . , Treasury bills negotiated directly on the market . . . , [and]

32. "China's Internal Loans," *Bulletin of the Government Bureau of Economic Information* 2, no. 19 (June 17, 1922): 7. The bureau was an English-language economic information agency of the Chinese Government, run by an Australian journalist, W. H. Donald (see Earl Albert Selle, *Donald of China* [New York, 1948], p. 224). A copy of this issue of the *Bulletin* was found in F.O. 371/9200.

33. F.O. 371/3188, 162953 (f88573), Despatch 353, Jordan to Balfour, Peking, July 25, 1918, confidential print, p. 2.

the debt to the Imperial Household, whose subsidy of 4,000,000 dollars is very much behindhand . . . , we get a figure of 364,000,000 [Mexican] dollars, which represents approximately the unsecured and unmanaged debt. . . . The annual interest charge on this debt at an average rate of 8 per cent comes to 29,120,000 dollars, some 4,000,000 dollars more than the total receipts for a year at the disposal of the Central Government. . . . [T]he debt must necessarily increase at an appalling rate, even if borrowing is entirely suspended."[34] The Peking government was sunk in an endemic and constantly worsening fiscal crisis.

The period of fiscal irresponsibility after Yuan's death had seen a lush flowering of new-style domestic banks; the period of fiscal crisis beginning in 1919 saw the emergence of the bankers to a role of extraordinary political influence. One of the most noteworthy features of Peking politics—and indeed of politics under the Kuomintang subsequently—was the extensive political influence enjoyed by the new-style banks despite their financial weakness. To understand the role of the new-style banks, it is necessary first to show how the fiscal structure of the Peking regime and of the domestic capital market placed them in a critical political position.

FISCAL STRUCTURE OF THE GOVERNMENT

Government revenues may be analyzed in four categories: domestic revenues collected without foreign protection, the salt and customs revenues, foreign loans, and domestic loans.

In imperial times, the central government was supported by small remittances from the provinces. Revenues were collected in the provinces and localities and expended there without passing through a central treasury. In the two years immediately after the revolution, the provinces cut off remittances to the central government, which turned to foreign loans for money. But in 1914 and 1915, the remittance of funds from the provinces was resumed. Furthermore, in 1915, the Yuan Shih-k'ai government took the unprecedented step of designating certain categories of revenue (chung-yang chuan-k'uan) as accruing entirely to the central government. These were the deed tax (yen-ch'i shui), stamp tax (yin-hua shui), wine and tobacco tax (yen-chiu shui), wine and tobacco certificate tax (yen-chiu p'ai-chao shui), and broker's license tax (ya-shui). In 1915, these taxes realized Mex. $11,150,000 for the central government.[35]

34. F.O. 371/6662, F4758/2635/10, Enclosure 2 in Peking Despatch 632 of October 31, 1921, confidential print: "Memorandum respecting Chinese Finance (continued)," Sir Francis Aglen, October 19, 1921, pp. 3–4. The well-placed journalist Rodney Gilbert estimated the total unsecured government debt at Mex. $376 million: NCH 1921.11.5.358.

35. Chiang Ch'i-chou, "Wo-kuo chün-fei tsai ts'ai-cheng shang chih ti-wei," Yin-hang yueh-k'an 4, no. 7 (July 1924), in GSK 1924.10.28. His figures seem to be based on W. W.

Even before Yuan's death, however, central control of revenues began to decline. Yuan's imperial movement of late 1915 provided the first impetus. Yunnan, Kweichow, Kwangsi, and Kwangtung declared independence of Peking and ceased their remittances. After Yuan's death, even the provincia¹ authorities who remained loyal to Peking gradually stopped remitting fund The provincial remittances declined from more than Mex. $5 million in 191ι to Mex. $900,000 in 1917 and then ended. Remittances of the special central government revenues also fell from a high of more than Mex. $17 million in 1916 to Mex. $4 million in the 1919–20 fiscal year, and zero by 1922.[36]

The wine and tobacco tax was separated from the special central government revenues in 1919 and placed under the National Wine and Tobacco Administration. In the first year, the administration remitted Mex. $2,673,000 to the government, but this declined year by year as funds were seized by local authorities. In 1925, the income was Mex. $1,060,000. The stamp tax was likewise made a separate item in 1919: of the approximately Mex. $3 million collected each year, only some Mex. $340,000 annually was remitted to the central government; the rest was spent on administration of the Stamp Tax Bureau or seized by local authorities.

In the years after Yuan's death, income that the government might have expected from the various enterprises of the Ministry of Communications—which made a profit of Mex. $41 million to $42 million per year after the payment of salaries, costs, and debt service and despite warlord interference with train and telegraph service—was virtually nil because local authorities seized the funds. The inland native customs (ch'ang-kuan) revenue, too, was usually seized by warlords, except for the portion levied within 50 li of the treaty ports,

Yen's Financial Readjustment Commission report of 1924: see The China Year Book 1924–5, pp. 736–41.

The list of central government revenues was revised in 1916 and again in 1917.

The discussion of the Yuan period is based on Chiang and also on Yang Ju-mei, "P'ing-lun min-kuo i-lai chih ts'ai-cheng ta-shih," Yin-hang chou-pao, no. 404 in GSK 1925.7.49–65; Yang Ju-mei, Min-kuo ts'ai-cheng lun (Shanghai, 1927), pp. 9–23; and Yun Tai-ying, "Chung-kuo ts'ai-cheng chuang-k'uang shu-p'ing," Hsin chien-she 1, no. 6 (May 20, 1924)· 118–40.

36. Figures from Yun Tai-ying, "Ts'ai-cheng chuang-k'uang," pp. 123–24. Yun's figur are based on the report of the Financial Readjustment Commission of 1924 (see note 35).

There was also a decline in the size of revenues that could be considered "seized with government permission," in the sense that they were assigned to the warlords by the central government because of its inability to enforce remittance. The figures were Mex. $14 million in 1917, Mex. $6 million in 1918, Mex. $5 million in 1919, Mex. $4 million in 1920, and Mex. $2 million in 1921. This meant an increase in the government debit column, since, when the funds were seized with permission, they were set off against funds that the central government ostensibly owed to its military subordinates; when simply appropriated by the warlord, they did not lighten the government's debt to the troops.

which was collected by the Maritime Customs Administration and safely remitted to the government, and the Mex. $2 million portion collected in the Peking area.[37] The one other steady source of income was the Peking Octroi (*Ch'ung-wen men shui*), a tax collected at the four gates of Peking; its annual earnings increased from Mex. $977,895 in 1916 to Mex. $2,698,163 in 1923.[38]

By the mid-1920s, Sir Francis Aglen was able to remark that "the financial relations between the provinces and the Central Government are to-day very much what they were in Imperial times"[39] —revenues collected in the provinces were largely retained and used there. To this principle, however, there were the two important exceptions where the powers had involved themselves in revenue collection and had thus disturbed the central-local balance: the salt and customs revenues.

We have already seen how a series of loan agreements between the powers and Peking in the late Ch'ing and first years of the republic had given the powers a stake in central government control of the salt and customs revenues. This stake was not merely financial: in differing degrees, the powers were directly involved in collecting and distributing the customs and salt revenues through the synarchic institutions of the Maritime Customs Administration and the Salt Gabelle.[40]

These revenues, however, particularly the salt revenues, were affected by political trends. As we have seen, the operation of the Salt Gabelle, and the political and legal status of foreign interest in the salt revenue, made these revenues much more susceptible to military seizure than those of the customs. Immediately upon the declarations of independence of the southern provinces in 1916, local seizures of the salt revenues began. Local seizures reached a level of about Mex. $30 million a year, leaving, after costs and debt services, some $40 million a year as the salt surplus revenue. This surplus was released each month to the central government by the salt inspectorate, the amount varying from

37. Chiang Ch'i-chou, "Chün-fei chih ti-wei," pp. 25–46; Yun Tai-ying, "Ts'ai-cheng chuang-k'uang," pp. 118–23; F.O. 371/11684, F1015/1001/10, Enclosure 2 in Peking Despatch 55 of January 21, 1926: "Statement of Customs and Salt Surplus Revenue and the Revenue of the Peking Octroi", memorandum by the Chinese Ministry of Finance, English translation, confidential print, p. 4.

38. During most of this period, the sum went directly to the support of the presidential offices, although in 1923 Feng Yü-hsiang managed to get control of the Octroi and for some time thereafter the money went to the support of his troops. *Chung-wai ching-chi chou-k'an*, no. 83, in *GSK* 1924.10.241; F.O. 371/11684, F1015/1001/10, Enclosure 2 in Peking Despatch 55 of January 21, 1926: "Statement of Customs and Salt Surplus Revenue and the Revenue of the Peking Ocrroi," confidential print, p. 4.

39. Sir Francis Aglen, "China and the Special Tariff Conference," *British Chamber of Commerce Journal*, n.d., pp. 376–79.

40. On the term "synarchic," see John King Fairbank, *Trade and Diplomacy on the China Coast: The Opening of the Treaty Ports, 1842–1854* (Stanford, Calif., 1969), p. 465.

month to month. But because of borrowing, a situation soon arose where the surplus was completely pledged in advance. By 1921, Mex. $18,270,767 worth of foreign bank advances and Mex. $22,680,250 worth of domestic bank advances had been obtained upon a pledge of repayment from the salt surplus. But no systematic debt service had been established to set up an order of priorities for repayment of the debts. Upon each release of the salt surplus there was a scramble for the funds, with the foreign banks, through whose hands the salt surplus passed, having the first opportunity to assert their claims. The government was paying out the salt surplus revenue as fast as it came in, without systematically retiring its debt pledged on the revenue, thus depriving itself indefinitely of the use of the cash released each month.[41] And the process of pledging the salt revenues went on unabated as long as banks would accept a pledge as the basis for a loan. Furthermore, local seizures of salt revenue jumped rapidly in 1925 and 1926 so that by the spring of 1926 the only salt revenue still under central government control was the Mex. $13 million yearly income of the salt depot at Ch'anglu near Tientsin.[42]

In the case of customs, as earlier described. the whole of the revenue was protected for the service of central government debts under the threat of intervention by the powers as creditors and trustees for the funds. In 1917, the customs receipts for the first time provided a surplus over what was needed to service the debts secured on them. This surplus of about 10 million Shanghai taels was handed over directly to the Chinese Government for general administrative expenses.[43]

In 1918, however, the diplomatic corps began to exert control over the surplus. Their position was based upon the 1912 agreement, which made them "trustee" of the customs receipts while these were lodged in foreign banks between collection and disbursement to China's creditors. Now that there was a surplus—a contingency not anticipated in 1912—the corps claimed a trusteeship relation to the surplus as well. Late in 1918, when the Chinese Government asked the corps to authorize the banks to release about half the 1918 surplus, the corps insisted upon earmarking the released funds for specific purposes, like

41. F.O. 371/6662, F4758/2635/10, Enclosure 2 in Peking Despatch 632 of October 31 1921, confidential print: "Memorandum respecting Chinese Finance (continued)," Sir Francis Aglen, October 19, 1921, p. 4. A report giving a similar aggregate figure of about Mex. $40 million borrowed on the security of the salt surplus is found in NCH 1921.10.29. 292; also see NCH 1921.11.26.560.

42. F.O. 371/11676, F2286/255/10, "Chinese Salt Tax," clipping from The Times (London) of May 28, 1926. The threatened seizure of this last source of revenue by Ch'u Yü-p'u at this point brought on a minor international crisis that was resolved when Ch'u agreed to a compromise under which he received a subsidy from the salt funds in return for noninterference with the debt service.

43. Wright, Collection and Disposal, p. 164.

service of internal debts, support of the diplomatic and consular services, support of education, and repayment of advances from banks. The powers imposed the condition that none of the releases be devoted to general administration or military purposes. To enforce these conditions, the powers threatened that they would "be guided in their future action by the good faith shown by the Chinese Government in carrying out this measure."[44]

Although the years 1917-20 saw the amount of the customs surplus increase dramatically, reaching a high of 22,356,050 Shanghai taels in 1920,[45] the powers' rigid control over the use of the surplus funds meant that they did little to relieve the financial demands on the government from warlords and politicians. In any case, the tremendous surpluses depended less upon the growth of China's foreign trade than upon the upward trend in the world price of silver, and this reversed itself in 1921, with a consequent decline in the size of the surplus.[46] In the same year, as we shall see below, the whole of each year's surplus was committed in advance to a fund administered by the Maritime Customs Administration for the service of the internal debt and thus removed on a permanent basis from the reach of the politicians. For better or worse, despite their substantial size, the customs surpluses were never available for direct use to relieve the politicians' and warlords' financial appetites.

With the breakdown of its control over domestic revenues, the Peking government tended to turn to foreign and domestic credit for income. During the later years of World War I, the international situation was favorable for the conclusion of foreign loans. The prewar consortium of foreign banks, which had prevented political competition for loans, had been dissolved, and international pressure no longer imposed bankerly conditions on loans. Japan was gorged with money earned in wartime trade and had few places to invest. The other powers had withdrawn their attention from the Chinese scene and were in no position to check and counter Japan's policies. China's natural resources had not yet been pledged as securities. Under the Terauchi cabinet (1916-18), Japanese policy favored the granting of generous loans to China, even on inadequate securities, as a way of securing an interest in Chinese natural resources. In the Nishihara Loans of 1917-18, Japan loaned China 140 million yen. Although the loans were ostensibly to be used for the development of resources and industrial enterprises, "the Japanese and Chinese parties to their conclusion

44. F.O. 371/3682, 42431 (f394), Copy of note to Wai-chiao pu [from Doyen], January 16, 1919, enclosure in Despatch 44, Jordan to Curzon, Peking, January 29, 1919; Wright, *Collection and Disposal*, Chapter 6.

45. Stanley F. Wright, *China's Customs Revenue since the Revolution of 1911*, 3d ed. (Shanghai, 1935), pp. 292-300.

46. China's revenue was in silver, but its foreign obligations were in gold. As the value of silver rose, it cost less to service the foreign debts. See *The China Year Book 1926-7*, p. 537, for the market value of silver dollars by year.

understood that practically the greater part of them would be diverted to military expenditure, bribery of members [of parliament], etc. Their titles were simply a nominal pretext."[47] There were also floated during this period the Marconi Wireless Loan of 1918 (£600,000), the Vickers Airplane Loan of 1919 (£1,803,200), two American loans secured in the wine and tobacco revenue in 1919 ($5.5 million each), and the Banque Industrielle de Chine loans.[48] None of these loans was adequately secured, and, beginning in 1920, the government defaulted on payments of its unsecured foreign obligations.

In 1918, the war ended and the Terauchi cabinet was replaced by the Hara Kei cabinet. Seeking accomodation with the other powers, who were now paying increased attention to China, Japan joined four-power negotiations on a new China consortium, which was organized in 1920. But China was already so disorganized that the political and financial conditions sought by the consortium for loans never materialized, and the consortium unintentionally became the instrument of a prolonged foreign financial boycott of the Chinese government. "The loan game in Peking was at an end."[49]

With domestic revenues declining, the salt and customs surpluses absorbed by loan service and other specific purposes, and foreign loans drying up, the Peking government had only one place to turn to raise funds for its upkeep and for political purposes: the domestic capital market.

Yuan Shih-k'ai's government had pioneered the exploitation of domestic capital through bond issues. China's first internal loans (the Merchants' Loan of 1894, the Chao-hsin Treasury Notes of 1898, the Fu-ch'ien Industrial Bonds of 1909, the Patriotic Bonds of 1911, the Eight Percent Military Loan of 1912 and the First Year Six Percent Loan of 1912) had been unsuccessful. The term of the bonds was too long, the interest too low, the security new and untried, and the amounts issued too large. Only a small proportion of each issue was sold. The loans were in fact forced contributions deducted from the salaries of government officials.[50] In 1914, however, the government decided to try again. With all the features of modern, Western commercial bond issues, including "prospectus, amortization tables, specifically pledged securities, elaborately engraved bonds, and all the machinery for a regular loan service,"[51] and with

47. F.O. 371/3190, 197672 (f150165), Enclosure 3 in Tokyo Despatch 362 of October 7, 1918: translation of *Kokumin* editorial of October 3, 1918.

48. For details, see Chia Shih-i, *Ts'ai-cheng shih, hsu-pien,* pien 4, pp. 132–34, 143–46, 174–78.

49. *NCH* 1920.6.26.808.

50. "China's Internal Loans," pp. 1–3; F.O. 371/3189, 100042 (f100042), Enclosure in Peking Despatch 109 of March 6, 1918: "Memorandum: Chinese National Loans of 1914 and 1915," Sir Francis Aglen, Peking, February 16, 1918, p. 1.

51. F.O. 371/3189, 100042 (f100042), Enclosure in Peking Despatch 109 of March 6, 1918: "Memorandum: Chinese National Loans of 1914 and 1915," Sir Francis Aglen.

shorter terms and more generous interest, the Third and Fourth Year Loans of 1914 and 1915 were fully or oversubscribed. Confidence in the government was high, and the attractive terms and sophisticated methods of underwriting heavily tapped a new source of funds for the government.

As the fiscal situation worsened after Yuan's death, domestic credit became increasingly crucial to the revenue-raising activity of a series of desperate ministers of finance. From 1913 to 1926, the government issued twenty-seven sets of internal bonds with a total face value of some Mex. $631 million.[52] Beginning with the Eighth Year Bonds in 1919, however, bankers' enthusiasm for government securities waned. The government was now deeply in debt; there was no reliable revenue left on which to secure the new bonds; and the political situation was regarded as insecure. Despite their low selling price and the small quantity issued, not all the Eighth Year Bonds were sold.[53]

Bankers were now able to exact harsh terms from the government for small advances of cash. Left-over First Year Bonds were sold by the government in Shanghai for Mex. $21.50 per Mex. $100 face value; unsold Seventh Year Bonds were sold for Mex. $54 per Mex. $100 bond. Banks made numerous short-term loans to the government at 16 to 25 percent per month, with unsold bonds, valued at 20 percent of face value, used as security. From 1912 to 1924, Mex. $46,740,062 worth of treasury bills (*kuo-k'u cheng-ch'üan*), payable in one or two years, were sold to banks at as little as 40 percent of face value, providing a handsome rate of return upon redemption.[54]

But the domestic banks were able to do more than establish advantageous terms for the short-term loans and advances they made to the government. Individually and collectively, the bankers became able to exert direct political influence on the government. They were able to participate in the making and unmaking of cabinets. Perhaps their supreme achievement was to force the government to allocate all future surplus customs revenues to a sinking fund for the service of the domestic debt. Before we show how the bankers' political power was exercised, we must briefly explain why, of all the institutions of the Chinese banking world, the new-style banks played the primary political role.

STRUCTURE OF CHINESE BANKING

The fundamental, if somewhat paradoxical, reason that the predominant political role in the domestic capital market was played by the new-style, sup-

Peking, February 16, 1918, p. 1b; for terms of these and subsequently discussed bond issues see Chia Shih-i, *Ts'ai-cheng shih, hsu-pien, pien* 4.

52. E. Kann, "Chinese Government Loans," *The China Year Book 1934* (Shanghai, 1934), p. 552.

53. "China's Internal Loans," pp. 6–7; Chia Shih-i, *Ts'ai-cheng shih, hsu-pien, pien* 4, pp. 13–14; *STSP* 1919.3.21.2

54. F.O. 371/3691, 145524 (f8369), Despatch 405, Jordan to Curzon, Peking, September 3, 1919, confidential print, pp. 2–3; Chiang Ch'i-chou, "Chün-fei chih ti-wei," p. 35.

posedly modern treaty-port banks instead of by the traditional money shops (*ch'ien-chuang, yin-hao*) was that the new-style banks were weaker. Within the world of Chinese banking, the new-style banks were flanked on the one side by the treaty port branches of the foreign banks, and on the other by the traditional money shops;[55] both types of institutions were financially stronger than the Chinese modern banks. The twenty-seven foreign banks with branches in China were immensely more powerful than the 119 (or more) Chinese banks.[56] They commanded three or four times the capital, virtually monopolized the lucrative foreign exchange and foreign trade markets, and enjoyed the privileges of issuing currency and of receiving several hundred million dollars per year in salt and customs receipts.[57] The foreign banks had the trust of Chinese and foreign businessmen alike and did the bulk of the banking business in the treaty ports. The innumerable money shops, on the other hand, were strongly entrenched in the fields of domestic currency exchange, securities speculation, and short-term loans. Their capital, while individually small, totalled more than that of the new-style banks, and because of their enjoyment of established channels of activity, they were more successful in maintaining liquidity than the modern banks. Indeed, the money shops served as a source of short-term capital for the new-style banks themselves.[58]

The new-style banks were financially weak institutions. With an aggregate authorized capital of Mex. $350 million, the 119 new-style banks on which data are available were able to raise only Mex. $150 million in paid-up capital. Because of low public confidence, they had to attract working funds, of which they were desperately short, by issuing paper money (if government authorization could be obtained), borrowing from the money shops at high interest, and accepting savings deposits at high interest. Then, in order to pay back the high-interest loans and deposits and support the value of their notes, the banks

55. There was a fourth type of financial institution, the joint Sino-foreign bank, of which there were about twenty. Except for three or four of the stronger ones, which were run by foreign personnel and enjoyed lucrative roles in foreign trade transactions, the joint banks were nearly bereft of capital and were established solely to take advantage of the ease with which, enjoying foreign involvement, they could get permission to issue currency. *SKJ*, pp. 195–96; Yang Hsien-chün, "Ti-kuo chu-i ching-chi ch'in-lueh hsia chih Chung-kuo," parts 5 and 6, *Shang-hai tsung shang-hui yueh-pao* 7, no. 9 (September 1927): 4–6. For the stories of two such banks, see *Ch'en pao* 1924.9.22 in *GSK* 1924.9.287–88, and *Ching pao* 1925.5.23 in *GSK* 1925.5.319–20. The bank referred to in the latter story, although not named, is clearly the Hua-wei yin-hang (Sino-Scandinavian bank); cf. Kōjima Shōtarō, *Daiji nempyō*, pp. 482, 514, 528.

56. *SKJ*, pp. 183, 191–92. According to Yang Hsien-chün, "Ti-kuo chu-i," there were 136 Chinese banks and he also gives a higher number of foreign banks. The *SKJ* figures for foreign banks exclude Manchuria.

57. Yang Hsien-chün, "Ti-kuo chu-i," pp. 1–5; *SKJ*, p. 192.

58. *SKJ*, pp. 199, 212–13.

were forced to seek highly profitable, and therefore speculative, investments.[59] In a vicious circle, the excessively speculative character of the loans and investments further compromised the banks' already inadequate liquidity and public confidence in them, increasing the cost of capital and forcing them into further speculative activities.

The new-style banks turned to government bonds and treasury notes as an investment in which it was possible to make huge profits, although at considerable risk:[60] by all accounts, they were the major holders of government bonds.[61] These bonds could be bought at a fraction of face value and often with the bank's own notes; the trouble was that they might never be repaid, and the value might continue to fall. On the other hand, the market value might leap at the news that new security had been found for the issue, or that a drawing would be held to redeem a portion of it, or that a new minister of finance was to be appointed. Bonds could prove a profitable investment because their market value rose and fell so violently. To speculate with success, however, it was necessary to anticipate or even influence the movements of the market. This required close political contacts.

The new-style banks already enjoyed close ties with the political world. Almost all of them had been founded under government or political auspices. The first new-style Chinese bank was the Imperial Bank of China, founded by the government in 1897 to marshal China's domestic capital resources and to compete with foreign banks in handling China's foreign trade.[62] The Bank of China was founded in 1905, the Bank of Communications in 1908, the Yien-yeh (Salt) Bank in 1915. All enjoyed governmental sponsorship. Bank foundings were particularly numerous in the years from 1917 to 1923. Government bond issues soared, and political factions rushed to establish banks to take advantage of the money and privileges the government had in its power to grant.[63] Of the fifty-four most prominent new-style Chinese banks, thirty-six were founded in these years.[64] These included six of the eleven "special banks"[65]—which,

59. Ibid., pp. 183–85. Yang Hsien-chün, "Ti-kuo chu-i," p. 5, gives Mex. $179,560,000 as the paid-up capital. By 1935, the banks' position had improved. See Leonard G. Ting, "Chinese Modern Banks and the Finance of Government and Industry," Nankai Social and Economic Quarterly 8, no. 3 (October 1935): 578.

60. Cf. NCH 1926.2.6.221.

61. See F.O. 371/12412, F3/3/10, Telegram 576, Lampson to F.O., Peking, December 31, 1926; F.O. 371/10920, F2809/2/10, letter from Sir Francis Aglen to Mr. Waterlow, London, July 2, 1925, p. 3; Yun Tai-ying, "Ts'ai-cheng chuang-k'uang," p. 120; Yin-hang chou-pao, no. 438 in GSK 1926.3.222; Ting, "Chinese Modern Banks," pp. 587–95.

62. Feuerwerker, China's Early Industrialization, pp. 225–41.

63. Ting, "Chinese Modern Banks," p. 585.

64. SKJ, p. 183.

65. The Ch'uan-yeh, Chung-kuo shih-yeh, Pien-yeh, Nung-shang, Meng-Tsang and

although privately owned in whole or in part, enjoyed privileges granted by the government—and many important private banks enjoying the sponsorship of political figures who were able to obtain banking licenses from the government and capital from commercial circles.[66] Two major Sino-foreign banks— the Sino-American Bank of Commerce and the (Sino-Japanese) Exchange Bank of China—were also founded in these years, with politicians' participation and special privileges granted by the government.[67]

Among the new-style banks, those with headquarters in Peking and Tientsin were most closely involved in Peking politics. The Shanghai banks, although they speculated in government bonds, also did considerable business in exchange transactions and industrial investments. In the sanctuary of Shanghai, they were free from undue political interference and their ties with industry moderated their reliance on the bond market and its political context. They were controlled primarily by local industrialists. Other treaty port banks, because of their distance from Peking, were more closely involved in local politics than in Peking politics.[68]

Like the political world, the banking world was heavily laced with connections and clientelist ties, which defined factions and clusters of banking personnel. Most prominent bankers came from one of three provinces: Kiangsu (Chang Chien, Chang Kia-ngau, Ch'ien Yung-ming, Chou Tso-min, T'an Li-sun, Wu Ting-ch'ang), Chekiang (Wang K'o-min, Ho Te-lin), or Kwangtung (Liang Shih-i, Feng Keng-kuang). These locality ties were mixed with bureaucratic connections among bank personnel whose early career experiences were in the Bank of China, those who were trained in the Bank of Communications, and those who came up in the Ministry of Finance.[69] The banks were also closely tied to major political factions. Banks tried to survive as institutions by retaining good relations with a number of political factions and by having on their boards of directors persons who had good connections throughout the political world.

Nung-kung banks. See *SKJ*, pp. 475–79, 572–75, 583–86, 593–96, 596–97, 597–601.

66. These included the Ch'uan-kuo shang-yeh yin-hang (*STSP* 1918.9.5.2), the Wu-tsu shang-yeh yin-hang (*SKJ*, pp. 586–90; *NCH* 1918.7.13.73), the Chung-hua ch'u-hsu yin-hang (*SKJ*, pp. 601–604), and the Tung-lu yin-hang (*SKJ*, pp. 492–95).

67. *STSP* 1919.4.26.2, 5.1.2; *SKJ*, pp. 618–22; *NCH* 1917.8.25.423, 425; *SKJ*, pp. 627–28. The privileges included note issue.

68. *SKJ*, pp. 212–16, 416–27, 469–71, 729.

69. *SKJ*, pp. 612–1 and 612–2 [*sic*]. Such ties in the banking world were extremely stable and persistent. What might loosely be called the "Bank of Communications faction" gave rise, under Liang Shih-i's aegis, to the four prominent banks that formed the core of what was known in the 1940s as the "Peiyang" banking clique. Many of the leading personnel of this Peiyang group had been prominent bankers during the period of this study. See Kagawa Shun'ichirō, *Sensō shihon ron* (Tokyo, 1948), pp. 24–27, 36–37, 213, 215–16, 217–19, 224–26.

The typical board of directors of a Peking or Tientsin bank was carefully composed. At its heart were usually a number of professional bankers who enjoyed excellent contacts with a variety of political factions—men such as Wu Ting-ch'ang, Wang Yu-ling, Chou Tso-min, and Ch'ien Yung-ming.[70] To these were added men of banking or other financial experience who were more closely identified with one political group or another—men such as Feng Keng-kuang and Wang K'o-min (Feng Kuo-chang faction), Ts'ao Ju-lin (New Communications Clique), and Kung Hsin-chan and Li Shih-wei (Tuan Ch'i-jui faction).[71] The purpose of such balancing was to provide banks with intelligence on the political facts that determined fluctuations in the market price of bonds and with friends in government who could obtain and protect privileges and government support for the bank, but to avoid a political imbalance in the bank's allegiances that might leave it utterly defenseless when the political situation changed in Peking.[72]

Despite the balance sought by new-style banks, the influence of one political faction in banking circles outdistanced that of the others. This was the Communications Clique. At the heart of its influence was control over the Bank of Communications, which performed the functions of a government bank, yet was controlled by private investors. The Bank had been established in 1908 by Communications Clique leader Liang Shih-i as an organ of the Ministry of Posts and Communications to handle the finances of the railway, post, telegraph, and navigation administrations. In 1914, it was empowered to issue currency and to share the control of public finance with the Bank of China.[73] Despite the bank's political power and special privileges, 70 percent of the shares were held after 1914 by private shareholders.[74] Liang Shih-i often controlled the government shares, and he also controlled most of the private shares through his associates among the directors.[75] In addition to the Bank of Com-

70. See Appendix for profiles of some major factions. Ch'ien, Wu, and Chou were still listed in the 1940s as enjoying among them thirty-one interlocking bank directorships or managerships. Kagawa Shun'ichirō, Sensō, p. 160.

71. For lists of bank directors, see SKJ, passim; and Yin-hang yueh-k'an 4, no. 9 in GSK 1924.10.317–20, 346–55.

72. However, banks could not achieve perfect balance and they were susceptible to the baneful effects of political shifts. Bank runs and closings sometimes followed wars in which Peking changed hands between rival warlord factions. On the other hand, a bank could be politically revived by recruiting new directors with political contacts more appropriate to the new circumstances.

73. LSINP, 1:65–67; Frank M. Tamagna, Banking and Finance in China (New York, 1942), p. 39.

74. The China Year Book 1921–2, pp. 274–79; LSINP, 1:67, says 60 percent.

75. Upton Close [Josef Washington Hall], "Closeups of China's 'Money Josses,'" China Review 4, no. 4 (April 1922): 199. Since capital for the Bank of Communications and other banks founded on Liang's initiative was raised by Liang's persuading others to invest,

munications, Liang founded "several tens" of private banks, including some of the most important in China (among them the Kincheng Bank, Yien-yeh Bank, Ta-lu Bank, and the Peiyang pao-shang Bank).[76] According to one source, Liang and his associates had an interest in "a majority" of the domestic banks to whom the government was in debt in the early 1920s.[77] The connections among these banks were many and complicated.[78] Thus, as of approximately 1920, when Liang was head of the Domestic Bond Bureau (Nei-kuo kung-chai chü), an organ established to "readjust" the domestic debt in order to reestablish the government's credit with the native banks,[79] and his lieutenants Yeh Kung-ch'o and Chou Tzu-ch'i were ministers of communications and finance, respectively, Liang held directorships not only on the Bank of Communications but on the boards of six private banks (of which three were members of the Chinese banking group, a consortium that made loans to the government), while other members of the faction held interlocking directorships on the same and other important banks.[80]

As the government became more and more impecunious after 1919, the political power of banks, and of political factions with influence in banking circles, increased. The Communications Clique, in particular, emerged as a powerful arbiter of the fate of cabinets.[81] At the same time, the ability of banks

---

capitalists with close personal relationships with Liang were more likely to invest than others, and Liang was therefore able to control the votes of the private shares. Reports of stockholder's meetings of banks might be valuable sources for pursuing the operation of Chinese factions in banking circles.

76. LSINP, 1:67. On the capital, directors, charters, etc., of the banks, see SKJ.

77. NCH 1922.2.4.289.

78. Tamagna, Banking and Finance, p. 42, Chapter 5, and elsewhere.

79. On the purposes and charter of the Bureau, see LSINP, 2: 75–78.

80. Upton Close, "Money Josses," p. 199; The China Year Book 1921–2, pp. 274–79; The China Year Book 1923, pp. 780–86. When, in 1922, the Communications Clique was temporarily driven from center stage in Peking, its visible influence on banking boards declined. For the sake of survival, the Bank of Communications loosened its ties with the Communications Clique and broadened the membership of its board of directors but Liang retained powerful influence on the board and among bank staff. SKJ, pp. 565–66, says that in 1922 the stockholders decided to change management policy from a considerable involvement with politics and government to an emphasis on ordinary banking business. This presumably was an adjustment taken because of Liang's fall from power. The board of directors as of 1925 (SKJ, p. 558), shows considerable representation from politically independent Shanghai banking circles, but it still includes Chou Tso-min and Ch'ien Yung-ming, both close to Liang Shih-i.

81. Communications Clique support was important for the survival of the Chin Yun-p'eng cabinets of 1919–21; the withdrawal of its support caused Chin's last cabinet to fall. See Chapter V and LSINP, 1: 75–78, 162–63, 175–204. During the years in which the Chihli Clique was dominant in Peking (1922–24), the Communications Clique's influence declined. Banks diversified their boards in order to remain on good terms with Peking, but the Com-

in general to enforce their interests on the government was strengthened. This ability was demonstrated by the circumstances surrounding the formation of the Consolidated Internal Loan Service in 1921.

The weakening of the government's financial position after 1919 had apparently been unexpected by the new-style banks, who were caught with heavy investments in bonds, whose value now showed a constant downward trend. Although the Third and Fourth Year Loans and the Seventh Year Short-Term Bonds were adequately secured and enjoyed relatively high market values, the First, Fifth, Seventh Year Long-Term, Eighth, and Ninth Year Bonds were all declining in value because their securities had all proved illusory.[82] Meeting at Shanghai in December 1920, the Chinese Bankers' Association decided to refuse to buy any more government bonds until the government "readjusted" means of paying the old ones.[83] They offered a proposal to the government for a satisfactory method of readjusting the domestic debt.

The proposal was not unwelcome to Finance Minister Chou Tzu-ch'i of the Communications Clique nor to President Hsu Shih-ch'ang, both of whom had interests and allies in the banks. In any case, the government had nowhere to turn for funds except the domestic banks. The proposal was accepted and put into effect by a presidential mandate of March 3, 1921.[84] In its final form,[85] the

munications Clique continued to play a political role. Financial assistance was extended to Sun Yat-sen as an element in an anti-Chihli alliance: Yeh Kung-ch'o became Sun's minister of finance and Cheng Hung-nien the vice-minister. See *LSINP*, 2:255-57. After the defeat of the Chihli Clique, the Communications Clique reemerged as a major supporter of the Tuan Ch'i-jui Executive Government (1924-26) and of the Peking military regime of Chang Tso-lin in 1927-28. Subsequently, many Communications Clique members (e.g., Yeh Kung-ch'o) and many of its allies in banking went over to the Nanking government and became influential figures there.

82. F.O. 228/2990, Memo by Sir Francis Aglen, January 19, 1921. For example, the Seventh Year Bonds were secured as a second charge on the collections of the native customs outside the fifty-*li* radius of the treaty ports (that within the radius was collected by the Maritime Customs Administration) but the revenue from this source was already inadequate to cover the bonds secured on it previously and was declining due to warlord seizures. The Eighth Year Loan was secured on the unpledged portion of the national goods tax, but apparently there was no revenue from this tax.

83. *SKJ*, p. 729; F.O. 371/6650, F1188/1188/10, Enclosure in Peking Despach 70: "Memorandum by Mr. A. Rose, Commercial Secretary to the British Legation, Respecting the Financial Situation in China," February 8, 1921, confidential print, p. 5. Building on their new unity, the Chinese bankers made a Mex. $6 million loan to the Ministry of Communications for railway cars and imposed unprecedentedly strict conditions on the control and disbursement of the funds. See the same memorandum of February 8, 1921; also F.O. 371/6636, F1300/314/10, Despatch 64, Alston to Curzon, Peking, February 3, 1921, confidential print.

84. The original idea of securing the domestic debt on a sinking fund made up from the surplus customs funds apparently came from customs Inspector General Sir Francis Aglen, who wished to remove the customs surplus funds from the control of the diplomatic

arrangement committed the customs surplus to a sinking fund called the Consolidated Internal Loan Service, administered by Inspector General of Customs Sir Francis Aglen. The First, Fifth, Seventh Year Long-Term, Eighth, and Ninth Year Bonds (other issues were later added) were revalued at a portion of face value and exchanged for two new bond issues, the service of which was guaranteed by the loan service.[86]

The establishment of the Consolidated Internal Loan Service was a great boon to the bankers. The bonds had been revalued below face value, but this did not matter because the bankers had originally purchased them at large

corps, to extend his own influence in the Chinese financial world, and most important, to seek "another anchor" besides the support of the powers to "prevent the wreck of the [customs] Service" in what he correctly foresaw as an approaching storm of nationalism. This other anchor, Sir Francis believed, "can be found in the interests represented by Chinese bondholders to the tune of about 300 million [Mexican] dollars [the estimated unsecured internal debt]" (F.O. 371/7986, F3568/59/10, Enclosure 2 in Peking Despatch 621, Aglen to Clive, Peking, September 25, 1922). Sir Francis spoke of his idea to Chang Kia-ngau of the Chinese Bankers' Association. The bankers were already looking for a scheme to adjust the internal debt. On January 28, 1921, Inspector General Aglen, managers of some of the Chinese banks, and the minister of finance met and agreed to the Consolidated Internal Loan Service proposal. Minister of Finance Chou Tzu-ch'i submitted a memorial embodying the proposal, which was put into effect by a presidential mandate of March 3, 1921. See F.O. 228/2990, Aglen to Alston, Peking, December 27, 1920; F.O. 228/2990, "Memorandum" by Aglen, December 27, 1920; F.O. 228/2990, "Memorandum: Chinese Finances (continued)" by Aglen, Peking, January 29, 1921; F.O. 228/2990, Aglen to Rose, Peking, February 5, 1921; Wright, *Collection and Disposal*, pp. 168–70, 239–42.

85. In the 1921 version, the Mex. $24 million required for the sinking fund was to be made up from fixed contributions from the salt surplus, the wine and tobacco tax, and the customs surplus. The contributions from the first two sources, however, soon stopped. Furthermore, the amount of the customs surplus decreased drastically because of the worldwide drop in the price of silver. In 1922, the cabinet therefore approved a proposal that the whole of the customs surplus be devoted to the sinking fund and that the government make no other calls upon it. This arrangement drew a protest from the powers because it meant that there was no hope of devoting any customs surplus funds to the service of government debts to foreign nationals, even though some of these debts predated some of the internal obligations serviced by the sinking fund. Despite the protest, however, the arrangement was continued. See Wright, *Collection and Disposal*, pp. 170–92; F.O. 371/7986, F3568/59/10, Despatch 621, Alston to Curzon, Peking, October 4, 1922, and enclosures; F.O. 371/7986, F3569/59/10, minutes by Campbell, Newton, Jordan; F.O. 371/9200, F586/81/10, Despatch 11, Clive to Curzon, Peking, January 10, 1923; F.O. 371/9200, F695/81/10, Despatch 216, Curzon to Macleay, London, April 4, 1923, and enclosure; F.O. 371/9203, F3591/81/10, Despatch 610, Hoare to Curzon, Peking, October 30, 1923.

It is interesting that although the powers claimed not to have foreseen that the sinking fund scheme might eventually prejudice the claim of foreign creditors on the customs surplus, Sir Francis was apparently aware of this possibility and pointed it out in a veiled fashion in a memorandum of December 27, 1920: F.O. 228/2990, Aglen to Alston, Peking, December 27, 1920.

86. Wright, *Collection and Disposal*, pp. 168–70; "China's Internal Loans," pp. 7–8.

discounts. Now, by waiting for the loan service to redeem the bonds, the banks could receive twice what they had paid for them; or, if they wished to trade the bonds, they could sell them at a higher price than they had paid. The assets of all the new-style banks that had so heavily invested in domestic bonds were magically increased. The government's credit was also enhanced, although the blessing of Sir Francis Aglen now became necessary for the success of any large government bond issues.[87]

In the Consolidated Internal Loan Service incident, the power of the domestic banks, which grew out of their very weakness and vulnerability to political influence, was turned against the government in its straitened circumstances and the new-style banks showed themselves able to dictate the conditions of their financial relations with the government. This situation demonstrated the pervasive influence, both political and fiscal, of the banks, which was one of the most insistent and important conditions of Peking politics.

87. See *NCH* 1921.3.5.579; "China's Internal Loans," p. 8. Paradoxically, although the new arrangement involved repudiation of part of the national debt, it raised the government's credit. New loans and bond issues whose service Sir Francis Aglen agreed to accept became especially attractive investments. These included the "$96 million" Bonds of 1921 and the Eleventh Year Short Term Bonds. See Wright, *Collection and Disposal*, pp. 152–53, 181–89; F.O. 371/9200, F586/81/10, Despatch 11, Clive to Curzon, January 10, 1923, enclosure; *NCH* 1923.11.10.395.

IV

THE RENEWAL OF LEGITIMACY, 1918

On July 1, 1917, Chang Hsun—known as the "Pigtail General" because he continued to wear the queue as a gesture of personal loyalty to the Ch'ing— announced the restoration of the Hsuan-t'ung Emperor, P'u-i.

It was the second survival crisis of the republic. The first, Yuan Shih-k'ai's effort to make himself emperor, had been defeated amid a national outcry of opposition capped by Yuan's death in June 1916. With general optimism, the republic had been restored—Li Yuan-hung replacing Yuan as president, Feng Kuo-chang succeeding Li as vice-president, and parliament, dissolved by Yuan in 1914, recalled. But so bitterly had president, parliament, and prime minister quarreled that the Pigtail General, summoned to intervene, declared the republic bankrupt. Perhaps the traditional system was after all the only one that would work.

This judgment was widely rejected; within twelve days, Chang's troops were defeated by those of other officers stationed near Peking. Feng Kuo-chang succeeded as president and Tuan Ch'i-jui returned to his post as prime minister. But parliament was not invited back. It was generally believed that the obstreperousness of the old parliament, dominated by radical politicians, had been the system's Achilles' heel, both in 1913–14 and in 1916–17. In any case, parliament had been elected four years earlier, had not renewed itself through elections, and probably no longer represented public opinion. The Provisional Constitution of 1912, of course, made no allowance for replacing a parliament under such circumstances. But the parallel between 1912 and 1917—two occasions when republicans overthrew the Hsuan-t'ung Emperor—sparked an ingenious solution. In 1912–13, after the Provisional Constitution had been promulgated but before parliament convened, a Provisional National Council (Lin-shih ts'an-i yuan) exercised parliamentary functions and prescribed the procedures for electing the permanent parliament. Treating this as the relevant precedent, it was possible to justify replacing only parliament among all the organs of government. Proponents argued that the government should "follow the precedent of the first revolution by convening a provisional national council to write a new Parliamentary Organic Law and parliamentary election laws, then convening a new parliament."[1]

Not only would the calling of a new parliament renew the legitimacy of the republican government, it would also provide an opportunity for the factions dominating the government—the Tuan Ch'i-jui faction and the Research Clique (*Yen-chiu hsi*)—to insure that the legislature would be more amenable to cooperation with them than the first one. Equally important, it would fall to the new legislators to elect a successor to Feng Kuo-chang, whose term would end on October 10, 1918. By controlling parliament, the dominant factions could try to control the presidency and thus bring all three elements of government into alignment and allow the republican system to work. There would, however, be several obstacles. First, other factions would contest the parliamentary elections and try in other ways to influence the presidential outcome. Second, even if these rivals were defeated, the ruling coalition would still need to combat its tendencies to split. Third, and most difficult to overcome, the members of the old parliament did not accept their fate quietly. Under Sun Yat-sen's nominal leadership, the old parliament and the warlords of the five southwestern provinces of Kwangtung, Kwangsi, Yunnan, Kweichow, and Szechwan declared their refusal to obey Peking and organized a military government at Canton dedicated to "protecting the constitution" (*hu-fa*). The constitution-protecting government denied the legitimacy of any new parliament and of any president such a parliament would produce. The expedient of electing a new parliament would have to be considered a failure if the South could not ultimately be persuaded to accept the resulting regime.

The Election of Parliament

The Provisional National Council, which convened in Peking on November 10, 1917, was dominated by the faction of Prime Minister Tuan Ch'i-jui—his follower, Wang I-t'ang, was elected Speaker—and by the Research Clique, whose leaders Liang Ch'i-ch'ao and T'ang Hua-lung and three of their associates were seated in the cabinet.[2] On February 17, 1918, the government promulgated

1. Li Chien-nung, *Chung-kuo chin-pai nien cheng-chih shih* (Taipei, 1959), 2: 502, quoting Liang Ch'i-ch'ao and T'ang Hua-lung. Also cf. Willoughby, *Constitutional Government*, p. 17.

2. The Provisional National Council was composed of persons appointed by the chief officials of the provinces and special regions; the five southwestern provinces sent no delegates; Ku Tun-jou, *Chung-kuo i-hui shih* (Taichung, 1962), pp. 145–48. For a list of its mem-

the new Parliamentary Organic Law (*Tsu-chih fa*) and House and Senate Election Laws (*Hsuan-chü fa*), which the council had prepared. As revised, these laws enhanced the ability of the dominant cabinet factions to control both the election and the resulting parliament. By reducing the size of both Senate and House, the new laws made parliament easier to manage. The privilege of electing senators was removed from the Kuo-min tang-dominated provincial assemblies and given instead to local electorates, with the aim of reducing radical representation. This effect was reinforced by sharply increasing the qualifications demanded of voters in both the House and Senate elections, producing a registered electorate that was both small (see Table 1) and presumably conservative. Finally, in case these provisions were not enough to guarantee parliamentary docility, each province's Senate delegation was halved to five, while the number of senators selected under various kinds of direct central government control was increased from fifty-four to fifty-eight.[3]

---

bers, see *Chih-yuan lu* 1918, no. 2, *ts'e* 1. On the Research Clique's role in the Tuan cabinet, see T'ao Chü-yin, *Pei-yang chün-fa t'ung-chih shih-ch'i shih-hua* (Peking, 1957–59), 4:3–6 (hereafter abbreviated *PYCF*).

3. This discussion is based on the old and new parliamentary organic and election law texts as given in Ku Tun-jou, *I-hui shih*, pp. 227–87. The first two changes are pointed out both by Ku, p. 149, and by Yang Yu-chiung, *Li-fa shih*, p. 279.

The size of the Senate was reduced from 274 to 168 members; that of the House from 596 to 406. (Since the five southwestern provinces did not participate, there were in fact only 143 senators and 327 representatives in the new parliament.)

In the old parliament, there had been ten senators elected from each of the twenty-two provinces, and fifty-four elected under direct central government supervision (twenty-seven from Mongolia, ten from Tibet, three from Tsinghai, eight from the Central Academic Group [*Chung-yang hsueh-hui*] under the minister of education, and six from the Overseas Chinese Election Assembly [*Hua-ch'iao hsuan-chü hui*] composed of one representative from each government-recognized overseas Chinese chamber of commerce). The Central Academic Group and the Overseas Chinese Election Assembly met in Peking under the direct supervision of central government officials. The Mongolia, Tibet, and Tsinghai elections were run by appointees of the central government's Bureau of Mongolian and Tibetan Affairs (*Meng-Tsang yuan*) who were unable to carry out thorough-going elections even if they wished to, due to the primitive state of transport and communications in these regions.

The fifty-eight centrally-influenced senators in the new parliament consisted of fifteen from Mongolia, six from Tibet, two from Tsinghai, one from each of the five special administrative regions (*t'e-pieh hsing-cheng ch'ü*) created under Yuan Shih-k'ai and placed directly under central government rule (see Table 1), and thirty from the central election assemblies (*chung-yang hsuan-chü hui*), six small groups meeting in Peking and consisting respectively of leading educators, former high officials, men of great wealth, rich overseas Chinese, Manchu princes, and Muslim princes. For an account of the central election assembly elections, see *CWCY*, pp. 439–41.

Under the old House Election Law, a voter could qualify if he was a male over twenty-five, resident for more than two years in the district, who paid Mex. $2 or more in direct taxes, owned Mex. $500 or more of real estate, had graduated from elementary school, or

TABLE 1. Registered Voters for Elections to 1918 Parliament

| | Registered voters[b] for election to: | |
Province or district[a]	Senate	House
Chihli	7,263	3,240,931
Fengtien	18,016	892,864
Kirin	9,188	232,050
Heilungkiang	2,219	137,100
Kiangsu	27,321	2,779,600
Anhwei	9,020	1,324,579
Kiangsi	4,575	425,065
Chekiang	15,268	1,642,633
Fukien	7,595	3,191,589
Hupei	12,813	5,923,346
Hunan	16,208	1,192,137
Shantung	5,680	1,623,566
Honan	15,864	2,861,725
Shansi	3,946	1,155,365
Shensi	6,237	4,361,526
Kansu	665	191,795
Sinkiang	1,260	22,860
Special administrative regions:		
Metropolitan District (Peking)	3,523	670,259
Jehol	2,776	705,222
Chahar	297	168,972
Kweisui (Suiyuan)	570	19,237
Ch'uanpien (Szechwan special border district)	245	1,243
Mongolia (Outer Mongolia)	64	
Tibet	24	54,983[c]
Tsinghai	18	
Central election assemblies		
1st section	444	
2d section	18	
3d section	397	
4th section	32	
5th section	15	
6th section	8	
Totals	172,469	36,508,647

Source: *T'ung-chi yueh-k'an*, no. 16 (July 15, 1919), pp. 137–42.

Note: The correct sums of the figures given are 171,569 (Senate), and 32,818,647 (House). No explanation is given for the discrepancy between figures and totals.

A rare view of one of the more hotly contested elections is provided by the reports of the British Consul in Nanking, Bertram Giles.[4] Late in 1917, Giles reported, voter registers were being compiled for the Kiangsu Provincial Assembly elections scheduled for 1918. These lists would later be used as the basis for compiling the House and Senate electoral registers. The compilation of the registers, said Giles, was "marked by many abuses," including the registration of minors, deceased persons, and fictitious names, or of one person under several names, so that in some districts the number of voters registered exceeded the total adult male population.[5] When registers were prepared for the House and Senate elections, those for the House were swollen to four to ten times the

[a]Figures were not submitted by Szechwan, Kwangtung, Kwangsi, Yunnan, or Kweichow, which did not recognize the central government at the time.

[b]The terminology, which has been translated here as "registered voters," is, in the case of the Senate, "electors at the election assemblies" (ko hsuan-chü hui hsuan-chü jen), and in the case of the House, "electors in the election districts" (ko hsuan-chü ch'ü hsuan-chü jen). Reference to Section 2 of the Senate Election Law and Subsection 1 of Section 1 of the House Election Law shows that this terminology is equivalent to "registered voters."

It should be noted that, because of the paucity of polling places, the number of registered voters is probably significantly greater thaa the number of people who actually voted, but, because of imperfect registration procedures, it is probably significantly smaller than the number qualified to vote. In some places, however, the figures may have been inflated by padding, as described in the text. Hunan, Hupei, and Shensi did not hold elections, although they submitted statistics (Ku Tun-jou, I-hui shih, p. 149; ATTA, chüan 1, p. 4).

While T'ung-chi yueh-k'an does not identify the source of its information, it was probably the voter registers, which election superintendants were directed in Article 28 of the Senate Election Law and Article 21 of the House Election Law to draw up as a preliminary to the election. These registers have not been found. They were supposed to contain the names, ages, addresses, and wealth or educational qualifications of all qualified voters.

[c]Article 98 of the House Election Law defines twenty-one election districts in these areas, for which T'ung-chi yueh-k'an gives separate breakdowns, not reproduced here.

had an equivalent educational qualification. The Senate was elected directly by the provincial assemblies. Under the new laws, educational qualifications for a voter in the House election remained the same, but the tax and property qualifications were doubled. To vote in the Senate election one had to be a male of at least thirty years of age who had graduated from a high-level technical school or had similar educational qualifications, or who had served in a government post of at least the chien-jen level (e.g., secretary to a government organ, director of a branch in a ministry), or who paid at least Mex. $100 in direct taxes or owned at least Mex. $50,000 in real estate.

4. Giles' reports are all the more valuable in light of the fact that the usually reliable PYCF, 4:144, contains a number of errors in its description of electoral practices. PYCF says the whole Anfu slate was elected in Shantung; yet this is the province in which the Anfu Club did worst. It speaks of election practices in Hunan, where elections were not held.

5. F.O. 228/3279, "Nanking Intelligence Report for the Quarter Ended December 31st, 1917," Bertram Giles, n.d., pp. 19–20.

size of those used in previous elections despite the more rigorous qualifications. Complaints were investigated, but the provincial authorities concluded that it would be too expensive to redo the registers, so the election proceeded on the basis of the existing ones.

The elections were conducted in two stages, the first one choosing electors who would meet later to select the M.P.'s. The dates for the primary and final elections were set on May 20 and June 10 for the House, and on June 5 and 20 for the Senate.[6] The first-stage elections for the House were characterized by Giles as "a veritable orgie [sic] of corruption and rowdyism." He wrote, "The quotations for votes and the daily market fluctuations were chronicled in the native press as that of a marketable commodity, on the same footing as rice or beancake or other articles of commerce." It was not unusual for an election supervisor to retain a large bloc of tickets that should have been handed out to registered voters, fill in the names of fictitious voters, and drop them into the ballot box or hire "beggars, hawkers, fortune-tellers, peasants and such small fry" to cast the votes. Alternatively, the election deputy could sell a packet of tickets to a candidate who would proceed in the same fashion. In Nanking, the chairman of the Government Property Office gave a holiday to the students in government schools and provided them with ballots so that they could vote for him. In another town, a candidate bought up all the ballots and engaged the police to supervise his hirelings in casting them. Some candidates, unable to buy enough tickets, hired toughs to seize them at the polling booth. In some cases, one candidate paid the others to withdraw. In the first-level Senate elections, Giles reported, things went more smoothly since the smaller number of electors made it easier to buy up all the votes.[7]

It was over the second-stage elections that the parties "began bidding against each other in earnest."[8]

It must be borne in mind that success at the primary elections only gave the right to vote, and to be elected, at the secondary elections. At these latter, however, votes change hands for much larger sums, and candidates successful at the primary elections look forward to reimbursing themselves, besides making a handsome profit, by the sale of their votes. . . . Many of the names of the successful candidates at the primary elections were entirely fictitious, individuals who possessed sufficient funds buying up enough tickets to secure election several times over under different names. The officials in charge of the elections, who were frequently candidates and who from their position had greater facilities than

6. F.O. 228/3279, "Nanking Intelligence Report for the Quarter Ended March 31st, 1918," Bertram Giles, n.d., p. 12. The dates given here for the Senate are June 6 and June 20, but in the report in the next footnote, Giles gives June 5 and June 20.

7. F.O. 228/3279, "Nanking Intelligence Report for the Quarter Ended July 31st, 1918," Bertram Giles, n.d., pp. 15–23.

8. Ibid., p. 23.

others, were in several cases so elected. As a result they could either cast several votes for themselves at the second election, or else make a large sum by the sale of all their tickets.[9]

Votes for the house in the second-level election went for Mex. $150 to Mex. $500. The elections were repeatedly postponed as bargaining over the price of votes went on.[10] If Kiangsu's cities were anything like Tientsin, from which we have a report, the business of teahouses, wine shops, and brothels recovered from their annual post-Spring Festival lull as candidates entertained potential supporters and used the premises to close deals on votes. The Tientsin author asks: "Who says elections don't benefit the little people?"[11]

Prime Minister Tuan's electoral machine was known as the Anfu Club. In Kiangsu, it had a branch called the Ya-yuan (Elegant garden), probably after the name of the building where Anfu emissaries entertained prospective supporters and exchanged money for ballots.[12] Giles reported that as a result of the second-level elections for the House, the Anfu Club won about three-quarters of the House seats despite the fact "that the bulk of the Province is strongly anti-Tuan."[13] Anfu's main rival in Kiangsu was the Research Clique (it had aligned itself with President Feng Kuo-chang after being dropped from the Tuan cabinet). After doing poorly in the House elections, the Research Clique made "a great effort" to win some Senate seats and, thanks to "a vigorous if unobtrusive campaign" by Feng's follower, Kiangsu Military Governor Li Ch'un, managed to buy several seats in the Senate at the final elections.[14]

The cost of the election for one senatorial candidate was reported at Mex. $40,000. The Anfu Club's investment in Kiangsu was estimated by one ob-

9. F.O. 371/6635, F3112/309/10, Enclosure in Peking Despatch 382 of July 6, 1921: "Nanking Intelligence Report for the Quarter Ended March 31st, 1921," Bertram Giles, April 15, 1921, p. 12. This describes the 1921 parliamentary elections, but the circumstances were the same in 1918.

10. F.O. 228/3279, "Nanking Intelligence Report for the Quarter Ended July 31st, 1918," pp. 23–24.

11. *AHKC*, 1:47.

12. *ATTA, chüan* 1, p. 4.

13. F.O. 228/3279, "Nanking Intelligence Report for the Quarter Ended July 31st, 1918," p. 24. However, according to *AHKC*, 1:60–61, the Anfu Club controlled only twelve of the twenty-seven Kiangsu seats in the House. *AHKC*, 1:56, also disagrees with Giles as to the number of Anfu senators: it finds two or three; he implies there were only two (see below). Some of the discrepancy might be due to changes of party affiliation during the interval between the election and the early days of the parliamentary session. Probably, however, Giles's information, which was presumably based upon the local press, exaggerated the size of the Anfu victory. Giles may also have exaggerated corruption because of his reliance on sensationalistic local newspapers.

14. F.O. 228/3279, "Nanking Intelligence Report for the Quarter Ended July 31st, 1918," p. 24. See the Appendix to this book for profiles of the factions mentioned here.

server as Mex. $100,000, by another as Mex. $160,000 for the senatorial election alone.[15] By providing financial support to candidates who could not afford to buy parliamentary seats, the club was able to ensure itself of more loyal support in the future parliament than it would have enjoyed if candidates of independent means had been elected under its banner. The Anfu Club's election purse came from funds raised by Tuan's follower Hsu Shu-cheng, although where he got the funds is unclear. Some sources imply that the funds were part of a large sum of money that the Communications Clique had donated to Tuan Ch'i-jui's campaign against Chang Hsun in mid-1917 and that Tuan had not used.[16] It is also possible that Hsu took the money from funds earmarked for the troops he led as vice-commander of the Fengtien Army. Hsu's peculation in the millions of yuan was discovered by Fengtien Commander Chang Tso-lin in August 1918, and was the pretext for Hsu's dismissal as vice-commander. Contemporary accounts state that some of the peculated funds were used for the Anfu Club election campaign.[17] In any case, the club allocated Mex. $1.5 million in cash for expenses of campaign personnel sent to the various provinces. Each emissary had a budget of Mex. $10,000 for entertaining and vote-buying.[18]

Although the Anfu Club spent a good deal of money on the election, in few provinces was the outcome as much in doubt as in Kiangsu. British Minister Sir John Jordan exaggerated only slightly when he reported, "The results in all cases comport with the views of the military leaders controlling the electoral area."[19] Of course, parliamentary seats were sufficiently lucrative and honorific to stimulate competition even among the supporters of the dominant local warlord, with the concomitant buying and selling of votes.[20] But in the majority of

15. *Ibid.*; F.O. 228/2982, Despatch 67, Giles to Jordan, June 18, 1918, p. 2; F.O. 228/2982, Despatch 72, Giles to Jordan, June 29, 1918, p. 2.

16. *ATTA, chüan* 1, p. 1; *AHKC,* 1:4. On the donation of the funds, see *LSINP,* 1:373–74; Yü Ch'eng-chih, *Hsia-an hui-kao (fu nien-p'u)* (Taipei, [1967?]), *nien-p'u,* p. 52.

17. On the so-called accounts controversy (*suan-chang feng-ch'ao*) of August 1918, see *STSP* 1918.8.14.2, 8.15.2, 8.16.2. Also see *CWCY,* p. 446. This was the source of Anfu Club funds according to Fei Hsing-chien, *Hsu Shih-ch'ang* (Taipei, 1967), p. 42 (hereafter abbreviated *HSC*).

18. *AHKC,* 1:5; *ATTA, chüan* 1, p. 4.

19. F.O. 371/3184, 162951 (f 16666), Despatch 351, Jordan to Balfour, Peking, July 24, 1918, confidential print. Also see *CWCY,* p. 441.

20. See, e.g., F.O. 371/6635, F3112/309/10, Enclosure in Peking Despatch 382 of July 6, 1921: "Mukden Intelligence Report for March Quarter 1921," no author, no date, but presumably by Wilkinson. Wilkinson is describing the 1921 elections, but what he says is valid for the 1918 elections as well. The control exercised by the warlords in certain provinces over their parliamentary delegations is illustrated by Wilkinson's report that one M.P. elected to the 1921 parliament whose views did not coincide with those of Chang Tso-lin resigned and was replaced by a man whose views did. F.O. 228/3290, F. E. Wilkinson,

provinces only the precise composition of the provincial delegation was in doubt. Its political alignment was ensured in advance.

Such thorough warlord control of local elections was unprecedented. Control by local authorities over the 1909 provincial assembly elections, the 1910 National Assembly elections, and the 1912–13 parliamentary elections appears to have been highly imperfect. Although bribery was reported in some provinces in 1909, in many provinces, the provincial assembly elections were openly conducted and the independence of the resulting bodies was illustrated by their leadership in the national movement to demand a faster implementation of constitutionalism.[21] The provincial assemblies in turn elected the 100 popular representatives in the 1910 National Assembly; although the Assembly was balanced with 100 court appointees, the elected members dominated and again demonstrated their independence by agitating for constitutionalism.[22] In 1912–13, members of the Senate were again elected by the provincial assemblies, which had not been reelected since 1909. Party affiliations of senators from each province frequently did not reflect those of the local warlords.[23] Although similarly detailed data are not available for the House, the fact that the proportions of members of the various parties were similar in the two houses of parliament suggests that local warlord control was not successfully exercised in the House elections either.[24]

Why did the warlords meddle as little as they did in these early elections? Several reasons may be suggested. First, most local regimes in the years between 1909 and 1913 were transitory and had not solidified their local control. Most of the military governors of 1913 would be replaced within the next few years—and expected to be. Second, the 1918 incentive for warlord interference—the presidential election that parliament was scheduled to carry out immediately after its election, the outcome of which would directly affect the interests of every warlord—was lacking in the 1909–13 elections. Third, in the early elections, a feeling of optimistic idealism about the working of democracy militated against interference in the elections.[25]

By 1918, these factors had changed. Although control of certain provinces

"Mukden Intelligence Report for June Quarter 1921," p. 7. Also cf. Robert H. G. Lee, *The Manchurian Frontier in Ch'ing History* (Cambridge, Mass., 1970), pp. 180–81.

21. P'eng-yuan Chang, "The Constitutionalists," pp. 148–49; John Fincher, "Political Provincialism," p. 197; Chūzō Ichiko, "The Role of the Gentry: An Hypothesis," p. 301, all in Mary Clabaugh Wright, ed., *China in Revolution: The First Phase, 1900–1913* (New Haven, Conn., 1968).

22. P'eng-yuan Chang, "The Constitutionalists," pp. 165–66.

23. Hsieh Pin, *Min-kuo cheng-tang shih* (Taipei, 1962), p. 49.

24. Yang Yu-chiung, *Chung-kuo cheng-tang shih* (Taipei, 1966), p. 61, gives party membership figures for the first parliament.

25. See, e.g., Lee, *Manchurian Frontier*, p. 180.

was contested, there was now a substantial number of provinces where local warlords were well entrenched. The general distribution of territory that Yuan Shih-k'ai had established among his followers in North China was generally accepted: open military struggle among the Peiyang warlords was two years in the future. The only territorial conflict was that between Canton- and Peking-allied armies in Shensi, Hunan and Hupei. Now, too, the presidency was at stake, for Feng Kuo-chang's term was near its end. Tuan Ch'i-jui and Feng were both candidates for the post, and local warlords allied with Tuan or Feng wanted their ally to be elected. Third, as a result of the behavior of the old parliament, idealism about the role of parliament had declined and interference in the election was cynically accepted.

But the most important factor was the new nature of provincial regimes. Until the end of the Ch'ing, such regimes were usually content with the limited power obtained by ruling in cooperation with the local gentry. The primary orientation of late Ch'ing local officials was to their official positions within the bureaucracy; these were the main source of their authority. The conditions of bureaucratic service normally included transfer from post to post. The period of local rule was limited and had limited goals—preservation of local order, production of tax revenue—which were well served by cooperation with the local elites.

With the breakdown of central authority (the death of Yuan Shih-k'ai in 1916 was perhaps even more important than the fall of the Ch'ing), the orientations of local authorities changed. They now attempted to establish permanent regimes. The source of their power was no longer official appointment but the military units that they controlled. Their primary goal therefore changed from fulfilling the centrally assigned functions of local rule to tightening their control over the resources of the countryside in order to raise money and manpower for military purposes. The warlord's relationship with the local gentry and fa-t'uan changed from one of cooperation to one of tension. The warlord now brought his men and his military and political machines into the province and challenged the influence of the local elite.

The conflict between warlord and local elite interests was most extreme when the military position of the warlord in the province was insecure. Then it was necessary for him to carry out his depradations as rapidly as possible, while his interest in maintaining good long-term relations with the local elite was secondary. Chang Ching-yao's brutal regime in Hunan was an example of such a situation. If the warlord was fairly secure in his control, as was, for example, Yen Hsi-shan in Shansi, his rule was more enlightened, but the effort to increase his hold on the manpower and grain resources of the countryside still necessarily involved strained relations with the local elite.[26]

26. Cf. Gillin, *Warlord*, pp. 51–58.

This change in the nature of local regimes was reflected in the composition of the new parliament. Membership of the late Ch'ing provincial and national assemblies and of the first republican parliament had shown considerable continuity: the members of these bodies had represented essentially the local gentry elites.[27] Of the 470 members of the new parliament of 1918, however, only ninety-eight, or 21 percent, were "old M.P.'s" who had participated in the late Ch'ing provincial or national assemblies, in the Provisional National Council of 1912, or in the 1913–14 or 1916–17 sessions of parliament (see Tables 2, 3 and 4). This ratio held good for both Anfu Club and non-Anfu members: 20 percent and 23 percent, respectively, were old M.P.'s. The sharp discontinuity in parliamentary membership is particularly striking in view of the continuity of personnel in other sectors of the Peking elite described in Chapter III.

In parliament, as in top local posts, the warlords had turned to new personnel who were loyal to them. (The trend was enhanced by the reaction of the members of the old parliament, who saw little opportunity of election under the new circumstances. Instead of returning home to contest the 1918 elections, most of them participated in the constitution-protecting parliament in Canton, promoting the view that the new parliament was illegitimate and should be dissolved and replaced with the reconvened old parliament. As the republican period continued, the chances that the members of the old parliament could be reelected continued to decline and they could base their political strategy only on arguing for the reconvening of the original parliament. As late as 1926, members of the old parliament mounted a substantial movement calling for their own reinstatement.)[28] Warlord control of the 1918 elections, and the election of a parliament consisting primarily of inexperienced members, was thus part of the broader warlord challenge to the power of local elites. In the 1918 parliament for the first time, many of the provincial delegations represented the local warlords rather than the local gentry and fa-t'uan.

Of the seventeen provinces that sent delegations to the new parliament, the warlords of thirteen were allied with Tuan Ch'i-jui. The delegations of eleven of these thirteen provinces joined the Anfu Club virtually as units (see Table 2), and functioned within the club as one-, two-, or three-province blocs or delegations under leaders responsive to the wishes of the home warlords. The bloc behavior of these allied delegations (Anhwei, Fengtien, Kirin, Heilungkiang, Hunan, Shensi, Shansi, Honan, Fukien, Sinkiang, and Kansu) reflected the close control the local warlords had maintained over the selection of the delegations.

As shown in Table 3, two provinces whose warlords were allied with Tuan

27. P'eng-yuan Chang, "The Constitutionalists," pp. 149–50; Chūzō Ichiko, "Role," p. 301.

28. See, e.g., *Ching pao* 1926.2.2 in *GSK* 1926.2.23–24; *Ching pao* 1926.2.4 in *GSK* 1926.2.50–54.

TABLE 2. Allied Delegations

Province (warlord)	Affiliation of M. P.'s	Senate New	Senate Old	House New	House Old
Anhwei	Anfu	5	0	14	2
(Ni Ssu-ch'ung)	Non-Anfu	0	0	3	0
Fengtien	Anfu	2	3	5	6
(Chang Tso-lin)	Non-Anfu	0	0	0	0
Kirin	Anfu	4	1	6	0
(Meng En-yuan)	Non-Anfu	0	0	1	0
Heilungliang	Anfu	3	2	5	2
(Pao Kuei-ch'ing)	Non-Anfu	0	0	0	0
*Hunan	Anfu	3	0	17	1
(Chang Ching-yao)	Non-Anfu	2	0	0	0
*Shensi	Anfu	4	1	8	1
(Ch'en Shu-fan)	Non-Anfu	1	0	6	0
Shansi	Anfu	1	3	16	1
(Yen Hsi-shan)	Non-Anfu	0	1	0	0
Honan	Anfu	4	1	14	7
(Chao T'i)	Non-Anfu	1	0	0	1
Fukien	Anfu	2	2	10	1
(Li Hou-chi)	Non-Anfu	1	1	2	3
Sinkiang	Anfu	3	0	7	0
(Yang Tseng-hsin)	Non-Anfu	2	0	0	0
Kansu	Anfu	3	2	8	1
(Chang Kuang-chien)	Non-Anfu	0	0	0	1

Sources: This listing is based upon identified members of parliament as found in sources described in bibliography under "Parliament List." In several cases, the total

(Chihli and Shantung) produced substantial non-Anfu strength in their delegations. The three provinces whose warlords favored Feng Kuo-chang for the presidency (Kiangsi, Kiangsu, and Hupei) and neutral Chekiang also produced mixed delegations.

The "nonprovincial delegations" (Table 4)—those of the special administrative regions, Mongolia, Tibet, Tsinghai, and the central election assemblies —produced strongly pro-Anfu delegations, because they were selected under strong central government influence.[29]

Parliament on the Eve of the Presidential Election

In mid-June 1918, the reports of election results flowed into Peking from the provinces[30] and it became clear that the Anfu Club had won a major victory. In a parliament of 470 members, the club controlled 342 seats. Of the remaining 128 seats, the Research Clique controlled about twenty, the Communications Clique perhaps fifty to eighty, and the rest were held by nonparty indepen-

---

number of names thus identified differs from the number of M.P.'s legally mandated for the province: Anhwei should have eighteen House members; Shensi should have five senators and fourteen members of the House; Honan should have five senators; Fukien should have five senators. It is not clear when such discrepancies are due to imperfections in the lists and when they are due to death or resignation of members.

Sources on warlords and their political affiliations:

Ni Ssu-ch'ung: *ATTA, chüan* 2, p. 14; *HSC*, p. 64; *GJMK*, 1924, p. 733.

Chang Tso-lin: There is so far no serious biography of this important figure. There are two more or less reliable popular biographies: Hakuun-sō shujin, *Chō Saku-rin* (Tokyo, 1928); and Yu-ming, *Chang Tso-lin wai-chuan* (Hongkong, 1967). See also Boorman and Howard, *Biographical Dictionary*, 1: 115–22; *GJMK*, 1932, pp. 235–36; *ATTA, chüan* 2, pp. 1–2; *HSC*, pp. 66–67.

Meng En-yuan: *GJMK*, 1932, p. 341; *HSC*, p. 67.

Pao Kuei-ch'ing: *GJMK*, 1932, p. 337; *MJTC, chüan* 9, p. 36.

Chang Ching-yao: *GJMK*, 1932, p. 231; *ATTA, chüan* 2, p. 13.

Ch'en Shu-fan: *GJMK*, 1932, p. 267.

Yen Hsi-shan: Gillin, *Warlord, passim.*

Chao T'i: *GJMK*, 1932, p. 250; *Who's Who*, p. 21; *ATTA, chüan* 2, pp. 6–7.

Li Hou-chi: *GJMK*, 1932, pp. 374–75; Wen Kung-chih, *Tsui-chin san-shih nien, pien* 2, pp. 233–35.

Yang Tseng-hsin: *Who's Who in China*, 3d ed. (Shanghai, 1925), pp. 912–13; Wen Kung-chih, *Tsui-chin san-shih nien, pien* 2, pp. 117–23 and chart ff. p. 444.

Chang Kuang-chien: *GJMK*, 1937, p. 328; Wen Kung-chih, *Tsui-chin san-shih nien, pien* 2, p. 111, and chart ff. p. 444.

*No election due to war conditions. Ku Tun-jou, *I-hui shih*, p. 149.

29. For further information on the composition of delegations and circumstances of their election, see Nathan, "Factionalism in Early Republican China," Chapter 6.

30. *CWCY*, pp. 440–41.

TABLE 3.   Contested Delegations

Province (warlord)	Affiliation of M.P.'s	Senate		House	
		New	Old	New	Old
Kiangsi (Ch'en Kuang-yuan)	Anfu	4	0	17	1
	Non-Anfu	1	1	5	2
Kiangsu (Li Ch'un)	Anfu	3	0	8	4
	Non-Anfu	2	0	10	4
*Hupei (Wang Chan-yuan)	Anfu	3	0	10	2
	Non-Anfu	2	0	6	0
Chihli (Ts'ao K'un)	Anfu	4	0	10	1
	Non-Anfu	1	0	8	4
Chekiang (Yang Shan-te)	Anfu	0	0	6	1
	Non-Anfu	4	1	18	2
Shantung (Chang Huai-chih)	Anfu	1	2	2	3
	Non-Anfu	2	0	13	3

Source: Parliament List (see Bibliography).

Discrepancies: List shows one extra senator and one extra representative for Kiangsi; one too few representatives for each of three provinces: Kiangsu, Chekiang, and Shantung.

Sources on warlords and their political affiliations:

Ch'en Kuang-yuan: *GJMK*, 1932, p. 263; Liu Feng-han, *Hsin-chien lu-chün* (Nankang, 1967), pp. 120–21; *ATTA*, *chüan* 2, p. 6.

Li Ch'un: *ATTA*, *chüan* 2, pp. 3–4; Liu Feng-han, *Hsin-chien*, p. 119; *PYCF*, 4: 12.

Wang Chan-yuan: *MJTC*, *chüan* 3, p. 37; *GJMK*, 1932, p. 32; *ATTA*, *chüan* 2, pp. 5–6; Liu Feng-han, *Hsin-chien*, p. 121.

Ts'ao K'un: *GJMK*, 1932, p. 201; *ATTA*, *chüan* 2, pp. 2–3; *HSC*, pp. 65–66; Liu Feng-han, *Hsin-chien*, pp. 115–16.

Yang Shan-te: Liu Feng-han, *Hsin-chien*, p. 122; Wen Kung-chih, *Tsui-chin san-shih nien, pien* 2, pp. 190–91.

Chang Huai-chih: *GJMK*, 1932, p. 226; Liu Feng-han, *Hsin-chien*, pp. 121–22; *PYCF*, 4: 137.

*No election due to war conditions. Ku Tun-jou, *I-hui shih*, p. 149.

TABLE 4.   Nonprovincial Delegations

Area	Affiliation of M.P.'s	Senate		House	
		New	Old	New	Old
Special administrative regions	Anfu	4	0	8	3
	Non–Anfu	2	0	3	0
Tsinghai	Anfu	1	1	2	0
	Non–Anfu	0	0	0	0
Mongolia	Anfu	9	3	9	7
	Non–Anfu	1	1	1	1
Tibet	Anfu	3	2	5	2
	Non–Anfu	0	1	0	2
Central election assemblies	Anfu	16			
	Non–Anfu	12			

Source: Parliament List.

Discrepancies: Special adminstrative regions should total five senators, twelve representatives; Mongolia should total fifteen senators, nineteen representatives; Tibet should have seven representatives; central election assemblies should total thirty senators.

dents.[31] The election had proved disastrous for the Research Clique, which had originally favored electing a new parliament because it hoped to improve on its poor position in the old one.

31. It is typical of the backwardness of republican China studies and of the frustrating character of the source materials that we do not know the exact party makeup of the Anfu parliament; indeed, it is impossible to be sure just how many members the Anfu parliament had. Thus, a word is needed here about how the figures for party membership are reached. First, as to the membership of parliament: if one adds the membership of the various delegations to the House and Senate as prescribed by Articles 2, 4 and 5 of the Parliamentary Organic Law, one arrives at the figures of 168 senators and 406 representatives, for a total of 574. (These are the figures given by Ku Tun-jou, *I-hui shih*, p. 149. Yang Yu-chiung, *Li-fa shih*, p. 279, with characterisitc unreliability, gives 168 and 353, for a total of 521.) Subtracting the prescribed delegation numbers for the five nonparticipating southwestern provinces, one arrives at the figure of 143 senators and 327 representatives, or 470 M.P.'s. Ku Tun-jou's list of members (pp. 306–310) contains only 139 and 326 names, totalling 465. The discrepancy of five names is understandable, since the list is dated "the end of 1918"

As the new members arrived in Peking in August 1918, the factions established clubs for liaison and mobilization. The clubs were to be the major organizations in parliament in the following two years. The largest, and the one
about which we have the most information, was the Anfu Club.

The Anfu Club was founded shortly after the promulgation of the revised
parliamentary election laws—the date usually given is March 7, 1918[32]—but in
its early months it appears to have had little formal organization. According to
what is by now an almost legendary account, the club evolved out of an eating
and recreational society, which had its premises on An-fu hu-t'ung (lane) in

---

when various personal accidents might have removed five M.P.'s who were not yet replaced
by alternates. The number of M.P.'s actually attending the session in early September
appears to have been 436 (the number voting at the presidential election on September 4;
STSP 1918.9.5.2 and other sources; see section below on the election). In this case, the
discrepancy might have been due to the lateness or absence of some members. Therefore
I adopt the number 470.

For the membership of the Anfu Club, I adopt the figure of 342, which is arrived at by
counting the number of names on the list of Anfu Club members in AHKC, 1:55–64. Although some of the names on this list do not appear in Ku Tun-jou's list of M.P.'s, I have
used the list in most of my generalizations about Anfu Club membership and adopt it here
for reasons of consistency. Generally, the list seems reliable. It appears to date from late
autumn 1918, since it does not contain the names of Communications Clique members who
participated in the Anfu Club only for the first few weeks of the session. This may explain
why at an early caucus of the club there were reported to be 384 members present (STSP
1918.4.2), and why AHKC, 1:27, says the club had more than 380 members. STSP 1918.
9.5.2 says that the pure Anfu membership, aside from temporarily cooperating members
of other cliques, was about 330.

We have no master list of Research, Discussion or Communications Clique members,
and so it is possible to identify only their core members in the 1918 parliament. The identifiable core members number five to ten for each clique. Various sources, however, give what
they allege to be the total strength of each faction without identifying their sources. Yang
Yu-chiung, Cheng-tang shih, pp. 108–109, says the Communications Clique had about 120
M.P.'s as of September 1918, later decreasing to about fifty, and the Research Clique had
about twenty. Li Chien-nung, Cheng-chih shih, 2: 517, says the Research Clique had about
twenty M.P.'s, the Communications Clique 120 or 130. Tokō Fumio, "Shina seitō no
genkyō," Chōsa shiryō, no. 10 (June 28, 1919) (hereafter abbreviated "SSG"), gives the
Communications Clique fifty or sixty (p. 7), and the Discussion Society twenty (p. 13),
while giving no definite number in its discussion of the Research Clique (pp. 20–21).

32. On the founding of the Anfu Club, see ATTA, chüan 1, pp. 1–12, and AHKC, 1:4.
On its purpose of electing Tuan: ATTA, chüan 1, p. 1; NCH 1918.1.22.685; F.O. 371/
3184, 162951 (f 16666), Despatch 351, Jordan to Balfour, Peking, July 24, 1918, confidential
print. On the date of founding, March 7, 1918, is given by Yang Yu-chiung, Cheng-tang
shih, p. 108, and by Kao Yin-tsu, Chung-hua min-kuo ta-shih chi (Taipei, 1957), p. 51. AHKC,
1:7, gives August 1917. ATTA, chüan 1, pp. 1–2, gives no date but says Tuan was prime
minister at the time of founding, which would exclude March 7, 1918 (Tuan became prime
minister on March 23, 1918). Since the club emerged as a full-blown organization only
when parliament convened in August 1918, there probably was no formal date of founding.

Peking.[33] In mid-1918, when it began to contest the elections on Tuan Ch'i-jui's behalf, it consisted of an informal group of some of Tuan's followers, led by Hsu Shu-cheng and Wang I-t'ang, together with a number of their political associates and the delegates of some of Tuan's warlord allies. Tuan himself took no direct part in founding or running the club. The word club (*chü-le-pu*) was considered preferable to party (*tang*) because the latter had come to connote divisiveness and lack of patriotism due to the fractious behavior of the parties in the previous two parliaments.[34]

The club emerged as a full-blown organization with hundreds of members only when parliament convened in August 1918. The headquarters at An-fu hu-t'ung were maintained, and a Secretariat was established at roomier quarters at T'aip'ing Lake, where plenary meetings of the club were also held.[35] The Secretariat was divided into five departments (*k'o*) each of which was subdivided into several sections (*ku*).[36] Each department was supervised by a standing cadre (*ch'ang-jen kan-shih*, a cadre with continuous administrative responsibility) who was a leading member of the club, and each section was supervised by several special cadre (*chuan-jen kan-shih*).

The Secretarial Department (*Wen-tu k'o*) was in charge of issuing club publications and announcements, sending and receiving letters, registering club members and issuing membership cards, conducting liaison with newspapers, and translating correspondence and telegrams to and from foreigners. The

33. This is the account given by *AHKC*, 1:4. In any case, it is clear that the word Anfu in the club's title came from the name of the lane in Peking, and not, as some have asserted, from the fact that many members of Tuan Ch'i-jui's entourage were from Anhwei and Fukien. On the terminological confusion over the phrase "Anfu clique," see Appendix, note 4.

34. In the first parliament, most political groups took the name "party" because this implied modern, Western, democratic practices. But after the experiences of 1913–14, the word resumed much of its traditional meaning of divisive, selfish, opportunistic politics, and Liang Ch'i-ch'ao and others called for nonparty politics (*wu-tang chu-i*). Li Chien-nung, *Cheng-chih shih*, 2: 482; *PYCF*, 3: 82; Tsou Lu, *Hui-ku lu* (Taipei, 1951), 1:80. In the 1916–17 and subsequent parliaments, the word ceased to be commonly used in the names of parliamentary groups.

35. The description of the formal organization of the club is based on two sources that often echo one another word for word: *ATTA*, *chüan* 1, 1–11; *AHKC*, 1:7–14. This was not a new type of organization for Chinese political groups. One precursor, perhaps not the earliest, was the Kuo-min tang of the first parliament. See its organizational charter in *Ko-ming wen-hsien* 41 (1967): 25–31.

36. The organization of the Secretariat was prescribed in "Rules for the Club Secretariat" (*Pen-pu kan-shih pu hsi-tse*). The text is given in *AHKC*, 1:9–10. Names of standing and special cadres are given in *AHKC*, 1: 15–16, and *ATTA*, *chüan* 1, pp. 7–9. With one or two differences, the two sources agree on these names. The names of the ordinary cadres were not preserved (*ATTA*, *chüan* 1, p. 5; *AHKC*, 1:17). The number of staff in the Secretariat is unknown.

standing cadre of this department was Liu En-ko,[37] the leader of the Fengtien delegation in parliament. The Liaison Department (*Chiao-chi k'o*) was in charge of the conduct of club relations and negotiations with M.P.'s within and outside the club and with other politicians in Peking and the provinces. Tseng Yü-chün, a follower of Tuan Ch'i-jui, was in charge of its work.

The Accounting Department (*K'uai-chi k'o*) was in charge of handling money, including the disbursement of the monthly gratuity received by each club member. This sensitive activity was supervised by Wang Chih-lung,[38] a leader of the Anhwei delegation in parliament. The remaining two departments were less important. The Club Affairs Department (*Shu-wu k'o*) was presumably in charge of running the club premises. The Recreation and Art Department (*Yu-i k'o*) was in charge of arranging lectures, debates, archery, painting, poetry-writing, lute-playing, and similar activities, and running the club library.

The club bylaws[39] provided elaborate institutions for internal governance. Chairman Wang I-t'ang was in charge of the Secretariat and of the various deliberative organs within the club. The Deliberative Assembly (*P'ing-i hui*) consisted of M.P.'s elected by provincial delegations[40] (each delegation elected one for every five of its M.P.'s), plus non-M.P. club members who were elected by majority vote of all M.P. members of the club. It was in charge of "deciding all the club's affairs."[41] The club also had a Members of Parliament Assembly (*I-yuan hui*), consisting of all M.P.'s in the club; it was supposed to meet to coordinate members' actions on issues coming before parliament. Finally, the club had a Political Affairs Research Council (*Cheng-wu yen-chiu hui*), composed of all club members who wished to join it. The council was organized in divisions corresponding to government ministries and was intended to study policy questions.

Despite its elaborately democratic decision-making apparatus, the club was actually run autocratically by the small group who had organized it and who

37. *GJMK*, 1932, p. 477; *Who's Who*, p. 165; "SSG," p. 4; Satō Saburō, ed., *Minkoku no seika* (Peking, 1916), p. 370.

38. *ATTA*, *chüan* 2, p. 17.

39. *AHKC*, 1: 7-9. The bylaws were not adopted until the club meeting of December 9, 1918, the meeting at which Wang I-t'ang was formally elected chairman (*STSP* 1918. 12.10.2).

40. An interesting feature of the bylaws was the provision that "those elected [to parliament] to represent districts other than their home districts shall for the purposes of the election [to the Deliberative Assembly] be counted with their provinces of origin" (Article 7a).

41. Article 6; cf. *ATTA*, *chüan* 1, pp. 10-11. All the known non-M.P. members of the Anfu Club did in fact belong to the Deliberative Assembly. See list of Deliberative Assembly members, *ATTA*, *chüan* 1, p. 12.

controlled its funds. Decisions about club policy were made in informal consultations among members of this group and between them and their political allies outside the club. Leaders of the provincial delegations then passed on the decision to informal meetings (*t'an-hua hui*) of the delegations held at provincial hostels (*chao-tai so*) scattered around Peking. Any problems were ironed out at these meetings, so that when the club formally assembled in caucus at its T'aip'ing Lake premises, the caucus usually consisted simply of speeches from the leadership and a near-unanimous straw vote.[42]

The club membership grumbled about this procedure, not out of outraged democratic sensibility, but because the leadership was so efficient that it deprived the members of a substantial portion of the income they had expected to reap in bribes from candidates for president, vice-president, Speaker and Vice-Speaker, and from nominees to cabinet posts.[43] The tight organization of the club and its dominance in parliament meant that lucrative contests seldom developed. When, for example, competition developed between Anfu members Liu En-ko and Wang Yin-ch'uan for the post of Vice-Speaker of the House and bribes began to be given, the club leaders decided to have Wang withdraw from the race. Many club members were disappointed, and Liu's election on August 22 was marred by the protest casting of thirteen spoiled ballots and seventy-seven ballots for twenty-four other persons.[44]

In the absence of extensive bribes, the income of M.P.'s came from their government salaries of Mex. $5,000 per year,[45] supplemented by the Mex. $300 received each month as a gratuity from the club, paid in the form of a check cashable only at the club's Accounting Department. The club paid an extra Mex. $300 to 400 to leaders of delegations and to members fulfilling other important tasks.[46] Income of prominent M.P.'s was further supplemented with salaries from government sinecures, such as advisorships to ministries or

42. Examples of this procedure are given below. For a description of the procedure together with complaints about it, see *STSP* 1918.8.27.2.

43. See *STSP* 1918.9.21.2.

44. *STSP* 1918.8.12.2, 8.15.2, 8.17.2, 8.18.2, 8.19.2, 8.20.2, 8.22.2, 8.23.2. Liu was presumably selected to run because he was backed by Chang Tso-lin. I surmise that most of the anti-Liu ballots were cast by Anfu Club members because at this early point in the session cooperative relations still obtained between the Anfu leadership and the leaders of other groups in parliament. Thus, Wang I-t'ang had been elected Speaker of the House on August 20 with only fourteen opposing ballots.

45. Article 92, part 1, of the Parliamentary Procedures (*I-yuan fa*; text in Ku Tun-jou, *I-hui shih*, pp. 230–38). These were promulgated September 27, 1913, and not revised for the new parliament. An extra allowance was provided for the Speaker and Vice-Speaker of each house, and a travelling allowance was given each M.P. in accordance with the distance and difficulty of travel from his home district to Peking.

46. *ATTA*, chüan 1, pp. 24–25; *AHKC*, 1:51.

seats on government advisory commissions. In addition, Anfu M.P.'s often were able to place relatives and friends on the nepotism-swollen staff of the House Secretariat.[47] Since club members were unable to recoup their investments in their parliamentary seats by the usual method of taking bribes, they were forced to work to preserve the club's dominance in parliament so that its leaders could retain the influence and government posts that were the ultimate source of the monthly gratuities and the sinecures. The club's dominance in parliament thus worked to reinforce its internal discipline in parliamentary maneuvers.

The Anfu Club budget seems to have been in the neighborhood of Mex. $140,000 per month.[48] Besides gratuities and the expenses connected with staff and building, the club needed funds to subsidize newspapers sympathetic to its cause, notably the *Kung-yen pao* owned by Wang Yu-ling, a sympathizer of the club.[49] As described earlier, the large sums used to fight the parliamentary election had been provided by Hsu Shu-cheng. But for its normal running expenses, the club relied on other friends in the official world. From the beginning of the parliamentary session until August 1920, three sympathetic ministers of finance held office (Ts'ao Ju-lin, Kung Hsin-chan, Li Ssu-hao) and reportedly provided the club with funds from the secret War Participation Loan from Japan.[50] The club may also have benefitted financially from the money-raising activities of some of its leaders. Such activities allegedly included the unauthorized issue of large sums of money by government ministries to Hsu Shu-cheng, Wang I-t'ang, and other pro-Anfu officials; the milking of an alleged Mex. $16 million from the coffers of the Peking-Hankow and Peking-Suiyuan railways by their director, Ting Shih-yuan; the sale to narcotics traffickers rather than medicine manufacturers of opium obtained by government authorities as part of an opium-suppression drive; and illegal export of rice to Japan from the rice-shortage provinces of Kiangsu and Anhwei.[51]

In addition to the Anfu Club, there were four political clubs in the new par-

47. *AHKC*, 1:53.

48. This is the figure given by *PYCF*, 5: 88–89. It seems to be in the right range, since *ATTA*, *chüan* 1, p. 24, says the budget for gratuities alone was 120,000 yuan per month.

49. "SSG", p. 5; *GJMK*, 1932, p. 43. I have not been able to locate copies of the *Kung-yen pao*.

50. *PYCF*, 5: 89. T'ao's version is supported by Li Chien-nung's statement that Tuan Ch'i-jui used part of the Nishihara Loans to create the War Participation Army, and part to create the Anfu-dominated new parliament. Li Chien-nung, *Cheng-chih shih*, 2: 517.

51. The first item was discovered when the accounts of the ministries were gone over after the defeat of the Anfu forces in 1920: Ch'ang An, *Min-liu hou chih ts'ai-cheng yü chün-fa* (Peking, [1922?]), pp. 2–4. The second is reported in the same source, pp. 53–55. The third is described in *ATTA*, *chüan* 1, p. 25; the fourth in *ibid.*, pp. 26–27, and is corroborated by F.O. 228/3279, J. T. Brenan, "Nanking Intelligence Report for Quarter ended September 30th, 1919," pp. 12–15.

liament in its early months. The membership of three of them overlapped with that of the Anfu Club because the early policy of the groups' leadership was to cooperate with the club. These were the Ch'iao-yuan (Ch'iao garden), the T'ao-yuan (T'ao garden), and the Discussion Society (T'ao-lun hui).

The largest and most powerful was the Ch'iao-yuan, a meeting place maintained by the Communications Clique for its members and sympathizers.[52] The Ch'iao-yuan probably had a strength of fifty to eighty M.P.'s. Its leadership was concentrated in the Senate delegation elected by the central election assemblies and included Liang Shih-i, Chou Tzu-ch'i, Chu Ch'i-ch'ien, Jen Feng-pao, and Chou Tso-min. Other important Ch'iao-yuan members were Pi Kuei-fang,[53] the former Heilungkiang military governor, and Ch'en Chen-hsien,[54] an agricultural expert who had served under Hsu Shih-ch'ang in Manchuria.

As a rival to the Ch'iao-yuan, the New Communications Clique (Hsin chiao-t'ung hsi) established a club called the T'ao-yuan.[55] Since none of the New Communications Clique core members had been elected to parliament, the T'ao-yuan were merely a club whose premises the clique made available to M.P.'s in general in order to build good will. It is doubtful that it had any independent strength.

Both the old and the New Communications Cliques were allied with the Anfu Club in the early days of the session, so the M.P.'s who frequented the Ch'iao-yuan or the T'ao-yuan were simultaneously Anfu members. The existence of the two rival clubs, however, alarmed the Anfu Club leaders, who demanded that they be closed to prevent weakening of M.P.'s ties to the Anfu Club. Both clubs formally closed,[56] but the two sponsoring cliques maintained their activities under other titles. The Ch'iao-yuan merely changed its name to the Number Seven Club (Ch'i-hao chü-le-pu) after the address of its premises, no. 7, Feng-sheng hu-t'ung.[57] Ultimately, as we shall see below, the Communications Clique split with the Anfu Club and shortly thereafter the Number

52. STSP 1918.9.18.2, 9.19.2. For a partial list of its members after it had changed its name, see Chu Ch'i-ch'ien, comp., Nan-Pei i-ho wen-hsien (in special issue no. 1 of Chin-tai shih tzu-liao, Peking, 1962), Document 21, p. 76 (hereafter abbreviated NPIHWH).

53. GJMK, 1937, p. 460; LSINP, 1:365.

54. Ch'en is listed in STSP 1919.6.16.2 as a member of the Chi-wei Club, a successor organization to the Ch'iao-yuan. I conclude he earlier belonged to the Ch'iao-yuan. Biographical references: GJMK, 1932, p. 224; HSC, pp. 62–63; Fei Hsing-chien, Tang-tai ming-jen hsiao-chuan (Shanghai, 1919) 1:41–42 (hereafter abbreviated TTMJ).

55. STSP 1918.9.18.2, 9.19.2.

56. STSP 1918.9.21.2, 9.22.2.

57. STSP 1918.12.20.2. Thus, the Communications Clique in this period was sometimes referred to as the "Number Seven Clique," or even the "Feng-sheng Clique" (see, for example, Yang Yu-chiung, Cheng-tang shih, p. 109).

Seven Club was merged into a larger organization called the Chi-wei chü-le-pu (1919 Club). The New Communications Clique closed the T'ao-yuan but continued its liaison with M.P.'s through another club that had already been established with its backing, the Discussion Society.

The Discussion Society was sponsored by Lu Tsung-yü of the New Communications Clique and Sun Jun-yü,[58] a Japan-trained lawyer and former member of the house from Kiangsu who had served under Lu in the Chinese mission in Japan. Both had belonged to an association in the 1916–17 parliament called the Constitutional Government Discussion Society (*Hsien-cheng t'ao-lun hui*),[59] which was also known as the Discussion Society or Discussion clique (*T'ao-lun hui, T'ao-lun hsi*). The earlier Discussion Society had been a small, temporary alliance of politicians who were either politically marginal or whose basic affiliations were with other factions.[60] The individual members had gone their own ways after the second dissolution of parliament, so despite the suggestion of organizational continuity in the name chosen by Lu and Sun for their 1918 organization, the Discussion Society in the new parliament was substantially a new group. In pursuance of the New Communication Clique's alliance with the Anfu Club, almost all the members of the Discussion Society whose names are known to us (except Sun Jun-yü) belonged to the Anfu Club as well.[61] Since the New Communications Clique did not split with the Anfu Club during the new parliament's life, the Discussion Society remained an unused potential.

The Research Clique operated in the new parliament under its old name, the Constitution Research Society (*Hsien-fa yen-chiu hui*).[62] The clique had been decimated in the elections; the only core members to be elected to the new parliament were Liang Shan-chi (Shansi), Huang Ch'ün (Chekiang), Lan Kung-wu (Kiangsu), and Chi Chung-yen (Chihli). Lin Ch'ang-min and Wang Chia-hsiang, although not in the new parliament, were also in Peking at this time. Liang Ch'i-ch'ao and T'ang Hua-lung were soon to go overseas (T'ang never to return).

When the House met on August 20 for its first business meeting, Wang

58. *GJMK*, 1932, pp. 207–208; "SSG", pp. 15–16; *MJTC, chüan* 6, p. 43; Satō Saburō, *Minkoku*, p. 186; *GJMK*, 1924, p. 652. Sun later associated himself with the Chihli Clique and served in various influential posts from 1924 to 1927.

59. Not to be confused with the *Hsien-fa t'ao-lun hui*, a name used by a portion of the Research Clique at the beginning of the 1916 parliament.

60. The main members besides Lu and Sun were Chiang T'ien-to, Chu Chao-hsing, Wu Tse-sheng, K'o-hsi-k'o-t'u, Chang Kuo-kan, and Chang Chih-t'an. See "SSG," pp. 12–20; Yang Yu-chiung, *Cheng-tang shih*, p. 92; Kokumin gikai, *Shina seitō no genjō* (n.p., n.d.), pp. 11–13; *PYCF*, 3: 54, 76.

61. This statement is based on analysis of the list of Discussion Society members given in *NPIHWH*, Document 21, p. 77.

62. See *NPIHWH*, Document 21, p. 76.

I-t'ang was elected Speaker by 262 of 276 ballots; Chi Chung-yen of the Research Clique received eleven votes, Wang Shu-nan (a venerable Confucian scholar in the Mongolian delegation) received two, and one spoiled ballot was cast.[63] Liu En-ko, leader of the Fengtien delegation and an Anfu leader, was elected Vice-Speaker on August 22.[64] At this early point in the session, as the vote illustrates, only the Research Clique had openly emerged in opposition to the Anfu Club and clearly it had few supporters.

A Dark Horse Emerges

Prime Minister Tuan Ch'i-jui and President Feng Kuo-chang had been running for president since the convening of the Provisional National Council in November 1917. Their rivalry had expressed itself not only in efforts to influence the composition of parliament, but also in struggles over policy toward the dissident South.[65] Tuan advocated a policy of "military unification" (wu-li t'ung-i), amounting to an effort to unify the country through territorial expansion of his own faction and its allies into areas controlled by the South. Feng's counter-policy of negotiation with the South, or "peaceful unification" (ho-p'ing t'ung-i), sought to achieve unification without the expansion of Tuan's power. Tuan's war policy had suffered a setback in late 1917 when his followers sustained military defeats in Hunan and Szechwan. Feng Kuo-chang's effort, between November 1917 and March 1918, to realize his peace policy had also failed, because he was unable to force it on the prowar northern allies of Tuan.[66]

Chihli Tuchun Ts'ao K'un commanded a large body of troops who were well placed to take up the cudgel in Hunan, and he controlled a section of the Peking-Hankow Railway, the only route for moving troops to the Hunan front. Ts'ao, known for his indecisiveness and dependence on subordinates' advice, had supported the war policy until April, but in that month his subordinate Wu P'ei-fu, dissatisfied with his rewards for several successful battles, refused to press his offensive beyond Hengchow, which he had just captured.[67]

63. STSP 1918.8.21.2. Parliament's joint opening session was held August 12; CWCY, p. 444. The texts of the president's and prime minister's addresses are printed in Sun Yao, comp., Chung-hua min-kuo shih-liao, pp. 396–97.

64. STSP 1918.8.23.2. See also note 44 above.

65. Liang Shih-i received a letter from a friend in Peking as early as January 1918, which described the implications of the policy struggle for the presidential election; LSINP, 1: 402.

66. Li T'ing-yü, comp., "Li T'ing-yü so-ts'en tien-kao" (reprinted in special issue no. 1 of Chin-tai shih tzu-liao, Peking, 1962), Documents 1–12; Lai Ch'ün-li, comp., "I-ho wen-hsien chi-ts'en" (reprinted in special issue no. 1 of Chin-tai shih tzu-liao, Peking, 1962), pp. 287–90.

67. T'ao Chü-yin, Wu P'ei-fu chuan (Taipei, 1963), pp. 18–19.

Ts'ao's attitude now became ambiguous. The loss of his support might cost Tuan the presidency.

In mid-June, Tuan's warlord supporters met in Tientsin and offered Ts'ao the honorific title of commissioner (*ching-lueh-shih*) of Kwangtung, Szechwan, Hunan, and Kiangsi in return for his undertaking to prosecute the war.[68] Hope was also held out to Ts'ao that he would receive the support of the Tuan party for the vice-presidency.[69] But although Ts'ao agreed to prosecute the war, Wu P'ei-fu, at the front in Hunan, refused to fight. A third Tientsin conference was convened on July 31 to consider this problem.[70] To spur Ts'ao, Hsu Shu-cheng and Ni Ssu-ch'ung now raised the suggestion that the vice-presidency be given to whoever could "earn merit" in the fight against the South in the month or so remaining before the election; Chang Tso-lin was mentioned as a possibility. Although he wanted the vice-presidency, Ts'ao could not compel Wu P'ei-fu to take the offensive, nor was Ts'ao willing to quit his territorial base in Chihli on the strength of a promise of high office. Ts'ao's solution to the dilemma was to agree to prosecute the war but to pose three superficially reasonable but actually impossible conditions: that the Peking government bear the expense of the campaign, that Chang Tso-lin advance the necessary ammunition, and that Ts'ao be given control over the Shanghai, Hanyang, and Techou arsenals.[71] By these means, Ts'ao kept his chances for the vice-presidency alive but the correspondent of the *North-China Herald* accurately evaluated the conference results when he wrote, "In the name of fighting against Canton, a policy was really decided upon that there should be no more fighting, and though there may be much strutting about as if the Northern Government were about to hurl itself upon the Infant Army of the South, no such dreadful occurrence will happen."[72]

Ts'ao's evasion spelled the end of Tuan Ch'i-jui's presidential hopes. Despite the Anfu Club victory in the parliamentary election, Tuan's position as a candidate was weakened by his failure to bring the military unification policy to fruition in time for the election. Those who opposed him—the South, the three Yangtze tuchuns, the Research Clique, and other groups—remained strong enough to make the presidency, which he could certainly win, untenable. In factional politics, it is only sensible to take office if a wide consensus of factions can be created for one's candidacy. While Tuan retained hopes of

68. Ts'ao, of course, did not get control over any of the four provinces named in the new title: two of them were under southern control, one was contested, and one was controlled by Ch'en Kuang-yuan.

69. *CWCY*, p. 437.

70. *PYCF*, 4:140; *STSP* 1918.8.1.2, 8.3.3.

71. *PYCF*, 4:141.

72. *NCH* 1918.8.17.389.

creating such a consensus eventually, the time was not ripe. To this extent, the political strategy of his enemies had been successful.

Tuan had already provided an alternate position for himself that would serve as an effective base from which to continue to pursue his military unification policy. He had secured loans from Japan for the training of a new army ostensibly to represent China in the world war. The War Participation Army was being recruited by Tuan's followers and trained near Peking. If he could not become president, Tuan would remain in Peking as commander of the War Participation Army and exert direct influence on Peking politics through his followers and the Anfu Club. Anfu control of parliament guaranteed that Feng Kuo-chang would not be elected, and upon retirement Feng would have no territorial or official base from which to operate. Tuan's interests would be served by Feng's retirement and by the selection of a suitable compromise candidate for the presidency.

Tuan's choice was Hsu Shih-ch'ang.[73] A *chin-shih* and Hanlin compiler who had held many high civil posts under the Ch'ing, Hsu was a prestigious elder bureaucrat. As the most senior of Yuan Shih-k'ai's surviving top aides, Hsu virtually personified Peiyang unity.[74] In his late Ch'ing posts of governor of Manchuria and president of the Ministry of Posts and Communications, Hsu had aided the careers of many important republican figures including Liang Shih-i, Yeh Kung-ch'o, Chu Ch'i-ch'ien, Hsu Shih-ying, Ni Ssu-ch'ung, Ts'ao K'un, Chang Hsun, Wang I-t'ang, Lu Yung-hsiang, and Chang Tso-lin.[75] He was widely respected throughout China and was personally acceptable to the South. He was "gentle and amicable by nature."[76] Lacking a territorial or organizational power base of his own, he would not be able to use the presidency to challenge Tuan's dominion in North China.

Tuan invited Feng Kuo-chang to support Hsu in exchange for a promise by Tuan not to continue as prime minister.[77] Feng, incapable of being elected, could hardly refuse to support the venerable Hsu. He could leave office with greater satisfaction under Tuan's formula of "stepping down simultaneously" (*t'ung-shih hsia-yeh*) than otherwise, even though Tuan would retain a hold on power and he would not. In mid-August, Feng instructed his chief secretary, Chang I-lin, to convey his agreement to Tuan's chief secretary, Fang Shu.[78] And on August 12, the day parliament opened, Feng issued a valedictory telegram noting that his term was almost up, taking all blame upon himself for the

73. Boorman and Howard, *Biographical Dictionary*, 2:136–40; *HSC, passim*.
74. Cf. *HSC*, pp. 33–40.
75. See *HSC*, pp. 56–73.
76. Li Chien-nung, *Cheng-chih shih*, 2:526.
77. *PYCF*, 4:140; *STSP* 1918.8.3.2; *NCH* 1918.8.10.321.
78. *STSP* 1918.8.20.2.

failure during his presidency to achieve peace and national unity, and calling
upon the new parliament to elect a person "of virtuous repute and capable of
restoring unity and peace" as president.[79] Feng's telegram was generally understood as an endorsement of Hsu Shih-ch'ang.[80]

Hsu, living in retirement in Tientsin where he often received his former students and subordinates, maintained public suspense on whether he would be
willing to serve.[81] But he privately let the political leaders know that he was
willing to take office in order to seek the reconciliation both of the Feng and
Tuan parties and of North and South.[82]

Election of Hsu Shih-ch'ang and Rejection of Ts'ao K'un

Although it had been agreed since the middle of August that Feng Kuo-chang
and Tuan Ch'i-jui would leave office together and Hsu Shih-ch'ang would be
elected president, suspicions accumulated as the date of the election approached.
Feng Kuo-chang and his supporters suspected Tuan Ch'i-jui of using Hsu's
name as a ruse, while planning to push through his own election at the last
moment.[83] Tuan's supporters, on the other hand, believed that Feng was behind
a series of telegrams issued by Wu P'ei-fu and other northern commanders at
the Hunan front between August 22 and 28 demanding a North-South truce
and the postponement of the presidential election, which would have kept
Feng in office.[84] But preparations for the election proceeded on schedule. A
joint session of parliament on August 31 approved a motion to hold the election
on September 4.[85] (It also decided to elect the vice-president on the following
day.) On August 31, Prime Minister Tuan issued a circular telegram to all
military commanders affirming his decision to step down after the election.
Noting that this would be the first transfer of the presidency by election in the
history of the republic, Tuan urged the military officers to guard against efforts
by the South to take advantage of the situation to create disorder.[86] As a matter

79. Text in LSINP, 1:426–27.
80. STSP 1918.8.14.2.
81. STSP 1918.8.5.2.
82. HSC, pp. 40, 42.
83. HSC, p. 40; LSINP, 1:431.
84. STSP 1918.8.29.2; CWCY, pp. 447–55. For the answering telegrams from Ts'ao
K'un, Chang Tso-lin, Tuan Ch'i-jui, Ni Ssu-ch'ung, etc., see PYCF, 4:146–50. Wu's move
may have been motivated by suspicion of Tuan and aimed at keeping Tuan's supporters
honest by emphasizing how unacceptable Tuan would be as president. Some observers,
however, thought that Feng was seeking through Wu to raise the possibility of postponing
the presidential election and perpetuating himself in office. HSC, p. 40; LSINP, 1:431;
STSP 1918.8.28.2 editorial, 8.30.2 editorial.
85. STSP 1918.9.1.2.
86. STSP 1918.9.1.2; CWCY, pp. 455–56.

of form, telegrams arrived from tuchuns allied with Tuan (Ts'ao K'un, Chang Tso-lin, Ni Ssu-ch'ung, Chang Ching-yao, Chao T'i, Pao Kuei-ch'ing, Ch'en Shu-fan) urging him to stay on as prime minister, but these were not considered politically significant.[87] At the presidential palace, Feng Kuo-chang's possessions were packed and removed for shipment to his home in Hochien, Chihli.[88]

A contemporary source offers a vivid account of the events leading up to the election. At the Anfu Club caucus on September 3:[89]

Wang I-t'ang had originally intended to speak [on behalf of Tuan Ch'i-jui] by arguing that Tuan was a man of resolve and character who could bring about the unification of the country. But in view of [the final decision to elect Hsu], he changed his theme to a discussion of the leading personalities of the day. There were only three who were suitable for election as president—[Hsu] Tung-hai, [Tuan] Ho-fei and [Feng] Ho-chien. Among the three, Ho-fei and Ho-chien agreed in urging the election of Tung-hai, for his virtue and accomplishments were respected by civil and military, old and new officials, and he was also acceptable to all the foreign countries. For these reasons, the Anfu clique regarded him as the most suitable candidate for the post.

A vote was taken, and of a total of 384 votes, there was one invalid ballot and 383 for Hsu Shih-ch'ang. Everyone was delighted, and applause rocked the room. Club member Kuang Yun-chin spoke: "In other countries parliament elects as president the leader of the majority party. Since today this club has unanimously endorsed Tung-hai for the presidency, Tung-hai is this club's leader. I request that the club chairman [Wang I-t'ang] convey to Tung-hai that he ought to regard this club as his political base; he must not regard the political parties with contempt in the manner of Yuan Shih-k'ai or Li Yuan-hung." . . .

In the days before the election, Wang I-t'ang and Liang Shih-i circulated among the Members of Parliaments' provincial hostels building up good will. The reason for the hostels was that the M.P.'s were solely concerned with money and had no political opinions to speak of, so instead of forming political parties [based on policy stands] they divided themselves up on the basis of provincial ties. Why did the two speakers [Wang and Liang] lower themselves to consort so eagerly with this flock of crows? It was because there was then a rumor current that Wang K'o-min had brought $1 million of Feng Kuo-chang's money and was secretly buying up M.P.'s. Wang and Liang's comings and goings at the reception centers, ostensibly for the purpose of good will, were really to spy out what was going on.

On the day of the election, September 4 plainclothes detectives circulated in each hostel. Ten automobiles provided by Hsu Shu-cheng transported the M.P.'s from each reception center to the parliament.[90]

87. STSP 1918.9.3.2; CWCY, p. 456.
88. CWCY, p. 456.
89. Cf. STSP 1918.9.4.2.
90. HSC, pp. 43–44; text mistakenly gives Kuang Yun-chin's name as Yun Chin-kuan. The invalid ballot of the Anfu caucus was probably cast by Liang Shih-i; see below. STSP 1918.9.2.2, 9.4.2 confirm the existence of the rumor about Wang K'o-min. Wang was reportedly offering Mex. $8,000 ($4,000 down and $4,000 after the election) to any M.P.

Troops provided by Police Chief Wu Ping-hsiang and Garrison Commander Tuan Chih-kuei—both Anfu allies—were visible throughout the city, and on Wu's orders the merchants of Peking had hung the national flag on their buildings. Over the gate of the House of Representatives hung a yellow banner reading "Presidential Election Meeting." At 10 A.M., the time scheduled for the meeting to begin, a quorum was still lacking, but by 10:22 a quorum was present. Liang Shih-i, as speaker of the upper house, opened the meeting but then, pleading "a slight indisposition," he ceded the chair to the speaker of the lower house, Wang I-t'ang. Wang selected sixteen members to count the votes. The onlookers withdrew and parliament closeted itself for the vote.

At 11:15 A.M. the doors opened and the observers streamed back in. The votes were counted out loud one by one. Of 436 votes cast, Hsu Shih-ch'ang had received 425. Tuan Ch'i-jui had received five votes; Wang Shih-chen, Wang I-t'ang, Ni Ssu-ch'ung, and Chang Chien one each; and there were two spoiled ballots. Wang I-t'ang announced that Hsu Shih-ch'ang was the victorious candidate, and then all present broke into applause. Wang then announced: "Today's business is over. The vice-presidential election will be conducted tomorrow." A group picture was taken, and at 1:10 P.M. the M.P.'s disbanded.[91]

The anti-Hsu votes were naturally the subject of speculation in the press. The seven votes cast for Anhweinese (Tuan Ch'i-jui, Wang I-t'ang, and Ni Ssu-ch'ung) were thought to represent a protest by several Anhweinese members of the Anfu Club against the club's failure to pay special gratuities on the occasion of the election. The vote for Wang Shih-chen, a Chihli native, Peiyang elder, and political ally of Feng Kuo-chang, was thought to have been cast by Feng's son, Senator Feng Chia-sui of the Chihli delegation. The vote for Chang Chien, the prominent Kiangsu gentry-industrialist, was interpreted as a protest cast by a Kiangsu M.P. who was dissatisfied with Anfu Club salaries.[92]

The behavior of Liang Shih-i throughout the caucusing and election process attracted some attention. Liang's Communications Clique was the most powerful rival to the Anfu Club in parliament, and it also enjoyed a rich network of connections in banking, communications, and senior Peiyang circles. Perhaps even more important for the immediate future, the Kwangtung-born Liang had recently exploited his links to southern leaders to investigate the possibilities for a negotiated peace. It seemed clear that Liang could erect several powerful obstacles to the ambitions of Tuan Ch'i-jui and the Anfu Club.[93] Hoping to

who would be willing to stay away from the election. The hope was allegedly to make a quorum impossible and thus to postpone the election indefinitely.

91. *STSP* 1918.9.5.2; *AHKC*, 1:20.

92. *STSP* 1918.9.5.2. According to another story on the same page, however, Feng Kuo-chang's son did not attend the session at all.

93. In July, Liang had gone to Hongkong to probe the attitudes of southern leaders.

induce Liang to cooperate, Anfu leaders had offered to back him for the post of Speaker of the Senate and to support his followeer, Chu Ch'i-ch'ien, for Vice-Speaker.[94] Liang had seemed reluctant to come north, as if to do so, and particularly to identify himself so closely with the new parliament, might damage his contacts with the South.[95] At the last minute, however, he bowed to Wang I-t'ang's and Hsu Shu-cheng's repeated requests and embarked for Peking.

Liang arrived on August 22.

The return of this notorious man to the north was one of the most dramatic incidents which has occurred within the knowledge of living man in China. He was met at Tientsin by a special train in the charge of the Vice-Minister of Communications, Mr. Yeh Kung-[ch'o], and hurried on to Peking as rapidly as possible. There he was met by a limousine and hastened directly to the parliament buildings. All the members of the upper house were sitting in their places in readiness and as soon as Liang arrived at the chambers, proceedings commenced and he was unanimously elected chairman of the upper house.[96]

Chu Ch'i-ch'ien was elected Vice-Speaker.[97] The next day, Liang invited Liang Hung-chih of the Anfu Club to serve as secretary-general of the Senate.[98]

Having accepted Anfu support for the Senate speakership and having invited

---

(LSINP, 1:415, erroneously states Liang went south in May 1918. But early in June, Liang was still in Peking [CWCY, p. 428], and British Consul Bertram Giles reported that he visited Li Ch'un in Nanking on July 7 on his way to Hongkong [F.O. 228/2982, Despatch 79, Giles to Jordan, Nanking, July 18, 1918].) He had already sent intermediaries to visit Lu Jung-t'ing, the tuchun of Kwangsi. These were Lin Shao-fei, a Kwangtung native, a general in the army, and former governor of Kwangsi; and Kuan Mien-chün, Liang's relative who came from Kwangsi and had served there as an official. Both were men whom Liang could trust and whom Lu would receive with respect. However, Lu's reply was not particularly encouraging. Liang, knowing the road to accommodation would necessarily be long and arduous, had continued his contacts with the southern leaders (LSINP, 1:415-16, 439; CWCY, pp. 443, 461; GJMK, 1937, p. 596; STSP 1918.8.22.7).

While pursuing probes in the South, Liang had also quietly arranged the election of "fifty or sixty" of his followers to the new parliament. Liang himself, Chu, and Chou were elected by one of the central election assemblies. Liang also rebuilt his power in banking circles: he, Chu, and Chou were elected to the board of the Bank of Communications at the stockholders' meeting in May, and Yeh Kung-ch'o and Kuan Mien-chün were elected as alternate directors. By the time parliament was due to convene, Liang was being spoken of as a possible prime minister, and Chu or Chou as possible ministers of communications ("SSG," p. 7; CWCY, p. 421; cf. LSINP, 1:416, which gives a date that is off by a month; NCH 1918.7.20.137; STSP 1918.8.4.2, 8.5.2).

94. STSP 1918.8.4.2, 8.5.2, 8.10.2, 8.16.3; NCH 1918.8.10.325, 381; LSINP, 1:425.

95. LSINP, 1:425; STSP 1918.8.9.2. Also cf. STSP 1918.8.22.2.

96. NCH 1918.9.7.563. Liang's election was not unanimous. He received 119 votes out of 123. STSP 1918.8.23.2; CWCY, p. 448.

97. STSP 1918.8.23.2.

98. STSP 1918.8.24.2.

an Anfu leader to serve under him as secretary-general, Liang seemed to have
thrown in his lot with the Tuan Ch'i-jui faction. His own partisans in parliament joined the Anfu Club, bringing attendance at club caucuses to about
380.[99] Yet Liang's attitude remained ambiguous. When interviewed by reporters on August 31, he said his main concern was with China's industrial development and refused to take a stand on the issue of whether or not the presidential
election should be held before the resolution of the North-South controversy.[100]
Although active behind the scenes in arranging Hsu Shih-ch'ang's election,[101]
Liang avoided strong public identification with the election process. As Speaker
of the Senate, he should have presided over both the Anfu Club caucus of
September 3 and the joint parliamentary session of September 4, but on both
occasions he claimed to be indisposed and passed the honor to Wang I-t'ang.[102]
(The one blank ballot that had turned up at the Anfu caucus was also understood
to be his.)[103] A few days after the presidential election, however, Liang's health
was better and he did not miss any of his subsequent official duties.[104] Obviously, his indisposition had been more political than physical, and this implied a
continued commitment to negotiations with the South that might yet spell
trouble for the Anfu Club.[105]

Events surrounding the vice-presidential election were soon to make Liang's
attitude clear. Although the Tientsin conference had offered the vice-presidency
to Ts'ao K'un, it was clear even before the conference dispersed that the
question was far from settled. The main imponderable was whether Ts'ao would
fulfill his part of the bargain and prosecute the war against the South despite the
opposition of his subordinates who were directly in command of the troops at
the front. As the date of the opening of parliament passed and that of the election approached, Ts'ao, who had remained in Tientsin discussing with emissaries
of Tuan Ch'i-jui the promised government provision of money and munitions
for his campaign, suddenly left on August 24 for Paoting, his headquarters,
and then returned to Tientsin.[106] Ts'ao's subordinate, Wu P'ei-fu, issued a
barrage of telegrams calling for a truce and a postponement of the presidential
elections.[107] In the confusion over Ts'ao's intentions, the Anfu Club leadership
was unable to decide whether or not to support him for the vice-presidency.[108]

99. STSP 1918.8.24.2; "SSG," p. 7. For attendance at caucuses, see, e.g., the caucus
before the presidential election, STSP 1918.9.5.2.

100. STSP 1918.9.1.2.

101. HSC, p. 40.

102. STSP 1918.9.4.2, 9.5.2; NCH 1918.9.7.556.

103. STSP 1918.9.5.2.

104. STSP 1918.9.9.2, 9.11.2.

105. So speculated the STSP 1918.9.5.2.

106. STSP 1918.8.21.2, 8.25.2; CWCY, p. 456.

107. CWCY, pp. 447-54.

108. STSP 1918.8.25.2, 8.29.2, 8.31.2.

It was in this context that the joint parliamentary session of August 31, which scheduled the presidential election for September 4, had also adopted the proposal that the vice-president be elected on September 5, rather than on the same day as the president, even though the Presidential Election Law (*Ta tsung-t'ung hsuan-chü fa*) provided the two should be elected the same day.[109] The September 4 joint meeting of parliament had ended after the election of the president, and Wang I-t'ang had announced that parliament would re-convene the next day at 10 A.M. to elect a vice-president. But on September 5, despite a lengthy delay to await late-comers, only twenty-nine senators and fifty-nine representatives arrived and the election could not be held for lack of a quorum.[110] The next day, parliament held a joint informal session (*t'an-hua hui*) and agreed to a proposal of Liu En-ko, Kuang Yun-chin, and others that the vice-presidential election be postponed until October 9, the day before the inauguration.[111]

This series of events was clearly the Anfu Club's riposte to Ts'ao K'un's procrastination. Ts'ao seemed to believe that if he could avoid taking an open stand until September 4, the Anfu Club would have no choice but to give him the vice-presidency. To avoid being forced to make an early decision, the club found these parliamentary devices to postpone rewarding Ts'ao until the last possible moment.[112]

By October 9, the day before the inauguration of the new president, when Ts'ao had still not clarified his position, the Anfu Club leadership decided to proceed with his election. A quorum for the election would be 383.[113] There had been an attendance of 384 at the Anfu Club caucus of September 3. On October 5, 390 M.P.'s attended a joint discussion session that agreed to order the Secretariat to prepare for a vice-presidential election meeting on October 9. At this session, it was announced that telegrams had been sent to the members who were still out of town urging them to return immediately.[114]

109. *STSP* 1918.9.1.2. The provision that the president and vice-president should be elected on the same day was never fulfilled during the early republic.

110. *STSP* 1918.9.6.2.

111. *STSP* 1918.9.7.2. Most of the discussion at this meeting involved the appropriate method to use for postponing the election in view of the lack of legal justification for not proceeding with it immediately. Liu's proposal was adopted. It provided that the secretariats of the two houses be given to understand that they should not issue announcements (*t'ung-kao*) of any meetings until October 9. This was considered preferable to taking a formal decision to "postpone" (*yen-hui*) the election because the latter step would require parliament to vote formally on setting the date for the next meeting, and this would leave the M.P.'s open to the charge of illegal procedure.

112. *STSP* 1918.9.1.2, 9.4.2, 9.6.2.

113. Two-thirds of the total legal membership of the two houses, 574, rather than of the actual membership of around 470, which reflected the absence of delegates from the five southern provinces.

114. *STSP* 1918.10.6.2.

On October 7, Anfu Club provincial delegation leaders gave banquets at the provincial hostels, explained Ts'ao K'un's qualifications, and argued for support of his candidacy.[115] On October 8, a club caucus was held at the T'aip'ing Lake headquarters to hear a speech by Wang I-t'ang urging the election of Ts'ao. Attendance at the caucus was 357, twenty-six short of a quorum, but it was expected that sufficient additional members would arrive in Peking by the next day to make up the shortage. Although Liang Shih-i did not attend the caucus personally, the other members of the Communications Clique did.[116]

But at the October 9 election session the Communications Clique "abruptly revealed its true face and came out against the Anfu Clique."[117] While Liang Shih-i, significantly reversing his previous practice, attended and chaired the session, the other Communications Clique members did not attend. Indeed, they did not remain in Peking, where it would have been possible for Wu Ping-hsiang's police to round them up and bring them to the meeting, but attended a luncheon at the Tientsin Zoological Gardens hosted by Chou Tzu-ch'i.[118] The Research Clique, of course, did not attend the parliamentary session nor did most independents. Three hundred and thirty-eight M.P.'s attended, but, with the defection of the Communications Clique, the Anfu Club was no longer large enough to command a quorum.[119] Over the protests of the Anfu Club members, Liang announced the lack of a quorum and adjourned the meeting.[120]

Liang later explained his motivations in a letter to various Peiyang leaders in which he attempted to soften their anger at his defection from the Anfu cause:

Those who advocated a quick election of a vice-president originally said that the election of Commissioner Ts'ao would help to compose the differences within the Peiyang Clique. Shih-i has humbly participated in the Peiyang Clique for years and has exerted every effort for its consolidation. But although one loves the Peiyang Clique, one loves the nation

115. *STSP* 1918.10.8.2.
116. *STSP* 1918.10.9.2.
117. *STSP* 1918.10.10.2.
118. *NCH* 1918.10.19.142. Also *NCH* 1918.10.19.135; *STSP* 1919.10.10.2.
119. The Anfu Club had 384 members at a caucus at the beginning of September (*STSP* 1918.9.4.2); now it could attract only 337 members (plus Liang Shih-i) to the election meeting. Of the loss of forty-seven, however, there is evidence that twelve were absent for reasons other than a split with the club (of 109 M.P.'s listed as boycotting the October 9 meeting in *STSP* 10.10.2, twelve are still listed as Anfu Club members in *AHKC*, 1: 55–64, a list that I have tentatively dated as compiled after the October 9 meeting [cf. note 31 above]). This would imply a permanent loss of thirty-five, presumably comprising the hard-core Communications Clique contingent in the club. The remaining sixty-two absentees on October 9 were probably Research Clique members and independents.
120. *NCH* 1918.10.12.72.

more. . . . Those who advocated a quick election in order to compose the differences within the Peiyang Clique were concerned solely with consolidating the clique and were unaware that this might split the nation [permanently]. . . . If Commissioner Ts'ao had been quickly elected as vice-president, the gentry and merchants of the country would have been very suspicious and would have said that the central government was again adopting a war policy, while the people of the Southwest would have taken it as a firm expression of enmity. This would have caused the peace, which was almost ripe, to fail to come to fruition . . . So long as no vice-president was elected, the Southwest had hopes that the seat would fall to them; so long as this hope was not cut off, the opportunity for peace and unity remained. But if we had suddenly elected a vice-president, this hope would have been cut off, and they would have proceeded to elect [their own president and vice-president], thus creating separate northern and southern governments and making the achievement of peace and unity impossible. . . . [121]

There had been rumors that Liang would split with the Anfu Club over the vice-presidency in the belief that it might serve as an important bargaining counter with the South. The Anfu Club leaders had apparently failed to credit these rumors, but they were true.[122] On the night of October 11, Wang I-t'ang and Hsu Shu-cheng met with Liang Shih-i and tried to persuade him to change his mind. But Liang was adamant and threatened to quit if Wang and Hsu continued to insist on their policy of war with the South. The meeting was apparently stormy and led to a final break.[123] Henceforth, Liang was to work openly for peace with the South.

A third attempt to elect a vice-president had been scheduled for October 16, but the attempt was clearly doomed to failure, and only 271 M.P.'s bothered to attend. Chou Tzu-ch'i had again entertained a large body of M.P.'s at lunch in Tientsin, while even a number of Anfu Club members stayed away from the session because it would not have mattered if they had attended.[124]

The last chapter of the "vice-presidency question" was written in November and December 1918, when the tuchuns assembled in Peking to discuss the emerging peace policy of the new president (see below). In an attempt to block the peace policy, the tuchuns tried to revive the idea of electing Ts'ao to the

121. *LSINP*, 1:432–33. No date is given for this document. It was probably written in November or December 1918.

122. *STSP* 1918.10.4.2, 10.8.2, 10.9.2. *STSP* 1918.10.10.2 noted that many persons had refused to believe reports that it had published about Liang's intentions toward the Anfu Club.

123. *STSP* 1918.10.14.2.

124. *STSP* 1918.10.15.2, 10.16.2, 10.17.2; *NCH* 1918.10.19.135. Comparison of lists in *STSP* 1918.10.10.2 and 10.17.2 shows that twenty-four additional Anfu Club members stayed away from the October 16 meeting, as did an additional thirty-three non-Anfu M.P.'s. Three Anfu and four non-Anfu M.P.'s who had missed the October 9 meeting attended that of October 16.

vice-presidency. Chang Tso-lin called on Liang Shih-i and, arguing that the nation must have a vice-president in order to avoid complications should the president become unable to serve, directly requested Liang to "sacrifice his own opinions" and accede to the judgment of others. This was not the sort of request that could be easily refused, but Liang avoided further pressures by removing himself to Tientsin. The tuchuns eventually returned to their posts, and the whole question died away, this time permanently.[125] Shortly thereafter, Liang submitted his resignation as a member of the Senate and went to Hongkong to pursue business and mediation with the South.[126] Chou Tzu-ch'i and Chu Ch'i-ch'ien also resigned from the Senate.[127] On January 9, 1919, the Senate elected Li Sheng-to, a senior former bureaucrat and Anfu Club leader, as its new Speaker.[128] No vice-president was ever elected to serve under Hsu Shih-ch'ang.

Hsu Shih-ch'ang and the Prospects for Peace

On the night of his election, the Peking house of Hsu Shih-ch'ang presented a scene of merriment. Old friends and followers thronged the residence to offer congratulations, while Wang I-t'ang visited with a delegation of M.P.'s to urge Hsu to accept office. Hsu told Wang and the others that he would be willing to take office provided he was assured of "support from all quarters."[129] To test this support, and in deference to precedent, Hsu on September 5 issued a circular telegram demurring from the post on the grounds of his inadequacy:

Having had this election thrust upon me, I search my soul as to whether [my desire to refuse the post] shows that I have less love for the people and for the nation than others have. At first, I did not wish to seem reluctant to sully myself with government affairs or afraid of the difficulties. But as I considered the disordered situation of our nation, as I observed the unrest of the merchants and people, and as I compared myself to the demands of the times, I concluded that this is not a job to which an old man like myself is equal.

I am not merely making a formal demur but speaking sincerely when I ask the gentle-

125. STSP 1918.12.2.2, 12.3.2, 12.9.2, 12.11.2; NCH 1919.1.11.56–57.

126. Liang's resignation was accepted by the Senate on December 21. STSP 1918.12.15.2, 12.17.2, 12.20.2, 12.22.2; LSINP, 1:439.

127. Their names are not found in the parliament list compiled at the end of 1918 and reprinted in Ku Tun-jou, I-hui shih, pp. 306–10.

128. STSP 1919.1.10.2. T'ien Ying-huang had been elected Vice-Speaker without opposition in December (STSP 1918.12.2.2). There was a desultory competition for the speakership, but Li was the Anfu leader in the Senate with the most seniority and the highest bureaucratic background, so he was easily elected. STSP 1918.12.29.2, 12.30.2, 1919.1.6.2 1.9.2.

129. STSP 1918.9.5.2.

men of the parliament, the senior civil and military officials of the provinces, and the re-tired officials to grant a hearing to my words. The republic has been unstable, disorders have followed fast upon one another, the desire for peace has become an empty hope, and the situation is a hundred times more dangerous than in ordinary times. The rule of virtue (*tao-te*) has not been established; authority is not effective; proper deference is no longer shown to superiors and seniors (*chi-kang pu-su*); the people are uneasy. The threat to national security increases daily; a worrisome situation of disorder is developing on the borders; and portentous changes are about to occur on the world scene with the end of the European war. . . .

Even a person with ten times my abilities and learning would be stymied in such a position. Precisely because I love the country but have no help for the country, I must hesitate and consider. . . . When I see the people homeless and in difficulties and have no art to better their situation, how could I bear to speak empty words about "govern-ing," fooling myself and cheating the people? Precisely because I love the people but have no protection for the people I must tremble and feel uneasy.

If I were in the prime of my youth, I would not lack the will to put things in order. But I am subject to continual ills and used to taking my ease; if on occasion I do take up the nation's affairs, I immediately feel exhausted. If despite my age I take up the high po-sition of president, although in spirit I love the nation and the people, my strength will not be adequate to what I would wish to accomplish. I would be unable to concentrate; I would be dangerously confused; I would be unable to plan ahead; and my negligence would immediately be manifest. I am afraid that, although I wish to save the country, I would undergo the shame of losing it, and despite my desire to help the people I would become an affliction to them. . . .

Lacking confidence in myself and not daring carelessly to take up the post, I respect-fully and sincerely report my anxieties. I hope you gentlemen of the parliament and you senior civil and military officials of the provinces will consider the situation and ponder daily; and I hope that each will do his duty so that together we may meet the dangers of the times.[130]

At sixty-four, of course, Hsu was by no means so ill, weak, and befuddled as he described himself. Instead of stating positively that he was unfit for the office, he merely brought up the possibility and in effect invited reassurances from the senior officials and members of parliament. Hsu's telegram was an effort to gauge the composition of the factional consensus under which he was taking office and to force those who supported him to commit themselves pub-licly. No one failed to understand these implications,[131] and from all corners of the northern official elite, including both pro-Tuan and pro-Feng factions, telegrams poured in urging Hsu to take the office.[132] The single exception was Wu P'ei-fu, who privately telegraphed Hsu urging him to postpone taking up

130. Text in *HSC*, pp. 45–46; *CWCY*, pp. 457–58.
131. *HSC*, p. 46; *STSP* 1918.9.6.2 editorial, 9.9.2 editorial; *NCH* 1918.9.14.631.
132. *HSC*, pp. 46–47; *CWCY*, pp. 458–59.

office until the agreement of the South to his doing so had been achieved.[133] But Wu was a relatively junior officer in northern ranks, and his opinion carried little weight.

But what would be the attitude of the South? The Canton government had stated in a circular telegram of August 3 that the new parliament was illegal and that "no matter who is elected by the illegal parliament, we absolutely will not recognize him."[134] But after Hsu's election there was no immediate southern reaction. This fact, combined with the knowledge of Hsu's excellent personal standing with the South, gave rise to rumors that an accomodation had already been reached. On September 11, it was rumored that Lin Shao-fei (one of the emissaries whom Liang Shih-i had sent to the South and who was now back in Peking) had received word from the South that the Canton parliament would elect Hsu president, thus making him the accepted president of both sides.[135] The next day the newspapers carried the story that one of the conditions the South had hoped to exact for this move was that the North agree to the election of a member of one of the prominent southern factions—probably Ts'en Ch'un-hsuan, chairman of the Canton government—as vice-president.[136]

Amid such rumors of negotiation and accommodation with the South, Liang Shih-i and Wang I-t'ang, the Speakers of the two houses of parliament, set off in ceremonial dress from the House of Representatives building on September 16, preceded and followed by troops of the garrison command. Proceeding to President-elect Hsu's home, the two Speakers entered the reception room and stood facing north. The president-elect, assisted by Minister of the Interior Ch'ien Neng-hsun, entered and sat facing south, as the emperor had done in granting audience. The two speakers ceremoniously handed Hsu the official notice of election (hsuan-cheng shu). The ceremony was concluded with a tradition of recent origin: the participants posed for a photograph.[137]

On the same day, the Canton government ended its hesitation by issuing a telegram politely but firmly refusing recognition to Hsu. In a private telegram (dated September 16 but not made public by Hsu until September 24),[138] two members of the ruling committee of the military government respectfully urged Hsu not to take office. The authors of the telegram, Ts'en Ch'un-hsuan and

133. *CWCY*, p. 463; *PYCF*, 4:156, has part of the text.

134. *LSINP*, 1:430.

135. *CWCY*, p. 461.

136. *Ibid.*, p. 463; *PYCF*, 4:156; Wu Hsiang-hsiang, "Ts'en Ch'un-hsuan," in Ts'en Ch'un-hsuan, *Le-chai man-pi* (Taipei, 1962), p. 15.

137. *STSP* 1918.9.17.2; *CWCY*, p. 465. More peace rumors: *CWCY*, pp. 463–65; *STSP* 1918.9.14.2, 9.15.2, 9.17.2.

138. *CWCY*, p. 470. Hsu had probably received the telegram on the 16th or 17th. *PYCF*, 4:156–57, also quotes a telegram of September 14 from Ts'en and other southern officials to Feng Kuo-chang, which had already made clear their nonacceptance of Hsu.

Wu T'ing-fang, were former senior northern bureaucrats and therefore had some standing with Hsu, although they were not personal friends or allies of his.[139] The telegram said:

From your circular telegram of the 5th, we have learned that the illegal parliament has elected you as president and that you are reluctant to take up the post for fear of ensuing disorders. May we say that your ability to perceive the people's desires and your unwillingness to take up the presidency without popular support is most deserving of respect! But in your telegram, although you grieve over the ruination of the nation, you neglect to touch upon its causes. This is something that we cannot allow to pass silently. For, although the causes of disorder are many, there is only one way to save the nation. It is, in a word, to receive and safeguard the law. . . . Since your election, the people have been plunged in melancholy because the northern government has no sincere remorse for the disasters it has brought on the nation through disregard of the Provisional Constitution and there has been no way to know your own intentions. If you would resolutely announce to the public that you will not take up the post to which you have been illegally elected and that you cannot act in accord with an election that perpetuates disorder, the people will praise your righteousness. . . . Regrettably, although you have refused the post, you have not spent so much as a word to point out the illegality of the election by the illegal parliament. We presume to express our anxiety that you have not thoroughly investigated the situation, that you are being misled by traitors, and that you will be unable to remain firm in your resolve not to take office. . . . We hope you will firmly close both ears [to flattery] and refuse to listen! . . . We have been so brazen as to call upon our old friendship with you and because of our love of the nation and of you, we have loyally reported to you [the situation as we see it]. May this receive your attention.[140]

The South's delay and the telegram's phraseology seemed to signal that, while the South was not willing to compromise without further negotiations, it had a favorable attitude to Hsu personally, objecting to the basis of his election but not to his qualifications for the presidency.

139. *HSC*, pp. 47, 86.
140. Text in *LSINP*, 1:433–34.

V

THE DRIVE FOR PEACE AND
THE ROAD TO WAR, 1918-20

On October 10, 1918, Hsu Shih-ch'ang was inaugurated as the fifth president of the Republic of China in the Great Ceremonial Hall (*Ta li-t'ang*) of the Presidential Palace. In the presence of the members of parliament and of high civil and military officials, Hsu repeated the oath of office prescribed by the Provisional Constitution and gave an address. He then received the congratulations of the diplomatic corps and the officials of the Ch'ing court. Echoing the imperial custom at the time of the accession of a new emperor, Hsu marked the occasion by issuing decorations to high officials.[1]

The president's inaugural address was issued as a circular telegram. It was dominated by his vision of the domestic and international dangers which continued division was causing China. Domestically, civil war was causing the stagnation of industry and commerce and a decline in popular welfare and was blocking China's progress toward wealth and power. But, Hsu pointed out, "arrangements for the improvement of domestic policies can be adopted at a pace consistent with the capacities of the nation." Much more urgent, in Hsu's opinion, was "the question of the international situation after the end of the European war." Hsu argued that if China did not compose its domestic differences immediately, it would not only be unable to reap the benefits at the peace conference for which it had entered the war in the first place, but would also be open to foreign economic encroachment or even to military intervention on the precedent of 1900:

I predict that when the fighting is ended, commercial competition will break out. Every little plot of ground, east and west, will attract the gaze of the industrialists. If we in China prolong the period in which our people's industry is not flourishing and domestic government is ineffective, we are going to be in straits a hundred times more dangerous than we are in today. The writ of the government must run throughout the country before the

1. Hatano Ken'ichi, *Gendai Shina*, p. 1182; *NCH* 1918.10.26.201.

power of the nation as a whole can develop and our international standing be protected. If instead we take our ease in the midst of these world developments and fail to adopt a policy, the foundations of the nation itself will be threatened, and it will be no use to speak of foreign affairs. This is a crisis of national existence. The officials, merchants and people of the nation must give it long and deep consideration.

In view of these dangers, Hsu announced that he would dedicate himself to the achievement of national unity:

My basic goals will be to save the nation and to save the people. I intend to work sincerely for progress toward unity, to seek resolutely to achieve the goal of peace. If both sides in the civil war will awaken, we may hope for a period of national convalescence, and the nation's future will be much brighter. Without such awakening, ending war and suppressing disorders will become empty words, the two sides will seek to cheat one another, and war will break out again. The people will complain of the depradations of the troops, and the allies will consider intervening to end the disorder. Should this happen, the fault will not lie at my door.[2]

The new president did not indicate in his inaugural telegram how he would seek unity. The tenor of his argument seemed to indicate a negotiated peace, and in several respects the situation in late 1918 seemed conducive to negotiations. At the front, a military stalemate had developed, and a truce had been declared by the front-line commanders, North and South, in Hunan. Northern troops had suffered defeats on the Fukien and Kwangtung borders, and the most recent Tientsin conference had revealed the lack of a northern warlord willing to commit his troops and resources to a new campaign against the South. The prospects for military unification therefore seemed darker than ever. Furthermore, the impending end of the European war, as Hsu had pointed out in his telegram, made national unity imperative if China was not to pay for its division with losses at the conference table.[3] Indeed, pressure for peace was beginning to come from the powers. Fearful of one another's ability to capitalize on China's disunity after the end of the war, they were beginning to exert diplomatic pressure for resolution of China's internal differences. On September 9, British Minister Sir John Jordan called on Foreign Minister Lu Chenghsiang and urged peace negotiations, predicting that if the division was not quickly healed the effects on China's international position would be serious.[4] President Wilson's telegram of congratulations to Hsu on the occasion of his

2. Text in *LSINP*, 1:435–37.
3. There was even a fear that the powers, no longer fighting one another, would decide to invade China; *NCH* 1918.11.2.257. On the specific fear of Japanese interference, see, e.g., Li T'ing-yü, comp., "Li T'ing-yü so-ts'en," Documents 21, 26, etc., pp. 13, 15, etc.— references to the danger to be expected from China's "strong neighbor" if disunity continued.
4. *NPIHWH*, Document 1, pp. 36–37.

inauguration contained a call for domestic peace in China, and U.S. Minister Paul Reinsch, returning from home leave a few days later, also urged peace.[5]

The prestige of the new president could serve as a powerful support to a peace strategy if he chose to follow one. Hsu had just been elected with the support of all the northern factions, and they could hardly fail to give at least initial support to whatever policy he adopted. But the factional consensus would be quickly dissipated if a statement of policy was not followed up by successful moves toward realizing it. Political skill was needed to capitalize on favorable conditions if the northern warlords' opposition to peace negotiations was to be overcome. An effort to initiate peace negotiations would face two potentially fatal dangers: first, that the South might not respond rapidly and enthusiastically enough to overcome the resistance of Tuan Ch'i-jui's followers and allies; and second, that public opinion within the northern elite might not provide sufficiently broad and visible support to maintain the high tide of factional consensus on which Hsu's power rested. Above all, Hsu could not reveal his policy until the ground was well prepared to ensure its success. This was the reason for his coy refusal to opt explicitly for negotiations either before his election or in his inaugural telegram, despite the widespread and accurate impression that he did favor negotiations. Hsu was still preparing the ground-work, probing southern attitudes and arranging an enthusiastic public response in the North.

Factional Alignments North and South

The most complex and important element in the situation facing Hsu was the shifting set of alignments of civilian and military factions in the southern government. At the time of its founding on August 31, 1917, the military government in Canton represented a combination of groups and factions whose interests converged on a policy of opposition to the Peking government under the titular leadership of Sun Yat-sen.[6] First, there was the old parliament as a whole, which claimed that it had been illegally dissolved by Li Yuan-hung just before the Chang Hsun restoration. According to those members of the old parliament who came south, the new parliament was illegal, while the old parliament—even though it now lacked a quorum or a presidential order to convene and had to operate in "extraordinary session" (kuo-hui fei-ch'ang hui-i) —represented legal continuity and "protection of the Provisional Constitu-tion" (hu-fa). Of the major parties in the old parliament, the most strongly represented at the extraordinary session was what had been called in 1913–14 the Kuo-min tang (Nationalist party), now split into three major sections, the I-yu she (Beneficial friendship society), the Political Study Group (*Cheng-hsueh hui*), and a group loyal to Sun Yat-sen.

A second element in the Canton government was the navy, which had a long history of cooperation with Sun Yat-sen and in this instance had elected, under the leadership of the then Navy Minister, Ch'eng Pi-kuang, and the commander of the First Fleet, Lin Pao-i, to come to Canton and join the military government.

The parliament and the navy, in coming south, were welcomed by the third element in the Canton coalition, the so-called Kwangsi warlord faction headed by Lu Jung-t'ing, inspector general of Kwangtung and Kwangsi.[7] In 1917, Lu's power, originally restricted to Kwangsi, was waxing in South China. Lu's interests clashed with those of Tuan Ch'i-jui when Tuan appointed his own follower, Fu Liang-tso,[8] a native Hunanese, as tuchun of Hunan. This move threatened Lu's influence in Hunan and the security of his territories, which bordered on Hunan. Preliminary to committing his troops to the battle in Hunan, he welcomed the old parliament to some south and establish a government to rival that dominated by Tuan in Peking.

A fourth element in the Canton government was the Yunnan warlord clique of T'ang Chi-yao.[9] T'ang's forces, the best in the South and equal in many respects to the best equipped and most modern of the Peiyang forces, had played an important role in the 1915–16 southern rising against Yuan Shih-k'ai. The end of the anti-Yuan war found Yunnan troops in Szechwan, Kweichow, and Kwangtung.[10] Not all of these troops were commanded by officers directly loyal to T'ang. In particular, the Yunnan forces in Kwangtung were under the control of Li Lieh-chün,[11] whose primary loyalty was to Sun Yat-sen. But despite his lack of control over this small portion of the Yunnan troops, T'ang Chi-yao's overall military position was extremely strong. T'ang's ally, Hsiung

7. This Kwangsi faction should not be confused with the Kwangsi faction of later Kuomintang history headed by Li Tsung-jen; the only link was a geographical one. Several years intervened between the defeat and break-up of the first and the dominance of the second in the province. See Wen Kung-chih, *Tsui-chin san-shih nien, pien* 2, pp. 344–46. On Lu Jung-t'ing, see Boorman and Howard, *Biographical Dictionary*, 2:447–49.

8. *ATTA, chüan* 2, p. 22; *HSC*, pp. 68–69; *GJMK*, 1924, p. 743.

9. On T'ang's life, see Boorman and Howard, *Biographical Dictionary*, 3:223–25; Wen Kung-chih, *Tsui-chin san-shih nien, pien* 2, pp. 374–89; *GJMK*, 1932, p. 292; and the adulatory biography, *T'ang Chi-yao* (Taipei, 1967).

10. Li Chien-nung, *Political History*, pp. 347–48.

11. Wen Kung-chih, *Tsui-chin san-shih nien, pien* 2, pp. 370–90; *GJMK*, 1932, pp. 386–87; Boorman and Howard, *Biographical Dictionary*, 2: 312–16.

K'o-wu, was for the moment predominant in Szechwan.[12] In the interests of his own territorial expansion into the areas contested between North and South, T'ang gave his support to the Canton government.

Fifth, the tuchun of Kweichow, Liu Hsien-shih,[13] also announced support of the Canton government. Kweichow was a poor and militarily backward province. Liu had come to control the province through the expansion of his locally raised militia. He could not aspire to power beyond the borders of the province and spent most of his career either seeking to avoid domination by neighboring Yunnan or defending himself against local rivals. In matters of national policy, Liu had no choice but to follow the lead of the powerful warlords of neighboring provinces, but he did not play an active role in the policy-making of the Canton government.

These were the major elements in the coalition that was the Canton government. The alliance, however, was uneasy. A divergence of interest soon became apparent. Sun Yat-sen wished to use the Canton government as a path to substantial power in the North—either through negotiations that would restore the Kuo-min tang dominated parliament, or through establishment of a viable alternate government that could defeat the northern government militarily and diplomatically. The southwestern warlords, however, were interested in expansion of their power locally, within the South. This implied a willingness to negotiate and settle with the northern government over issues of local power, territory, and office and a willingness to sacrifice the old parliament and ultimately to accept the domination of the government in Peking by the northern warlords. In April 1918, parliament, under the influence of the Political Study faction, which had thrown in its lot with Lu Jung-t'ing, legislated a reorganization of the Canton government designed to reduce the power of Sun Yat-sen. The most influential members of the new ruling committee when Hsu Shih-ch'ang took office were Lu Jung-t'ing and Chairman Ts'en Ch'un-hsuan. Ts'en's role was that of a respectable, senior, civilian representative of the interests of Lu Jung-t'ing, his former subordinate who now held military control of Kwangtung and Kwangsi.[14]

The complexity of the political calculations facing Hsu in dealing with the southern factional alliance is suggested by a secret report to the Peking government from Chou T'ing-li, an emissary who was sent to size up the southern situation when Hsu took office. Chou wrote:

The factional situation in the military government and old parliament is complex. Ts'en Ch'un-hsuan and Lu Jung-t'ing are in favor of peace [negotiations], with the Political

12. Wen Kung-chih, *Tsui-chin san-shih nien, pien* 2, pp. 312–13.
13. *Ibid.*, pp. 396–403.
14. Wu Hsiang-hsiang, "Ts'en Ch'un-hsuan," appendix; Boorman and Howard, *Biographical Dictionary,* 3:305–8.

Study Group and the neutral [i.e., non–Political Study, non–Kuo-min tang] M.P.'s supporting them. Sun Yat-sen and Wu T'ing-fang are in favor of continuing to fight, and the extremist Kuo-min tang M.P.'s support them. As for the rest, such as the navy, and the representatives of Yunnan, Kweichow, and of the mass of small warlords, their views are not fixed. At times they ally themselves with Sun and Wu, at times with Ts'en and Lu, but they never make their position explicit. . . . Now since Kwangtung is the center of the rebellion, if we could deal with the portions of the Kwangsi and Yunnan armies that are in Kwangtung and with the powerful elements in the Kwangtung forces, then the navy and parliament would have no financial support and the so-called southwestern idea would disintegrate. Therefore, to solve the problem of the Southwest, one must take Ts'en and Lu as the essence. . . . [15]

Hsu Shih-ch'ang was well aware of these developments. The Peking government, indeed, had never been wholly out of touch with the South. A constant flow of mediators had been maintained ever since the split.[16] When Hsu decided to allow his name to be proposed for the presidency, he began his own private contacts with the southern leaders. We do not know the content of their communications, but there are scraps of evidence to indicate Hsu's activities. According to one report, in mid-September he requested Chang Chien, a former high official now retired from politics, to act as a mediator, but Chang refused because of his age.[17] Another source says that Hsu sent Jen K'o-ch'eng and Chang Ping-lin, a politically retired Kuo-min tang elder, to Canton with a message for the southern leaders.[18] In mid-September, when delegates of northern and southern warlords arrived in Nanking to help him celebrate his birthday, Li Ch'un took the opportunity to carry on multilateral negotiations on a possible North-South peace conference.[19] In late September, Liang Shih-i told a Japanese diplomat in Peking that President Hsu was dealing with the South through intermediaries and that the prospects of agreement were

15. Chou's report is dated November 28, 1918, but the situation it described was true in October and was presumably understood in outline by northern officials even before they received Chou's report. *NPIHWH*, Document, 5, pp. 47–49.

16. See, e.g., Li T'ing-yü, comp., "Li T'ing-yü so-ts'en," Documents 1–20, pp. 1–13; Lai Ch'ün-li, comp., "I-ho wen-hsien," Documents 1–3, pp. 287–90; *LSINP*, 1:415–16, 439–40; *CWCY*, pp. 419, 422, 431, 436, 443, 461; F.O. 228/2982, Despatch 79, Giles to Jordan, July 18, 1918, p. 1; *ATTA*, *chüan* 2, pp. 3–4.

17. *STSP* 1918.9.17.2.

18. *PYCF*, 4:180. Chang's autobiographical *nien-p'u* states that he regarded Hsu's election as illegal and considered Hsu the source of all the difficulties between North and South: Chang Ping-lin, *T'ai-yen hsien-sheng tzu-ting nien-p'u* (Hongkong, 1965), p. 39. If so, it is hardly likely that he would have been willing to run a political errand for Hsu. But T'ao is usually reliable about such matters, and Chang's reminiscences may have been colored by the ultimate failure of Hsu's peace policy.

19. *STSP* 1918.9.18.2.

good.[20] In early October, Britain's Nanking Consul, Bertram Giles, learned from Li Ch'un's English physician that Li viewed peace prospects as bright.[21]

Between Hsu's election and his inauguration, rumors of negotiations and accommodations with the South were rife.[22] Although apparently exaggerated, the rumors reflected an appreciation of the fact that Hsu was in touch with the southern leaders and that their attitude to him personally was not unfavorable. On October 9, the Canton parliament announced that the military government would take over the duties of the presidency as of the end of Feng Kuo-chang's term on October 10. Far from being an obstacle to negotiations, this was the minimum action necessary for the South to preserve its position that the Anfu parliament was illegal. In refraining from electing a rival successor to Feng, Canton showed a willingness to negotiate.[23]

In Peking, the withholding of the vice-presidency from Ts'ao K'un was a public signal to the southern leaders of Hsu's sincerity in pursuing negotiations. By mid-October, Hsu's probes had apparently satisfied him that he understood the positions of the various southern factions toward peace and that there was a reasonable certainty of a favorable southern response to a public move toward negotiations.

In the North, meanwhile, Hsu took steps to assure a quick, loud, favorable public response to a peace initiative. Specifically, Hsu had Liang Shih-i organize the Peace Promotion Society (*Ho-p'ing ch'i-ch'eng hui*),[24] which was to provide vociferous public backing of prestigious men for Hsu's policy and thus create an impression that "public opinion" (*yü-lun*) supported Hsu.

Liang began to organize the Peace Promotion Society immediately after his final break with Wang I-t'ang and Hsu Shu-cheng. On October 13, in Tientsin, he gave a banquet for 100-odd M.P.'s who had boycotted the vice-presidential election of October 9 and mentioned the idea of forming a peace promotion society. By the 15th, the society was reportedly formed, with Liang, Chou Tzu-ch'i and Chu Ch'i-ch'ien as the main leaders, and with the support of the Research Clique members of parliament. Wu Chi-sun, a follower of Hsu who had served as his secretary in Manchuria, came to Tientsin to provide liaison

20. Telegram 1269, Yoshizawa to Gotō, September 23, 1918, in *Nihon gaikō bunsho*, 1918, vol. 2, pt. 1 (Tokyo, 1969): 31–32. According to *STSP* 1918.10.8.2, Li Ch'un told a reporter that Liang was working for peace and that Hsu was in secret contact with Lu Jung-t'ing and Ts'en Ch'un-hsuan.

21. F.O. 228/2982, Telegram 108, Giles to Jordan, Nanking, October 4, 1918.

22. *CWCY*, pp. 461–70; *STSP* 1918.9.14.2, 9.15.2, 9.17.2.

23. *PYCF*, 4:179.

24. In the first few weeks, also referred to as *Ho-p'ing ts'u-chin hui* and *Ho-p'ing ts'u-ch'eng hui*. Eventually a single designation came to be accepted. T'ao Chü-yin implies that there were two different organizations by these two names (*PYCF*, 4:181). This seems to be wrong.

with the president. Within the space of another week, the nascent organization had gained the support of a wide variety of prestigious public figures and, although it had made no public move, it was being treated in the press as a potentially powerful political force. The society held its first publicly announced meeting on November 3.[25]

The board of directors of the Peace Promotion Society was so constituted as to create an impression of an overwhelming demand for peace negotiations from almost all sectors of the elite.[26] Its membership can be divided into four categories: first, prominent and prestigious bureaucrats and politicians without strong factional identifications, lending an air of nonpartisanship; second, representatives of all major northern factions except that of Tuan Ch'-jui, demonstrating the breadth of the consensual factional support for negotiations; third, southern members of the old parliament who had not gone to Canton and whose presence therefore challenged the monopoly of the Canton M.P.'s over the right to speak for the old parliament; and fourth, prominent southerners whose membership on the board showed that the desire for peace was national.

The chairman of the society was Hsiung Hsi-ling,[27] a recently retired official just embarking on a new career as a philanthropist. Hsiung, a *chin-shih* and former Hanlin compiler, although never intimately tied into the Peiyang network, had a good reputation and high personal standing with the northern bureaucracy. At the same time, because he had worked with Liang Ch'i-ch'ao at the Hunan Current Affairs Institute in 1898 and had helped form the T'ung-i tang (Unity party) of 1911 and the Chin-pu tang (Progressive party) of 1913, he was respected by the members of the old parliament and was particularly close to the Research Clique. Furthermore, he was a native of Hunan, the province which had been most severely ravaged by the civil war.

The Vice-Chairman, Ts'ai Yuan-p'ei,[28] principal of Peking University, was

25. *STSP* 1918.10.14.2, 10.15.2, 10.16.2, 10.18.2, 10.20.2, 10.22.2 editorial, 10.22.2, 10.23.2, 11.4.2; *ATTA, chüan* 2, pp. 30–31. According to *STSP* 1918.10.17.2, the Discussion Society also joined, but judging from an analysis of the lists of directors (see below), this was not correct. On Wu Chi-sun, see *HSC*, p. 60. The November 3 meeting in Tientsin was attended by about 100 M.P.'s and some 130 or 140 other public figures. The meeting elected the chairman and vice-chairman, who appointed the seventy-five board members (*chih-yuan*) of the society. The board's first meeting was held on November 11 in Peking, and after this steps were taken to establish branch societies in the provinces. *STSP* 1918.11.11.2, 11.12.2.

26. List of the board members: *STSP* 1918.11.12.2. The seventy-five members had been invited to serve by the chairman and vice-chairman and had accepted the invitation by letter.

27. *MJTC, chüan* 7, p. 89; *TTMJ*, 1:25–27; *GJMK*, 1924, p. 934; "SSG," pp. 33–34; Chia Shih-i, *Min-kuo ch'u-nien ti chi-jen ts'ai-cheng tsung-chang* (Taipei, 1967), pp. 8–22; Boorman and Howard, *Biographical Dictionary*, 2:108–10.

28. *GJMK*, 1932, p. 139; Boorman and Howard, *Biographical Dictionary*, 3:295–99.

influential in the South because of his participation in the late Ch'ing revolutionary movement, and in the North because of his academic credentials (*chin-shih*, Hanlin) and official position. Other prominent northern politicians and bureaucrats on the board included Sun Pao-ch'i,[29] a former minister to Austria, Germany, and France with the status of a respected elder in Peking circles; Chuang Yun-kuan,[30] head of the Audit Bureau (*Shen-chi yuan*) of the Peking government since 1915, who had good relations with the Kwangsi warlord clique; and Wang Ch'ung-hui,[31] a Cantonese who had been active in the revolutionary movement and who was now serving as head of the Peking government's Law Codification Bureau (*Hsiu-ting fa-lü kuan*).

The Communications Clique was represented among the directors by Liang Shih-i, Chou Tzu-ch'i, Chou Tso-min, Wang Yu-ling, Ch'en Chieh, Kuan Mien-chün, and Lin Shao-fei. The last two had been involved in the earlier efforts to plumb Lu Jung-t'ing's opinions. The fact that they now came out and took a public position on the issue of peace instead of preserving anonymity conveyed the impression that they had reason to believe the time ripe for open negotiations. Chu Ch'i-ch'ien, although he had at first been mentioned as one of the founders of the society, was not among its directors; since Chu was shortly to be chosen by Hsu Shih-ch'ang as the chief northern delegate to the peace conference, we may infer that he wished to avoid association with the group in order to deprive the warlords of a pretext for opposing him as chief negotiator.

The Research Clique was represented by Hsu Fo-su, Chang Chia-sen, Chi Chung-yen, Wang Chia-hsiang, Liang Shan-chi, Ling Wen-yuan, and Ch'en Kuo-hsiang. Several of these men were members of the new parliament.

The Political Study faction, which was influential within the Canton parliament, was represented by three members who had not gone to Canton but who retained close connections with their faction-mates there: Ku Chung-hsiu, Wen Ch'ün, and Li Chao-fu.

Three prominent members of the board were identified in the public mind as

29. *MJTC*, *chüan* 6, p. 39; Chia Shih-i, *Min-kuo ch'u-nien*, p. 96; *GJMK*, 1932, p. 211; *Jimbutsu jihyō* (August 1924), pp. 17–18, and (September 1925), pp. 1–3; Boorman and Howard, *Biographical Dictionary*, 3:169–70.

30. *GJMK*, 1924, p. 644; 1932, p. 202. In May, the rumor had gone around Peking that President Feng had sent Chuang to Nanking to negotiate with Lu Jung-t'ing (*CWCY*, p. 419). Chuang presumably knew Lu from the days when Chuang served as a military commander in Kwangsi; Chuang's former subordinate, Niu Yung-chien, was an ally of Ts'en Ch'un-hsuan and Lu Jung-t'ing and served from 1917 to 1920 as Shanghai military representative of the Canton government. Wu Hsiang-hsiang, ' Ts'en Ch'un-hsuan,'' p. 16; *Saishin Shina yōjin den* (Osaka, 1941), pp. 114–15.

31. *GJMK*, 1932, p. 34; *MJTC*, *chüan* 3, p. 57; Boorman and Howard, *Biographical Dictionary*, 3:376–78.

followers of Feng Kuo-chang, who had been mentioned as a backer of the society.[32] These were Chang I-lin,[33] a former bureaucrat who had served as Feng's chief secretary during his presidency; Wang K'o-min,[34] a wealthy banker and financier who enjoyed Feng's patronage; and Feng Keng-kuang,[35] a Cantonese who had served under Feng as a military officer and had succeeded Wang K'o-min in 1918 as manager of the Bank of China.

The support of other major figures was also clear from the board membership. Two followers of Li Yuan-hung were on the board: Hsia Shou-k'ang,[36] Li's secretary during most of his vice-presidency and presidency; and Ting Shih-to,[37] presidential secretary-general in 1916–17. Board member Shih Yü[38] was a subordinate of Li Ch'un. Ch'en Chen-hsien was a former subordinate of Hsu Shih-ch'ang in Fengtien.

Several members of the board were southern members of the old parliament who had not joined the Canton extraordinary session. These included[39] Chao Ping-lin (Kwangsi),[40] Yu Ts'ung-lung (Yunnan),[41] Huang Ts'an-yuan (Hunan),[42] and Wang Jen-wen (Yunnan).[43] Such names were useful on the board, both because they indicated that the desire for peace was national, and because they seemed to illustrate the fact that the interests of the old parliament and those of the peace forces in Peking were not opposed. As a reward for this and anticipated future services, Wang and presumably others as well were given seats on the Postwar Economic Investigation Commission (Chan-hou ching-chi tiao-ch'a wei-yuan hui) in January 1919. This commission had the ostensible purpose of investigating world economic conditions in the aftermath of the World War and the actual purpose of providing sinecures for politicians whose services were useful for one reason or another to President Hsu.[44]

32. E.g., STSP 1918.10.20.2.

33. MJTC, chüan 5, p. 12; Kuo-shih kuan kuan-k'an 1, no. 4 (November 1948): 88–93.

34. MJTC, chüan 3, p. 91; Chia Shih-i, Min-kuo ch'u-nien, pp. 71–74; TTMJ, 1:51–52; ATTA, chüan 2, p. 30; Boorman and Howard, Biographical Dictionary, 3: 386–88.

35. GJMK, 1932, p. 322.

36. MJTC, chüan 4, p. 28; GJMK, 1924, p. 532.

37. "SSG," pp. 52–53.

38. GJMK, 1937, p. 197; AHKC, 2:124.

39. There were probably others who fit this description. I have not been able to identify twenty-five members of the board.

40. GJMK, 1937, p. 357; Satō, Minkoku, p. 344.

41. GJMK, 1932, p. 344.

42. GJMK, 1937, p. 179; Satō, Minkoku, p. 271.

43. GJMK, 1937, p. 37; Satō, Minkoku, p. 11.

44. STSP 1920.4.2.2, 4.12.2; LSINP, 2:2, gives January 20 as the date of founding; Kao Yin-tsu, Ta-shih chi, p. 57, gives January 18. The word "Postwar" was eventually dropped from the commission's title.

A final feature of the makeup of the board of directors was the heavy representation of i. .ı who, either because of their provincial origin or because of their political associations, had high prestige (if not direct political influence) in the southern provinces as well as in the North. These included Wang I-shu,[45] a "Hunan elder" who had also served in Kwangsi; Wang Wen-pao,[46] a Hunanese with a long official career; Chiang Han,[47] a former Szechwan salt commissioner; Liu Kuei-i,[48] a Hunanese who had participated in the foundings of the Hua-hsing hui (Society for China's revival) and the T'ung-meng hui (Revolutionary alliance); Liang Ch'i-hsun,[49] a Cantonese banker living in Peking; Fan Chih-huan,[50] a Hunanese official; Chang Chih-chang,[51] a journalist who had worked with Yü Yu-jen (the southern commander in Shensi); and T'an Jui-lin,[52] a Cantonese member of both the old and the new parliaments. Besides lending a national cast to the board, such men served to influence southern politicians and military officers to take a favorable attitude toward negotiations, and, by being seen to influence the South in this way, helped to create the impression in the North of a strong, viable peace movement with a good chance of success.

Hsu's Peace Offensive

His preparations completed, Hsu revealed his policy toward the South. The move came in the form of a barrage of telegrams on peace, triggered by an October 23 telegram from his follower, Acting Prime Minister Ch'ien Neng-hsun,[53] to Ts'en Ch'un-hsuan and the other members of the Canton government, offering peace negotiations.[54] This was followed, on October 24, by a presidential mandate ordering respect for peace. Hsu took as his text President Woodrow Wilson's repeated calls for world peace, noting that China's purpose in entering the European war was precisely to secure eternal world peace. Now that the European nations had ceased fighting one another, ought not Chinese,

45. *GJMK*, 1932, p. 40.
46. *GJMK*, 1924, p. 442; *MJTC*, chüan 3, p. 6.
47. *GJMK*, 1932, p. 119.
48. *GJMK*, 1932, p. 393.
49. *GJMK*, 1937, p. 586.
50. *GJMK*, 1937, p. 454.
51. *GJMK*, 1932, p. 238.
52. Satō, *Minkoku*, p. 421; Parliament List.
53. *GJMK*, 1924, p. 1094; *HSC*, p. 58; *TTMJ*, 1:35–37. Ch'ien was a *chin-shih* of 1886, the same year as Hsu.
54. Text: *LSINP*, 1:437–38. Li Chien-nung, *Cheng-chih shih*, p. 527, mistakenly dates the telegram November 23.

who are all brothers, also cease to fight? He hoped that all the people of the nation would cooperate to put an end to war and to plan for the development of the country in peace.[55]

Also part of the opening salvo was a circular telegram issued on October 23 by twenty-four leaders of the Peace Promotion Society. The telegram an-nounced the formation of the society and urged all who agreed with its aims to join the nonpartisan effort for peace.[56] The telegram drew favorable answering wires from many sectors of public opinion—for example, from Feng Kuo-chang, Wang Chan-yuan, Ts'ao Ju-lin, K'ang Yu-wei, "the citizens of Ning-po," the "United Association of Organizations of Hankow," and provincial peace committees that were established in October and November.[57]

The southern reaction was rapid: on October 30, Ts'en Ch'un-hsuan tele-grammed Peking advocating the opening of a peace conference with an equal number of representatives from each side. On November 12, the Peking cabinet formally passed the policy proposal for a peace conference. On the 16th, Peking ordered a front-line armistice in Hunan (thus legitimizing an informal truce that had been in force for some time). On November 30, the southern leaders wired asking for a quick opening to the conference.[58]

The next step was to overcome the resistance of the prowar tuchuns. Early in November, President Hsu sent invitations to the major northern warlords in-viting them to attend a conference in Peking on the question of policy toward the South.[59] One by one, the warlords arrived in Peking: Chang Tso-lin (Feng-tien), Meng En-yuan (Kirin), Chao T'i (Honan), Chang Huai-chih (formerly of Shantung, recently assigned to the Hunan front), Yen Hsi-shan (Shansi), Ts'ai Ch'eng-hsun (Suiyuan), Ch'en Kuang-yuan (Kiangsi), Ni Ssu-ch'ung (Anhwei), Yang Shan-te (Chekiang), Wang Chan-yuan (Hupei), Lu Yung-hsiang (com-mander of the Shanghai region).[60] According to T'ao Chü-yin, it was the great-

55. Text in *LSINP* 1:438–39.

56. *STSP* 1918.10.24.2. Chang Chien was the only signer of this telegram who did not become a director of the society.

57. *STSP* 1918.10.29.2, 11.11.2, 11.19.2, 11.24.2.

58. Kao Yin-tsu, *Ta-shih chi*, pp. 55–56; for the dates October 30 and November 12, I am indebted to Professor Kuo T'ing-i. The telegram of November 30 was one of a series of wires exchanged in November and December between the two sides not only through normal telegraphic channels but also through the medium of the British consulates in the South and the legation in Peking, apparently as a form of insurance against the unreliability of the telegraph service. The British kept English translations of the documents, which are collected in F.O. 228/2985. The text of the November 30 telegram may be found in this volume, in Telegram 44, Canton to Peking, December 1, 1918.

59. E.g., *STSP* 1918.10.31.2. On the conference generally, see *PYCF*, 4:184–86, 191–92.

60. *STSP* 1918.11.16.2. This is the list of warlords who actually attended the November 15 meeting. The list differs from that given by *PYCF*, 4:184–85, in that *PYCF* omits the

est number of tuchuns to attend a military conference since the founding of the republic.[61] The tuchuns who did not come to Peking personally sent delegates. Only Ts'ao K'un, smarting from the humiliation of his rejection by parliament, sent no delegate and refused to come, claiming to be ill. The meeting was delayed until a series of messengers from the president succeeded in persuading Ts'ao to come to Peking on November 14.[62]

As the tuchuns awaited Ts'ao K'un, they debated and discussed the question of policy toward the South among themselves and with President Hsu.[63] Two of the tuchuns—significantly, the two who were most insecure in their provincial positions and who were rumored to be interested in getting cabinet or army staff positions in Peking[64]—quickly went on record as favoring negotiations with the South. These were Ni Ssu-ch'ung, who said that the military, as the physicians of the national health, had been unable to cure the division of the country by means of war and should try the new physic of peace; and Chang Huai-chih, who said that North and South were like elder and younger brothers who could hold no permanent grudge against one another.[65]

More common, however, was the uncompromising attitude exemplified by Chang Tso-lin. At a banquet given by the Anfu Club for the visiting warlords on November 7, Chang drew applause when he answered Wang I-t'ang's toast with a speech pointing out that southern provinces could by no means be considered commensurate with the northern provinces in number, size, or completeness of central government apparatus. In a democracy, the majority rules. Therefore, Chang concluded, there should be no thought of "peace" negotiations as if between equal powers. And rather ominously, but to the delight of his hosts, he added, "there is definitely no reason to dissolve the new parliament as part of a compromise with Canton. Parliament is the organ which elected the president. If we can't preserve the parliament, we can hardly continue to uphold the president."[66]

---

names of Yang Shan-te and Ts'ai Ch'eng-hsun. The provincial posts are those given by Wen Kung-chih, *Tsui-chin san-shih nien, pien* 2, chart ff. p. 444; except that in the cases of Chang Huai-chih and Lu Yung-hsiang, the affiliations given are those reported in *GJMK*, 1932, pp. 226 and 424. Lung Chi-kuang and Wu Kuang-hsin were also in Peking (*STSP* 1918.11.8.2) but are not listed as attending the November 15 meeting.

61. *PYCF*, 4:185.

62. *STSP* 1918.11.4.2, 11.15.2.

63. *STSP* 1918.11.12.2, 11.13.2.

64. *PYCF*, 4:184; see also *STSP* 1918.9.6.2, 9.18.2, 10.14.2, on Ni's d sire for cabinet office. Ni, however, remained in Anhwei until 1920, after which he retired d died shortly thereafter. Chang was transferred to a post as chief of staff in Peking on January 11, 1919.

65. *STSP* 1918.11.12.2.

66. *STSP* 1918.11.8.2.

But the news of the November 11 European armistice strengthened Hsu's position. Combined with Hsu's prestige and with the effects of the peace propaganda barrage of late October, it forced the warlords to adopt the grudging position that "we are soldiers; therefore we do not interfere in government. At this stage, we will follow the president's orders and stick to the business of being soldiers."[67] The conference itself, held at the Presidential Palace on the morning of November 15, merely formalized this position. The tuchuns' complaisance, however, was more apparent than real. While agreeing to negotiations, they set conditions that would make the success of the negotiations unlikely. The negotiations must not take a form that would grant equal standing to both sides— it should not be a "peace" conference but a "reconstruction" (*shan-hou*) conference between the government on the one side and several provinces on the other. There could be no compromise on the continued existence of the Anfu parliament. And if the South stuck to its "unreasonable" position, the warlords retained the option of taking up arms again.[68] The warlords also made it clear that they did not think the military balance of power made it wise or necessary to concede the contested provinces of Hunan and Fukien to the South.[69] Ts'ao and the other warlords announced the formation of the Wu-wu (1918) Comrades' Association (*Wu-wu t'ung-pao she*), ostensibly to restore the deteriorating unity of the Peiyang group, but in fact for the purpose of showing solidarity in the face of the moves toward peace. The association adopted a platform to the effect that the South should disband its troops first and the North would disband an equal number afterward.[70] Finally, as reported above, the tuchuns took the opportunity of their stay in Peking to revive the vice-presidential question and vainly tried to persuade Liang Shih-i to permit the election of Ts'ao K'un, which of course would have severely harmed the peace possibilities.

Because of their intransigence, President Hsu did not dismiss the warlords from Peking but kept them there for further consultations. Meanwhile, Hsu was faced with obstructionism on the part of the Anfu Club in parliament. On October 10, the day of his inauguration, Hsu had accepted the resignation of Tuan Ch'i-jui as prime minister and had appointed his own follower, Ch'ien Neng-hsun, already minister of the interior, as acting prime minister.[71] In early

67. *STSP* 1918.11.13.2; see also *NCH* 1918.11.16.393.

68. *PYCF*, 4:186; *STSP* 1918.11.16.2, 11.22.2.

69. *STSP* 1918.11.21.2, 11.22.2.

70. *STSP* 1918.11.26.2, 11.27.2 editorial, 12.3.2. The name was later changed to War Participation Comrades' Association (*Ts'an-chan t'ung-chih she*) (*STSP* 1918.12.2.2). After the tuchuns left Peking, this organization was not heard from again.

71. Hsu offered the prime ministership to a number of other men, but this was merely a polite gesture and they all refused, fully aware of Hsu's preference for Ch'ien. *AHKC*, 1:65; *LSINP*, 2:1.

November, when Hsu began his contacts with parliament on the allocation of cabinet seats, he found that although the non-Anfu M.P.'s were willing to confirm Ch'ien, there was heavy opposition on the part of the Anfu Club. The fundamental reason for Anfu opposition to Ch'ien's nomination was, of course, the peace policy that Ch'ien was carrying out on behalf of Hsu, the success of which would threaten the very existence of the new parliament. In addition, there was strong personal animosity to Ch'ien among Anfu leaders because of his long-standing propeace leanings and his role in the vice-presidential fiasco. To block submission of Ch'ien's name, several Anfu members brought before parliament a bill calling for Ch'ien's impeachment for alleged abuse of authority in connection with government policy toward virgin lands during his tenure as minister of the interior in the preceding cabinet.[72]

The deadlock between Hsu on the one hand and the tuchuns and Anfu Club on the other was dramatically resolved on December 2. On that day, the ministers of the five allied powers (Britain, Japan, the United States, France, and Italy) were received by President Hsu. They handed him an aide-mémoire, which urged that "while refraining from taking any steps which might obstruct peace, both parties [Peking and Canton] . . . seek without delay, by frank confidence, the means of obtaining reconciliation."[73] The consuls of the five powers meanwhile delivered an identical note to Canton's foreign minister, Wu T'ing-fang. British Minister Sir John Jordan telegraphed home, "after reading document and expressing his warm appreciation of its contents President stated that of twenty-two provinces of China the seventeen attached to Peking Government all desired peace. The five which favoured Southern cause equally desired it but there were divergent views amongst them which would retard the negotiation of a settlement. He thought however that presentation of Aide-Mémoire would have salutary effect on hastening matter in South."[74]

On December 3, Japan made the additional announcement that "loans supplied to China, under the existing conditions of domestic strife in that country, are liable to create misunderstandings on the part of either of the contending factions, and to interfere with the re-establishment of peace and unity in China, so essential to her own interests as well as to the interests of foreign Powers. Accordingly, the Japanese Government have decided to withhold such financial assistance to China, as is likely, in their opinion, to add to the complications of

72. *STSP* 1918.11.2.2, 11.5.2, 11.7.2, 11.18.2, 11.19.2, 11.22.2, 11.23.2, 11.26.2, 11.28.2. On Ch'ien's role in the vice-presidential election, see *STSP* 1918.8.5.2, 11.5.2; also cf. *STSP* 1918.11.2.2.

73. Reinsch, *American Diplomat*, p. 326.

74. F.O. 371/3184, 199393 (f16666), Telegram 978, Jordan to Balfour, Peking, December 2, 1918.

her internal situation."[75] This statement explicitly spelled the end of the era of Japanese loans on which Tuan Ch'i-jui had relied for the establishment of his War Participation Army and for the election of the Anfu parliament.

Hsu's pleasure, reported by Jordan, at receiving the December 2 note was hardly surprising in view of the fact that it came at such a convenient time for his domestic policies. Indeed, the note's timing, although not controlled by Hsu, had been influenced by him through informal contacts with the sympathetic Japanese. The Terauchi cabinet, whose policy had been to back Tuan Ch'i-jui financially and politically, had just given way to the Hara Kei cabinet, which adopted a foreign policy of cooperation with the Western powers and an end to active support of any single faction in China.[76] When in September, British Ambassador in Tokyo Sir Conyngham Greene approached the Japanese with the suggestion for a joint representation by the powers to the two sides in China, he was told that the Japanese were in touch with Liang Shih-i and felt on the basis of what they had learned that the time was not ripe for foreign action.[77] Through October and November, Liang and President Hsu kept the Japanese informed of progress in constructing the northern peace bloc and conducting intermediary negotiations with the South. They asked that the powers' note be delayed until peace terms were ripe. The powers' shared desire to exert pressure for peace finally resulted in agreement on a text, and the note could not be delayed beyond December 2.[78]

75. English text attached to Telegram 1090, Uchida to Hayashi, November 30, 1918, in *Nihon gaikō bunsho*, 1918, vol. 2, pt. 1, pp. 110–11.

76. Akira Iriye, *After Imperialism: The Search for a New Order in the Far East, 1921–1931* (Cambridge, Mass., 1965), p. 9.

77. F.O. 371/3184, 164101 (f16666), Telegram 1023, Greene [to Balfour], Tokyo, September 27, 1918. The conversation is reported from the Japanese side in Telegram 544, Uchida to Chinda, September 30, 1918, in *Nihon gaikō bunsho*, 1918, vol. 2, pt. 1, pp. 32–33.

78. For Hsu Shih-ch'ang's and Liang Shih-i's conversations with Japanese representatives, see *Nihon gaikō bunsho*, 1918, vol. 2, pt. 1, Documents 35, 65 (here the source is Chou Tzu-ch'i), 81, 94, 109. Despite Hsu's efforts to postpone the powers' initiative, the Japanese on October 23 started the process of drafting the joint note by informing the other powers that they thought the Chinese leaders were ready to make peace if given the lead by the powers (Telegram 587, Uchida to Chinda, October 22, 1918, in *Nihon gaikō bunsho*, 1918, vol. 2 pt. 1, pp. 58–59). The record does not show that Japan had any inside information to justify this conclusion. But Japan, Britain and the United States had been informally pressuring the Chinese to make peace (for example, American Minister Reinsch and Japanese Minister Hayashi had each urged peace upon President Hsu when they called on him to resume their posts; early in November Japanese banks had stopped paying advances on already contracted loans to China; and, in November 1918, the powers, as reported in Chapter III, refused to release the customs surplus to the Chinese Government without strings attached, giving China's internal differences as the main reason [Reinsch, *American Diplomat*, pp. 317–22; Telegram 1550, Hayashi to Uchida, November 9, 1918, in *Nihon gaikō bunsho*, 1918, vol.

For Hsu the timing, if imperfect, was still powerful. The joint note and the Japanese statement of December 3 crushed his opposition. The warlords remaining in Peking—Ts'ao K'un, Chang Tso-lin, Wang Chan-yuan, Meng En-yuan, Ni Ssu-ch'ung and Chang Huai-chih—together with Tuan Ch'i-jui and the cabinet, were summoned on December 3 to the Presidential Palace, where Hsu read them a translation of the five-power note. The warlords immediately dropped their opposition to the policy of negotiations with the South and promised their support to Hsu.[79]

A New Cabinet and Peace Delegations

The same day, President Hsu sent parliament the formal nomination of Ch'ien Neng-hsun as prime minister. On the urging of Tuan Ch'i-jui and Chang Tso-lin, the sponsors of the bill for the impeachment of Ch'ien withdrew the bill. Meeting in caucus at T'aip'ing Lake on December 9, the Anfu Club heard an hour-long speech by Wang I-t'ang urging approval of Ch'ien's nomination. Wang pointed out that Tuan Ch'i-jui now backed this course. The nomination passed the house, 234 to 16, on December 14; the Senate, 105 to 4, on the 18th; and was gazetted on the 20th.[80]

As Ch'ien's nomination passed through parliament, the cabinet members who remained from the preceding Tuan Ch'i-jui cabinet followed precedent and submitted their resignations.[81] Ch'ien, however, reluctant to trigger political struggle over the allocation of seats, made only two new appointments. A minister of war had to be appointed to replace Tuan Ch'i-jui, and Ch'ien decided to replace Wang K'o-min, the minister of finance, who was perhaps too closely associated with Feng Kuo-chang to be acceptable to parliament. For the war post, Ch'ien nominated General Chin Yun-p'eng[82] and, for the finance post, Anhweinese financier and bureaucrat Kung Hsin-chan.[83] Both were mem-

2, pt. 1, pp. 91–93; F.O. 371/3184, 187343 (f 16666), Telegram 931, Jordan to Balfour, Peking, November 11, 1918]). Wishing to be seen to take the initiative in the developing situation, the Japanese may have considered the launching of President Hsu's peace offensive on October 23 sufficient justification for their move.

79. NCH 1918.12.7.582; PYCF, 4:191–92.

80. STSP 1918.12.4.2, 12.5.2, 12.6.2, 12.9.2, 12.10.2, 12.13.2, 12.15.2, 12.19.2, 12.21.2.

81. STSP 1918.12.14.2.

82. GJMK 1924, p. 918: GJMK, 1932, pp. 87–88; ATTA, chüan 2, pp. 22–23; Boorman and Howard, Biographical Dictionary, 1:382–84. Chin had served in the Yunnan military with T'ang Chi-yao and other southern leaders. Cf. Wen Kung-chih, Tsui-chin san-shih nien, pien 2, p. 372.

83. MJTC, chüan 2, p. 27; ATTA, chüan 2, p. 21; Chia Shih-i, Min-kuo ch'u-nien, pp. 83–86. Kung had serevd under Ts'en Ch'un-hsuan in Kwangtung. See TTMJ, 1:54–56.

bers of the Tuan Ch'i-jui faction but were not involved with the Anfu Club; and both, perhaps not coincidentally, had been bureaucratic colleagues of some of the southern leaders in the late Ch'ing.

The Anfu Club was in a weak position to bargain over cabinet seats because it was under pressure from Tuan and Chang Tso-lin to give approval to the cabinet. Ch'ien's war and finance appointments adroitly drove a wedge between Tuan and the club on the cabinet issue. Although the club was particularly anxious to gain control of the Ministry of Interior, which might be a critical post if negotiations with the South led to the election of a new parliament, Ch'ien decided to continue to serve as concurrent minister of interior himself. Anfu attempts to persuade Ch'ien to give the post to Wang I-t'ang came to nothing. Ch'ien's cabinet list passed the House on January 7 and the Senate on January 9 and was gazetted on January 11.[84]

The Ch'ien cabinet was not heavily political in composition. Most of its members had incumbencies dating back to late 1917 or early 1918. The ministers of Foreign Affairs (Lu Cheng-hsiang),[85] Navy (Liu Kuan-hsiung)[86] and Education (Fu Tseng-hsiang)[87] were nonpolitical representatives of the respective bureaucracies they superintended. Minister of Agriculture and Commerce T'ien Wen-lieh[88] was a senior Peiyang figure who stayed aloof from internal squabbling within the Peiyang group. Minister of Communications Ts'ao Ju-lin, although an Anfu Club member, had considerable experience in the ministry and had been in his post in successive cabinets since July 1917. Chu Shen,[89] the minister of justice, an Anfu Club leader, was at the same time a Japanese-trained lawyer, with high standing in legal circles. Ch'ien, Kung, and Chin completed the list.

With the deadlock in Peking broken, President Hsu quickly announced the makeup of the northern peace delegation before it could become an issue of

84. *STSP* 1918.12.14.2, 12.28.2, 1.8.2, 1.10.2, 1.12.2. In the House, Ts'ao Ju-lin and Kung Hsin-chan passed with significantly fewer votes than the other nominees. The opposition vote on each of these candidates apparently came from certain provincial delegations who had locally-related grievances against the two. Ts'ao was opposed by the Fengtien delegation because of actions taken by him during his previous incumbency of the post. The identity of the opposition to Kung is unclear. See *STSP* 1918.12.28.2, 12.31.2; *NCH* 1919.1.11. 74.

85. Lo Kuang, *Lu Cheng-hsiang chuan* (Taipei, 1967); *TTMJ*, 1:28–29; *GJMK*, 1932, p. 389; Boorman and Howard, *Biographical Dictionary*, 2: 441–44.

86. *GJMK*, 1924, p. 387.

87. *MJTC, chüan* 7, p. 128; *GJMK*, 1924, p. 744; *TTMJ*, 1:56; Boorman and Howard, *Biographical Dictionary*, 2:46–47.

88. *GJMK*, 1924, p. 875; *TTMJ*, 1:57.

89. *MJTC, chüan* 8, p. 32; *ATTA, chüan* 2, pp. 10–11; *GJMK*, 1932, pp. 150–51.

factional struggle. As in the cases of his other political decisions since taking office, advance preparation and quick, decisive action robbed his opponents of a chance to obstruct the development of his policy.

Only days after delivery of the five-power note, the Anfu Club sent a delegate to President Hsu to argue that the head of the northern delegation should be a man "able to represent four elements: President Hsu, Tuan Ch'i-jui, the northern warlords, and the majority in parliament"; and that only Wang I-t'ang fit these qualifications. Hsu answered that a chief delegate had already been selected. It would be awkward to change him, but Wang would be welcome to serve as one of the other delegates on the negotiating team. Wang, of course, could not accept the invitation to serve as a negotiator under someone else.[90] Hsu in fact had already arrived at a preliminary list which differed by only two names from the delegation ultimately to be appointed.[91] The names of the delegates were made public on December 11, and by the time some warlords got around to sending telegrams urging that each province (i.e., each major warlord) be allowed to appoint its own representative,[92] it was too late.

The composition of the delegation reflected the importance of connections in the selection of go-betweens and negotiators. The delegates were chosen first of all for their ability to represent the interests and keep the confidence of one or preferably several of the warlords and factions without whose cooperation no peace agreement would be honored. Second, within the context of this requirement, it was necessary to select delegates who would not be offensive to the South because of open association with the military unification policies of the past. Third, the delegates had to be men of personal prestige adequate to their ambassadorial role. The ten delegates were as follows.[93]

Chu Ch'i-ch'ien, chairman of the delegation, was a member of the Communications Clique. He was also a former subordinate and adopted son of President Hsu. Chu's name had been conspicuously absent from the board of directors of the Peace Promotion Society, which suggests that he had been chosen as the future head of the northern delegation as early as October. In November, President Hsu had used Chu as a semisecret delegate to negotiate with southern

90. *STSP* 1918.12.10.2.

91. *Ibid.* The list printed here had the names of Wang Chih-lung and Sun Jun-yü and lacked those of Shih Yü and Chiang Shao-chieh. Also see *STSP* 1918.12.11.2.

92. *STSP* 1918.12.16.2.

93. Lists of the delegates together with characterizations as to the factions they represented may be found in Hsieh Pin, *Cheng-tang shih*, p. 85; *AHKC*, 2:124; *NPIHWH*, Document 20, pp. 75–76. In the last source, the affiliations were provided by Yeh Kung-ch'o (the editors do not make clear whether he provided this information at the time or later). Since these sources do not agree on all the attributions, I rely ultimately on my own interpretation of biographical data about each man.

propeace elements.[94] Chu was acceptable to the South because he was a native of Kweichow and because of his identification with the pronegotiations movement in the North. He was a personal friend of T'ang Shao-i, who was expected to be the chief southern delegate.[95]

Wu Ting-ch'ang,[96] born in Szechwan, was a banker and financial bureaucrat who had served under both Chou Tzu-ch'i and Ts'ao Ju-lin. Wu apparently had the confidence of Tuan Ch'i-jui, the Anfu Club (of which he was a non-M.P. member), and Hsu Shih-ch'ang and the Communications Clique. In his later career, he operated as a banker ally of the Communications Clique.

Wang K'o-min, the newly retired minister of finance, represented the interests of Feng Kuo-chang and of the pro-Feng warlords of the Yangtze basin.

Shih Yü,[97] a Szechwanese, was a *chin-shih* who had served in the secretariat of Li Ch'un and had been one of Li's major political messengers in the search for peace that had been going on for a year and a half. It was appropriate that Li, as the major mediator between North and South, have his own representative on the northern delegation.

Fang Shu,[98] an Anhweinese, was a follower of Tuan Ch'i-jui. Although not a member of the Anfu Club, he was considered sympathetic to its interests. Fang, however, was also a former member of Hsu Shih-ch'ang's secretariat. As a Waseda-educated lawyer and former head of the Legislative Drafting Bureau (*Fa-chih chü*), Fang was qualified to help resolve the legal questions between North and South.

Wang Yu-ling,[99] another Japanese-educated lawyer, was a senator from Chekiang in the new parliament. Although he had not joined the Anfu Club, he published the newspaper that served as the major Anfu organ in Peking, the *Kung-yen pao*. He was a former subordinate of Liang Shih-i and loosely connected with the Communications Clique.

Chiang Shao-chieh,[100] like Wang Yu-ling a law graduate of Hōsei University, was a senator and a member of the Anfu Club. A *chin-shih,* Chiang had held high judicial and administrative posts in the Ch'ing bureaucracy. He was a

94. *STSP* 1918.11.10.2.

95. *LSINP*, 2:10.

96. *GJMK*, 1932, p. 114; Boorman and Howard, *Biographical Dictionary*, 3: 452–53; *Who's Who*, 1936, p. 265; "SSG," pp. 18–19; *SKJ*, p. 612–2 [*sic*]. Hsieh Pin lists him as representing Hsu Shih-ch'ang at the conference; *NPIHWH*, Document 20, has the annotation, "Anfu clique;" *AHKC* considers him a representative of both the New Communications Clique and the "Anfu clique."

97. *GJMK*, 1937, p. 197.

98. *ATTA, chüan* 2, pp. 21–22; "SSG," pp. 31–32; *GJMK*, 1937, p. 475.

99. "SSG," p. 5; *GJMK*, 1932, p. 43.

100. *GJMK*, 1937, p. 162.

native of Anhwei and represented Ni Ssu-ch'ung as well as the Anfu Club at the negotiations.

Liu En-ko, the head of the Manchurian delegation in Parliament, represented both the Anfu Club and, more importantly, Chang Tso-lin.

Li Kuo-chen and Hsu Fo-su, finally, represented the Research Clique on the delegation.

In his selection of the delegation, President Hsu had skillfully managed to give the Anfu Club superficially strong but potentially weak representation. Each of the Anfu-related members on the delegation had other loyalties that might, under certain circumstances, supersede loyalty to the club. Wu Ting-ch'ang was essentially a banker with ties to the Communications and New Communications cliques; Chiang Shao-chieh represented Ni Ssu-ch'ung; Liu En-ko was loyal to Chang Tso-lin; Fang Shu was a non-Anfu Club follower of Tuan Ch'i-jui, and Wang Yu-ling, although sympathetic, was only loosely connected with the club. The dissolution of parliament, should that be necessary to achieve peace, would not threaten the power base of any of these delegates. Thus, while the Anfu Club was assured at least of reports of the progress of the negotiations in the early stages, it could not be sure of uncompromising support at the conference.

The makeup of the delegation also reflected the expectation that secret negotiations would probably be carried out between the two chief delegates, assisted by whichever delegates were sympathetic to them, and that *faits accomplis* would be presented to the delegates hostile to the solution taking shape. In fact, the chief northern negotiatiors in practice were to be Chu Ch'i-ch'ien, Wu Ting-ch'ang, and Wang Yu-ling.[101] The pro-Anfu delegates and the delegates of prowar tuchuns were, predictably, to make an effort as soon as the two delegations reached Shanghai to persuade the southerners that Chu could not speak for the whole delegation.[102] In view of this sort of foreseeable division within the delegation, it was important for Hsu's man to be head of the delegation.

On December 29, the names of the members of the southern delegation were released.[103] The chairman was T'ang Shao-i.[104] One of the first Chinese educated in the West, T'ang had been Yuan Shih-k'ai's chief foreign affairs expert; he had served under Hsu Shih-ch'ang in Manchuria, and his coprovincial Liang Shih-i had served as his aide on a trip to India to negotiate over Tibet. T'ang's

101. *STSP* 1919.4.1.2.

102. *LSINP*, 2:43.

103. They were formally appointed in January. *CWCY*, p. 483.

104. *GJMK*, 1932, p. 294; *MJTC*, *chüan* 1, p. 107; *Kuo-shih kuan kuan-k'an* 1, no. 2 (March 1948): 79–80; *TTMJ*, 1:20–23; Boorman and Howard, *Biographical Dictionary*, 3: 232–36.

friendly relations with Hsu and Liang were still strong.[105] In 1911, T'ang had been the chief northern delegate to the Shanghai peace conference. After serving as the first prime minister of the republic, T'ang had gone to Shanghai and engaged in commerce. There, he actively opposed Yuan Shih-k'ai's imperial movement and associated himself with Sun Yat-sen. Since then, he had been considered a Kuo-min tang elder statesman.

The other southern delegates can be described by quoting the notations found next to their names in the private papers of Chu Ch'i-ch'ien.

Chang Shih-chao. Hunanese, studied in England. Represents Ts'en Ch'un-hsuan, Political Study Group.

Hu Han-min. Sun Wen's representative. Studied in Japan. Early member of the T'ung-meng hui. . . . Former *tutu* [military governor] of Kwangtung.

Miao Chia-shou. Former advisor of T'ang Chi-yü [brother of T'ang Chi-yao], went with him to Kwangtung. Served as commander of the second division of the Yunnan Army. . . .

Tseng Yen. Kwangsi representative. Has served as an M.P. and as head of the Kwangtung Provincial Finance Office. Formerly belonged to Political Study faction, . . . now Wu-ming [i.e., Lu Jung-t'ing] faction.

Kuo Ch'un-sen. Kwangtung representative, chief of staff of the Kwangtung tuchun [Mo Jung-hsin]. . . . Native of Kweichow. . . .

Liu Kuang-lieh. Szechwan representative—tuchun Hsiung [K'o-wu] of Szechwan. Said to be close to the Political Study Group.

Wang Po-ch'ün. Kweichow native, studied in Japan. Nephew of tuchun Liu [Hsien-shih], elder brother of Kweichow Division Commander Wang Wen-hua. . . .

Li Shu-ying. Shensi native. Member of the old parliament. Represents Shensi. Political Study Group.

Jao Ming-luan. Fukienese. Represents Fukien and the navy. Chief of staff of the navy.

P'eng Yun-i. Hunanese. Studied in Japan. Political Study Group.[106]

After being named, the northern peace delegation (except for Shih Yü who was in Nanking)[107] collected in Peking and began a ceremonious round of banquets for the ostensible purpose of soliciting the opinions of the various factions in Peking about the shape the peace settlement should take. On December 23, the delegation entertained five Anfu Club representatives at lunch; on the 24th, it banqueted six representatives of the Number Seven Club (Communications Clique); that evening, it met with five members of the Research Clique; at noon on December 25, the delegation entertained eleven delegates of the

105. *PYCF*, 4:188; *NPIHWH*, Document 34, p. 92.

106. *NPIHWH*, Document 55, pp. 107–8.

107. His absence is mentioned in *NPIHWH*, Document 24, p. 84. We learn Shih was in Nanking from F.O. 228/2982, Despatch 127, Giles to Jordan, Nanking, December 6, 1918, p. 2; and from *STSP* 1918.11.21.2.

Discussion Society; and that evening it dined with representatives of various peace groups, including the Peace Promotion Society. On the afternoon of the 26th, the peace delegation met with sixty or seventy Chinese and foreign journalists—not for a news conference but for an exchange of speeches between the two sides about their hopes for the shape of the settlement. On the 27th, the delegation was feted by the cabinet; on the 28th, it met with the President; and on the 29th, Chu and some of the other delegates departed for Nanking, Li Ch'un's capital, where they hoped to meet with the southern delegation.[108]

Progress at Shanghai

Hsu Shih-ch'ang had made skillful use of political resources in the first months of his presidency. The factional consensus behind the new president and his personal prestige enabled him to seize the policy initiative. Skillful use of connections and control over the timing of initiatives allowed him to prepare responses from the South and from northern public opinion. Foreign intervention was turned to advantage. Once made public, Hsu's peace-through-negotiations policy was pushed as rapidly as possible to avoid loss of momentum.

The second phase would be more difficult. The advantage now lay with the policy's opponents, who could see where Hsu's plans were headed clearly enough to throw obstacles in the path. From the beginning, the prowar northern tuchuns dragged their feet. They wanted a "reconstruction conference" (shan-hou hui-i), a term implying the reordering of affairs after a rebellion or insurrection;[109] the South insisted on a "peace conference" (ho-p'ing hui-i), as between two equal governments. The warlords wanted the conference in Nanking, the capital of a province that recognized Peking; the South insisted on Shanghai, a foreign concession that was neutral ground and had been the site of the 1911 negotiations between the revolutionaries and the Ch'ing (the

---

108. STSP 1918.12.23.2, 12.24.2; NPIHWH, Documents 22–24, pp. 80–82, 84. According to Document 22, p. 80, at the dinner on the 25th, representatives of two groups besides the Peace Promotion Society attended. The groups were called the Peace and Unity Association (Ho-p'ing t'ung-i hui) and the Five Races Peace Society (Wu-tsu ho-p'ing hui). I have not found these groups mentioned in any other source (with one exception; see below) nor can I identify the eleven representatives of the two groups who are listed as attending. Lists of the delegates from each clique may be found in NPIHWH, Document 21, pp. 76–78. Here, the Peace and Unity Association is listed but the Five Races Peace Society is not. Instead, a group called the Society for the People's Economic Advancement (Kuo-min ching-chi hsieh-chin hui) is listed. This group is not mentioned in any other source I have seen.

109. STSP 1918.11.26.2, 12.14.2. In line with this view, the Peking government's preparatory organ for the conference was at first called the Reconstruction Preparation Office (Shan-hou ch'ou-pei ch'u). NPIHWH, p. 90, note 1.

South's appointment of T'ang Shao-i as its chief negotiator reinforced the echo of 1911, since T'ang had been a chief delegate then as well, albeit for the North). The South insisted that each side have an equal number of delegates, while the North argued that each delegation should have a number of representatives equal to the number of provinces and districts under its control. (This would have produced a twenty-man northern delegation and a five-man southern delegation.) Lengthy negotiations through mediators, especially Li Ch'un, were required to deal with these issues. Finally, in light of the powers' pressure to begin negotiations, Hsu was able to concede these issues to the South without further warlord opposition.[110] The conference would be called the Shanghai Peace Conference, and each side would send a ten-man team.

There remained, however, a more fundamental issue between the two sides —the question of a truce on all the fronts where northern and southern troops were fighting.[111] Peking had ordered a truce in Hunan, but its commanders in Shensi (Ch'en Shu-fan) and Fukien (Li Hou-chi) continued their operations against the southern forces in those provinces (led by Yü Yu-jen and Ch'en Chiung-ming respectively).[112] The South complained of these operations and insisted on a truce on all fronts before the start of negotiations.[113] Eventually, Peking agreed to order a truce in Fukien but refused to do so in Shensi, where it claimed to be engaged in bandit suppression. This meant that the North refused

110. On Li Ch'un's role, see F.O. 228/2982, *passim*; Li T'ing-yü, comp., "Li T'ing-yü so-ts'en," Documents 21–72, pp. 13–34; *NPIHWH*, Documents 13–15, 19, 28–30, 37, 39–40, pp. 24–25, 26–30, 70, 73–75, 88–100; *STSP* 1918.11.26.2 (Li's appointment as authorized negotiator for the North). On mediators, see *STSP* 1918.11.2.2, 11.22.2, 11.23.2, 11.24.2, 11.25.2, 11.28.2 and *LSINP*, 1:439–41 (on the second trip of Lin Shao-fei and Kuan Mien-chün to see Lu Jung-t'ing); *STSP* 1918.11.23.2 (Chang Shih-chao in Nanking as delegate of the South); F.O. 228/2982, Despatch 120, Giles to Jordan, November 7, 1918, p. 2 (on the arrival in Nanking of Leng Yü-ch'iu, a military representative of the Canton government); *STSP* 1918.12.15.2 (on Kuo T'ung, a delegate of T'ang Chi-yao); *CWCY*, p. 478. On the direct exchange of telegrams between the two governments, see F.O. 228/2985, English translations of telegrams exchanged between the two sides through the courtesy of the British Legation and consulates in November and December 1918.

111. The South also made the disbandment of the War Participation Army a precondition for opening negotiations but eventually went ahead without its fulfillment.

112. The military situations in these provinces, particularly Shensi, were complex. The concept of northern and southern sides in the conflict is merely a convenient simplification. It would be more accurate to say that there was a multiplicity of local commanders and brigands, many of whom nominally adhered to one side or the other in order to get supplies, allies, and so forth. There were more fundamental issues involved in their battles than that of loyalty to Peking or Canton. See "A Special Correspondent" [Rodney Gilbert], "Real Conditions in Shensi as Seen by an Eyewitness," *Peking Leader*, April 5, 1919; clipping in F.O. 371/3683, 90955 (f394).

113. Telegram of November 29, Ts'en Ch'un-hsuan to Ch'ien Neng-hsun, contained in F.O. 228/2985, Telegram 42, Canton to Peking, November 30, 1918.

to recognize Shensi as a contested province and would not permit the province to be a subject of the negotiations. Peking's intransigence was due to the belief of the northern warlords that Shensi was essential to their territorial security.[114]

After two months of preconference negotiations, the delegates at Shanghai agreed to a formula for a Shensi truce and formally opened the Shanghai peace conference on February 20. But the truce in Shensi proved fragile. Receiving reports of an offensive by the troops of Ch'en Shu-fan, chief southern delegate T'ang Shao-i addressed a strong inquiry to the northern delegation with a deadline of forty-eight hours for a satisfactory reply. Chu Ch'i-ch'ien referred the ultimatum to Peking and received no answer. So, on March 2, T'ang broke off negotiations and Chu offered his resignation to Peking.

Despite the appearance of a confrontation between the northern and southern delegations, these events represented in fact a joint effort of chief delegates T'ang and Chu to strengthen the hand of President Hsu in an effort to force the prowar tuchuns to respect the truce that the Peking government had declared in Shensi.[115] The threatened breakup of the conference gave Hsu the cudgel necessary to force Shensi Tuchun Ch'en Shu-fan and his backer, Tuan Ch'i-jui,[116] to respect the truce order. In response to the crisis at the conference, public pressure, especially in the form of telegrams from Wu P'ei-fu and the three Yangtze tuchuns, and foreign pressure, in the form of visits to Hsu by various foreign diplomats, mounted for a reopening of the conference.[117] Hsu appointed Chang Jui-ch'i, a retired official with good relations with both Ch'en Shu-fan and Yü Yu-jen and with local officials in Shensi,[118] to visit the battle area and supervise and verify the establishment of a truce. During March, Chang visited several places in Shensi and sent telegrams certifying to the satisfaction of both sides that a truce had actually been established there.[119] With this, contacts

114. *STSP* 1919.3.4.2; cf. *STSP* 1918.12.21.2.

115. F.O. 228/2982, Despatch 31, Giles to Jordan, Nanking, March 21, 1919; F.O. 371/3682, 62492 (f394), Despatch 85, Jordan to Curzon, Peking, March 4, 1919, p. 1.

116. Because of the strategic importance of Shensi, Tuan provided financial support and munitions to Ch'en. *STSP* 1919.3.4.2.

117. *PYCF*, 5:12.

118. Chang was a *chü-jen* who had served as a *hsien* magistrate in Shensi for nine years before and after the revolution. He enjoyed widespread respect in the province and was a friend of both Yü and Ch'en. As a former bureaucrat, he was acceptable to the northern elite; as a member of the Kuo-min tang in the 1913–14 parliament and an opponent of Yuan Shih-k'ai's imperial movement, he was acceptable to the South. *GJMK*, 1928, p. 156; *STSP* 1919.3.8.20.

119. *STSP* 1919.3.4.2, 3.13.2, 3.22.2, 3.27.2, 3.28.2. According to Rodney Gilbert (see note 112), the areas visited by Chang had seen no fighting for some time. But even if only a formality, Chang's visit to Shensi did serve the purpose of bringing the southern delegation back to the conference.

resumed between the two delegations with a view to reopening the peace conference and at last beginning substantive negotiations in earnest.

The process of direct and indirect contacts between North and South through the five-month period had already brought the two sides to the verge of agreement on most of the issues between them.[120] The establishment of truces in most of the contested areas signified that a broadly acceptable distribution of territory had been achieved. In this atmosphere, issues like the allocation of titles and the amount of funds to be supplied by Peking to the southern military leaders could be easily settled. While the issue of the fate of the War Participation Army was still knotty, Peking had partially satisfied southern demands by publication on March 14 of the text of the Sino-Japanese Military Cooperation Agreement. This left the problem of the fate of the two parliaments.

It had been recognized from the beginning that the issue of parliament would present the final obstacle to a settlement. As Ch'ien Neng-hsun had written in his October 23 telegram to the southern leaders launching the peace policy:

Although the problem of the constitution was the *casus belli*, the solution of matters of principle is difficult, and if in the present urgent state of our foreign affairs we set aside practical questions and debate the constitutional issue, we will waste a great deal of time. . . . I believe it is appropriate first to find a way to solve the practical problems, and to leave the constitutional issue for subsequent discussion by the public. . . . [121]

With "practical questions" of territory, titles, and finance near settlement, the "constitutional issue" bulked large.

The problem of parliament was the most difficult part of the constitutional issue. Both sides had always claimed to be operating in accord with the Provisional Constitution, so that the adoption of a formula satisfactory to the South, by which the Provisional Constitution was "restored" or a new constitution adopted, was no serious obstacle to the North. Since October, the South had been willing to accept Hsu Shih-ch'ang's presidency as part of an overall agreement. The difficult part of the constitutional problem was what to do with the two parliaments—both containing many politicians who depended upon their parliamentary positions for income and status.

On the parliament issue, the leaders of the two delegations and their respective principals—Hsu Shih-ch'ang and his allies in the North, Lu Jung-t'ing and his allies in the South—shared a common interest. Propeace forces both North and South had little stake in the two parliaments and indeed regarded them as obstacles to the extension of their power. Far from being willing to sacrifice the

120. The delegates did not realize late in March or early in April how quickly agreement could now be reached on practical details of most issues, but this became clear to them as talks began. See, e.g., *NPIHWH*, Documents 221, 230, and ff.

121. *LSINP*, 1:437–38.

budding peace agreement in a struggle to preserve the respective parliaments, they had a positive interest in agreeing to their dissolution. In this, the chief delegates and their principals were opposed by most of the M.P.'s in the two parliaments and their principal backers—Tuan Ch'i-jui in the North, Sun Yat-sen in the South.[122] With peace negotiations nearing a climax, these alignments became more important than the North/ South split.

In order to facilitate agreement, the two chief delegates agreed that the second series of meetings, unlike the first, should be held in closed sessions. The first meeting, held on April 9, was devoted to a discussion of the agenda. After the meeting, Chu Ch'i-ch'ien wired to Wu Ting-ch'ang—whom he had sent to Peking to consult with the president and the prime minister—that it had been decided to discuss the parliament question but to leave it to the end of the negotiations. "I can think of no other way to deal with this than the fundamental solution [i.e., dissolution of both parliaments and election of a new one]," Chu wrote. "However, it is still hard to know what Hsiao-ch'uan's [i.e., T'ang's] latest position on this is. . . . Please consult with the president and prime minister as to how we should deal with this so that we will have a policy prepared."[123]

The same day Chu received a telegram from Wu, who had already consulted with President Hsu and Prime Minister Ch'ien. "Both strongly feel that the fundamental solution is desirable and would be worthwhile even though it involves the sacrifice [of the Anfu parliament]," Wu wrote.[124]

On April 13, Chu wired that the other items on the agenda were being settled so fast the parliament question would shortly be up for solution. Failure to solve this question would render the solution of all the other problems useless. Chu urged Wu to obtain from the government a final position on the parliament question and to return to Shanghai to help him with the negotiations.[125]

On April 18, Ch'ien Neng-hsun sent Wu Ting-ch'ang back to Shanghai with the proposal that some seventy members from each parliament's constitutional drafting committee combine to form an organ that would meet in Nanking to prepare and pass upon a new constitution and new parliamentary electoral laws. If the South could agree to such an arrangement, Ch'ien felt confident that he could carry it over the opposition of the Anfu Club in the North.[126]

122. Not enough research has been done on the internal politics of the South to untangle confidently the relationships among and policies of the southern factions. Although an ally of Sun Yat-sen, T'ang Shao-i, in his role as chief southern delegate, seems to have been more responsive to Lu Jung-t'ing and was influenced to follow Sun's uncompromising position only at the end of the negotiations.

123. *NPIHWH*, Document 241, p. 231. Also see Document 237, pp. 224–29.

124. *NPIHWH*, Document 239, p. 229. Also see Documents 240, 242, and 243.

125. *NPIHWH*, Document 250, pp. 234–35. See *STSP* 1919.4.15.2.

126. *NPIHWH*, Document 267, pp. 242–43, and Document 268, p. 243.

The Anfu Club Counteroffensive

Meanwhile, however, the Anfu Club had mounted a counteroffensive to try to block a solution that would lead to parliament's dissolution. (Fang Shu had recently returned to Peking from Shanghai and had presumably informed the club leaders of the trend of events.)[127] After a series of meetings to discuss the deteriorating situation,[128] the club released to the public the text of a telegram sent on April 17 to Chu Ch'i-ch'ien by more than 250 M.P.'s headed by Anfu's Wang Chih-lung.

Recently we have read in the newspapers that your conference is now actually touching upon the constitutional question. Now the constitutional question is essentially the parliament question. The parliament is based upon the Provisional Constitution; it elects the president; it approves the cabinet; and both in China and abroad parliament is regarded as intimately connected with the foundations of the nation. Anything that shakes the parliament affects the whole government. The competence of a delegate of the cabinet cannot extend beyond administrative questions. Parliament is the nation's legislative organ and definitely does not fall within the bounds of matters that a delegate of the administrative branch can discuss. If he exceeds his powers and discusses [parliament], then the responsibility for disordering the constitution and shaking the national foundation is his. We make this declaration in order to uphold the constitution and strengthen the national foundation, and we request your attention to it.[129]

On April 18, Prime Minister Ch'ien told the House that the government would accept neither a settlement requiring it to brand the Anfu parliament as illegal nor one providing for the restoration of the old parliament, but that the delegates could not be excluded from discussing the constitutional question at the peace conference. Hardly satisfied with this answer, which amounted to a rebuttal of the previous day's telegram, the M.P.'s proceeded to attack the government on the always handy issue of the declining value of bank notes and Eighth Year Bonds. Ch'ien angrily responded that if parliament did not like his policies it should impeach him. A motion was entered to impeach the cabinet, but the speaker declared a quorum lacking and the meeting was adjourned.[130] Non-Anfu M.P.'s, it should be noted, were as active as Anfu Club members in this attack on the cabinet, for on the issue of the life of parliament the interests of M.P.'s tended to converge.[131]

The Anfu Club now began negotiations with a group of members of the

127. *STSP* 1919.4.17.2.

128. *STSP* 1919.4.14.2; *NCH* 1919.4.19.147.

129. *STSP* 1919.4.21.2; Lai Ch'ün-li, comp., "I-ho wen-hsien," Document 32, pp. 311–12.

130. *STSP* 1919.4.19.2; *NPIHWH*, Document 269, pp. 243–44; according to one rumor, the cabinet was so furious at this encounter that it considered resigning: *STSP* 1919.4.21.2.

131. *STSP* 1919.4.19.2: see also *STSP* 1919.4.18.2.

old parliament under the slogan, "a solution carried out by the two parliaments themselves" (*liang-hui tzu-hsing chieh-chueh*). The club argued that only the legislative organs had the right to arrange a settlement of the constitutional question. In the latter half of April, "several tens"[132] of old parliament M.P.'s engaged in talks first with the Anfu Club leaders and then with the leaders of the other parliamentary factions. Of these several tens, we have the names of only seven:[133] Ho Wen (Anhwei), Han Yü-chen (Hupei), Ching Yao-yueh (Shansi), Kuo Jen-chang (Hunan), Ch'en Ming-chien (Honan), T'ao Pao-chin (Kiangsu), and Sun Chung (Honan). Of the seven, four (Ho Wen, Ching Yao-yueh, Ch'en Ming-chien, and T'ao Pao-chin) had not joined the Canton parliament; the other three had but were among a group who had recently come to Peking to establish relations with the Peking authorities in hopes of getting seats in the next parliament.[134]

A noteworthy characteristic of the group was that their parliamentary posts seem to have been the highest political posts most of them had achieved. Han Yü-chen, for example, had been a clerk in the Hupei Provincial Justice Department, then a section head, and finally, with an official's patronage, "he went with a leap up to senator."[135] Ch'en Ming-chien was a lawyer and later a Peiping city official. Ching Yao-yueh went no higher outside of parliament than the post of lecturer in law at Peiping University. As professional politicians who depended upon parliamentary seats for their income and status, their main concern was to preserve and extend their parliamentary service as long as possible. (Han Yü-chen was prominent in a group of old parliament M.P.'s who as late as January 1926 called for the recall of the old parliament as the solution to China's political woes.)[136]

132. *STSP* 1919.4.20.2.

133. These names are gleaned from *STSP* 1919.4.19.2, 4.20.2, 4.22.2, 5.4.2. Some biographical information on the seven is taken from the Parliament List. Other sources are as follows:

Ho Wen: *Shen pao* 1924.8.3 in *GSK* 1924.8.172; Hsieh Pin, *Cheng-tang shih*, chart ff. p. 176.

Han Yü-chen: Hsieh Pin, *Cheng-tang shih*, p. 183; Chiang Yü-sheng, "Hu-fa," Document 7, pp. 364–66.

Ching Yao-yueh: Yang Yu-chiung, *Cheng-tang shih*, p. 69; *GJMK*, 1937, p. 118; Hsieh Pin, *Cheng-tang shih*, chart ff. p. 176.

Kuo Jen-chang: Yang Yu-chiung, *Cheng-tang shih*, p. 69.

Ch'en Ming-chien: *GJMK*, 1937, p. 395.

T'ao Pao-chin: *GJMK*, 1937, p. 428.

Sun Chung: Kokumin gikai, *Shina seitō no genjō*, p. 11.

134. In mid-April, a small migration of old parliament M.P.'s from Canton to Peking was reported. *STSP* 1919.4.18.2.

135. Chiang Yü-sheng, "Hu-fa," Document 7, p. 365.

136. *Chiao-t'ung jih-pao* 1926.1.12 in *GSK* 1926.1.115.

The contact between the old parliament M.P.'s and Wang I-t'ang was probably Ho Wen, who had a connection with Wang as a fellow native of Anhwei, and with some other Anfu Club leaders as a former colleague in the parliamentary Chung-ho chü-le-pu (Harmony club) of 1917. On April 17, Ho and several of the other old parliament M.P.'s were feted by Wang I-t'ang at the Anfu Club headquarters. At later meetings, held through April and in early May, leaders of non-Anfu factions were also involved. One plan that was discussed called for both parliaments to dissolve, then to reconvene jointly as a citizens' convention (kuo-min ta-hui) to write and pass a permanent constitution.[137] At the rate at which constitutions had been written by parliaments in the past, this should provide secure seats for everyone virtually as long as a government agency could be found to pay salaries.

The great defect of such discussion was the inability of the few old parliament M.P.'s present to represent the majority of the Canton parliament.[138] Not only were the pro-Sun Yat-sen groups in Canton opposed to any accomodation with the Anfu parliament, but the so-called 1919 elements (min-pa fen-tzu) were vociferous in oppostition to any arrangement that did not provide for their own continuation as M.P.'s. (The 1919 elements were the 325 M.P.'s in Canton who had been selected to fill the seats of those members of the old parliament who had not gone south to "protect the constitution." The existence of several non-hu-fa M.P.'s in the negotiating group at Peking suggested that any solution reached in Peking would provide for official positions for members of the old parliament as it existed in 1917 rather than as it existed in 1919.)[139] A bill to reprimand Kuo Jen-chang for his involvement in these negotiations was introduced into the Canton parliament on May 2, prominently supported by 1919 elements but, due to the lack of a quorum, was not taken up.[140] Given the inability of the Peking group to represent the Canton parliament, the main usefulness of the negotiations lay in demonstrating for the benefit of Ch'ien Neng-hsun and Chu Ch'i-ch'ien that a peace settlement that countenanced the dissolution of the two parliaments would meet with strong opposition.[141]

Ultimately, however, the rigid stance of the "two Sun factions" (liang-Sun-p'ai, the Sun Yat-sen and the Sun Hung-i factions) in demanding the restoration of the 1917 parliament and the dissolution of the Anfu parliament brought about the collapse of the Shanghai peace talks. Rumors of a budding accord between

137. STSP 1919.4.19.2, 4.20.2, 4.21.2, 4.22.2.

138. STSP 1919.4.22.2.

139. Within the Canton parliament, of course, there were various views as to the form in which the old parliament should be restored. T'ang Shao-i was shortly to demand restoration of the 1917 form of parliament. The status of the 1919 elements became a major problem in 1922 when the old parliament finally was restored in Peking; see Chapter VI.

140. STSP 1919.5.8.7.

141. This effect was achieved. See NPIHWH, Document 283, p. 252.

Chu and T'ang had reached Canton as well as Peking. Public and private pressure was mounted by M.P.'s of the two Sun factions on T'ang to refuse to compromise on the parliament question.[142] In late April, therefore, T'ang's position stiffened.[143] At the formal meeting of May 13, he presented an ultimatum consisting of eight points. Point five demanded that "the peace conference should declare invalid the order issued by former President Li Yuan-hung on June 13, 1917."[144] Since this was the order by which President Li had disbanded the old parliament, its invalidation would recall the parliament of 1917. Chu Ch'i-ch'ien could not agree to this, and both delegations submitted their resignations to their governments.[145] Chu Ch'i-ch'ien and Wu Ting-ch'ang left Shanghai on the 20th. The other northern delegates returned to Peking one by one, and the southern delegation likewise dispersed.[146]

The failure to achieve unity was a severe blow to Hsu Shih-ch'ang. Virtually in a stroke, it reduced him to a figurehead lacking the prestige or power to solve the immense problems his government faced. The final nail in his political coffin was now to be driven by Peking's students.

The Peking Government and the Incident of May 4

The last days of the Shanghai peace conference overlapped with the early stage of a new crisis. On April 30, the international peace conference in Paris dashed Chinese hopes by confirming Japan's possession of the former German rights in Shantung; the student protest demonstrations of May 4 turned into a great national movement whose passion and power caught the Peking factions

142. *STSP* 1919.4.20.2, 4.21.2, 4.25.2.

143. *STSP* 1919.4.26.2, 4.27.2, 4.30.2, 5.1.2, 5.1.2 editorial, 5.3.2; *NPIHWH*, Document 283, pp. 251–52; F.O. 371/3683, 77728 (f394), Telegram 280, Jordan to Curzon, Peking, May 17, 1919. According to Jordan, the North had by now agreed to all the major southern demands, including disbandment of the Border Defense (formerly War Participation) Army and removal of high officials whose administration was contrary to the wishes of the people. While I do not find corroborating evidence of northern agreement to these terms, it seems certain that a satisfactory compromise was within reach.

144. For the text of the proceedings, see *NPIHWH*, Document 300, pp. 260–64. On T'ang's motives, see *NPIHWH*, Document 311, pp. 269–70; *STSP* 1919.5.16.2.

145. *NPIHWH* Document 301, pp. 264–65. The text of the northern resignation is not among the *NPIHWH* documents, but it is mentioned in Document 308, p. 268.

146. *STSP* 1919.5.21.2, 5.24.2, 5.25.2, 5.26.2. There were further contacts between the two sides, especially between Hsu Shih-ch'ang and Lu Jung-t'ing, both of whom remained anxious to reach a settlement. See Wu Hsiang-hsiang, "Ts'en Ch'un-hsuan," p. 16; *T'ang Chi-yao*, p. 97; *STSP* 1919.5.18.7, 5.19.2; F.O. 371/3683, 87235 (f394), Telegram 310, Jordan to Curzon, Peking, June 6, 1919. In August 1919, Wang I-t'ang was appointed as chief northern delegate and, in June 1920, there was a brief revival of interest in the negotiations on the part of T'ang Shao-i, but these events came to nothing.

by surprise. The activities of the student participants in the May Fourth Movement have been thoroughly chronicled; the politicians' responses, however, were less unified and clear-cut than they have been portrayed.[147] As the factions scrambled to profit politically from the crisis and to avoid becoming tainted with the label of traitor, strains appeared within the two major factional alliances centered respectively on Hsu Shih-ch'ang and Tuan Ch'i-jui.

President Hsu and Prime Minister Ch'ien were unwavering at the eye of the storm. They opposed the May Fourth Movement and its objectives on principle. Although Hsu and Ch'ien had not been involved in making the original secret agreements with Japan that caused China's diplomatic defeat at Paris, they had been in office since the beginning of the Paris negotiations and had supervised the Chinese role by cable. They believed that it was in China's interest to sign the peace treaty despite the unsatisfactory provisions regarding the Shantung problem. President Hsu had long argued for China's entry into the war and for the resolution of North-South differences on the grounds that China would enhance its international standing through involvement in the peace negotiations. He believed that China would lose its improved standing if China alone refrained from signing the treaty. Nor could he see how refusing to sign would help to achieve a satisfactory solution of the Shantung problem.

In addition to their disagreement with the aims of the May Fourth Movement, Hsu and Ch'ien considered student demonstrations illegitimate disorders that ought to be firmly and forcefully suppressed. "Schools," as President Hsu expressed it in a mandate of May 8, "were established [by the government] chiefly for the purpose of training and developing the ability of men with a view to rendering service to the nation at some future date. As the students at schools are yet youthful, and as their nature and character have not yet been fixedly shaped, it is essential for them to devote their whole heart to their studies; it is inconceivable that they should be allowed to intervene in politics and disturb our public peace."[148] Hsu blamed the educational officials for their failure properly to control the students, and issued a series of mandates praising Ts'ao Ju-lin, Chang Tsung-hsiang, and Lu Tsung-yü—the objects of the students' rage—for meritorious service to the country.[149]

147. Chow, *May Fourth Movement*, chapters 4–6, describe the events of May and June from the student viewpoint. But Chow oversimplifies when he writes, for example, that "The Anfu clique . . . was in control of the government and backed Ts'ao Ju-lin . . . " (p. 118), or that "The dispute . . . soon became . . . a struggle between a pro-Japanese faction of warlords . . . and the population of the country . . . " (p. 127). Chow views the government as a unified entity and ignores the splits between Hsu and the Anfu Club, between the Anfu leaders and the Anfu Club members, and between Wu Ping-hsiang and the other Anfu leaders.

148. Quoted in Chow, *May Fourth Movement*, p. 134.

149. Chow, *May Fourth Movement*, pp. 134–35, 148.

Hsu's erstwhile allies, the Research Clique, broke with him on the issue of how to respond to the incident of May 4. Their strategy was to tar Tuan and his followers, especially the Anfu Club, with the brush that the students had directed solely at the "three traitors," Ts'ao Ju-lin, Chang Tsung-hsiang, and Lu Tsung-yü of the New Communications Clique. In speeches and articles, Research Clique politicians promoted the view that the "sell-out" of the three traitors to Japan was part of the larger sell-out by the "pro-Japanese" Anfu clique headed by Tuan.[150] This strategy enjoyed considerable success. Although the May Fourth Movement did not drive Tuan and his followers from power, it did administer a permanent blow to their prestige, and succeeded in identifying them for posterity as pro-Japanese and responsible for the defeat at Paris.

Tuan Ch'i-jui did not take an active part in the response of his faction to the incident of May 4. He seems to have believed simply that the students should be suppressed and the president allowed to carry out his foreign policy.[151] His followers, however, were presented with a political dilemma. On the one hand, they felt it was necessary to dissociate themselves as much as possible from their former allies, the three traitors. On the other, failure to support the administration might lead to the fall of the government, increased disorder in Peking, and a victory for the students.

The confusion among Tuan's followers is illustrated by the controversy surrounding the actions of Police Commander Wu Ping-hsiang, a member of Tuan's faction, on May 4. Wu apparently felt that it would not be wise to suppress the demonstrating students too forcefully, and the police did not prevent the students from marching on Ts'ao Ju-lin's house. The inadequate police detail guarding the Ts'ao house failed to prevent the students from invading the house, setting it on fire, and beating Chang Tsung-hsiang, whom they found there. Wu arrived on the scene only after most of the demonstrators had dispersed. On his orders, thirty-two students were arrested but Wu had them released on bail on May 7 without the prior knowledge of Prime Minister Ch'ien.[152]

150. See, for example, Ts'ao Ju-lin, *I-sheng chih hui-i* (Hongkong, 1966), pp. 202–3 (the politician referred to here is clearly Lin Ch'ang-min); Chow, *May Fourth Movement*, pp. 90, 92, 124, 128 note m; Boorman and Howard, *Biographical Dictionary*, 2:390; *STSP* 1919. 5.12.2; *NCH* 1919.5.24.491. The opportunism of the Research Clique position is clear in historical perspective. In 1917, members of the Research Clique had been allies of Tuan, and Liang Ch'i-ch'ao had participated in the negotiations for the Nishihara Loans (Li Chien-nung, *Political History*, p. 383). In 1925, Lin Ch'ang-min was again to become a prominent supporter of Tuan. Failing to understand the shifting nature of alignments of the period, historians have tended to call the Research Clique "anti-Japanese" or "pro-American and -British," although the description is valid only for the immediate May Fourth period.

151. *PYCF*, 5:46.

152. Chow, *May Fourth Movement*, p. 111, footnote c', and pp. 113, 114, 128; *NPIHWH*,

Wu's lack of severity caused shock and outrage throughout officialdom,[153] including Tuan's followers. On the day of the demonstrations, Tuan's follower, Garrison Commander Tuan Chih-kuei, complained to the prime minister that Wu was not doing an adequate job of suppressing the students.[154] On the 6th, President Hsu issued a mandate explicitly taking Wu to task for "seriously blunder[ing] in the . . . handling of the affair."[155] On the 8th, the cabinet submitted its resignation in protest against what was considered Wu's virtual insubordination in releasing the arrested students without cabinet authorization.[156] The post of prime minister was offered to several prominent individuals in order to ascertain whether they still supported the cabinet. Tuan Ch'i-jui, refusing to organize a cabinet, agreed with Hsu and Ch'ien that the thirty-two students should be taken to court and that Wu Ping-hsiang should be punished and responsibility for the security of Peking turned over to the garrison command.[157]

The Anfu Club responded disunitedly to the political crisis. Immediately after the incident of May 4, a number of Anfu Club members attempted to dissociate themselves and the club from the three traitors. A bill to impeach the cabinet for exceeding its power and harming national sovereignty with regard to the Shantung question was circulated in parliament over the signature of Li Chi-chen, an Anfu Club member from Hupei. Other members of the house, presumably Anfuites, submitted a bill to investigate possible wrongdoing on the part of the delegates to the Paris peace conference. Fu Ting-i, an Anfu member of the house from Hunan, addressed the May 5 meeting of students at Peking University in support of their cause.[158]

Ch'ien's resignation over the insubordination of Wu Ping-hsiang on May 8, however, forced the club leadership to adopt a clear policy toward the cabinet. The leaders did not wish the Ch'ien cabinet to fall, since they did not themselves wish to form a cabinet to deal with the knotty student and treaty problems. On May 10, Wang I-t'ang and Li Sheng-to, the Anfu Club leaders and speakers of the two houses of parliament, visited President Hsu and urged that the resignation of the Ch'ien cabinet be rejected. Support for the cabinet also came

---

Document 292, p. 255; NPIHWH, Document 296, p. 259; Ts'ao Ju-lin, I-sheng, pp. 196–98. Other signs of Wu's soft attitude toward the students included participation of Police Academy students in the incident of May 4 and Wu's reception of the chancellors of the thirteen Peking colleges and universities on May 5. Chow, May Fourth Movement, p. 124 and p. 387, note b.

153. NPIHWH, Document 291, p. 255.

154. Ts'ao Ju-lin, I-sheng, p. 196.

155. Chow, May Fourth Movement, p. 133.

156. NPIHWH, Documents 291–92, 296–97, pp. 255, 259–60.

157. NPIHWH, Document 298, p. 260.

158. STSP 1919.5.9.2, 5.10.2, 5.13.2; Chow, May Fourth Movement, p. 121. For biographical data on Fu, see Hashikawa Tokio, Chūgoku bunkakai jimbutsu sōkan (Peking, 1940), p. 531.

from Tuan Ch'i-jui; telegrams of support arrived from provincial officials as well. The cabinet stayed in office.[159]

As national opposition to the Versilles treaty mounted, however, the Anfu Club found it increasingly difficult to maintain its support for the government. In response to the general strike called by the students on May 19, the government finally acceded to the student demand for the removal from office of the "three traitors,"[160] but remained obdurate in its intention to order its negotiators to sign the treaty. The Research Clique had succeeded in identifying the Anfu Club as the force behind the alleged Paris sell-out of the nation. Seeking to evade this label, the Anfu Club on June 10 issued its first public statement on the treaty, a telegram denouncing its Shantung provisions and announcing the club's intention to follow the "popular will" on the issue.[161]

The Anfu Club's action precipitated a fresh government crisis. Hsu Shih-ch'ang regarded the Anfu action as a repudiation of earlier promises to support him on the issue. In addition, since parliament would have to approve the treaty, the Anfu defection made it impossible for Hsu to lay in place the keystone of his foreign policy. On June 11, Hsu submitted his resignation to parliament and issued a public telegram accepting the blame for the government's failure to adopt a foreign policy meeting with the nation's approval. Referring to his age and physical weakness, Hsu stated that he could no longer bear the rigors of office. He urged parliament to elect a successor, promising to conduct the necessary business of the presidency in the interim.[162] The cabinet also submitted its resignation.[163]

159. *STSP* 1919.5.11.2, 5.12.2, 5.14.2, 5.16.7.

160. Chow, *May Fourth Movement*, pp. 140–41, 145–46, 163. Ts'ao Ju-lin writes in his autobiography that Hsu had long wished to remove him and the others from office in order to cut off Tuan Ch'i-jui's close ties with Japan and simply waited until the time was ripe to issue the mandate (*I-sheng*, pp. 200–1). But, in my view, Hsu was in fact reluctant to let the "three traitors" go and only did so under strong duress more than a month after the students demanded it. One may speculate that even if he would have liked to see Ts'ao out of office before May 4, he now felt that the authority of the government to make appointments was at stake.

161. *STSP* 1919.6.13.2; NCH 1919.7.14.691. The club, at a meeting of May 16, had agreed to a stance of rejection of the Shantung portion of the treaty but had not made any public statement to this effect (*STSP* 1919.5.17.2). Ch'ien Neng-hsun knew of the Anfu position from direct consultations (*NPIHWH*, Document 306, p. 267). Apparently, however, the club had later been swayed by administration arguments and had promised its support for the policy of signing the treaty, for several news stories state that the club had promised Hsu support on the treaty (*STSP* 1919.6.11.2, 6.12.2).

162. *STSP* 1919.6.12.2.

163. *STSP* 1919.6.11.2, 6.12.2 editorial, 6.13.2, 6.14.2. Some people believed that the club issued its June 10 telegram in order to topple the Ch'ien cabinet and replace it with an Anfu-dominated cabinet (*STSP* 1919.6.12.2; *NCH* 1919.6.21.757), but this interpretation is not

The time was not right for Tuan Ch'i-jui to try to win the presidency. Hsu's fall would precipitate an untimely struggle for control of the government. Now that Hsu was powerless, he was an acceptable president to the Anfu Club. Meeting on June 11, the House found a technical reason to reject Hsu's resignation: it had not been countersigned by Prime Minister Ch'ien, who had already made up his mind to resign when Hsu drew up his resignation.[164] Tuan Ch'i-jui visited Hsu to urge him to stay on and issued a public telegram calling for support for the president. Telegrams poured in from many tuchuns and officials urging Hsu to stay in office. On June 24, President Hsu permitted the cabinet to issue a circular telegram announcing that he had cancelled his intention to resign. Despite the continued opposition from the students and citizens of the striking cities, Hsu instructed the delegates to proceed with the signing of the treaty at Versailles.[165]

The treaty, however, was not signed—either because of the delegates' own decision to disobey their instructions, as claimed by the chief delegate, Lu Cheng-hsiang, or because, as some historians believe, the delegates were prevented from attending the signing on June 28 by Chinese students and workers who surrounded Lu's residence in Paris. The demands of the student strikers, in any case, were satisfied, and the May Fourth political crisis in Peking came to an end.[166] But the crisis had completed the political emasculation of Hsu, whose key domestic and foreign policies for dealing with China's problems in the postwar world had come to naught in the first nine months of his term.[167]

Tuan Ch'i-jui's Dilemma

With the decline of Hsu Shih-ch'ang, Tuan Ch'i-jui was once again the most powerful figure in Peking but his leading position was as ambiguous an advantage now as it had been in 1918 when he abandoned his hopes for the presidency because his strength was not enough to crush the opposition evoked by his preeminence. In the latter half of 1919, Tuan was faced with a choice: either seek to eradicate rival centers of influence in North China, or maneuver to gain their support, thus emerging at the crest of a new consensus.

consistent with subsequent Anfu Club actions. Wang I-t'ang, for example, who was being mentioned as a possible successor to Ch'ien, left Peking "to nurse an illness" in order to make it clear that he would not accept the prime ministership (*STSP* 1919.6.13.2).

164. *STSP* 1919.6.12.2.

165. *STSP* 1919.6.13.2, 6.18.2, 6.25.2; Chow, *May Fourth Movement*, p. 165.

166. Chow, *May Fourth Movement*, pp. 165–67; Lo Kuang, *Lu Cheng-hsiang chuan*, pp. 113–14.

167. Since Hsu's presidency from mid-1919 onward was a weak one, Hsu has become known, somewhat oversimply, as a weak president. See, e.g., Boorman and Howard, *Biographical Dictionary*, 2:138.

The rival centers of influence were Ts'ao K'un and Chang Tso-lin, the rulers respectively of Chihli and Manchuria. The two had been Tuan's allies throughout the period of his rivalry with Feng Kuo-chang and his conflicts with President Hsu. But with Hsu's decline, they were aspirants for the power that would derive from control of Peking and Tuan, if he wished to preserve his alliance with them, would have to offer them more influence in Peking than they had enjoyed before.

Tuan's followers were split on the question of what policy to follow toward Ts'ao and Chang. An aggressive policy of seeking military predominance in North China was advocated by Hsu Shu-cheng, one of the founders of the Anfu Club and commander of the Northwest Border Defense Army (*Hsi-pei pien-fang chün*), which he had recruited and trained under the aegis of Tuan's War Participation Army (after June 24, 1919, Border Defense Army). The Border Defense Army's dual purpose was to provide a rubric for the continuation of army-building now that the end of the Great War made the title "War Participation Army" anomalous and to capitalize on developments in Mongolia in order to extend Tuan's influence into that region.[168] Hsu was armed with powers sufficient to enable him to establish a military-political base in underpopulated Mongolia. As northwest border commissioner (*hsi-pei ch'ou-pien shih*), he enjoyed the virtual power of civil rule in Mongolia and the right to take steps necessary to colonize the region and develop mining, forestry, salt production, and education.[169] After participating at Urga in negotiations leading to the renunciation of Mongolia's independence on November 22, 1919, he was also appointed supervisor of Outer Mongolian affairs (*Wai-Meng shih-i tu-pan*).[170]

Hsu's expansion into Mongolia alarmed Ts'ao K'un and Chang Tso-lin. In a memorial asking for the establishment of the office of northwest border commissioner, Hsu had written, "Now, the Northwest extends from Ch'ech'enkan in the east, to the Altai in the west, and from the Russian border in the north, to Chahar and Suiyuan in the south."[171] This description defined a vast area that

168. Hsu Tao-lin, *Hsu Shu-cheng hsien-sheng wen-chi nien-p'u ho-k'an* (Taipei, 1962), pp. 225–27, 237; *STSP* 1919.3.21.2; *PYCF*, 5:91. Mongolian developments included the decline of Russian influence in Outer Mongolia (independent since 1911) during the confusion of the Russian revolution; the consequent increase of Japanese influence there; and the turning of some Mongol kings and princes to China in hopes of checking Japan and countering the growing influence of the Dalai Llama.

169. Hsu Tao-lin, *Hsu Shu-cheng nien-p'u*, pp. 227–31; the text of the regulations of the office of northwest border commissioner is quoted in part in *ibid.*, pp. 245–46; they were promulgated on July 18, 1919; also see *PYCF*, 5: 91–92. These regulations had to be passed by the House, where the Chi-wei Club made an unsuccessful effort to block them; *STSP* 1919.7.6.2; *Tung-fang tsa-chih* 16, no. 8 (August 1919): 224.

170. *PYCF*, 5: 92; Hsu Tao-lin, *Hsu Shu-cheng nien-p'u*, pp. 231–61.

171. Hsu Tao-lin, *Hsu Shu-cheng nien-p'u*, p. 227.

amounted to present-day Outer Mongolia and parts of Inner Mongolia and Sinkiang. Ch'ech'enkan, a huge region in eastern Outer Mongolia, bordered on Heilungkiang, where Chang Tso-lin had only recently solidified his control. Hsu's self-assigned southern border was threatening to Ts'ao K'un because Chahar, itself militarily weak, touched upon Chihli in the north.[172]

To counter Hsu, Ts'ao and Chang turned to Hsu's main rival among Tuan Ch'i-jui's followers, Chin Yun-p'eng, a man with whom both men enjoyed connections and who was the chief advocate of a policy of peacefully seeking a new consensus. Chin had served as Tuan's aide in War Participation Army headquarters, where he had found himself competing for influence with Hsu Shu-cheng. Competition had engendered mutual dislike.[173] Chin was related by marriage to Chang Tso-lin, was a sworn brother of Ts'ao K'un, and came from the same province (Shantung) as Ts'ao's follower, Wu P'ei-fu. Having served as an instructor in the Yunnan Military Academy in the late Ch'ing, he had ties with a number of the southern military leaders. In short, Chin was exceedingly well placed in the network of connections to pursue a policy of consensus-building and negotiation on behalf of Tuan Ch'i-jui. In the autumn of 1919, Ts'ao and Chang threw their support to Chin, precipitating a struggle within the Tuan faction over the policy it should follow.[174]

The immediate trigger was Kung Hsin-chan's resignation as acting prime minister (Kung had succeeded Ch'ien Neng-hsun). Central government salaries were more than two months in arrears; issuance of the Eighth Year Bonds had been postponed because of controversies surrounding them; loan negotiations with the foreign banking consortium were not progressing well; warlords continued to press for funds; and the Autumn Festival, when the government would be expected to pay at least part of the back salaries of its employees, was approaching. On September 4, 1919, Kung called on President Hsu and informed him that he would like to resign.[175]

Kung's resignation would reduce the number of full cabinet members in

172. *PYCF*, 5:92–96, 129; *NCH* 1920.3.13.677; Boorman and Howard, *Biographical Dictionary*, 2:145. On Ts'ao's fears of Hsu, cf. *NCH* 1919.7.19.154; Wen Kung-chih, *Tsui-chin san-shih nien, pien* 3, p. 97. Ts'ao's fears were justified, as shown by the use of Hsu's troops against Ts'ao in the Anfu-Chihli war; *ibid*, pp. 97–99. My interpretation of Ts'ao K'un's political position differs somewhat from that of Li Chien-nung and T'ao Chü-yin. These authors take Ts'ao's opposition to Tuan Ch'i-jui as needing no explanation, growing naturally out of Feng Kuo-chang's opposition to Tuan. Actually, Ts'ao was pro-Tuan for a considerable time until he broke with Tuan. See Appendix.

173. *PYCF*, 5:79; *AHKC*, 1:70.

174. Cf. *PYCF*, 5:130.

175. *STSP* 1919.9.7.2, 9.19.2, 9.20.2. The Autumn Festival, the fifteenth day of the eighth lunar month, fell on October 8, 1919.

Peking to four,[176] making a complete renegotiation of cabinet seats almost mandatory. Hsu sent secret telegrams to the major warlords to ask their opinion on whether the cabinet should be reorganized. He hoped that in order to avoid a cabinet crisis they would answer supporting Kung and would decrease their pressure on him for funds.[177] Prompt replies were received from Ts'ao K'un and Chang Tso-lin. Instead of supporting Kung, however, the two telegrams argued in similar language that it was not healthy for the government to continue long without a prime minister approved by parliament. They had heard that Kung wished to resign and that Chin Yun-p'eng was being mentioned as a successor. Chin was a capable person who would certainly satisfy the people's wishes for a prime minister. If Kung insisted upon resigning, Chin would be a most satisfactory candidate to organize a formal cabinet.[178]

When these telegrams were received, Kung visited the president and reiterated his request to resign, which Hsu granted. Chin took office on September 25 amid a flurry of congratulatory telegrams from Chang, Ts'ao, Wu P'ei-fu, and others.[179] Communications Clique bankers, who had withheld their assistance from Kung, swiftly lent the Chin cabinet sufficient funds to tide it over the Autumn Festival.[180] The outlook for conclusion of a $5.5 million loan from the Pacific Development Corporation brightened; Chou Tzu-ch'i hurried to Tientsin to negotiate with the visiting American financiers.[181]

176. Foreign Minister Lu Cheng-hsiang was still in Europe. Of the other cabinet members originally approved by parliament, only Chin Yun-p'eng, Liu Kuan-hsiung, Chu Shen, and T'ien Wen-lieh were still serving.

177. STSP 1919.9.23.2.

178. STSP 1919.9.27.2.

179. STSP 1919.9.24.2, 9.25.2, 9.27.2, 9.28.2.

180. STSP 1919.10.5.2, 10.7.2, 10.12.2, 10.13.2. The banks mentioned are the Bank of China, the Bank of Communications, the Yien-yeh (Salt) Bank, and the Exchange Bank of China. The sum loaned was around Mex. $4 or $5 million. The reported participation of the New Communications Clique in these loans, if true, would indicate that they had broken with the Anfu Club in the aftermath of the May 4 events. STSP 1920.1.8.2 reports a formal decision of the Communications Clique leaders to ally with Chin. Also cf. NCH 1920.2.14. 416. This strategy was to prove rewarding. Chin survived the Chihli-Anfu war as prime minister, and the Communications Clique became the financial basis of a series of Chin cabinets that lasted until December 1921.

181. STSP 1919.10.13.2; PYCF, 5: 89. Known as the Wine and Tobacco Loan because it was secured on the wine and tobacco taxes, the loan was concluded at the end of November. At the same time, another loan was concluded with the Continental and Commercial Trust and Savings Bank of Chicago, but this was only a refinancing of a previous debt. The Pacific Development Corporation Loan represented free funds for governmental and political use. Thus, because it violated the consortium agreement, it was strongly opposed by the powers. See Kōjima Shōtarō, Shina saikin daiji nempyō, pp. 450–51; Chia Shih-i, Ts'ai-cheng shih, hsu-pien, pien 4, pp. 143–46.

To win quick parliamentary passage of his nomination, Chin promised the Anfu Club the posts of finance, justice, communications, and perhaps interior in his cabinet.[182] After his approval by parliament, however, Chin made several changes in his cabinet nominations calculated to reduce the Anfu role. He now proposed to shift incumbent Minister of Agriculture and Commerce T'ien Wen-lieh, a political neutral, to the sensitive interior post for which the Anfu Club had favored Wu Ping-hsiang, replacing T'ien with his subordinate, Chang Chih-t'an.[183] Most important, instead of appointing Anfu's Li Ssu-hao as minister of finance, Chin now proposed to appoint Chou Tzu-ch'i.[184]

Chin's desire to solidify his emerging alliance with the Communications Clique and to reward the clique for its recent financial support was understandable, but equally understandable was the Anfu Club's vociferous opposition to the appointment of its enemy, Chou, to the post where he would be able to control the club's major source of funds. Chin's tactic of reneging on his word after the Anfu Club had supported him in parliament was also infuriating. Furthermore, before announcing his nominations for the cabinet posts, Chin had secretly wired the major tuchuns asking their support for his nominees, so that, by the time he revealed his preferences to the Anfu Club, he had received or was about to receive telegrams of support for his list from several major

182. Parliament, having ended its 1919 session on August 31, had reconvened on September 10 in a "provisional session" (*lin-shih hui-i*) necessitated, so he M.P.'s said, by unsettled business such as the need to establish a formal cabinet (cf. *STSP* 1919.8.13.2, 8.28.2). Before submission of his own name to parliament for approval, Chin promised to Anfu Club members the ministries of Finance (Li Ssu-hao), Justice (Yao Chen), and Communications (Chu Shen); said he was considering Wu Ping-hsiang for the Ministry of the Interior; and promised the post of cabinet secretary-general to Tseng Yü-chün of the Anfu Club. In most of the other posts, he said he intended to retain the incumbents. (*STSP* 1919.10.25.2, 10.26.2, 10.27.2; *PYCF*, 5:88). Chin's name was submitted to parliament on October 28, was approved by the House on October 31, by the Senate on November 4, and was gazetted on November 5 (*STSP* 1919.10.29.2, 10.31.2, 11.2.2, 11.5.2, 11.6.2).

183. *MJTC*, *chüan* 5, p. 107; *GJMK*, 1932, pp. 236–37; "*SSG*," pp. 13–14; *PYCF*, 5: 87–88; *AHKC*, 1:72; Hsu Tao-lin, *Hsu Shu-cheng nien-p'u*, p. 212, note 3.

184. The cabinet secretary-generalship, which had been promised to Tseng Yü-chün, went instead on November 6 to Hsu Shih-ch'ang's aide, Kuo Tse-yun (for biographical information, see *GJMK*, 1924, p. 721; *STSP* 1919.11.7.2). Chin also decided to retain incumbent Minister of Justice Chu Shen, instead of replacing him with Yao Chen, and to appoint Tseng Yü-chün rather than Chu as minister of communications. Chu, Yao, and Tseng were all Anfu Club members, so the net effect of these changes was to deprive the Anfu Club of one position, the secretary-generalship of the cabinet.

Furthermore, Chin decided to replace Minister of the Navy Liu Kuan-hsiung with another naval officer, Sa Chen-ping, instead of retaining Liu as originally planned. This was a noncontroversial decision. Chin also changed his nominee for minister of education from Chang Chih-t'an to Hsia Shou-k'ang. This at first drew no political fire but later became a political issue, as recounted below. *STSP* 1919.11.2.2, 11.4.2. 11.5.2, 11.6.2.

warlords.[185] The struggle between the two wings of the Tuan faction was now in the open, with Chin appealing outside the boundaries of the faction for support against the Anfu Club, and the club reflecting Hsu Shu-cheng's opposition to the growth in Chin's influence.

When the Anfu Club learned of Chin's new cabinet nominations, therefore, there was considerable sentiment for rejecting the whole list and demanding that Chin n j   ce precisely those persons he had promised to name prior to his approval by parliament. Finally, however, the club decided to focus its opposition on four of the nominations, those of Chou Tzu-ch'i, Chang Chih-t'an, T'ien Wen-lieh (although they would support him for minister of agriculture and commerce), and Hsia Shou-k'ang, the proposed minister of education. The club threatened that if Chin did not revise his list to meet its objections, it would block parliamentary action on the nominations. Chin, however, refused to yield. Negotiations were frozen.[186]

The deadlock called forth intervention by Tuan. Utilizing as emissaries several members of his faction who had not become involved in the dispute,[187] Tuan obtained Chin's and President Hsu's agreement to nominate Li Ssu-hao after all for the finance post while appointing Chou Tzu-ch'i to the important job of head of the Currency Reform Bureau.[188] He then persuaded the Anfu Club to accept Chin's cabinet list with this single change.[189] The nominations came before the House on November 28 and the Senate December 2; all passed except—as a final protest—the inessential nominations of Chang Chih-t'an and Hsia Shou-k'ang.

Chin's cabinet, however, was soon plunged again in crisis brought on by Anfu enmity. The fuse of the new conflict was the "Honan tuchun question" of February 1920.[190]

Honan was controlled by Chao T'i, who was allied with Tuan Ch'i-jui. But Chao was not considered a reliable ally, nor were his troops adequate to stand in the way of those of Wu P'ei-fu, who was threatening to withdraw his troops

185. STSP 1919.11.10.2, 11.11.2, 11.13.2; PYCF, 5: 88.

186. STSP 1919.11.8.2, 11.9.2, 11.10.2, 11.11.2, 11.12.2, 11.13.2, 11.16.2, 11.17.2; AHKC, 1:72. Hsia Shou-k'ang was a follower of Li Yuan-hung and had won high academic credentials during the Ch'ing. MJTC, chüan 4, p. 28; GJMK, 1924, p. 532.

187. These were Ch'ü Ying-kuang, a follower of Tuan's and governor of Chin's home province, Shantung; Wang Chih-lung, the Anfu Club leader who was secretary to Anhwei Military Governor Ni Ssu-ch'ung; and Fu Liang-tso, chief of staff of Tuan's Border Defense Affairs office and a trusted former subordinate of Hsu Shih-ch'ang. On Ch'ü, see GJMK, 1924, p. 726; GJMK, 1932, p. 89; Who's Who, p. 69; on Fu, see ATTA, chüan 2, p. 22; GJMK, 1924, p. 743; HSC, pp. 68-69; STSP 1918.9.12.2.

188. STSP 1919.11.18.2, 11.19.2, 11.20.2, 11.21.2, 11.22.2, 11.23.2, 11.29.2, 12.3,2, 12.4.2.

189. STSP 1919.11.26.2, 11.29.2; PYCF, 5:90.

190. See PYCF, 5:130-33.

from the Hunan front toward Peking via Chao's province. (Although Peking probably did not know it, the Canton government had made Wu a positive offer of financial support for the expenses of removing his troops north.)[191] Tuan prevailed upon the cabinet to pass an order elevating Chao to a sinecure in Peking and replacing him with Tuan's relative, Wu Kuang-hsin.[192]

The decision to replace Chao naturally aroused vociferous opposition from Wu P'ei-fu and other anti-Anfu warlords. Chao T'i decided to resist any attempt to replace him, broke off his alliance with Tuan, and openly joined the anti-Anfu camp (now known as the "eight-province alliance" because it consisted of Chihli, the three Yangtze provinces, Chang Tso-lin's three Manchurian provinces, and Honan). The effort to appoint Wu Kuang-hsin had ultimately to be abandoned.

Chin Yun-p'eng's role in the affair drew the Anfu Club's ire. After Wu Kuang-hsin's appointment had passed the cabinet, it was sent to President Hsu for promulgation, but Hsu refused to seal and publish it. Chin had submitted his resignation in protest on February 27 and had been given two days' leave. What the Anfu Club objected to was that, after taking this brief leave and receiving a number of emissaries from President Hsu urging him not to resign, Chin had agreed to continue in his post and had resumed his duties in March. The Anfu Club claimed that Chin's resignation was an inadequate gesture of protest and betrayed insufficient loyalty to Tuan. What was really at stake, of course, was the policy to be followed by the Tuan faction with respect to Ts'ao K'un and Chang Tso-lin. Chin's failure to fight more vigorously on the Honan question reflected his reluctance to see the faction adopt a policy of military confrontation with the two warlords. To clear the way for such a policy, the Anfu Club felt it would be necessary to remove Chin from the prime ministership.[193]

On March 4, the three Anfu members of the Cabinet—Chu Shen, Tseng Yü-chün, and Li Ssu-hao—absented themselves from a regularly scheduled cabinet meeting.[194] When Chin telephoned to remind them of the meeting, he

191. PYCF, 5:131. Wu's followers confirm his acceptance of this bribe in Wu P'ei-fu hsien-sheng chi (Taipei, 1960), p. 337.

192. On Wu Kuang-hsin, see MJTC, chüan 8, p. 149; GJMK, 1932, p. 790; ATTA, chüan 2, pp. 14–15; Jimbutsu jihyō 2, no. 8 (December 1924): 8–10.

193. STSP 1920.2.29.2, 3.1.2, 3.2.2, 3.3.2, 3.4.2; PYCF, 5:133. T'ao's account of this controversy is uncharacteristically inaccurate. He states that the three cabinet members submitted their resignations on March 4; in fact, they did not do so until March 9. T'ao states that on March 4 Tuan Ch'i-jui ordered the three to return to their cabinet duties and that the crisis therefore ended that day; in fact, the crisis continued nearly to the end of March.

194. STSP 1920.3.5.2. These ministers, with most of the others, had also been absent from the March 2 cabinet meeting, but since that was the first meeting after Chin's return to

learned that Li Ssu-hao had asked for a leave of absence, while Chu and Tseng gave excuses for being unable to attend. Chin reported these events to Hsu Shih-ch'ang, and when Hsu sent his aide, Wu Chi-sun, to interview the three ministers, it emerged that they were offended by Chin's "lack of sincerity" in offering his resignation over the Honan question and wanted him to "reflect" (*fan-hsing*) on his lack of any good policy to meet the need of the times.[195] If Chin did not arrest his drift toward cooperation with the Anfu Club's enemies and adopt a more complaisant attitude toward the club, they would resign and topple the cabinet.

Chin sought a solution to the impasse through mediators. Tuan Ch'i-jui, who could have offered decisive support for Chin, for the moment refused to take sides in the dispute. Finally, on March 8, T'ien Wen-lieh took up the mediator's burden, making visits to Chin, Tuan, Hsu, and the three Anfu ministers. But T'ien carried no conciliatory message from Chin to the three ministers. He could only urge them to abandon their boycott of the cabinet meetings. Therefore, the next day, the three ministers called on President Hsu and submitted their resignations. These were returned to them the next day. The three, however, announced that as long as Chin continued as prime minister, they would repeatedly offer their resignations and stay away from cabinet meetings, meanwhile continuing to fulfill the necessary ministerial duties on an interim basis.[196]

Chin, however, was the epitome of coolness. Cabinet meetings were held as usual on Tuesdays, Thursdays, and Saturdays. Before each meeting, Chin politely telephoned the absent ministers to remind them of the meeting in case they had forgotten. The discomfited ministers gave pretexts for being unable to attend.[197]

Chin's confidence was doubtless founded on the knowledge that Ts'ao K'un and Chang Tso-lin supported him. Probably it was also based in part on the knowledge that the Anfu Club position in parliament was weakening. The 1920 parliamentary session, which had opened March 1, had as yet no quorum;[198] in the meantime, Chin had taken steps to woo some of the M.P.'s away

---

office, it was presumed that they had not realized there would be a meeting that day, and no attention was paid to their absence; *STSP* 1920.3.3.2.

In addition to the three Anfu ministers, Acting Minister of Foreign Affairs Ch'en Lu stayed away from the March 4 cabinet meeting and asked for a leave of absence. At first, it was thought he was cooperating with the Anfu ministers but it turned out that his action was connected with developments in foreign affairs and was unrelated to the Anfu ministers' action. Ch'en returned to his cabinet duties on March 6; *STSP* 1920.3.5.2, 3.7.2.

195. *STSP* 1920.3.5.2, 3.6.2.

196. *STSP* 1920.3.6.2, 3.7.2, 3.8.2, 3.9.2, 3.10.2, 3.11.2, 3.12.2.

197. E.g., see *STSP* 1920.3.10.2, 3.12.2, 3.15.2.

198. *STSP* 1920.3.3.2, 3.15.2. It did not get a quorum until May. See *STSP* 1920.5.12.2, 5.14.2.

from the club. During the cabinet crisis of late 1919, Chin had revived an anti-Anfu parliamentary group called the Chi-wei Club.[199] In May, when the house finally achieved a bare quorum, the Fengtien and Chihli delegations deserted the Anfu Club en masse.[200] At that point, the strength of the pro-Chin forces reached about 100, a more significant figure than it would have been a year earlier because the number of M.P.'s in Peking was now much reduced: for example, at one reported meeting of the House, there were only 202 members present (out of 327), and seventy of them voted against the Anfu Club position.[201] Chin's confidence gave the three rebellious ministers pause. Their expected second submission of resignations was postponed.[202]

On March 13, Chang Tso-lin's follower, Wang Nai-pin,[203] arrived in Peking with a lengthy letter from Chang to Tuan Ch'i-jui.[204] The letter, solicited by Chin Yun-p'eng, urged Tuan to give strong support to Chin in the cabinet

199. Founded early in 1919, the Chi-wei Club was a blanket organization for anti-Anfu members of parliament. It consisted mainly of former members of the Communications Clique's Number Seven Club (which seems to have closed after Liang Shih-i resigned from the Senate), supporters of Hsu Shih-ch'ang, members of the Research Clique, and other miscellaneous oppositionists. We have no list of Chi-wei Club members. A partial list of members is provided in the form of the list of those signing a telegram issued by the club in June 1919: *STSP* 1919.6.19.2, but the telegram was signed only by senators. The size of the Chi-wei Club fluctuated from well over 100 in its earlier days, to a very few members after the fall of the Ch'ien Neng-hsün cabinet, to 100 or more again when it was taken over and supported by Chin Yun-p'eng during his struggles with the Anfu Club in late 1919. The figure of "over 100" is suggested by *STSP* 1918.11.10.2, which reports that Liang Shih-i held a meeting of M.P.'s opposing the Anfu Club and 157 attended. Probably most of these would have joined the Chi-wei Club. On the decline of the club, see *STSP* 1919.9.17.2, 9.20.2, 9.23.2. On its revival, see *STSP* 1919.11.12.2, 11.14.2.

The account of the Chi-wei Club given by Yang Yu-chiung, *Cheng-tang shih*, p. 109, is incorrect in most respects. Yang says the club was founded by an alliance between Ch'ien Neng-hsun and Chin Yun-p'eng; he thus telescopes the events of early 1919 with those of late 1919 and early 1920. He lists Huang Yun-p'eng as a leader of the club. Huang was an active leader of the Anfu Club, and I find no evidence he was involved in the Chi-wei Club.

Like the Anfu Club, the Chi-wei Club was supported with government funds. Members of the Chi-wei Club received appointments to the Postwar Economic Investigation Commission, which had been established by the cabinet on January 20, 1919 (*LSINP*, 2:2), and was under the direction of Ch'ien Neng-hsun's nephew-in-law, Yü Pao-hsien (*GJMK*, 1932, p. 6). The commission salaries of about Mex. $200 per month served as club "gratuities" for the Chi-wei Club members. Other club expenses were met through a "secret fund" drawn in the name of the commission (*STSP* 1919.4.2.2, 4.12.2).

200. *STSP* 1920.5.20.3, 5.21.2.

201. *STSP* 1920.5.14.2, 5.19.2.

202. *STSP* 1920.3.14.2, 3.5.2.

203. *MJTC, chüan* 3, p. 68; *GJMK*, 1924, p. 469; *STSP* 1919.11.22.2, 12.14.2.

204. *PYCF*, 5:134. *PYCF* gives the date as March 14. *STSP* 1920.3.16.2 gives the date as March 13, but without mentioning Wang Nai-pin.

crisis. It was difficult for Tuan to ignore this direct demand from the powerful Manchurian warlord, and he ordered Tseng Yü-chün, Chu Shen, and Li Ssu-hao to end their boycott of the cabinet meetings. (The three ministers returned to their duties at the next meeting.)[205] But Tuan also summoned Chin and took him to task for calling on outside help to settle a dispute within the ranks of the faction. He instructed Chin to wait until the crisis had settled down and then to "make his own decision whether to stay in office or go"—i.e., to quit the prime ministership.[206]

Tuan's dismissal of Chin signalled a fateful decision to eschew the route of compromise and conciliation, which Chin propounded, and to move toward a military test of strength with Ts'ao K'un and Chang Tso-lin. As the British chargé in Peking, Miles Lampson, observed, the March crisis "has brought out with remarkable precision the existence of two distinct military parties in the North. On the side of the President and Premier stand ranged the Military Governors of Fengtien and Chihli, with whom, for the time being at least, the three Yang-tsze Tuchuns, headed by the well-known Li [Ch'un] of Nanking, are allied. Opposed to them are Marshal Tuan and his satellite 'little Hsu' [Hsu Shu-cheng]. . . ."[207]

The Outbreak of War

Tuan's refusal to repudiate Hsu Shu-cheng and the Anfu Club brought an increase of pressure on him by the anti-Anfu tuchuns. When Tuan proved obdurate, events moved rapidly toward a military confrontation.

Early in March, Wu P'ei-fu cancelled leaves among his troops and began to send the military baggage of his forces north. Ts'ao K'un sent six telegrams urging Peking to grant Wu permission to come north. Representatives of the warlords of the eight-province alliance met in Mukden late in March and in Paoting (Ts'ao's headquarters) early in April. They decided to support Chin Yun-p'eng, to oppose the Anfu Club and Hsu Shu-cheng, to refrain from opposition to Tuan Ch'i-jui personally, and to back the policy of northward withdrawal of Wu P'ei-fu's army from the Hunan front.[208]

Chin Yun-p'eng made one more effort to persuade Tuan. On the basis of letters and telegrams of support from the tuchuns around the country, he sent T'ien Wen-lieh to ask Tuan whether he should still plan to quit his post after twenty days. Tuan replied that, in his opinion, Chin could not solve the many

205. *STSP* 1920.3.15.2, 3.16.2, 3.17.2.
206. *STSP* 1920.3.16.2.
207. F.O. 371/5338, F865/865/10, Despatch 177, Lampson to Curzon, Peking, March 25, 1920, confidential print, p. 1.
208. *PYCF*, 5:134–35.

difficulties with which he was faced and might as well resign. On March 28, Tuan removed himself from Peking to the resort town of T'uanho, on the pretext that he wished to relieve his friends of the obligation of making an elaborate observance of his birthday. Chin now showed his loyalty to Tuan by verbally submitting his resignation to President Hsu on March 30. Despite extensive efforts by Hsu Shih-ch'ang to use mediators to persuade Tuan to return to Peking, Tuan remained in T'uanho. Chin therefore submitted a written resignation May 8 and a second resignation on May 9. On May 14, Hsu granted Chin ten days' leave, appointing Minister of the Navy Sa Chen-ping as acting prime minister.[209]

Tuan now prepared for military confrontation. He ordered Hsu Shu-cheng to transfer his Northwest Border Defense Army to the Peking area. On May 20, Wu P'ei-fu began to bring his troops north from the Hunan border, reaching Hankow on May 31. With Wu's withdrawal, the southern forces under T'an Yen-k'ai flowed northward through Hunan and easily overran the province with no resistance from the numerous but demoralized troops of Tuan's ally, Chang Ching-yao. Wu's forces reached Chengchow (Honan) on June 7. Wu went to Ts'ao K'un's headquarters on June 15 for a conference with representatives of the anti-Anfu provinces. On the following day, Ts'ao K'un telegrammed Peking asking to be relieved of the post of high inspecting commissioner of Szechwan, Kwangtung, Hunan, and Kiangsi—the prestigious appointment he had received from Tuan Ch'i-jui to cement their alliance two years earlier.[210]

In the midst of the war preparations, the House of Representatives met on June 17 and incongruously decided to extend its 1920 session for another two months.[211] In Shanghai, there was ironically a stir of life at the long moribund North-South peace conference. Because the existence of the Anfu parliament was now threatened by the aggressive posture of the eight-province alliance and the Canton parliament had recently fallen out with its military sponsors, the interests of the two parliaments suddenly converged on reaching an agreement that would buttress their legal standing and stay the hands of their enemies. Wang I-t'ang, who had been appointed chief northern delegate in August to guarantee that no agreement would be reached, and whom chief southern delegate T'ang Shao-i had consistently refused to see, was now received by T'ang, and the Anfu Club telegrammed urging the rapid conclusion of peace. Lu Jung-t'ing, however, quickly pricked the bubble by replacing T'ang with Lu's ally, Wen Tsung-yao.[212]

209. *STSP* 1920.3.23.2, 4.1.2, 4.2.2, 4.3.2, 4.4.2, 4.5.2, 4.6.2, 4.7.2, 4.8.2, 4.11.2, 4.14.2, 5.7.2, 5.10.2, 5.11.2, 5.13.2, 5.14.2, 5.15.2.

210. *PYCF*, 5:142–47, 152–54; *ATTA, chüan* 4, 1962 reprint ed., pp. 71–80.

211. *STSP* 1920.6.18.2.

212. Li Chien-nung, *Political History*, pp. 398–99; *STSP* 1920.6.9.2, 6.10.2; *PYCF*, 5:

In a final attempt to avoid a military confrontation, President Hsu summoned Ts'ao K'un, Li Ch'un, and Chang Tso-lin to Peking. Only Chang, however, arrived on June 19, impressively accompanied by two battalions of guards and a company of machine gunners. Upon his arrival, Chang adopted the mediator's role, calling first on Hsu Shih-ch'ang, then on Tuan Ch'i-jui, and achieving their agreement on what he presented as the central issue, the retention of Chin Yun-p'eng as prime minister. Chang then proceeded to Paoting, where Ts'ao K'un, Wu P'ei-fu, and representatives of their allies were meeting, and was told that, in addition to the retention of Chin, the Paoting group demanded the removal of the three Anfu ministers from the cabinet, the disbandment of the Anfu Club, the recall of Wang I-t'ang as chief northern delegate in Shanghai, and the placing of the Border Defense Army under the direct control of the Ministry of War. Chang returned with these unacceptable demands to Peking. On July 7, he returned to Fengtien.[213] On July 5, Tuan ordered the Border Defense Army, rechristened the National Pacification Army (*Ting-kuo chün*), to move south toward its confrontation with the troops of Ts'ao and Wu. Each side issued a barrage of telegrams exposing the crimes of its adversaries.

The conflict was over almost before it began. In light fighting, assisted by Chang Tso-lin's troops, the Chihli troops defeated those of the National Pacification Army at several locations between July 14 and July 18 and forced one of Tuan's commanders, Ch'ü T'ung-feng, to surrender. On the 19th, President Hsu issued an order for a cease-fire and Tuan Ch'i-jui, recognizing his defeat, asked the president to deprive him of all his posts and honors.[214]

Prominent Anfu Club leaders and followers of Tuan fled "like dogs of a dead master" to legation quarter refuges—the Japanese Legation, the German Hospital, the Hôtel des Wagon-Lits. The pro-Anfu newspaper, the *Kung-yen pao*, which had been predicting a victory for Tuan's forces, ceased publication. Ten Anfu leaders—Hsu Shu-cheng, Tseng Yü-chün, Tuan Chih-kuei, Ting Shih-yuan, Chu Shen, Wang Chih-lung, Liang Hung-chih, Yao Chen, Li Ssu-hao, and Yao Kuo-chen—were ordered proscribed and their houses searched—fruitlessly, since they had fled with their property to the legation quarter or Tientsin.[215] Tuan Ch'i-jui himself was treated courteously and permitted to go into dignified retirement in Tientsin, where he was to concentrate on Buddhist studies and await an opportunity to return to politics. He was joined in political exile by many of his followers.[216] The Border Defense Army was ordered

80, 84-85; *NCH* 1920.6.12.643-45; *GJMK*, 1932, pp. 46-47.

213. *ATTA, chüan* 5, pp. 1-17; *PYCF*, 5:153-58.

214. *ATTA, chüan* 6 and 7, 1962 reprint ed., pp. 88-103; *PYCF*, 5:162-69; Li Chien-nung, *Political History*, pp. 396-97.

215. *ATTA, chüan* 7, pp. 14-15, *chüan* 8, pp. 7-18.

216. See Wu T'ing-hsieh, *Ho-fei chih-cheng nien-p'u* (Taipei, 1962), pp. 82-83. Followers who went with Tuan included Wang I-t'ang, Yao Chen, Yao Kuo-chen, Li Ssu-hao, and Tseng Yü-chün.

disbanded,[217] and so was the Anfu Club—although when Tuan and his faction reemerged in Peking politics late in 1924, Wang I-t'ang issued a circular telegram announcing the dissolution of the club, as if to suggest rather triumphantly that it had never been affected by the government order of 1920.[218]

Factionalism and Frustration, 1918–20

In the events of 1918–20, Peking's political leaders experienced both the seductive accessibility of factional forms of organization and the frustrating way in which factionalism kept solid political accomplishments just out of reach. Taking the opportunity of the dissolution of the old parliament in the Chang Hsun restoration and the impending election of a new president, the Tuan Ch'i-jui faction worked hard to construct a military and parliamentary alliance that could unify control of the government and overcome the paralyzing contentiousness that had been the cause of the restoration. But the fruit could not be grasped: although the Tuan faction was able to control parliament, it could not match this achievement with the extraparliamentary consensus necessary for a successful presidency, and Tuan had to cede the office to a dark horse, Hsu Shih-ch'ang.

Seizing the initiative, Hsu in turn worked skillfully to construct a factional consensus behind the policy of a negotiated peace with the South. Just when success seemed close, factions both north and south broke away from the emerging agreement and caused it to crumble. Hsu's damaged prestige, his only political resource, suffered further attrition in the factional free-for-all that followed the outbreak of the May Fourth Movement.

It was now once again Tuan Ch'i-jui's turn to act. He could make another effort to unify power either by bargaining with rival factions or by confronting them on the field of battle. He chose the latter strategy, and it failed.

In the mosaic of motivations and tactics making up these events, two themes form the ruling pattern. First, the recurrent recourse to the ideals and procedures of the republic, with the hope that these will provide the key to political unity and national strength. And second, the recurrent effort to organize consensus around these ideals and procedures in the form of factions and factional alliances. The frustrating contradiction lay in the incompatibility of the goal and the means adopted to achieve it: the very imminence of success was each time the signal for factional defections, and, with the deterioration of each arduously constructed factional alliance, the task of making the republic work had to start over again.

217. F.O. 371/5339, F2552/865/10, Despatch 578, Clive to Curzon, Peking, August 16, 1920, confidential print, p. 1.
218. Kao Yin-tsu, *Ta-shih chi*, p. 71; *AHKC*, 1:1; *Ching pao* 1924.11.25 in *GSK* 1924.11.331.

VI

THE RETURN TO CONSTITUTIONAL ORTHODOXY, 1922

For two years after the Anfu-Chihli war of 1920, Peking hung in placid suspension between the poles of Paoting and Mukden. Prime Minister Chin Yun-p'eng held the balance between his relative by marriage, Chang Tso-lin, and his blood brother, Ts'ao K'un, assuring central government performance of essential diplomatic and administrative tasks without attempting to aggrandize from his official base. The Communications Clique kept the government solvent in exchange for the communications and finance portfolios. President Hsu Shih-ch'ang retreated to a ceremonial role. With no parliament in session to complicate matters, contretemps were minor. Political adjustment occurred through civil wars in the provinces.[1]

The situation was necessarily temporary: Peking was too valuable a resource to remain indefinitely outside the political struggle. Beneath the surface, the North China military balance was shifting and, in the spring of 1922, it moved toward a major test of strength. The Chihli-Fengtien war ended with Chihli victory. Peking was thrust again to center stage.

War had a cleansing effect on the political atmosphere and seemed to offer a final opportunity to make the republic work. The belief grew that if only the point where the republic had left the rails could be located, it could be "put back on the right track" (*shang cheng kuei-tao*). Let constitutional orthodoxy (*fa-t'ung*) be restored, and a stable republic might yet emerge.

Chihli's Proposal and the Response

The Chihli-Fengtien war broke out in the Peking area late in April 1922; a few days into May, the fighting stopped, with the Chihli Clique victorious.[2] Victory

---

1. For a detailed account of these two years, see *PYCF*, 5: 171–224 and 6: 1–97. There was a relatively noisy minor political crisis when the cabinet was reorganized in May 1921.

2. Kao Yin-tsu, *Ta-shih chi*, p. 94; Li Chien-nung, *Political History*, p. 413. For telegrams,

put the Chihli leaders in a position to attempt national reunification. With Chang Tso-lin's defeat, the chief obstacle was Sun Yat-sen. Sun's Canton government, with which Hsu Shih-ch'ang had tried to negotiate for national reunification in 1919, had gone through a number of metamorphoses but still existed as a rival to Peking; and Sun, after leaving Canton in 1919, had returned to the city late in 1920 to be elected "president of China" by the extraordinary session of the old parliament.[3]

The Chihli leaders now advanced a generous proposal to deal with Sun. They would concede all the demands upon which the Canton government based its claim to existence—the restoration of the Provisional Constitution in its pristine form,[4] the recall of the old parliament, the discarding of President Hsu Shih-ch'ang, and his replacement with Li Yuan-hung, the last president whose legitimacy Canton recognized. The proposal was launched by one of the Chihli leaders, Sun Ch'uan-fang,[5] in a public telegram. "The split in national unity between North and South is a calamity that arose from the constitutional problem (*fa-lü wen-t'i*)," Sun wrote, "and the direct way to reunify the country is to restore constitutional orthodoxy. We should invite Li Huang-p'i to return to office, convene the old parliament of 1917 and have it quickly complete the constitution and elect a vice-president."[6] On May 28, Sun issued a second telegram (this time addressed to Hsu Shih-ch'ang and Sun Yat-sen) in which the proposal and its rationale were set forth more fully:

Since the break in constitutional continuity [in 1917], politics have been in disorder. The South brought together the members of the old parliament, elected President Sun, and organized the Canton government as a rallying point. The North elected the new parliament and President Hsu and used the Peking government as a basis to resist the South. Whose actions were legal and whose were illegal will be argued by later generations. But so long as North and South oppose one another, we will continue to have the uninterrupted civil war and internal disorder, the mass poverty and national instability that threaten our national existence. If we seek the origins of all this, how can it be anything other than

---

battle reports, etc., see *Chih-Feng ta-chan shih* ([Shanghai], 1922), *passim*; and [Chang] Tzu-sheng, "Feng-Chih chan-cheng chi-shih," *Tung-fang tsa-chih* 19, no. 8 (April 25, 1922): 59–88. Although brief, the fighting was reported to have been severe and the casualties were estimated in the thousands; see F.O. 371/7997, F2139/84/10, Despatch 259, Alston to Curzon, Peking, May 9, 1922, confidential print, pp. 2–3; *Chih-Feng ta-chan shih*, pp. 70, 84–86.

3. Sharman, *Sun Yat-sen*, p. 213; Li Chien-nung, *Political History*, pp. 414–15. Sun was elected in April 1921.

4. That is, without the changes in the Parliamentary Organic Law and House and Senate election laws made in Peking in 1918.

5. *GJMK*, 1932, p. 209; Li Chien-nung, *Political History*, p. 421; *PYCF*, 6: 122.

6. This portion of the Sun telegram of May 15 is quoted in *LSINP*, 2: 227. On the Paoting conference, which preceded this, see *STSP* 1922.5.11.2, 5.13.2, 5.14.2, 5.15.2, 5.16.2, 5.25.2. For the whole course of events in May and early June, see Chang Tzu-sheng, "Li Yuan-hung fu-chih chi," *Tung-fang tsa-chih* 19, no. 12 (June 25, 1922): 53–57.

the dissolution of parliament [in 1917] and the breaking of constitutional law that began the disaster!

In my telegram of May 15, I advocated restoring constitutional continuity, hastening unification, and seeking national survival. Now I have received answers from various quarters, most of them agreeing with my proposal. . . . President Sun of Canton stands for restoration of the constitution; once it is restored, his responsibility will be over and he can retire covered with glory—why delay? President Hsu of Peking was elected by the new parliament; when the old parliament is restored and the new parliament disappears, his claim to the office loses its validity. I hope that both gentlemen, embodying the virtue of heaven, taking pity on the people's plight, discarding empty honors like wornout sandals, will resign immediately.[7]

The only problem with such sweet reasonableness was that the Chihli "concessions" had a very different significance in 1922 from what they would have had in 1917 when the demands were first advanced by the South. They now cost the Chihli leaders nothing they valued but, if accepted, would deprive Sun Yat-sen of his position as president, the Canton government of its right to exist, and Sun's nascent Northern Expedition of its *casus belli*.[8] Nonetheless, Sun Ch'uan-fang's proposal struck a deeply responsive chord in public opinion. As Lyon Sharman has written, "new hope awoke in the hearts of old patriots that China was about to find the lost path to constitutional government."[9] The famous good-government manifesto, "Our Political Proposals" ("Women ti cheng-chih chu-chang"), had just been published by sixteen eminent writers, lawyers, and educators, including Hu Shih and Ts'ai Yuan-p'ei—men with no vulgar political stake in the restoration of the constitution—demanding very nearly what the Chihli clique was offering.[10] Although their proposals went far beyond Sun's telegram, the two documents agreed that the first step

7. Text in Wang Ching-lien and T'ang Nai-p'ei, *Chung-hua min-kuo fa-t'ung ti-shan shih* ([Shanghai?], 1922), p. 111; partial text in *LSINP*, 2: 227.

8. Strictly speaking, the matter was more complicated. With the election of Sun as president in the context of a "formal" (*cheng-shih*) government with its own constitutional document (the *Chung-hua min-kuo cheng-fu tsu-chih ta-kang*), the Canton government no longer stood merely for the restoration of the status quo of 1917. It now implicitly regarded itself as a legitimate evolution from the last government under the Provisional Constitution and thus superior in legitimacy to any order that might be established in Peking on the basis of revived adherence to the Provisional Constitution. Thus, from this standpoint, Peking's revival of the Provisional Constitution could no longer undermine the legitimacy of the Canton government. Cf. *PYCF*, 6:15 (but T'ao's formulation of the matter seems to me misleading); *Kuo-fu nien-p'u* (Taipei, 1965), 2: 767–68; [Dazai Matsusaburō], *Chūka minkoku daijūnenshi* (Dairen, 1922), pp. 273–79. But this legalism did not suffice to stem the course of events; the public still regarded Canton in terms of "constitution-protection."

9. Sharman, *Sun Yat-sen*, p. 214.

10. The manifesto was published in Hu Shih's journal, *Nu-li chou-pao*, no. 2 (May 14, 1922), pp. 1–2. It had already come out in *Tung-fang tsa-chih* 19, no. 8 (April 25, 1922): 138–40.

in solving China's problems was to establish a constitutional regime: one with a proper constitution, a proper parliament, and a proper president. Once these institutions were in place, they would take on a vitality of their own, serving as bulwarks against disorder and a source of peace and prosperity. As twenty-two military officers argued in a public telegram on June 2,

Once constitutional orthodoxy is reestablished, all disorders can immediately be resolved. The completion of the constitution and the election of a new president can be completed in due order, and all issues such as the local government system and provincial autonomy can subsequently be solved. Once the nation has a unified governmental authority, political questions are susceptible to resolution through discussion.[11]

There were variant proposals, but all reflected the same basic assumptions. One suggestion was offered in a telegram of May 22 signed by Liang Ch'i-ch'ao, Ts'ai Yuan-p'ei, Sun Pao-ch'i, Ch'ien Neng-hsun, and eight other prestigious citizens. The telegram said that the 1917 parliament should be recalled to finish its original task of preparing a permanent constitution, while provincial delegates meeting in some neutral place could settle remaining concrete issues between North and South.[12] Another view, reflecting the public mistrust the old parliament had earned by its years of contentious bickering, was that the old parliament had outlived its legitimate term of office and that the institutions of the republic should therefore be renewed by a national convention (*kuo-shih hui-i*) representing all elements of the public. "The basic goal of the national convention," argued one proponent, "would be to abolish the rules and organs laid down by our present Provisional Constitution and laws, such as the parliament, courts, president, cabinet, tuchuns, provincial governors, and high inspecting commissioners, and set up all new ones."[13]

The difficulty with this sort of proposal, however, was exposed by critics. "Suppose you nine organizations in Shanghai can convene a national conven-

11. *STSP* 1922.6.7.3; text also in Wang Ching-lien and T'ang Nai-p'ei, *Chung-hua min-kuo*, pp. 116–18. The chief signer was Ch'i Hsieh-yuan.

12. For text, see *STSP* 1922.5.25.2 or Ting Wen-chiang, *Liang Jen-kung hsien-sheng nien-p'u ch'ang-pien ch'u-kao* (Taipei, 1962), 2: 616. For other examples of similar public responses at this time, see [Dazai Matsusaburō], *Chūka minkoku daijūichinenshi* (Dairen, 1923), pp. 206–7.

13. The quotation is from *STSP* 1922.5.13.2 editorial, paraphrasing or quoting Hsu Fo-su's "Kuo-shih hui-i lun" (On a national convention), of which I have been unable to find a copy. The editorial notes that similar proposals at this time were rife. Hsu was a member of the Research Clique; see Appendix. Another example of this odd combination of legalism and extralegalism is found in a proposal to have the various *fa-t'uan* and provincial assemblies, rather than the president, shoulder the responsibility of convening parliament, on the grounds that the convening of parliament under such national-popular auspices would avoid all arguments about parliament's right to exist. See *Tung-fang tsa-chih* 19, no. 6 (March 25, 1922): 3–4 (editorial).

tion in Shanghai," wrote one, "what is to prevent me from setting up some organizations in Hankow, gathering some vagabonds and beggars, and opening a big national convention? What if Chang San and Li Ssu set up their own national conventions in Canton or Loyang? Then who is discussing real 'national affairs' and who isn't? On the one hand, you want to put government back on the right track, and on the other hand you go about it in an illegal fashion; you use a method that is off the proper track to put government on the track. Isn't this a contradiction? Your carriage is facing south but heading north." The only way to create respect for law, it was argued, is persistently to restore the parliament every time it is dissolved illegally.[14]

The Sun Ch'uan-fang proposal, in short, carried the day with public opinion. One legal scholar buttressed it with a resourceful rationale for the recall of the 1917 parliament. The Canton parliament was illegal, he reasoned, because, as an "extraordinary" continuation of the second session rather than the beginning of a new, third session, it should have utilized Article 80 instead of Article 7 of the Parliamentary Procedures (*I-yuan fa*) to replace absent members; since Article 80 requires a quorum of half the membership, and since the Canton parliament lacked such a quorum, it used Article 7 and thus committed an offense that made it illegal. The 1917 parliament could therefore legally reconvene without worrying about the acts committed in its name in the interval.[15]

Although public opinion was overwhelmingly in favor of restoring constitutional orthodoxy,[16] there remained the scheme's targets, Sun Yat-sen and Hsu Shih-ch'ang, who tried to evade the logic of events. On May 5, when Chihli victory was clear, Hsu issued an order for both sides to return to their original positions, meanwhile recruiting a cadre of prominent political figures as mediators, in hopes of making an early and more militarily balanced peace.[17] He floated the idea of a political or reconstruction conference (*cheng-wu hui-i* or *shan-hou hui-i*) to meet in Peking to determine the postwar political structure;[18] such a conference would represent the voices of other factions besides the Chihli Clique and would therefore allow Hsu to play a mediating role. And he promoted the nomination of Peiyang elder Wang Shih-chen as prime minister, both by seeking support for Wang at Paoting and by urging Wang to take up

14. Fei Chueh-t'ien, "Chung-kuo cheng-chih pu-neng shang cheng-kuei ti chen-yin chi chin-hou ying-tsou ti tao-lu," *Tung-fang tsa-chih* 19, no. 11 (June 10, 1922): 9–10. The proposal to which Fei was responding may have been that of eight Shanghai organizations reprinted in Wang Ching-lien and T'ang Nai-p'ei, *Chung-hua min-kuo*, pp. 154–56.

15. Ch'en Ch'eng-tse, "Fa-t'ung wen-t'i ti yen-cheng chieh-shih," *Tung-fang tsa-chih* 19, no. 15 (August 10, 1922): 128–29.

16. For other telegrams. see *STSP* 1922.5.17.3, 5.19.2, 5.20.3, 5.28.2; Liu Ch'u-hsiang, *Kuei-hai cheng-pien chi-lueh* (Taipei, [1967]), pp. 5–21; *LSINP*, 2: 227–28.

17. *STSP* 1922.5.6.2.

18. *STSP* 1922.5.7.2, 5.10.2, 5.16.2.

office.[19] If Ts'ao K'un, out of respect for Wang's seniority in the Peiyang group, could be brought to back Wang's candidacy instead of insisting on his own puppet prime minister, it would complicate the political situation to Hsu's advantage and give him greater room for maneuver.

Hsu's efforts, however, were unavailing. The Fengtien defeat was irreversible; the idea of an aftermath conference did not catch on; and Wang judged the situation inhospitable to his political emergence.[20] On May 31, Hsu issued a public telegram describing his pleasure at the "loyal and intelligent" plan put forward by Sun Ch'uan-fang, which would enable him to retire to the countryside for a life of peace.[21] He moved his possessions out of the Presidential Palace to a private residence; on June 2, he took the train to retirement in Tientsin.[22] Hsu left behind him in Peking a caretaker cabinet headed by Chou Tzu-ch'i. The cabinet, doubtful of its legality when the president who had appointed it had been forced to resign because of questions about his legal standing, adopted the dual posture of a caretaker cabinet exercising the powers of an absent president and of a citizens' committee to uphold the peace.[23]

This left Sun Yat-sen to be disposed of. Sun had formally launched his Northern Expedition on May 4 and had no intention of resigning to the advantage of Ts'ao K'un and Wu P'ei-fu but on June 16 his hopes were dashed by a rebellion at the rear by a supporter, Ch'en Chiung-ming. Whatever Ch'en's motives for this betrayal, Sun Ch'uan-fang's suggestion for Sun's resignation provided the pretext. As Li Chien-nung has written:

The Chihli Clique's proposal for restoration of legal continuity received widespread enthusiastic support. Everyone hoped that Sun Yat-sen would now be able to roll up the banner of "constitution-protection," abolish the Canton presidency, and put an end to the war between North and South. This was a universal way of thinking on the part of a people anxious for peace and unity. . . . When Yeh Chü [a subordinate of Ch'en Chiung-ming] surrounded the Presidential Palace in Canton and issued a telegram declaring that Sun should resign together with Hsu in view of the fact that the task of restoring the con-

19. *STSP* 1922.5.13.2, 5.14.2, 5.17.2, 5.18.2, 5.19.2, 5.21.2, 5.25.2, 5.31.2.

20. *STSP* 1922.5.17.2, 5.18.2, 5.19.2.

21. Text: *LSINP*, 2:228; Wang Ching-lien and T'ang Nai-p'ei, *Chung-hua min-kuo*, pp. 112–13.

22. *STSP* 1922.6.2.2, 6.2.3. In departing, Hsu issued an interesting telegram summing up his view of his years in office. Ironically, in view of posterity's nationalistic rejection of his foreign policy, he regarded as his prime achievement the resolution of the Shantung issue and the raising of China's international standing. His major disappointments were the failure of the Shanghai peace conference, the outbreak of the Anfu-Chihli war, and the growth of militarism. For the text of the telegram and other details on Hsu's departure from Peking, see *STSP* 1922.6.4.2; *Hsu Shih-ch'ang ch'üan-chuan* ([Shanghai?], 1922), pp. 64–70; Wang Ching-lien and T'ang Nai-p'ei, *Chung-hua min-kuo*, pp. 113–15.

23. Chang Tzu-sheng, "Li Yuan-hung," pp. 57–58; also see *STSP* 1922.5.2.2, 5.3.2, 5.7.2, 6.2.2, 6.3.2; *LSINP*, 2:225.

situation was completed, various circles within the country, seeing that Hsu Shih-ch'ang had resigned and the constitution had been restored, also telegrammed supporting unification and urging Sun to step down; scholars and prominent figures like Ts'ai Yuan-p'ei all expressed the same sort of opinions.[24]

Sun was defeated militarily by Ch'en and, even more importantly, in the field of public opinion by Sun Ch'uan-fang's proposal: by August 9, when he fled Canton for Shanghai, the old parliament and Li Yuan-hung had already been restored in Peking.

The Old Parliament's Agitation for Restoration

There were four different conceptions of the meaning of "restoring parliament," each defended by a group of M.P.'s whose careers were tied to a particular embodiment of parliament. The ultimately successful group was the one whose quest had always seemed the most quixotic.

This group's leader, Wang Chia-hsiang,[25] had been the Senate Speaker in 1913–14 and 1916–17 but had not gone south to join the extraordinary session. He was not elected to the Anfu parliament (it is not clear whether or not he ran), and he was among 325 members expelled from the Canton parliament for not coming south. In 1918–22, Wang pursued a part-time business career, but because he lacked a bureaucratic or military base, his political future was tied to the hope of restoring the old parliament in its 1917, rather than 1919, form. The nucleus provided by Wang and others like him was from time to time augmented by waves of migrants from Canton, motivated either by the hostile political environment Canton intermittently provided or by the superior opportunities they believed were unfolding in Peking. For example, early in 1920, when the Canton military authorities were displaying a marked lack of enthusiasm for parliament, and the Peking government was toying with the idea of merging the new and old parliaments in a constitutional convention, two or three hundred old parliament M.P.'s gathered in Peking and Tientsin, where they were reportedly supported with funds from the government's Economic Investigation Bureau.[26] When the Anfu-Chihli war put an end to the hopeful scheme, most of the newly assembled M.P.'s dispersed.

On October 30, 1920, the hopes of the Wang group had suffered a blow. Still seeking a formula to resolved Peking's differences with Canton, President

24. Li Chien-nung, *Cheng-chih shih*, 2: 572–73. On the course of events, also see *PYCF*, 6:133–34. For text of the telegram issued by Ts'ai and other scholars, see *STSP* 1922.6.4.3.

25. *GJMK*, 1932, p. 18; *MJTC*, *chüan* 3, p. 60; *Who's Who*, p. 243; "SSG." pp. 21–22; *Kuo-shih kuan kuan-k'an* 2, no. 1 (January 1949): 67–70. Although *MJTC* says Wang joined the Canton parliament, *GJMK* and *Kuo-shih kuan kuan-k'an* make it clear that he did not.

26. *STSP* 1920.3.12.2, 3.25.2, 3.26.2, 3.28.2. The Economic Investigation Bureau was formerly called the Postwar Economic Investigation Commission.

Hsu issued an order that both northern and southern parliaments be dissolved and that a third parliament be elected. As a concession to the South, Hsu ordered that the new parliament be elected in accordance with the original, rather than the 1917 revised, electoral laws.[27] Ts'en Ch'un-hsuan, the southern leader who had agreed to Hsu's plan, was shortly driven out of Canton by Ch'en Chiung-ming, so the Canton parliament was not dissolved, but Peking nonetheless proceeded with the elections during the summer of 1921.[28] There was wide-spread public opposition;[29] warlords who belonged to neither of the dominant northern military groups refused to carry out the elections; and the Chihli-Fengtien war broke out before the elections were completed. The result was a curious entity known as the "New-New Parliament" (Hsin-hsin kuo-hui), which consisted solely of delegates to the House from eleven provinces and special districts, relatively few of whom seem to have been parliamentary veterans or nationally known politicians.[30] This group was another rival to the Wang Chia-hsiang group, taking the position that the only resolution of the republic's constitutional tangle lay in completing the "New-New Parliament" elections and convening it in Peking.

Sometime during 1921, on the other hand, the Wang group gained an important new ally, Wu Ching-lien. Wu was Speaker of the Canton parliament's House and leader of its largest club, the I-yu she, which was led by members of the original Kuo-min tang and enjoyed some 200 adherents.[31] Neither the reasons for Wu's defection from Canton nor its exact date are clear,[32] but its

27. Kōjima Shōtarō, Daiji nempyō, p. 457; for background, see PYCF, 5:202 and 6:1–5. The text of Hsu's order is printed in Wang Ching-lien and T'ang Nai-p'ei, Chung-hua min-kuo, p. 96.

28. See Cheng-fu kung-pao, ming-ling (orders), t'ung-kao (announcements), and kung-tien (public telegrams) sections, from August 1920, through November 1921, for numerous entries on the subject. Peking communicated with twenty provinces about the elections during this period. In many provinces, provincial assembly elections were conducted at the same time as those for the third parliament. I am indebted to Abraham T. C. Shen for searching Cheng-fu kung-pao for relevant entries.

29. F.O. 371/6615, F2861/81/10, Despatch 323, Alston to Curzon, Peking, June 14, 1921, confidential print, p. 1.

30. Roughly sixty New-New Parliament respresentatives signed a telegram that is reprinted in Wang Ching-lien and T'ang Nai-p'ei, Chung-hua min-kuo, pp. 103–5. The eleven districts or provinces listed here are Kiangsu, Anhwei, Shantung, Shansi, Shensi, Fengtien, Kirin, Heilungkiang, Sinkiang, Mongolia, and Tsinghai. One hundred and sixty-seven names can be gleaned from the election reports of eight provinces and two Mongol banners contained in Cheng-fu kung-pao, April 14, 19, 23, May 28, and June 27, 1921. A spot check indicates that relatively few of the names are found in the biographical references used for this study.

31. See Appendix; Kokumin gikai, Shina seitō no genjō, p. 9; "SSG," pp. 37–42; Yang Yu-chiung, Cheng-tang shih, p. 122; Hsieh Pin, Cheng-tang shih, pp. 81–82. Estimates of the size of parliamentary factions are notoriously unreliable.

32. Wu's activities throughout 1920 in connection with the Canton parliament are chroni-

political effects were pronounced. The manpower and prestige of Wang's forces were considerably increased, and the argument that the original old parliament, rather than the Canton version, ought to be restored suddenly became far more serious than it had been at any time since the extraordinary session began.

In 1922, even before the end of the Chihli-Fengtien war, Wang and Wu sent telegrams to members of the old parliament throughout the country urging them to gather in Shanghai.[33] As soon as the outcome of the war was clear, they and their followers began an energetic program to persuade the Chihli leaders to include restoration of the 1917 parliament in the postwar arrangements. As it happened, the Chihli strategy of out-constitution-protecting Sun Yat-sen dovetailed with the Wang-Wu group's proposals, and Sun Ch'uan-fang's first telegram (May 15) indicated provisional Chihli support for their program. Wang Chia-hsiang hastened to Tientsin to establish a headquarters (t'ung-hsin ch'u, lit., "communications office") for coordinating the effort to gather the scattered parliamentarians. On May 20, 1922, this was transformed into a more formal "preparatory office" (ch'ou-pei ch'u), with one or more M.P.'s from each province appointed as "preparatory personnel" (ch'ou-pei yuan). Firm Chihli Clique backing was indicated by the fact that the new preparatory office had its headquarters not in the offices of a private company, where the former communications office had been, but in the offices of the Chihli Provincial Assembly, whose speaker, Pien Shou-ch'ing, was a follower of Ts'ao K'un.[34] Simultaneous with the establishment of the preparatory office, Wu Ching-lien issued a telegram urging that, since the old parliament was the constitutional legislative organ of the nation, restoring it was the only way to unify the country.[35] Reception offices (chao-tai so) were established in Shanghai and Hankow to distribute financial aid to enable M.P.'s to travel to Tientsin. By the time Sun Ch'uan-fang's second telegram was issued on May 28, several hundred M.P.'s had reportedly gathered in the Peking-Tientsin area and there were another eighty or ninety in Shanghai.[36]

---

cled in *PYCF*, 5: 118–25. The last date on which I can identify Wu as working within the framework of the Canton parliament is January 5, 1921 (Wang Ching-lien and T'ang Nai-p'ei, *Chung-hua min-kuo*, p. 97; cf. further Dazai, *Daijūnenshi*, p. 278). It is not until May 1922, after the Chihli-Fengtien war, that Wu can be positively dated as working with Wang Chia-hsiang. The events of the intervening year and a half remain unclear, pending a close study of the politics of the Canton parliament.

33. *STSP* 1922.5.1.2.

34. *STSP* 1922.5.15.2, 5.22.2, 5.24.2. The formal roster of preparatory personnel did not consist of men actively engaged in preparing the convening of parliament; it was a representative listing of prominent members of all major factions in the old parliament, including one group that was later to oppose restoration vigorously (the left wing of the Kuo-min tang).

35. *STSP* 1922.5.23.2.

36. *STSP* 1922.5.25.2, 5.27.2. The number 400 given in *STSP* 1922.5.27.2 must be treated as an extremely rough estimate; cf. note 41 below.

All three rival bodies of M.P.'s tried to block the trend of events. The most feckless of these efforts was that of some 100 members of the disbanded and discredited Anfu parliament to defend the legitimacy of that body and argue for its recall.[37] Not surprisingly, this proposal gathered no momentum. Meanwhile, members of the New–New Parliament advanced the argument that they should be the ones to serve, since the old parliament had already exhausted its legal term in office. A telegram was sent to Wu P'ei-fu, and made public, quoting a July 1920, denunciation he had made of the old M.P.'s as traitors, and pointing out that his new position contradicted his former one. President Hsu was urged to order the remaining stages of the New–New Parliament election carried out. Since Hsu had issued the order for the New–New Parliament's election, it could not survive unless he continued as president. With his resignation, the hopes of the New–New Parliament died.[38]

The most considerable opposition came from within the old parliament. During May, when Wang and Wu were building support for the idea of restoration, the Canton parliament, which had elected Sun Yat-sen president, was still in session. For Wang and Wu to get a quorum[39] and make the Peking restoration a reality, they had to attract most of the M.P.'s still meeting in Canton. But many of these remained loyal to Sun. On June 3, the Canton parliament issued two public telegrams. The first rehearsed the arguments for the illegality of the 1917 parliament, and the exclusive legality of the Canton version, and pointed out that Wang Chia-hsiang had long ago been deprived of his seat in the body for his failure to come south. The second attacked Wu Ching-lien as ambitious, unscrupulous, and in league with the warlords. It claimed to be signed by 377 members of the extraordinary session, indicating Canton's continued ability to deprive Peking of a quorum.[40]

Ch'en Chiung-ming's coup against Sun on June 16 changed the calculus fundamentally. Ch'en announced his support of the Peking restoration, and the Canton M.P.'s fled the city. Accepting travel expenses and free rail passes from the preparatory office in Tientsin, many M.P.'s proceeded to Tientsin and Peking, where, in the last part of June, the number of M.P.'s rose dramatically.[41]

37. STSP 1922.6.5.2, 6.13.2. Text in Wang Ching-lien and T'ang Nai-p'ei, Chung-hua min-kuo, pp. 107–10.

38. STSP 1922.5.8.2, 5.16.2, 5.17.3, 5.20.2, 5.29.2, 5.30.2 editorial. See STSP 1922.7.13.2, for a memorial of some twenty members to new President Li, asking him to declare that, when the next parliamentary elections were held, their seats would be regarded as valid and requesting that in the meantime they be given government posts.

39. A quorum was a majority of the membership of 870, i.e., 436.

40. STSP 1922.6.14.3; texts in Wang Ching-lien and T'ang Nai-p'ei, Chung-hua min-kuo, pp. 119–20. A smaller group of M.P's loyal to Sun but resident in Shanghai issued a similar declaration. STSP 1922.5.12.2; Wang Ching-lien and T'ang Nai-p'ei, Chung-hua min-kuo, pp. 120–21.

41. Dazai, Daijūichinenshi, p. 200. The number given is 353.

Some 100 M.P.'s still loyal to Sun Yat-sen gathered in Shanghai, where early in July they formed an organization called the Society to Support Constitutional Orthodoxy (*Fa-t'ung wei-ch'ih hui*) and issued telegrams and declarations attacking the move to restore the 1917 parliament.[42] But it was too late, and they were too few to stop the momentum of the restoration movement.

The Return of Li Yuan-hung

Would Li Yuan-hung agree to take up office, and, if so, what did the law have to say about his term?[43] A disinterested discussion of the latter issue appeared in the pages of *Tung-fang tsa-chih*. The author pointed to Article 6 of the Presidential Election Law, which read, "The president should leave office on the day on which his term of office ends. If the succeeding president has not yet been elected, or has been elected but has not taken office, and if furthermore the succeeding vice-president is unable to take office as acting president, then the presidential powers should be exercised by the cabinet." This statement that under no circumstances may a president serve beyond the last day of his five-year term

42. *STSP* 1922.7.5.3, 7.7.2; Dazai, *Daijūichinenshi*, p. 201; Wang Ching-lien and T'ang Nai-p'ei, *Chung-kua min-kuo*, pp. 157–58. The number 100 is a rough estimate. The correct number may have been anywhere between 58 (a number given by *STSP*) and 180 (the figure given by Dazai).

When the restored old parliament convened in Peking, this small group of Sun's followers decided to return to Peking, take up their seats, and follow a strategy of disruption. Although few of the actual "1919 elements" seem to have come to Peking in 1922, this group of Sun's followers disrupted parliament meetings throughout 1922 by repeatedly bringing up the issue of the "1919 elements" from the floor, by holding demonstrations in front of the parliament building, and by engaging in a war of words with the parliamentary leadership in telegrams, letters, and the press. The consistent response of the Peking authorities was to seek some way to pension off the few 1919 elements who had come to Peking. Late in the year, a Political Reconstruction Discussion Commission (*Cheng-chih shan-hou t'ao-lun hui*) was established to pay the 1919 elements monthly salaries and the issue died down. After parliament moved to Shanghai in July 1923, the 1919 elements issue was briefly revived, but when the strong Ts'ao K'un candidacy for the presidency emerged, the issue finally died. Sun's followers were now primarily interested in preventing Ts'ao's election. They had no choice but to abandon the argument of parliament's illegality and throw their weight behind Li Yuan-hung's position, which stressed the lack of a quorum in Peking (see below), thus tacitly accepting the assumption that parliament was legal. The issue of the 1919 elements, of no further use to Sun, was abandoned. Sources: Tsou Lu, *Hui-ku lu*, 1:121–28; Hsieh Pin, *Cheng-tang shih*, pp. 88–90; Shen Yun-lung, *Li Yuan-hung p'ing-chuan* (Nankang, 1963), p. 181; *PYCF*, 6:184, note 3; Yang Yu-chiung, *Cheng-tang shih*, pp. 134–35; and *STSP* 1922.6.24.2, 6.28.2, 7.2.2, 7.3.2, 7.10.2, 7.25.2, 7.28.3, 8.2.3, 8.31.2, 9.4.2, 9.5.3, 9.6.2, 9.7.2, 9.9.2, 9.11.2, 10.3.2, 10.9.2, 10.12.2, 10.29.2, 11.15.3.

43. The issue of Li's legitimate term in office was debated both before and after he took office. Some of the sources used in this section date from July and August but are discussed here because they represent positions in the debate.

reflected the concern of the authors of the Provisional Constitution to avoid the imposition of a dictatorship. Li Yuan-hung had become president by succession to Yuan Shih-k'ai, who took office on October 10, 1913. Yuan's term, filled out by Li and by Feng Kuo-chang, ended on October 9, 1918. The law did not provide for Li to serve as president after that date on any pretext whatever.[44]

This straightforward conclusion, of course, had attraction only to those who were enemies of the Chihli Clique and opposed Li's restoration. For pro-Li politicians, the issue was not whether Li should return to office but what legal rationale could be found for that return and what its implications would be for his length of service. A number of ingenious positions were advanced. Chihli's Chang Shao-tseng argued that, since Li Yuan-hung had been driven from office illegally by Chang Hsun in 1917, the period served subsequently in office by Feng Kuo-chang was *de facto* (*shih-shih shang*) but not *de jure* (*fa-lü shang*). There- fore, Li's term still had a little more than one year and three months to run (the period of time served by Feng). According to another view, Feng Kuo-chang's term in office was legitimate, but the eighty-three days in 1916 during which Yuan Shih-k'ai suspended the republic and declared the Hung-hsien imperial era, plus the seven days in 1917 of Chang Hsun's restoration of the Hsuan-t'ung Emperor were illegal and remained to be filled out by Li. A third interpretation was that Yuan Shih-k'ai's tenure from the first day of Hung-hsien until his death was illegal, and thus Li had some 160 days left to serve. A fourth view said that Yuan had been illegitimate from the moment in 1914 when he summoned the Constitutional Conference to rewrite the Provisional Constitution, giving Li more than two years yet to serve.[45]

Resolution of this issue, however, was postponed until Li could be persuaded to return to office. Since his political retirement in 1917, he had been living in Tientsin, "shutting his door, turning away guests, and not asking about the affairs of the world."[46] If Li seemed reluctant to return to politics, it was perhaps because, as his career thus far showed, he was not ideally suited for it by temper- ament. His personality was summed up by a pair of hanging calligraphic scrolls donated by Chang Ping-lin at Li's funeral, reading, "His nature was pure and virtuous," and "Benevolent and unwarlike."[47] In other words, in a less euphe-

44. Ch'en Ch'eng-tse, "Fa-t'ung wen-t'i," p. 125. A foreign legal advisor to Li Yuan- hung reportedly gave him the same interpretation of the Presidential Election Law; *STSP* 1922.6.5.2. For a discussion supporting this view, see Willoughby, *Constitutional Govern- ment*, pp. 22–24. For text of the Presidential Election Law, see Wang Ching-lien and T'ang Nai-p'ei, *Chung-hua min-kuo*, appendix, pp. 13–14.

45. For these views, see Liu Ch'u-hsiang, *Kuei-hai cheng-pien*, pp. 24–25; Shen Yun-lung, *Li Yuan-hung*, pp. 139–41; *STSP* 1922.6.2.2.

46. Shen Yun-lung, *Li Yuan-hung*, p. 130. "The affairs of the world" means politics. Li had business involvments during this time.

47. Quoted by Shen Yun-lung, *Li Yuan-hung*, p. 205.

mistic description circulated during Li's lifetime, "Loyalty and generosity, has extra; ability and intelligence, not enough."[48] Li was sometimes referred to as "Li P'u-sa" (Bodhisattva Li), both to indicate his placid mien and stolid temper, and because in most dialects the nickname sounded like *"ni P'u-sa"*, mud Bodhisattva, calling to mind the old saying, "When the mud Bodhisattva is carried across the river, it can't even protect itself [much less the devotees]."[49] Li commanded national respect for his integrity, but he was one of the least skilled politicians to hold high office in the republic.

With the retirement of Hsu Shih-ch'ang on June 2, there was a stepped-up flow of telegrams and visitors to Li's Tientsin home urging him to take up office, and pointing to the dangers of allowing the republic to continue for long without a president.[50] Li's home was so crowded with politicians, the rumor went, that members of his staff had to repair to a public theater-restaurant to work on drafts of telegrams for him.[51] Li hesitated, however. He wanted to be sure his support went beyond the voluminous but frothy telegram-and-delegations campaign whipped up by Chihli Clique politicians[52] and included some of the other elements on the national political scene, especially the South and a quorum of the old parliament.[53] And in this respect, there were some disturbing signs. Lu Yung-hsiang and Ho Feng-lin issued telegrams opposing Li's return to office.[54] Chang Tso-lin's opposition came in the form of a telegram from the provincial assemblies of the three eastern provinces advocating that parliament meet in Shanghai to avoid interference from warlords.[55] The Canton parliament was still meeting and refused to support Li's restoration. A particularly stinging rebuke was delivered by a group in Shanghai, which telegraphed, "You are the person who dissolved parliament [in 1917]. To take office again now—would not that be to put your own crimes on display?"[56] Perhaps most impressive, because disinterested, was a telegram from the retired revolutionary elder, Chang Ping-lin, which argued, "At this moment, when the military are overbearingly arrogant, you can hardly accept the post. . . . It would be well to

48. Ku Hsiu-sun, *Chia-tzu nei-luan shih-mo chi-shih* (Tientsin, 1924), p. 39.

49. Interview with Professor Shen Yun-lung, Nankang, February 19, 1968.

50. *STSP* 1922.6.4.2, 6.6.2.

51. *STSP* 1922.6.8.2.

52. For direct evidence of Chihli politicians' orchestration of the campaign, see *Nu-li chou-pao*, no. 6 (June 11, 1922), Telegram 3, p. 1. There is much indirect evidence in the identity of the telegrammers and petitioners.

53. *STSP* 1922.6.4.2, 6.5.2.

54. Chang Tzu-sheng, "Li Yuan-hung," pp. 64–66; Wang Ching-lien and T'ang Nai-p'ei, *Chung-hua min-kuo*, pp. 121–22.

55. *STSP* 1922.6.6.2.

56. *STSP* 1922.6.8.2. The telegram is signed Chung-hua p'ing-min she (Association of the Chinese masses). Judging from its name and stance, it was a pro–Sun Yat-sen group.

select a plot of ground in Wuchang or Nanking [whence to retire]. A return to office is indeed nothing to wish for. Peking is a prison."[57]

By one report, such negative reactions tempered Li's initial interest in going to Peking but, within a matter of days, the situation had gotten out of his control.[58] Peking continued without a president, and the nervous caretaker cabinet bombarded Li with requests to take office.[59] As the only candidate for the post, Li was in a sense responsible for every day in which Peking remained in a "governmentless condition" (wu cheng-fu chuang-t'ai), a situation regarded as dangerously enticing to the foreign powers. Li had already been involved in conversations with various politicians about the prime ministership,[60] enmeshing himself in a web of half-promises and understandings. Finally, Li had privately articulated a number of stiff conditions to Paoting—e.g., a free hand in government with no military interference—and Paoting had readily assented to all Li's demands.[61] On June 6, Li sealed the compact of cooperation with the Chihli leaders. He issued a public telegram laying down as conditions for his acceptance of the presidency that the post of tuchun be abolished and the number of troops in the nation cut.[62] These demands were quickly acceded to in public telegrams by the Chihli leaders,[63] and, without waiting for other answers or for the Chihli leaders to put the promised measures into effect,[64] Li on June 11 proceeded to Peking to shoulder again the presidential burden.

Escorted by members of the caretaker cabinet and other dignitaries who had come to Tientsin to accompany him, Li arrived by train at Peking station at 11:05 A.M. the morning of June 11. After resting briefly at his private Peking residence, he proceeded to the Presidential Palace, went through a brief ceremony of assumption of office, and received the official seals. His speech alluded to the still unsettled question of his term of office: "In the five years since I left the capital, the nation has become dispirited; most recently, since I was pressed to do so on all sides, I was obliged to come and temporarily exercise the powers of the presidency, in order to uphold China's international position. With

57. STSP 1922.6.6.2. For a paraphrase, see Chang Ping-lin, T'ai-yen hsien-sheng tzu-ting nien-p'u, p. 47. For more anti-Li public opinion, see STSP 1922.6.13.3.

58. Chang Tzu-sheng, "Li Yuan-hung," p. 59.

59. STSP 1922.6.4.2, 6.5.3, 6.8.2, 6.10.2.

60. See Nu-li chou-pao, no. 6 (June 11, 1922), pp. 1–2; STSP 1922.6.5.2.

61. STSP 1922.6.5.2, 6.7.2.

62. STSP 1922.6.8.3; Sun Yao, comp., Chung-hua min-kuo shih-liao, pp. 433–38.

63. STSP 1922.6.8.2, 6.11.2.

64. A point stressed by T'ao Chü-yin, in PYCF, 6:130. The timing of events makes it clear that the telegram of June 6 was not so much a serious effort to elicit support for the idea of abolition of tuchunships and reduction of troops (fei-tu ts'ai-ping) as an attempt, after the decision to go to Peking had been effectively made, to provide Li with a popular banner under which to launch his new venture into politics.

respect to all other matters [the term of office], I will await their resolution by by the people."[65] That evening, Li issued his first order, relieving the caretaker cabinet of its duties and appointing a new, interim cabinet under the diplomat W. W. Yen (Yen Hui-ch'ing).[66] Then, on June 13, Li issued an order cancelling the June 12, 1917, dissolution of the old parliament.[67]

Li's return to Peking and the cancellation of the 1917 dissolution order spurred the efforts of the old parliament's preparatory office in Tientsin to gather a quorum. With Ch'en Chiung-ming's coup in mid-June, decisive numbers of M.P.'s made the decision to come north. Travelling funds were issued; rumors were circulated about the payment of large amounts of back salaries; and guarantees were given that the 400 yuan monthly M.P. stipend would be renewed as soon as parliament opened. Through the month of July, parliamentarians arrived in Tientsin, until by the end of the month, 414 members of the house and 171 senators had reported in.[68] On August 1, in a chamber stirred by "twenty big ceiling fans . . . play[ing] on the bunting below . . . [and] 300-odd members [waving] their fans, which must have been of as many shapes and kinds as the number of men present," the two houses held their opening meetings of the new sitting.[69]

65. Chang Tzu-sheng, "Li Yuan-hung," p. 73; also see *STSP* 1922.6.12.2. Here, Li's accession speech is reported as phrased more explicitly but still ambiguously: "Once parliament is formally opened and elects someone else who is able and virtuous [as president], I shall, at the end of my term, of course yield the post."

66. "The Cabinet headed by Regent Chow handed over the Government to President Li, who astonished me by an invitation to form a new Cabinet. His reason for doing so was simple: he did not at all feel certain that the Powers would be as easily satisfied as our people by the rather specious reasoning of the legitimists, and might hesitate in giving his regime recognition, which would create an awkward position for him. As he put it, he wanted me to 'ferry' him across the stream, as I was favorably known to the Legation Quarter, and my willingness to act as his Premier would be a strong argument in his favor. Although official life in Peking was beginning to pall on me, I consented to help him and the country at the critical moment, only on the understanding that he would permit me to retire as soon as the crisis became easier. A cabinet was therefore formed by me, with myself remaining at the President's request as Foreign Minister and including two close friends of Marshal Wu Pei-fu's (he was now a national figure), besides a few independent persons of ministerial rank. . . . " W. W. Yen, "An Autobiography," manuscript, p. 219.

67. Chang Tzu-sheng, "Li Yuan-hung," p. 73; *STSP* 1922.6.14.2.

68. *STSP* 1922.6.8.2, 6.9.2, 6.13.7, 6.15.2, 6.25.2, 6.26.2, 6.28.2, 7.8.2, 7.14.2, 7.15.2, 7.16.2, 7.20.2, 8.2.2; Dazai, *Daijūichinenshi*, p. 193.

69. *Peking Leader*, August 2, 1922; clipping enclosed in F.O. 228/2998, Despatch 515 of August 10, 1922; *STSP* 1922.8.2.2, 8.2.3; *NCH* 1922.8.5.367 (giving slightly different figures for attendance at the opening meetings); the houses did not meet in joint session because, legally, this was not the opening of a new session (*hui-ch'i*) of parliament but a continuation of the interrupted second; the third session would open in due course on October 11, and at that time the two houses would conduct joint ceremonies; see, e.g., F.O. 228/2999, "Opening of Parliament, Peking, 11th October, 1922."

THE RETURN TO CONSTITUTIONAL ORTHODOXY   191

A burst of presidential energy in the first month in office enhanced the sense of political upswing. Four days after taking office, Li issued an order calling on all front-line commanders around the nation to stop fighting and he also issued permission for the Fengtien troops to withdraw to Manchuria, ending their skirmishes with Wu P'ei-fu's forces.[70] Toward Sun Yat-sen—this was before the final success of Ch'en Chiung-ming's coup—and toward the South in general, Li made several conciliatory moves. One of his first acts in office was to cancel an order issued by an earlier government for the arrest of Sun. Another gesture was to appoint a cabinet in which southern politicians and technocrats respected by the South were heavily represented (W. W. Yen as prime minister, T'an Yen-k'ai as minister of interior, Li Ting-hsin as navy minister, Wang Ch'ung-hui as minister of justice, and Huang Yen-p'ei as minister of education).[71] Li sent telegrams to Sun and his followers and allies Wu T'ing-fang, Ch'en Chiung-ming, Li Lieh-chün, Ts'en Ch'un-hsuan, T'ang Shao-i, and T'an Yen-k'ai, inviting them to Peking to discuss national policy, and he let it be known that he would like to appoint as his first formal prime minister Sun's close follower, Wu T'ing-fang, who had been the last prime minister under Li's former presidency.[72]

Li moved with apparent energy to "reduce troops and abolish tuchunships." In Kiangsi, he replaced defeated tuchun Ch'en Kuang-yuan with a new civil governor (sheng-chang), Hsieh Yuan-han, instead of another tuchun. In Chekiang, Lu Yung-hsiang still withheld recognition of Li's presidency but had long been an advocate of abolishing tuchunships; he now held a convention of the provincial assembly and provincial professional associations, which changed his title from tuchun to Chekiang military affairs reconstruction commissioner (Che-chiang chün-wu shan-hou tu-pan). The tuchuns of Honan, Shantung, Anhwei, and Shansi followed suit in adopting the more acceptable title, and a few even announced the disbandment of small portions of their troops. In Peking, a Citizens' Association to Encourage Troop Reduction (Pei-ching kuo-min ts'ai-ping t'su-chin hui) was formed and attracted a large, prestigious membership.[73]

Other actions contributed to a new-broom atmosphere. In addition to his cabinet, Li appointed eight provincial governors and sixteen vice-ministers and

---

70. Chang Tzu-sheng, "Li Yuan-hung," p. 74; Kao Yin-tsu, Ta-shih chi, pp. 96–99.

71. The cabinet was appointed in an acting (shu) capacity pending parliamentary approval. A number of the appointees refused to serve.

72. Chang Tzu-sheng, "Li Yuan-hung," pp. 73–74; PYCF, 6:132–34; Kao Yin-tsu, Ta-shih chi, pp. 96–99: STSP 1922.6.13.2, 6.23.2. Wu had distinguished himself by refusing to sign the parliamentary dissolution order that Li issued under Chang Hsun's pressure in 1917. Ironically, Wu died on June 23, 1922.

73. Chang Tzu-sheng, "Li Yuan-hung," pp. 74; PYCF, 6:134–37; Kao Yin-tsu, Ta-shih chi, p. 98; STSP 1922.7.1.3; Tung-fang tsa-chih 19, no. 4 (July 25, 1922): 153. Of course, changes of title and marginal troop disbandments were to prove inadequate measures to end warlordism.

other central government officials.[74] Under the rubric of improving president-cabinet communications, Li inaugurated a practice of sitting in on cabinet meetings as a nonvoting observer.[75] Several ministries energetically effected an order, which Hsu Shih-ch'ang had issued late in his term, to reduce the number of officials (*ts'ai-kuan*).[76] The Communications Ministry abolished the practice of giving financial subventions to newspapers and took several other economy steps.[77] Minister of Finance Tung K'ang issued a report, on which a commission had been working since 1921, revealing and criticising irregularities in the issue of the controversial "$96-Million" Bonds of 1921.[78] And as if to signal that corruption in the future would not be tolerated, Peking police on June 18 seized, searched, and put under guard the Peking home of former Minister of Communications Ts'ao Ju-lin on grounds of suspected corruption.[79]

When Li entered office, innumerable small financial crises awaited his attention.[80] Most politicians and officials had not grasped the implications of the structural weakness of government finance described in Chapter III. The pattern, which is clear in retrospect, was obscured by uncertainty about whether or not the consortium financial boycott would persist and whether or not the price of silver would continue its unfortunate fall; by the unusually good relations the Chin Yun-p'eng cabinets of 1920–21 had enjoyed with the domestic banks; and by the conviction that disorders that cut off taxes and harmed government credit were merely episodes that could be overcome.

There was widespread hope that President Li could put the government back on its financial feet. The public was willing to credit the widespread rumors that bankers of "a certain" foreign country were going to break the

---

74. *PYCF*, 6: 137; *Tung-fang tsa-chih* 19, no. 13 (July 10, 1922): 142, and 19, no. 14 (July 25, 1922): 151–52; *STSP* 1922.6.19.2. Only two of the provincial governors were able to take up office; Li had neglected to clear the appointments with the local military authorities.

75. *STSP* 1922.6.16.2; *PYCF*, 6:134–35. The practice soon became contentious and was stopped on August 8.

76. *Nu-li chou-pao*, no. 7 (June 18, 1922), p. 2; no. 8 (June 25, 1922), pp. 1, 4; *NCH* 1922.6.3.657; *STSP* 1922.5.29.2, 5.30.3, 5.31.3. The ministries of Communications and Finance, under Wu P'ei-fu followers Kao En-hung and Tung K'ang, were especially efficient in this respect, firing several thousand officials between them. It may be that these dismissals of officials appointed under the old Communications Clique-dominated regimes were meant to clear the way for Chihli Clique followers.

77. *Nu-li chou-pao*, no. 8 (June 25, 1922), pp. 1–2.

78. *Nu-li chou-pao*, no. 5 (June 4, 1922), pp. 1–3; *STSP* 1922.5.19.2. The dollars in the slogan are Mexican dollars.

79. *STSP* 1922.6.20.3; *PYCF*, 6: 139; Ts'ao Ju-lin, *l-sheng*, pp. 226–27.

80. Funds were lacking to make foreign loan payments that were coming due; troops' pay was months in arrears all over the North, and until troops were paid they could not be disbanded and were prone to mutiny and looting; provincial officials and warlords were submitting a stream of requests for money; the central government's own staff had not

financial boycott and aid the new government;[81] they were willing to repose some hope in the new Financial Discussion Commission (*Ts'ai-cheng t'ao-lun wei-yuan hui*), which Li appointed under the chairmanship of Wellington Koo to determine ways of improving the government's financial position.[82] A contemporary observer wrote, "If Koo, together with [the acting ministers of finance and communications] Tung K'ang and Kao En-hung, can avoid corruption and the pitfalls of the old finance, then perhaps the financial future of the government is not entirely hopeless."[83] Meanwhile, as expediencies, the government received some short-term funds from the salt and customs surpluses and from several domestic banks.[84] The financial crisis would return to beset the Li government, but in its early days the government created on this issue, as on many others, a salutary sense of motion.

The Rise and Fall of the "Able Men Cabinet"

Li's appointment of a technocratic cabinet of talents was another hopeful sign of republican vitality. Too many cabinets in the past had been merely factional balancing acts or warlord puppets. When Li's first choice as prime minister, T'ang Shao-i, drew opposition both in parliament and from the Chihli leaders

been paid for months, and Ministry of War personnel even held a demonstration on the matter, roughing up Minister of Finance Tung K'ang, who promptly resigned. *STSP* 1922.6.23.2, 6.27.2, 7.8.2 (Paoting mutiny of July 6), 7.9.2, 7.14.2, 7.16.2 (Ministry of War personnel demonstration of July 15), 7.17.2, 7.18.2. Also see *PYCF*, 6: 152, on mutinies. On Tung's resignation, see also Appendix.

81. For the rumors, see *STSP* 1922.6.18.2, 6.19.2, 6.23.2. They were not unfounded. British banking representatives E. G. Hillier and S. F. Mayers had in fact recommended to the London office of the consortium that a loan be made in support of the new government. The argument was that Wu P'ei-fu's strong influence made this a rare opportunity for unification and for reforms of a sort acceptable to Britain; without financial support, the new government would wither and the opportunity be lost. Meanwhile, members of the diplomatic corps in Peking agreed to recommend to home governments that the powers offer a loan to Peking if a stable government under Wu's tutelage emerged. But ultimately neither the Japanese Government nor the British Foreign Office was enthusiastic about such a loan, and negotiations with the Chinese Government were not continued. F.O. 371/7984, F1712/59/10, letter from Stabb of China Consortium to Under-secretary of State, May 12, 1922; F.O. 371/7984, F1850/59/10, Telegram No. 175, Alston to Curzon, May 24, 1922; F.O. 371/7984, F1850/59/10, Telegram 161, Balfour to Alston, May 26, 1922; F.O. 371/7985, F1996/59/10, Telegram 198, Alston to Curzon, June 8, 1922; F.O. 371/7985, F2045/59/10, Telegram 156, Eliot to F.O., June 12, 1922; F.O. 371/7985, F2675/59/10, Telegram 268, Clive to F.O., August 16, 1922; F.O. 371/7985, F2815/15/10, letter from Jones of China Consortium to Wellesley, August 31, 1922.

82. *STSP* 1922.7.7.3, 7.10.2.

83. Chang Tzu-sheng, "Li Yuan-hung," p. 74.

84. Kao Yin-tsu, *Ta-shih chi*, p. 98; *STSP* 1922.7.8.2.

and refused to serve,[85] Li turned to Acting Prime Minister Wang Ch'ung-hui. Wang, although acceptable to Chihli, was no Chihli tool. A prestigious Western-trained lawyer, diplomat, and educator, he had recently been among the signers of the good-government manifesto, "Our Political Proposals." Two other members of Wang's cabinet—Lo Wen-kan and T'ang Erh-ho—were also signers of the manifesto. Oxford-educated Lo,[86] appointed minister of finance, had served on the Law Codification Bureau since 1916 and had taught law at Peking University and at the Judges' Training Institute (*Fa-kuan hsun-lien so*) in Peking; he resigned as a vice-chief justice of the Supreme Court to join the cabinet. T'ang,[87] the new minister of education, was a medical doctor and president of the Government Medical College in Peking. Other prestigious cabinet members included Wellington Koo,[88] minister of foreign affairs, the famous diplomat just returned to Peking from the Washington Conference; Hsu Ch'ien[89] (George Hsu), minister of justice, a prominent legal specialist under the Ch'ing and lately minister of justice in the Canton government; and Li Ting-hsin,[90] minister of the navy, a senior naval officer, retired from active duty, who had served in consecutive cabinets as navy minister since the spring of 1921 (and would continue to serve, through a total of eight cabinets, until October 1924).

Finally, there were four ministers who had Chihli factional affiliations. Chang

85. Immediately upon taking office, Li appointed Yen Hui-ch'ing as acting prime minister and sent delegates to sound out four southern candidates on their willingness to take the post. At the end of July, Yen insisted on resigning and was replaced by Wang Ch'ung-hui, already acting minister of justice. At about the same time, the cabinet lost its ministers of finance, education, and interior in various squabbles (see Appendix profile of Chihli Clique). The deterioration of the interim cabinet forced Li's hand. Although T'ang Shao-i had not agreed to serve, Li submitted his name to parliament on August 5. T'ang announced he did not want the job, and Wu P'ei-fu campaigned against approval, but Li's supporters in parliament tried to push the nomination through anyway. When this failed, the nomination was returned on a procedural pretext to the executive branch and Li, on September 19, upgraded Wang Ch'ung-hui's appointment from *tai* (acting pending selection of another appointee) to *shu* (acting pending formal approval by parliament). STSP 1922.6.23.2, 6.25.2, 6.26.2, 6.28.2, 7.5.2, 7.16.2, 7.17.2, 7.18.2, 7.19.2, 7.22.2, 7.25.2, 7.26.2, 7.30.2, 8.1.2, 8.1.3, 8.6.3, 8.9.2, 8.10.2, 8.16.2, 8.17.2, 8.18.2, 8.20.2, 8.29.2, 9.14.2, 9.15.2, 9.20.2, 9.20.3. Dazai, *Daijūichinenshi*, pp. 240, 245–48; W. W. Yen, "Autobiography," p. 220.

86. *GJMK*, 1932, p. 367; *Who's Who*, p. 177; Boorman and Howard, *Biographical Dictionary* 2:438–41.

87. *GJMK*, 1932, p. 297; *Who's Who*, p. 222; Boorman and Howard, *Biographical Dictionary*, 3:228–30.

88. Boorman and Howard, *Biographical Dictionary*, 2: 255–59.

89. *GJMK*, 1932, p. 165; *Who's Who*, p. 92; Boorman and Howard, *Biographical Dictionary*, 2: 118–22. Hsu refused to take office.

90. *GJMK*, 1932, p. 381. Li can be considered to have served in eleven consecutive cabinets if every shift in prime minister, including acting prime ministers, is counted.

Shao-tseng,[91] a retired general appointed minister of war, was a relative by marriage and a political ally of Wu P'ei-fu. Kao Ling-wei, minister of agriculture and commerce, was a senior bureaucrat and politician and a political follower of Ts'ao K'un. Kao En-hung, minister of communications, and Sun Tan-lin, minister of the interior, were natives of Wu P'ei-fu's home county, P'englai, Shantung, and followers of Wu. Of these four Chihli Clique politicians, both Chang and Kao Ling-wei were widely respected, the former because of his support for the revolutionaries in 1911 and 1917, and the latter for his competence as a bureaucrat.

The new cabinet commanded widespread public support, and became known, because of its distinguished composition, as the "able men cabinet" (hao-jen nei-ko).[92] Nu-li chou-pao expressed confidence that as soon as the government got over the financial crisis of the impending Autumn Festival, the reforms advocated in "Our Political Proposals" would begin to be carried out.[93] Thanks to the prestige of the cabinet and his own abilities, new Finance Minister Lo Wen-kan was able to achieve the support of the domestic banks for a government bond issue, which, together with other devices, provided enough money to bring the new cabinet through the festival financial crisis with considerable "merit."[94]

91. *GJMK*, 1932, p. 239; *MJTC*, *chüan* 5, p. 65; *PYCF*, 6: 128.

92. A write-in poll conducted a few weeks earlier by the *Shun-t'ien shih-pao* had shown Wang Ch'ung-hui, Kao En-hung, and Wellington Koo to be among those viewed by the paper's readers as ideal cabinet members. The results of the poll were as follows: president, Sun Yat-sen (276 votes), Li Yuan-hung (199), Tuan Ch'i-jui (56); vice-president, Li Yuan-hung (180), Ts'ao K'un (163), Wu P'ei-fu (90), Tuan Ch'i-jui (87); prime minister, T'ang Shao-i (324), Tuan Ch'i-jui (116), Sun Hung-i (62). In the cabinet, the first-place winners were as follows: interior, Sun Hung-i (305 votes); foreign affairs, Wellington Koo (344); finance, Wellington Koo (90); communications, Kao En-hung (79); education, Ts'ai Yuan-p'ei (252); war, Wu P'ei-fu (235); navy, Sa Chen-ping (411); justice, Wang Ch'ung-hui (329); agriculture and commerce, Chang Chien (404). *STSP* 1922.8.10.7.

While it would be fallacious to take the poll as representative of the electorate's precise level of support for various political figures, the overall composition of the list probably reflects the mood of politically articulate Peking residents. A number of points are striking: the preference for technocrats in the cabinet; the high prestige of both Ts'ao K'un and Wu P'ei-fu, and especially the latter; Li Yuan-hung's prestige; the continued public regard for Tuan Ch'i-jui despite his political retirement and charges of pro-Japanism; and the ideologically inconsistent (or innocent) granting of support both to Peiyang types like Ts'ao K'un and Tuan Ch'i-jui and to Kuo-min tang leaders like Sun Yat-sen and Sun Hung-i. An image of technical competence and/or personal moral rectitude (as in the cases of Sun, Tuan, and Li) seems to have been the major qualification for support, while ideological or policy differences among candidates were unimportant.

93. *Nu-li chou-pao*, no. 22 (October 1, 1922), p. 1. The Autumn Festival, falling on the fifteenth day of the eighth lunar month (October 5, 1922) was an occasion for the payment of debts, including wages and troop rations owed by the government.

94. *STSP* 1922.9.21.2, 9.24.2, 9.26.2, 10.4.2, 10.5.2.

Finance Minister Lo soon achieved another success in renegotiating the so-called Austrian Loans, a government debt of some £5 million originally incurred in an armaments contract with two Austrian firms on the eve of World War I. Because of the war, most of the arms had never been delivered, nor had the Chinese payments been completed, and meanwhile ownership of the two Austrian firms had come into French and Italian hands. Early in 1921, agents of the firms had come to Peking to seek settlement of the problem and, on November 14, 1921, the Ministry of Finance and the Sino-Italian Bank (representing the European principals) signed an agreement fairly favorable to the Chinese side. The Chinese were able to resist the demand that they take delivery of the remaining portion of the order, and as a result the debt was reduced by some £2 million. Payment of the rest of the obligation was rescheduled. Meanwhile the desperately cash-short Ministry of Finance was given a check for £80,000 as a share of the money saved for both sides by juggling details of tax payments owed on the transaction in Britain.[95] The money was immediately used to defray some of the government's pressing obligations.[96]

Little could Minister Lo or his colleagues have suspected that this happy outcome would lead within eleven days to the fall of the cabinet. Here is Lo Wen-kan's bitter account of what happened next:

At midnight on the evening of the 18th, a certain T'ien from the police commander's office suddenly arrived at my residence on Nanch'ang Street and sent in his card asking to see me. I received him immediately; a throng of policemen came crowding in with him. T'ien said, "Please come to the Presidential Palace; there is an important matter [the President] wants to discuss with you." I said I would go as soon as my car arrived. T'ien replied that there was already a car waiting outside. So we went out together and got into the car; with more than ten policemen in and on the car guarding me, we drove off.

95. F.O. 371/9179, F89/6/10, Despatch 733, Clive to Curzon, November 25, 1922, confidential print, 3 pp.; F.O. 228/3000, "Arrest of Lo Wen-kan," notes of a conversation between Wang Ch'ung-hui, Wellington Koo, and "W.H.D.", n.d.; for Chinese text of accord, see STSP 1922.11.20.2. In evaluating the loan agreement as favorable to the Chinese, I am following the British judgment, which was obviously affected by discussions with Lo's cabinet colleagues, who were English-speaking, and by the fact that Lo was Oxford-educated. From another perspective, it might be argued that the agreement was not so favorable, for, although the Chinese Government had managed to reduce its obligation to some degree, it had still been forced, because of its diplomatic weakness, to pay out a considerable sum of money for which it received nothing. The French and Italian legations had pressured the government for a resolution of the dispute that would favor their nationals, and Clive, in his despatch cited above, noted rather righteously that one "merit" of the "transaction . . . would appear to be the lesson it should impart to [the Chinese] to keep out of the hands of continental money-lenders" (p. 2).

96. Clive despatch, cited in preceding note, p. 2, says that the money was used to make the payments then due on the Canton-Kowloon Railway Loan; PYCF, 6:173, says that £50,000 was remitted to Wu P'ei-fu for troop upkeep.

When we had exited from Nanch'ang Street, T'ien ordered the driver to change his course for the police headquarters. As soon as we got there, a crowd of police escorted me to a back room. . . . The commander arrived shortly and announced in a loud voice, "Today I have received a direct oral order from the president that, on the strength of a report contained in a letter sealed with the official seal of the House of Representatives on the personal authority of Speaker Wu Ching-lien and Vice-Speaker Chang Po-lieh, I should arrest you and bring you before the court"; and he showed me the letter.[97]

The letter, which Wu Ching-lien and Chang Po-lieh had submitted to President Li earlier that evening, made the following accusations against Lo: first, that the Austrian Loan accord signed four days earlier was disadvantageous to the nation because all Chinese obligations to Austria and Germany had been cancelled by the Treaty of Versailles as part of the postwar settlement; second, that Lo had neglected to seek approval of the accord by the parliament, as required by the Provisional Constitution, or by the cabinet or president, as required by the accord; third, that a check for £80,000 had been issued to the Ministry of Finance by the Sino-Italian bank and personally endorsed for cashing by Minister Lo—implying that the money had gone to line Lo's pockets.[98]

These accusations, as it turned out, had little validity. On the first point, Wu and Chang ignored the fact that the original bonds held by the Austrian creditors had come into the hands of nationals of other countries who had been China's wartime allies, so that the obligation was not cancelled under the Versailles treaty. On the second point, the article of the Provisional Constitution referred to did charge parliament with deciding on bond issues and other government debts, but it could be argued that the wording did not imply parliamentary approval for the readjustment of already existing obligations, especially involving a net reduction.[99] Although the cabinet had not formally discussed the matter, Prime Minister Wang had authorized Lo to proceed.[100] Although Lo had apparently failed to get the president's approval, and to this extent the charges were justified, this was a relatively minor point, both legally and in terms of the real impact of the accusations. The central point was the alleged peculation, and here, it was later to be shown, Lo was entirely innocent.[101] Wu and Chang relied on the innuendo that the £80,000 paid to the Ministry of

97. *STSP* 1922.11.22.2. The commander referred to was Police Commander Hsueh Chih-heng; cf. *PYCF*, 6: 169; *STSP* 1922.11.24.2; *GJMK*, 1937, p. 272.

98. *STSP* 1922.11.20.2.

99. See Provisional Constitution, Article 19, Section 4, in Wang Ching-lien and T'ang Nai-p'ei, *Chung-hua min-kuo*, appendices, p. 5.

100. *PYCF*, 6:171.

101. See sources cited in note 95; also F.O. 228/2999, copy of letter to Chargé [Clive] from Major Augustine Barker of Arnhold Bros. and Co., Ltd., the agents in China of the creditors, Peking, November 21, 1922. On June 29, 1923, Lo Wen-kan and an implicated colleague were found not quilty by the courts and released; *NCH* 1923.7.7.12.

Finance had been improperly used but had no evidence to support this accusation.[102] Nonetheless, the rather naive and emotional president had responded to Wu's and Chang's urgent pleas and, on the strength of their presentation, had ordered the immediate arrest of Lo.

The arrest created a public furor. Revealingly, most people took it for granted that the alleged embezzlement had occurred and rumors began to build as to the quantity of money involved.[103] But the bulk of the public discussion, whether pro- or anti-Lo, focused on procedural issues of whether the arrest was justified as carried out. Lo's defenders pointed out that Speaker Wu and Vice-Speaker Chang had exceeded their powers of office in using the seals of the House of Representatives to seal the letter in which they accused Lo; that the case should have been brought to court, not to the president; that the president had not adequately investigated the facts before ordering the arrest; and that the president had not taken the prior step of dissolving the cabinet or asking the cabinet to remove Lo from office and had therefore trespassed upon the immunity of a cabinet member.[104] Those who defended the arrest attacked not only Lo's presumed corruption but especially the allegedly favoritistic treatment he was receiving from the local procurator-general, who was a former subordinate of his, and the failure of the cabinet to resign in the face of evidence of corruption in its ranks.[105]

The cabinet's failure to resign in turn reflected the feeling of most of its members that not they, but the president and Speakers, were at fault, and that they should stand behind Minister Lo.[106] Informed of the arrest during the night, the cabinet members called on President Li the next morning and pressed him to issue an order, the prepared text of which was carefully worded so as to refrain from directly repudiating Li's previous actions, while still recognizing the aggrieved position of the imprisoned finance minister. The proposed presidential order read:

It is brought to my attention by Acting Prime Minister Wang Ch'ung-hui that Acting Minister of Finance Lo Wen-kan has been arrested on the strength of a joint letter to the

102. Wu and Chang's presentation to President Li was made more impressive because they were accompanied by a compradore of the Sino-Italian Bank, who told the president about the £80,000 cash payment to the ministry and Lo's personal endorsement of the check as if there were something wrong with the situation. Inside information from the bank gave the president the impression of a discovered secret. PYCF, 6: 166–67, 173.

103. STSP 1922.11.20.2, 11.20.2 editorial, 11.22.2, 11.23.2, 11.26.2.

104. E.g., STSP 1922.11.24.2, a telegram from Wu P'ei-fu.

105. E.g., STSP 1922.11.25.2, a telegram from Ts'ao K'un. Also PYCF, 6:175–77. On Lo's relations with the Peking procurator-general, see PYCF, 6:172. Also see PYCF, 6: 170–72, for a discussion of trespasses of law committed by all parties.

106. The exceptions were Chang Shao-tseng and Kao Ling-wei. Taking their lead from Paoting, they favored resignation. STSP 1922.11.20.2, 11.23.2 (text of cabinet telegram not signed by Chang and Kao); PYCF, 6: 168.

president from House Speaker and Vice-Speaker Wu Ching-lien and Chang Po-lieh stating that he improperly took upon himself the authority to sign the accord extending the repayment of the Austrian Loan; but I am informed that the said minister did in fact get the approval of the cabinet. I am further informed that the said minister refuses to leave the court [where he is imprisoned] until "the water recedes and the stones are revealed"; and that, since his arrest was conducted without the proper legal procedures, the cabinet is very concerned. These considerations all have merit. I order that, since the said minister is unwilling to leave the court, the case be dealt with by the court in accordance with law. I hope that the truth will be fully revealed, right and wrong clarified, and justice served.[107]

Li, the cabinet members later claimed, had been on the verge of putting his seal to this quasi-apologetic document when Wu Ching-lien, Chang Po-lieh and some twenty other M.P.'s burst into the room and prevented him from doing so.[108]

Over the next two days, the cabinet continued to press Li to issue the order, while Li wavered under counterpressure from parliament and many anticabinet warlord telegrams. To conciliate the cabinet, Li sent Chin Yung-yen, vice-minister of war, several times to Lo's place of imprisonment to urge Lo to return home to await resolution of the case, but Lo, all outraged innocence, refused. Finally Li sent several senior political figures in his official car to urge Lo to come take up imprisonment as the president's guest at the Presidential Palace. This offer Lo accepted, but it was not enough to satisfy his cabinet colleagues. As warlord telegrams and parliamentary pressure built up, guaranteeing President Li would make no further concessions, the cabinet on November 5 offered its resignation. Lo Wen-kan was sent back to the Peking procurator's office to continue his imprisonment, and, on November 29, Research Clique elder Wang Ta-hsieh was appointed the new acting prime minister.[109]

Why had the "able men cabinet," on which so many hopes had been placed, come to such a quick and ignominious end? Precisely because the "able"—that is, the apolitical—character of the cabinet unsuited it to survive. The heavy proportion of technocrats meant that there was not a single representative of a parliamentary faction, while among factionally aligned cabinet members, Chihli's Loyang group was disproportionately represented in comparison with the Paoting wing. Even so, parliament's and Paoting's early hostility to the new cabinet would not have been insuperable obstacles if the cabinet had satisfied Paoting's demand for funds and had actively cultivated the support of parliament. Instead, the cabinet took an "above-party" stance toward parliamentary

107. *STSP* 1922.11.23.2; this text is embedded in the slightly longer text of the cabinet's circular telegram of November 21.
108. *Ibid.*; also see *PYCF*, 6: 167–68.
109. *STSP* 1922.11.21.2, 11.22.2, 11.23.2, 11.25.2, 11.26.2, 11.30.3; *PYCF*, 6: 169, 174–77.

confirmation and gave what financial support was available to Loyang, not Pao-ting.[110] As time passed without the cabinet coming before parliament for confirmation, a series of harassing interpolations were lodged and a bill of impeachment of the cabinet was circulated for signatures.[111] This was the context in which the assistant manager of the Sino-Italian Bank, Hsu Shih-i—said by one source to be a relative of the anti-Wu P'ei-fu Chihli Clique politician Pien Shou-ch'ing[112]—came to Wu Ching-lien with the text of the Austrian Loan accord and the £80,000 check endorsed by Lo Wen-kan. The opportunity to harass the uncooperative cabinet was eagerly seized, and Li Yuan-hung's credulity enabled the ploy to succeed beyond its sponsor's hopes.

Lo remained in jail to await trial and eventual exoneration. To pass the time, he wrote a book, *Yü-chung jen yü* (Words from prison), in which he analyzed the ills of the republic. In the section on the institution that had brought him to grief, Lo wrote, "The depravity of our members of parliament today is basically due to the inadequacy of the electoral laws."[113] Ironically, despite his personal experience with the destructive effects of factionalism, Lo continued to search for the solution to political problems in constitutional arrangements.

110. *STSP* 1922.9.27.2, 9.28.2, 10.3.2, 10.7.2, 10.12.2, 11.10.2; *PYCF*, 6:173, 176. The cabinet was not entirely unresponsive to Paoting; for example, it did appoint a Paoting nominee, Hsiung Ping-ch'i, as governor of Shantung; *STSP* 1922.10.1.3; on Hsiung, see *PYCF*, 6:138; *GJMK*, 1932, p. 346.

111. *STSP* 1922.11.7.2, 11.13.2, 11.14.2, 11.16.2, 11.17.2, 11.19.2. The cabinet was quite willing to resign, but President Li kept rejecting the proffered resignations. *STSP* 1922.10.13.2, 10.14.2, 10.15.2, 10.16.2, 10.21.2, 10.28.2, 10.29.2, 11.3.2. 11.6.2, 11.10.2.

112. *PYCF*, 6:173; Hsu is also mentioned in *STSP* 1922.11.21.2 and Liu Ch'u-hsiang, *Kuei-hai cheng-pien*, p. 33. T'ao uses this information to argue that the Tientsin group had been actively seeking the collapse of the cabinet. This is not confirmable from other sources, but in any case the hostility of Paoting to the new cabinet became relevant after the arrest of Lo, when Ts'ao K'un chose not to defend but to attack the cabinet and, after a few days, forced Wu P'ei-fu to stop defending it too.

113. Lo Wen-kan, *Yü-chung jen yü* (Taipei, [1967?]), pp. 199–200.

VII

THE REPUBLIC DEBASED, 1923

The spectacular collapse of the "able men cabinet" spelled a victory—easier than anyone had expected—of disintegrative factionalism over the integrative efficacy of constitutionalism. Whether one believed Lo Wen-kan corrupt or the president gulled, the incident was equally depressing. Worse, the cabinet's fall opened the door to an even more disheartening series of events connected with the issue of presidential succession.

It was no secret in Peking late in 1922 that Ts'ao K'un wanted to become president. Since October, if not earlier, Ts'ao's agents had been buying the votes of M.P.'s for the next presidential election, both by enrolling M.P.'s as advisors (*ku-wen*) to the Office of High Inspecting Commissioner and by giving money to parliamentary leaders to establish pro-Ts'ao political clubs.[1] (The large number of M.P.'s willing to accept such bribes formed a proliferating number of small clubs with overlapping membership, thus squeezing maximum payments from Paoting.)[2] Ts'ao's urgency increased early in 1923, when troops loyal to Sun Yat-sen ousted Ch'en Chiung-ming from Canton and Sun returned to declare himself marshal of a military government dedicated to freeing the nation from warlordism. Ts'ao needed the presidency, he felt, to counter the threat; in any case, Li had outlived his utility as a cat's-paw since Sun no longer marched under the banner of constitution-protection.

A Duel of Wits: Li Versus Ts'ao

The trouble was that Li Yuan-hung had come to Peking with his term of office unfixed. Although Li claimed to have no interest in lingering as president,

1. *STSP* 1922.10.12.2, 12.7.3, 12.9.2, 1923.1.9.2, 1.14.2; *PYCF*, 6:183–84; Yang Yu-chiung, *Cheng-tang shih*, pp. 125–33; Liu Ch'u-hsiang, *Kuei-hai cheng-pien*, p. 23.
2. This point is made by *PYCF*, 6:183; and Yang Yu-chiung, *Cheng-tang shih*, p. 125.

neither did he push the issue of a successor. On taking office, he stated that he expected parliament to determine the term of his service, and when parliament convened in August, Li put the problem before it in the form of the resignation he had not been able to submit when he went into retirement in 1917. If parliament rejected this belated 1917 resignation—and they could hardly accept it— Li's resumption of the presidency would be legitimized and plausibility would accrue to the notion that he was resuming the unfilled fifteen months of his term. Instead, the M.P.'s cannily found a procedural pretext for not acting on the resignation.[3] They seemed reluctant to set any term to Li's service because they expected to be dismissed after electing his successor. Remembering that Yuan Shih-k'ai had dissolved parliament soon after being elected president and before the constitution was completed, most M.P.'s argued for completing the constitution before dealing with the problem of the presidency.[4] Li made no effort to force the issue.

Paoting-sponsored efforts to have parliament resolve the issue met with frustration; it was immensely difficult to bring parliament to the point of action. Since October, when Wang Chia-hsiang's term as Speaker ended, the Senate had been embroiled in an endless, crippling struggle over the election of a new Speaker. Many scheduled meetings of the House had broken up for lack of a quorum, and others had been disrupted by demonstrations by "1919 elements" or fights among members. Unable to accomplish anything, parliament had twice granted itself emergency extensions of its term in office. Although parliament's major task was to complete the constitution, meetings of the Constitutional Drafting Committee (a joint committee of the whole) seldom commanded the required two-thirds quorum.[5]

When the pro-Ts'ao forces finally mounted a serious threat to Li, Li's allies resourcefully turned it aside. A strongly supported bill suggesting that Li's term of office had already been exceeded and proposing an urgent presidential election, was put forward in May by Ts'ao's backers. Rather than debate the issue directly, the anti-Ts'ao M.P.'s called for completion of the constitution before election of the next president. They backed this up by carrying through an amendment permitting discussion of the constitution with a quorum of only three-fifths of the members of parliament, with decisions to be made by a two-thirds vote. The rules were further revised to impose a 20 yuan fine on any member who missed a Constitutional Drafting Committee meeting without leave and to pay a 20 yuan fee to all who attended each meeting. The necessary funds were allocated by President Li from the Maritime Customs' Construction

3. STSP 1922.8.8.2, 8.9.2, 9.14.2; Shen Yun-lung, Li Yuan-hung, p. 141. For another interpretation, see Nu-li chou-pao, no. 15 (August 13, 1922), p. 1.

4. Liu Ch'u-hsiang, Kuei-hai cheng-pien, pp. 23–24; STSP 1923.1.7.2.

5. STSP, October 1922 through May 1923, passim; STSP 1923.2.1.2, 2.3.7, 6.9.3.

Fund. Since the 20-yuan-per-meeting inducement could be accepted without forfeiting the income funnelled to M.P.'s from Paoting sources through their parliamentary clubs, an unprecedented 667 M.P.'s attended the first Constitutional Drafting Committee meeting after the new rule was passed. The election threat was stymied.[6]

Nor did cabinet politics fall out to Ts'ao's advantage. An extended crisis following the fall of the able men cabinet might have forced Li to resign, but he manged to avoid that by turning to Chang Shao-tseng, already minister of war, to serve as the new prime minister.[7] A Peiyang ex-general in his fifties, a graduate of Paoting Military Academy and the Japanese Officers' Training School, and a relative by marriage of Wu P'ei-fu, Chang was a mediating figure in Peiyang ranks, politically useful because of his seniority, connections, good personal reputation, and lack of troops. Both Paoting and Li Yuan-hung hoped to profit from his appointment—Paoting because of his Chihli leanings, Li because Chang's political ambition and skill might enable him to shield Li from cabinet crises. Not that Chang had been Li's first choice for the post—his Chihli connections were too strong, and, although he had made himself conspicuously available in August,[8] Li at that time preferred Wang Ch'ung-hui. But the choice, now that he was driven to it, was to prove an inspired one from Li's point of view.

Chang knew how to deal with parliament, and he went about the politics of confirmation with energy. His name was approved on December 18 by the House, on December 29 by the Senate, and was gazetted on January 4, 1923.[9] On the same day, Chang announced his nominees for the other cabinet posts. Although Chang was personally more closely identified with Wu P'ei-fu than

6. *STSP* 1923.5.1.3, 5.16.2, 5.18.2, 5.22.2, 5.27.2, 5.28.2, 6.3.2, 6.3.2 editorial; Liu Ch'u-hsiang, *Kuei-hai cheng-pien*, pp. 25, 35. The position in favor of constitution-writing gained support from four overlapping groups: Li's supporters, those who opposed Ts'ao without particularly favoring Li, those who simply believed in the priority of constitution-writing as an obligation of parliament, and those who wanted to write into the constitution provisions for local self-government that the Chihli warlords opposed.

7. In the immediate aftermath of the fall of the "able men cabinet," Li filled the cabinet gap with two acting prime ministers, Wang Ta-hsieh and Wang Cheng-t'ing, both prestigious jurists and diplomats. Wang Ta-hsieh agreed to hold office only in order to complete negotiations then going forward with the Japanese over Shantung. He resigned when the formalities were completed and was succeeded by Wang Cheng-t'ing, who agreed to serve only until Chang's nomination could be approved by parliament, and only on condition that nothing important be done during his tenure. See *STSP* 1922.11.30.2, 11.30.3, 12.1.2, 12.2.2, 12.10.2, 12.11.2, 12.12.2, 12.13.2, 12.14.2, 12.22.2, 1923.1.6.3; "Chō Shō-sō naikaku to sōtō kaisen mondai," *Shina jōhō*, no. 3 (June 30, 1923), pp. 1–2.

8. *STSP* 1922.8.12.2, 8.13.2, 8.18.2, 8.30.2.

9. *STSP* 1922.12.8.2, 12.9.2, 12.10.2, 12.12.2, 12.14.2, 12.16.2, 12.17.2, 12.19.2, 12.30.2, 1923.1.6.3.

with Ts'ao K'un, the cabinet makeup realistically reflected Wu's waning involvement in Peking politics and the increasing influence of Paoting.[10] In addition to Kao Ling-wei, retained from the last cabinet but shifted to the more influential post of minister of the interior, Paoting was represented by two cronies of Ts'ao K'un, Liu En-yuan as minister of finance and Wu Yü-lin as minister of communications. Both were Chihli natives and former Peiyang military officers who had long enjoyed lucrative patronage posts in Ts'ao's sphere of influence. The Political Study faction received two posts in exchange for its support in parliament: the Ministry of Agriculture and Commerce went to Li Ken-yuan and the Ministry of Education to P'eng Yun-i. Chang Shao-tseng retained the Ministry of War himself and kept Li Ting-hsin as minister of the navy. In the two remaining posts, Chang appointed technocrats: Alfred Sao-ke Sze (Shih Chao-chi) as foreign minister, and C. T. Wang (Wang Cheng-t'ing) as minister of justice.[11] On January 7, Chang Shao-tseng hosted a luncheon for M.P.'s, at which a number of cabinet nominees spoke and answered questions. Gifts of 200 yuan for each M.P. were issued to encourage support for the cabinet. On January 19, the cabinet passed the House and, on the 24th, it was confirmed by the Senate (with the exception of Alfred Sze). The appointments were gazetted on January 25.[12]

Chang's cabinet was the first to have gone through the legal process of parliamentary approval since the Chin Yun-p'eng cabinet of late 1919. Once approved by parliament, a cabinet could be unseated only by a major crisis. Furthermore, by passing Li's nominee Chang, parliament dropped the pretense of suspending judgment on the legality of Li's position as president.[13]

The ambitious Chang almost called down a crisis on his own head with one of his first official acts, a public telegram of January 8, 1923, addressed to the

10. *STSP* 1923.1.6.2; also see "Chō Shō-sō," pp. 3–9, for an analysis of the cabinet's composition. The declining involvement of Wu was due to a combination of factors. The fall of the Wang cabinet, which Wu had strongly backed, constituted a rebuke to his efforts to play Peking politics, and Sun Yat-sen's return to Canton drew Wu's attention more closely to military confrontations with the South.

11. Wang refused to take up the post and was replaced with Ch'eng K'o, a former M.P. and bureaucrat who was probably recommended to Chang Shao-tseng by Feng Yü-hsiang. See "Chō Shō-sō," pp. 11–12; *GJMK*, 1932, p. 281; *MJTC*, *chüan* 8, p. 167; *PYCF*, 6: 182. Dr. Sze's nomination was not approved by parliament, so he was replaced with Huang Fu, who was later replaced with Wellington Koo. "Chō Shō-sō," pp. 12–14, 18–19.

12. *STSP* 1923.1.8.2, 1.12.2, 1.14.2, 1.15.2, 1.20.2, 1.25.2, 1.26.3; also cf. *PYCF*, 6: 183. Although there are various interpretations of the reasons for parliament's rejection of Sze's nomination, I find most plausible the argument that Sze foresaw the failure of forthcoming Sino-Japanese negotiations, and, wishing not to be associated with them, sent a message to the Senate that he was ill and could not serve. See "Chō Shō-sō," pp. 12–13; *STSP* 1923.1.25.2.

13. *PYCF*, 6:182.

feuding parties in the South, calling for an end to the fighting, completion of the constitution, and a national conference to resolve disputes and determine methods to cut troops, regulate national finances, and promote education and industry.[14] Harmless enough in its sentiments, the inaugural expression of high goals happened to be extraordinarily timely from the viewpoint of Sun Yat-sen, whose allies had just driven Ch'en Chiung-ming out of Canton. A truce would stave off the threat from Wu P'ei-fu's ally, Shen Hung ying, who was bearing down from Kwangsi, and give Sun time to return to Canton and re-establish his base. The delighted Sun replied favorably to Chang's proposal, as did a broad range of other military and political figures who were interested in blocking Wu's military expansion.[15] Chang seemed intoxicated by an unrea is-tic belief that peace was near and continued to pursue it through telegrams and envoys,[16] to the discomfiture of Wu P'ei-fu and Ts'ao K'un. Wu demanded the appointments of Shen Hung-ying and Sun Ch'uan-fang as *tuli* (military governors) of Kwangtung and Fukien, respectively, wishing by the appoint-ments to legitimize invasions of the two provinces. The organization of Sun's military government on March 2 made these appointments all the more urgent.[17] But Chang, publicly committed to the pursuit of a truce, could not do this small favor without great embarrassment. To escape the dilemma, he submitted his cabinet's resignation on March 8. But eleven days out of office to demonstrate sincerity were sufficient to enable Chang to return to office with face more or less intact. On his return, Chang countersigned the two contenti-ous appointments, ending the crisis.[18]

The incident of the Fukien-Kwangtung military governorships was only the most spectacular of several shocks the cabinet managed to survive. In January, student demonstrations in Peking attacked Minister of Education P'eng Yun-i for his part in formulating the policy of recommitting Lo Wen-kan to jail for a second trial, but P'eng stayed in office and the demonstrations died out.[19] Late in March, a motion of no confidence in the cabinet was submitted to parliament, where it continued to be discussed and considered, a constant threat to the cabi-

14. Text in *LSINP*, 2:241.

15. *LSINP*, 2:242–46; *STSP* 1923.2.2.2. Those responding included Tuan Ch'i-jui, Chang Tso-lin, and Lu Yung-hsiang.

16. *STSP* 1923.1.18.2, 2.2.2, 2.3.2, 2.4.2, 2.5.2; *PYCF*, 6:201–5. Chang went so far as to issue an order on February 8 cancelling the proscription of Wang I-t'ang that had been issued after the Anfu-Chihli war and restoring Wang's ranks and decorations (*Tung-fang tsa-chih* 20, no. 5 [March 10, 1923]: 136). But amnesty orders for the other Anfu "criminals" were delayed because of opposition from Wu P'ei-fu (*STSP* 1923.2.15.2). Li Ssu-hao's amnesty was issued on March 26 (*STSP* 1923.3.28.3).

17. *STSP* 1923.2.26.2, 3.7.2, 3.8.2; "Chō Shō-sō," p. 16.

18. *STSP* 1923.3.9.2, 3.10.2, 3.20.2, 3.21.2; *PYCF*, 6: 205–8.

19. "Chō Shō-sō," pp. 14–15; *PYCF*, 6: 210–11.

net.[20] In May, the government was deeply embarrassed by the "Lincheng incident," in which bandits in Shantung seized some 200 passengers, including twenty-six foreigners, from the northbound Pukow-Tientsin passenger train and successfully held them for ransom for more than a month.[21]

And the ever-tightening financial noose hung around the cabinet's neck. In April, troops and officers of the Peking garrison demonstrated to demand payment of Mex. $1.5 million in back pay.[22] In June, employees of the ministries of Interior and Education held meetings to demand back pay.[23] A government scheme to earmark a large part of the customs surplus for administrative costs was blocked by the bankers and Inspector General Aglen.[24] An effort to raise money from foreign banks failed.[25] The garrison troops, pacified in April by a promise of payment of their back wages in installments, surrounded the residence of the minister of finance on May 10 to demonstrate against the delay in making these payments. But the minister had already fled and, with his two vice-ministers, submitted his resignation.[26]

Despite these tribulations, the weakened cabinet survived. And as long as the cabinet survived, so did Li Yuan-hung.

Toppling Li Yuan-hung

At a cabinet meeting on June 6, 1923, Kao Ling-wei pulled from his pocket prepared copies of a resignation statement and a circular telegram, which he proposed the cabinet should issue, and read them to his colleagues. These recalled that in the past few days Li Yuan-hung had encroached on the cabinet's authority three times: first, by not seeking cabinet approval before ordering that funds from the Maritime Customs Construction Fund be allocated to pay parliament's constitution-writing fees; second, by refusing to appoint a person nominated by the cabinet to be garrison chief inspector;[27] and, third, by refusing to promulgate the appointment of Feng Yü-hsiang's subordinate,

20. Text, STSP 1923.3.24.3. For general discussion of this bill and its fate, see "Chō Shō-sō," pp. 22–24. For key incidents, see STSP 1923.5.4.2, 4.10.2, 4.12.2, 4.26.2, 5.3.2, 5.17.2.

21. PYCF, 6: 224–31.

22. STSP 1923.4.3.2, 4.27.7. For related stories, see STSP 1923.2.11.7, 3.7.2, 3.30.7, 3.31.2, 4.17.7, 4.18.4, 4.29.3, 5.3.2, 5.4.2, 5.4.3; PYCF, 6: 233–34.

23. STSP 1923.5.5.7; PYCF, 6:234. Also see Sheridan, Chinese Warlord, pp. 125–26, for further evidence of financial stringency.

24. Stanley F. Wright, Collection and Disposal, pp. 182–83; STSP 1923.4.7.2.

25. STSP 1923.5.2.2.

26. STSP 1923.5.10.2, 5.11.3. Finance Minister Liu was replaced on May 12 by Chang Ying-hua, another Chihli Clique financier. STSP 1923. 5.13.2; GJMK,1932, p. 224; MJTC, chüan 5, p. 120; Chia Shih-i, Min-kuo ch'u-nien, pp. 93–94.

27. The cabinet had nominated one Chang Kung-chen for this post, while Li preferred

Hsueh Tu-pi, as director of the Peking Octroi.[28] The statements argued that the president was creating confusion about the role of the cabinet under a responsible cabinet system. To prevent the country from slipping into constitutional confusion, the cabinet must resign in protest. Wu Yü-lin, Ch'eng K'o, and Chang Ying-hua—all Paoting followers—agreed with Kao that the cabinet should resign. Whether the rest of the cabinet resigned or not, the four of them would do so. "If there are going to be resignations, we should all resign," said Prime Minister Chang. The other ministers perforce bowed to their colleagues' will, and the resignation was sent to the president.[29]

This was the first salvo in a more determined effort by Ts'ao K'un's lieutenants to sweep Li Yuan-hung from the Peking stage.[30] Potential successors to Chang Shao-tseng understood the situation was now untenable. Li turned first to Wellington Koo, who thought for a day, then declined; W. W. Yen was unwilling to serve if Li intended to remain in office. To reinforce the message, Army Inspecting Commissioner Feng Yü-hsiang and Garrison Commander Wang Huai-ch'ing brought several hundred garrison officers and troops to

---

to appoint his own follower, Ha Han-chang; *PYCF*, 6: 238.

28. The Peking Octroi was a gate tax of 3 percent, worth roughly 2 million yuan per year. The income customarily went to support the expenses of the presidential office as well as certain educational expenses and payments on certain short-term bonds. The post of Octroi director (*chien-tu*) was usually held by someone close to the president. The incumbent, T'ao Li, had been recommended by Wu P'ei-fu and apparently continued to supply the Presidential Palace with its share of the Octroi income. When the cabinet decided to appoint Hsueh Tu-pi to the post, Li, fearing it meant the diversion of Octroi funds from the support of his office, refused to promulgate the appointment. *STSP* 1922.6.5.2, 1923.2.11.3, .6.4.2; *NCH* 1924.4.12.46; *Ching-shih shui-wu yueh-k'an*, no. 1 (n.d.), tables section, pp. 1–2; Sheridan, *Chinese Warlord*, pp. 126–27; *PYCF*, 6:238. On July 4, after Li had left Peking, the caretaker cabinet promulgated Hsueh's appointment to the post. *STSP* 1923.7.5.3.

29. Liu Ch'u-hsiang, *Kuei-hai cheng-pien*, pp. 36–38.

30. My interpretation of the events of June 1923 differs in certain respects from those of *PYCF*, 6: 232–48 and Liu Ch'u-hsiang, *Kuei-hai cheng-pien*, pp. 33–43, who view the June events as having been planned in advance by Ts'ao K'un. I suspect that these events proceeded incrementally—first with an intention merely to cause a cabinet crisis, and then, when Li refused to resign, turning to direct action to force him out of office. On a related point, I interpret the cabinet crisis strategy as a new one, initiated at the beginning of June, while *PYCF*, 6: 232–36, argues that the effort to topple the cabinet dates from the end of April. It is true that late in April and early in May three Chihli Clique cabinet members, Kao Ling-wei, Wu Yü-lin, and Ch'eng K'o, absented themselves from cabinet meetings for about a week and Chang Shao-tseng offered his resignation to President Li. But the three members returned to the cabinet in return for the replacement of cabinet Secretary-General Lü Chün with Feng Yü-hsiang's follower Hsueh Tu-pi. The Chihli Clique also provided Chang Ying-hua to replace Liu En-yuan as minister of finance. It is therefore hard to believe that this was a serious effort to topple the cabinet. See *STSP* 1923.5.3.2, 5.6.2, 5.7.2, 5.8.2, 5.9.2, 5.10.2, 5.11.2.

demonstrate at the Presidential Palace on June 7, demanding back pay. On June 9, the police announced that they were going on strike. Although in fact the police continued to patrol in plainclothes, the implication of the strike was that the president could not guarantee public order in Peking or protect merchants and foreigners.[31]

The message was clear to all but the stubborn Li. Declaring that he had come into office in accord with the law and would leave it in the same way, he sent a letter to parliament urging it to determine when he should leave office. At the same time, Li pressed the hopeless search for a prime minister and issued a series of public telegrams—one defending himself against the charges made by the retiring Chang cabinet, others making public the steps he was taking to find a prime minister and placing the blame for the deteriorating situation on Feng Yü-hsiang and Wang Huai-ch'ing. Summoning the dean of the diplomatic corps, Li explained that the police strike was part of a Ts'ao K'un plot to drive him from office and said he refused to leave until the constitution was completed. Li even telegrammed twice to Ts'ao K'un and Wu P'ei-fu, describing how he was being persecuted and asking them, "as senior officers near the capital," to take steps to help him.[32]

In response to Li's resistance, his enemies only tightened the screws. Pien Shou-ch'ing arrived from Tientsin and organized a series of "citizens'" demonstrations, which surrounded the president's private residence from June 10 through 13, displaying signs saying, "The people are hungry, the president fat," "Reform the government," "Retire the president," and "Greedy for office." A second demonstration by the troops of the garrison on June 10 also surrounded the president's home and cut off the water and telephone. And on June 12, Feng Yü-hsiang and Wang Huai-ch'ing submitted their resignations, abandoning their responsibility to protect the president..[33]

Li could no longer operate in Peking. On June 13, he issued a telegram reviewing the demonstrations, the resignations of the officials responsible for public order, and the inaction of the nearby senior military officials. "From the Wuchang uprising until now," Li wrote, "I have neither raised troops nor established political parties. I have tried to serve the popular will with sincere public spirit. When I returned to office last year, I urged parliament to elect a successor; all I wished for was early completion of the constitution. Not only have I never tried to prolong my term in office or contest the election, but I

31. Liu Ch'u-hsiang, *Kuei-hai cheng-pien*, pp. 39, 43–45; *STSP* 1923.6.8.2, 6.8.3, 6.9.2, 6.10.2, 6.10.3, 6.11.2.

32. Liu Ch'u-hsiang, *Kuei-hai cheng-pien*, pp. 39, 43–46; *STSP* 1923.6.10.2, 6.11.2; F.O. 228/3001, Circular No. 146, Dean of Diplomatic Corps to Ministers, June 9, 1923.

33. Liu Ch'u-hsiang, *Kuei-hai cheng-pien*, pp. 40–45; *STSP* 1923.6.9.7, 6.10.2, 6.11.2, 6.13.2.

have never thought of doing it: how can I be suspected of it? Now my personal freedom has been wantonly restricted, and I am unable to conduct the duties of my office. I have no choice but to move temporarily to Tientsin [to carry on as President]."[34]

Li Ken-yuan had assisted Li throughout the difficult week. The president now drew up a series of orders appointing Li Ken-yuan as prime minister and Chin Yung-yen as minister of war; abolishing all offices of tuchun, tuli, high inspecting commissioner, and the like, and putting all troops under the direct control of the Ministry of War; calling for the punishment of "those persons initiating and directing" the disorders in Peking; and announcing a date for the abolition of likin. The orders abolishing tuchuns and likin and ordering the punishment of malefactors were, of course, hopelessly quixotic. They constituted no more than efforts to harass Li's warlord enemies and establish a platform for seeking future public support. Li also dispatched a message to the two houses of parliament, withdrawing the resignation he had submitted as a formality the preceding August,[35] and sent a message to parliament and the diplomatic corps announcing that he was proceeding to Tientsin to continue in his duties as president. Li then boarded a special train for Tientsin.[36]

As soon as Li had gone, the Chihli politicians began to take control of the city. Feng Yü-hsiang and Wang Huai-ch'ing cancelled their resignations and undertook to keep the peace. The police strike and demonstrations ended. Surveillance was placed over the movements of members of parliament to ensure that a quorum remained in Peking to elect the next president. The seven orders that Li had issued before leaving were held up at the Office of Printing and Engraving and not published. The remaining cabinet members in Peking, led by Kao Ling-wei, held a meeting to discuss taking over the government as a caretaker cabinet pending the presidential election. In all respects, the Chihli politicians treated the situation as though Li Yuan-hung had resigned.[37]

The trouble was Li had not resigned and, it soon became evident, he had neither handed over nor, apparently, left behind the seals of office without which the caretaker cabinet could not issue orders. Alerted by phone, Chihli Governor Wang Ch'eng-pin met the president's train at Yangts'un, outside of Tientsin.

34. Liu Ch'u-hsiang, Kuei-hai cheng-pien, pp. 40–41.

35. Since parliament had refused to act on the resignation and had returned it to Li, there was no need to withdraw it. But this did serve to underscore the president's determination to continue in office. It also was probably meant to deprive parliament of a pretext that it might have used to undercut Li's claim to the presedency.

36. STSP 1923.6.14.2; texts of orders and messages in Liu Ch'u-hsiang, Kuei-hai cheng-pien, pp. 47–48.

37. STSP 1923.6.13.3, 6.14.2, 6.14.7, 6.15.7, 6.16.2; Liu Ch'u-hsiang, Kuei-hai cheng-pien, pp. 41, 51–52.

Troops were put aboard, and the presidential train proceeded to Tientsin with Li a virtual prisoner. Governor Wang, at first polite, became increasingly explicit. Li would not be released until he handed over the presidential seals. When Li's son and the foreign consuls in Tientsin came to the station to see him, they were prevented from entering the train. Furious, Li reportedly tried to shoot himself but was prevented by a foreign adviser.

Some nine hours after leaving Peking, Li, who was hungry, tired, and in pain from diabetes, finally revealed to Governor Wang that before leaving Peking he had given the seals to one of his wives and instructed her to go to the French Hospital in the diplomatic quarter and remain there until she had further instructions. After several telephone calls from Li, his wife handed over the seals. Li was then compelled to sign a series of telegrams announcing his resignation and charging the cabinet with exercising the presidential powers. Only then, in the early morning hours of June 14, was he allowed to leave the train and go to his private residence in the Tientsin British concession.[38]

As soon as he was safely home, Li issued a series of telegrams repudiating his forced resignation and reiterating his appointment of Li Ken-yuan as acting prime minister.[39] In Peking, these messages were ignored. The cabinet under Kao Ling-wei declared itself a caretaker cabinet and, a few days later, on parliamentary authorization, proclaimed invalid all orders and telegrams issued by Li Yuan-hung beginning on June 13.[40] With Paoting's support, the cabinet was able to pay government officials two months' arrears and give a 500-yuan bonus to the members of parliament. Money to pay the garrison troops and other government employees became available from salt funds, government banks, and government-connected private banks.[41]

Although Li continued to claim to be president,[42] Peking was now securely in the hands of Ts'ao K'un's followers. In terms of public opinion and the legitimacy of Peking, it had been a costly victory.[43] Although history blames Ts'ao and his followers for the June 1923 coup, it would not have come about if parliament had performed its duty of resolving the presidency issue, nor would

38. This account is a composite drawn from several souces, which conflict on details. Liu Ch'u-hsiang, *Kuei-hai cheng-pien*, pp. 49–51; F.O. 228/3001, Despatch 95 from Tientsin Consulate-General to Peking, June 13, 1923; F.O. 228/3001, Despatch 99 from Tientsin to Peking, June 15, 1923, and enclosure; F.O. 228/3001, Dean's Circular No. 154, June 14, 1923; *STSP* 1923.6.14.2, 6.15.2; Shen Yun-lung, *Li Yuan-hung*, pp. 162–70.

39. *STSP* 1923.6.16.2; Liu Ch'u-hsiang, *Kuei-hai cheng-pien*, pp. 73–74.

40. Liu Ch'u-hsiang, *Kuei-hai cheng-pien*, pp. 52–53, 60–62; *STSP* 1923.6.15.2, 6.16.2, 6.17.2, 6.18.2.

41. *STSP* 1923.6.16.2, 6.18.2; Liu Ch'u-hsiang, *Kuei-hai cheng-pien*, p. 59.

42. See Liu Ch'u-hsiang, *Kuei-hai cheng-pien*, pp. 73–75, 166–71; *LSINP*, 2: 261–65.

43. See, e.g., *STSP* 1923.6.18.2, 6.20.2; "Chō Shō-sō," pp. 45–49.

it have been so destructive if Li Yuan-hung had not held on to his office so stubbornly. Each played a part in dissipating whatever optimism remained about making constitutionalism work in China. The prize for which Ts'ao had fought was much devalued by the events of June. And he had yet to persuade parliament to make his victory final.

Ts'ao K'un Buys the Presidency

Not since the death of Yuan Shih-k'ai had the warlords' grail of national unification seemed so close to being grasped by a single faction. The Chihli warlords now controlled the heartland of China—Chihli, Shantung, Honan, Kiangsu, Hupei, Anhwei, Kiangsi, and Fukien. Their major enemies, though still dangerous, were geographically dispersed—Chang Tso-lin in Fengtien, Sun Yat-sen in Canton, Lu Yung-hsiang in Chekiang, and T'ang Chi-yao in Yunnan. Hunan, Szechwan, Chekiang, and Kwangtung were already under military pressure.[44] Command of the presidency would add crucial financial, diplomatic, and symbolic resources to complete the drive toward unity. So, at least, the situation appeared to Ts'ao K'un and his advisors: Wu P'ei-fu had favored postponing the election until military unification was more nearly complete, but with the expulsion of Li Yuan-hung this was no longer an option, and Wu lapsed into silence.[45] Ts'ao's agents in Peking, Pien Shou-ch'ing and Wang Yü-chih, quickly negotiated the price of votes and the date of the election with Wu Ching-lien and the parliamentary clubs. Five thousand yuan per vote was agreed upon, with the election set for July 26 and the constitution to be completed in the interim and promulgated on August 1.[46]

44. "Chihō seikyō (ichi)" *Shina jōhō*, no. 9 (April 16, 1924), p. 29. For more information on the Chihli Clique's military base, see Wen Kung-chih, *Tsui-chin san-shih nien, pien* 2, pp. 8–49. In the warlord context, such global strategic statements must always be taken to assume the qualification that "control" of a province usually meant only an unchallenged position as the chief official of the province and not necessarily full control over all of its territory, which might contain virtually autonomous pockets ruled by local officials or bandits.

45. On Wu's attitude, see T'ao Chü-yin, *Wu P'ei-fu*, pp. 83–84; *Wu P'ei-fu hsien-sheng chi*, pp. 226–27; Shen Yun-lung, *Li Yuan-hung*, p. 146; Odoric Y. K. Wou, "Militarism in Modern China as Exemplified in the Career of Wu P'ei-fu, 1916–1928," (Ph.D. diss., Columbia University, 1970), p. 256.

46. *STSP* 1923.6.20.2, 6.24.2, 6.25.2, 6.26.2. There is also a report of a June 28 meeting of Chihli politicians to establish an office to manage the election, but the authenticity of the report is doubtful because the list of those attending includes the names of some politicians who do not seem to have been closely involved in Ts'ao's election—particularly Wellington Koo, W. W. Yen, and Ch'ü Ying-kuang; see *STSP* 1923.6.29.7. Also contributing to the sense of haste toward the election in Peking in late June was the publication of a telegram

But no sooner had the arrangements been completed than it became clear that parliament lacked the quorum to complete either the constitution or the presidential election. The election required two-thirds of the total 870-man House and Senate membership, or 580 members. The constitutional quorum was three-fifths of the joint membership, or 522. This meant that 290 members could block the election and 348 could block consideration of the constitution.[47] As early as the joint session of June 16, which met to determine what to do in the aftermath of Li's flight, it proved impossible to get a three-fifths quorum and the members present could only proceed on the basis of a quorum of one-half the members—an action later denounced as illegal by those who opposed the day's decisions.[48] Subsequent constitutional committee meetings also failed to obtain quorums. It soon became clear that this was not merely because of postcoup excitement; in fact, M.P.'s were fleeing in large numbers to Tientsin, where by early July some 350 had gathered.[49]

What lay behind such rapid, unified action by members of the usually demoralized and atomized old parliament? The Chihli threat of military and political dominance had produced a coterie of strange bedfellows known as the "three-corner alliance" (san-chiao t'ung-meng), to whose leaders many M.P.'s were allied. The three "corners" of the alliance were Sun Yat-sen, Chang Tso-lin, and Lu Yung-hsiang. Although not formally allied, the three had regularly exchanged emissaries since 1922 to discuss their shared interest in preventing unification under Ts'ao K'un's auspices—an interest also shared by Tuan Ch'i-jui, T'ang Chi-yao, and the old Communications Clique, who were involved in the anti-Chihli consortium although not popularly counted among its corners.[50] So long as Li Yuan-hung was president, there had been utility in having anti-Chihli M.P.'s in Peking to back Li against Ts'ao; now that Ts'ao K'un's presidential aspirations were before parliament, their major utility lay in being

---

Wu P'ei-fu allegedly sent to Ts'ao K'un urging Ts'ao to order the garrison command to prevent M.P.'s from leaving the city so that the election could be completed within a week. Wu denied having sent the telegram. T'ao Chü-yin believes the telegram was authentic, but in view of Wu's general coolness to the election, it seems more likely the wire was a forgery. For the text, see Liu Ch'u-hsiang, *Kuei-hai cheng-pien*, p. 79, and *LSINP*, 2: 266; for discussion, *PYCF*, 6: 248; T'ao Chü-yin, *Wu P'ei-fu*, p. 90; Wou, "Militarism," p. 256.

47. This assumes that all M.P.'s were alive and well and in Peking. In fact, the antielection forces probably started with an advantage of five or ten members who were no longer active.

48. *STSP* 1923.6.17.2; Liu Ch'u-hsiang, *Kuei-hai cheng-pien*, pp. 60–73.

49. *STSP* 1923.6.16.2, 6.22.2, 6.23.2, 6.24.2, 6.25.2, 6.26.2, 7.1.2, 7.5.2, 7.7.2.

50. Ku Hsiu-sun, *Chia-tzu nei-luan shih-mo chi-shih*, pp. 24–25; *Kuo-fu nien-p'u* (Taipei, 1965), 2:523–24; *Chih-Feng ta-chan shih*, pp. 40–41; *PYCF*, 6:189; Li Yun-han, *Ts'ung jung-kung tao ch'ing-tang* (Taipei, 1966), 1:165; F.O. 371/9181, F1807/2/10, Fletcher to Stubbs, April 25, 1923; F.O. 371/9203, F1245/85/10, Macleay to Curzon, February 17, 1923, enclosure, extracts from Mukden Intelligence Report, December quarter, 1922.

withdrawn to destroy parliament's quorum. Sun's followers in parliament, Chang's Fengtien delegation, Lu's Chekiang delegation, and Tuan's followers from the old Anfu Club leadership, each constituted a group of some twenty to sixty members. The core anti-Ts'ao group was completed by the addition of twenty or thirty Political Study faction members, who had become Li Yuan-hung's closest supporters during the preceding year. The opposition core group thus numbered in the neighborhood of 275 members.[51] The great political issue of the next three months was to be whether the anti-Ts'ao forces could bring their strength up to the 290 necessary to block the election.

Parliamentary leaders on both sides conducted a letter-and-telegram debate laying out the arguments for leaving or staying in Peking.[52] In a letter to their colleagues still in Peking, a group of anti-Ts'ao M.P.'s argued:

Except for the Lincheng incident, we have not in recent times seen such an extreme case of disruption as this latest instance of wanton behavior and usurpation in the capital. If you gentlemen don't look into this carefully, you may think we are putting it too strongly. But how can one believe parliament still has the freedom to carry out its duties, if one hasn't looked into the facts of the conduct of this latest coup? How can one believe there is still any hope of completing and promulgating the constitution in light of the discussion sessions of June 13 and 16 [in which parliament decided that all Li Yuan-hung's orders since June 13 were invalid]? How can one read over the various telegrams [e.g., a secret telegram allegedly written by Wu P'ei-fu] urging [police officials in Peking to assure] rapid completion of the election and to forbid work on the constitution in the meantime, and believe that parliament has the power to punish the perpetrators of the coup? And how can it not have occurred to you that when the legal position of the cabinet is that of men who have seized and usurped their office, they will be unable to balance right and wrong, weigh profit and harm, for our vast nation with its 400 million people? Gentlemen, what do you say? We, your colleagues, when faced with this coup, could only decide to move our meetings to Shanghai. This was the way to preserve our stature as M.P.'s and, indeed, to preserve our stature as citizens. Moreover, all the heavy duties which we have undertaken and which we cannot now complete in Peking, such as finishing the constitution and electing the president, will be easily completed there.

The letter went on to urge the M.P.'s in Peking not to associate themselves with bribery, as it was rumored they had been doing, because of the harm this would do the the reputation of parliament and the health of the republic.[53]

51. Hsieh Pin, *Cheng-tang shih*, pp. 110–14; STSP 1923.7.7.2; Liu Ch'u-hsiang, *Kuei-hai cheng-pien*, p. 77; inspection of list in *ibid.*, pp. 90–100, and of lists of signers of various telegrams in *ibid.*; my rough estimates of faction strength.

52. For extensive documentation of this debate, see Liu Ch'u-hsiang, *Kuei-hai cheng-pien*, pp. 118–34, and Sun Yao, comp., *Chung-hua min-kuo shih-liao*, pp. 464–501.

53. Liu Ch'u-hsiang, *Kuei-hai cheng-pien*, pp. 80–81. No date given; the probable date is approximately July 1. Although there were claimed to be 285 signers, only 13 names were actually listed. They constituted a good sample of the leadership of the major anti-Ts'ao factions.

A typical response to such arguments was the July 8 declaration of the M.P.'s in Peking:

Recently, because Li Yuan-hung has left Peking, there are some powerful figures outside the capital who wish to take advantage of the situation and use parliament to cause trouble. At the same time a number of our colleagues have become excited by temporary political appearances and, without thinking the matter through carefully, have given vent to emotional impulse and called for a move to the South. Without regret, they throw themselves into the vortex. As a result, successive meetings of the Constitutional Drafting Committee have lacked a quorum. Divisions within parliament may encourage the outbreak of civil war among the various factions of North and South. It is easy to cause disorder but difficult to bring it to an end. The tragic consequences are unbearable to consider. We cannot rely on war to settle our national political disagreements. . . . War will plunge us into an eternal anarchy, with multitudes of soldiers confronting one another, bandits filling the mountains, and foreigners stationing troops in the country, carrying out "joint supervision" and seizing our sovereignty in order to protect their investments. . . . And the reason for all this will be the reckless division of our parliament. . . .

Li Yuan-hung's recent departure from office was neither a change in the form of government nor a dissolution of parliament. . . . Surely it shows a lack of proportion to sacrifice parliament on the bier, destroy the nearly-completed constitution, and cut off legal orthodoxy just when it has been restored, all because of the comings and goings of one man, Li Yuan-hung. If it be argued that Li's departure was under compulsion of militarists, then parliament can decide to have an investigation to ferret out the culprit and with the administration's cooperation the man can be impeached. There is adequate room for dealing with the situation within the scope of the law. . . . Recall that parliament has been twice dissolved and dispersed. In the nation-protecting war, [Yuan Shih-k'ai's] imperial order was overthrown and parliament restored. In the constitution-protecting war, the false president [Hsu Shih-ch'ang] was overthrown and parliament restored. [Parliament is] the carefully preserved fruit of our efforts, for which we have sacrificed countless lives and treasure, for which many of us have gone to war and undergone hardships. Those who now suddenly turn around and scheme to cooperate with those who would destroy parliament are consulting with the tiger about getting his skin: in the end, it is he who will bite them. . . .

We deeply hope that our colleagues who have left Peking will think carefully, look closely at the political situation, consider where it started and how it will end, and hurry back to Peking to complete the constitution, thus discharging the responsibility borne by us M.P.'s for ten years.[54]

54. Liu Ch'u-hsiang, *Kuei-hai cheng-pien*, pp. 118–20; signed by more than 200 members. "Joint supervision" (*kung-kuan*) refers to a scheme promoted by the powers, in the aftermath of the Lincheng incident, to put Chinese railways under the powers' joint supervision in order to reform railway fiscal and management policies and thus prevent warlord or bandit seizure of money slated to pay off foreign obligations. The scheme was never put into effect, but the discussion of it caused a strong nationalist reaction—combined with a self-interested concern in official circles about the fate of one of their most lucrative sources of money. See further Chapter III, note 6.

Loath to rely solely on the merits of their arguments, both sides resorted to a tried device: money. Publishing the decision to move parliament to Shanghai to complete the constitution, the anti-Ts'ao leaders let it be known that M.P.'s would receive 500 yuan "travel money" on arrival in Tientsin and 300 yuan per month salary in Shanghai.[55] By July 14, when ceremonies were held to establish the new parliamentary offices at the Hupei Guild (*Hu-pei hui-kuan*) in Shanghai, nearly 300 M.P.'s were present and the number was rising steadily.[56] But how many could be kept from returning to Peking?

In Peking, Ts'ao K'un told visiting parliamentary leaders that he favored "the consitution first and the election afterward" (*hsien-hsien hou-hsuan*).[57] This brought back to Peking some M.P.' s who felt strongly about parliament's responsibility to complete the constitution. Constitutional Drafting Committee meetings were convened three times a week and just as regularly failed to get a quorum. While political observers carefully charted rising and falling attendance at these meetings, Ts'ao's agents in Peking and Tientsin worked to persuade more M.P. 's to return.[58] Some M.P. 's went back and forth between Tientsin and Peking, accepting travel money in one place and Constitutional Drafting Committee attendance fees and monthly salaries and bonuses at the other.[59]

As July wore into August, the tide seemed to turn clearly against Ts'ao K'un. Attendance dropped steadily from 459 on July 14, to 435 at the end of July. On August 4, 536 members showed up in Peking to receive their salaries for July, but many of them returned directly to Shanghai to receive salaries there. Thus, on August 14, attendance in Peking was down to 385; in Shanghai a few days later, an equal number were present to receive their wages.[60]

---

55. *STSP* 1923.6.23.2; Liu Ch'u-hsiang, *Kuei-hai cheng-pien*, p. 135. The source of the money is not clear. T'ao says part of the money was provided by Li Yuan-hung, part by Lu Yung-hsiang (*PYCF*, 6:246; 7:6).

56. Liu Ch'u-hsiang, *Kuei-hai cheng-pien*, pp. 80, 101. Also see F.O. 228/3002, Despatch 112, Barton to Macleay, July 20, 1923. The Hupei Guild was outside the foreign settlement, within which political activity was forbidden. It is not clear precisely why the Hupei Guild was available or why it was chosen. In general, Shanghai public opinion was strongly against the Ts'ao coup in Peking and the M.P.'s coming to Shanghai received the support of most of the *fa-t'uan* there. Cf. *STSP* 1923.6.26.2, 6.26.3.

57. *STSP* 1923.7.5.2, 7.7.2; Liu Ch'u-hsiang, *Kuei-hai cheng-pien*, pp. 134–40. Ts'ao also pursued an abortive negotiation to win the support of Sun Yat-sen. Sun Hung-i served as mediator in this effort. *STSP* 1923.7.5.2, 7.6.2, 7.7.2; Liu Ch'u-hsiang, *Kuei-hai cheng-pien*, pp. 140–45.

58. E.g., see *STSP* 1923.7.11.2, 7.12.2, 7.13.2, 7.14.2, 7.15.2, 7.17.2.

59. *STSP* 1923.7.5.2, 7.7.2, 7.7.3.

60. *STSP* 1923.7.15.3, 8.1.2, 8.7.2, 8.15.2, 8.15.3, 8.26.2. This last source gives the number as 386, but Liu Ch'u-hsiang, *Kuei-hai cheng-pien*, p. 80, says 385. Since Liu was a leader of the Shanghai parliament, and since he claims that 385 is the greatest number ever to have

Wu Ching-lien, managing Ts'ao's campaign in parliament, now further revised his tactics.[61] The presidential election law allowed a maximum interval of three months in which a caretaker cabinet could perform the presidential functions; by September 13, a new president must be elected.[62] The law also provided that the date of the election meeting of parliament was to be set by a joint caucus of the two houses. In consultation with other parliament and Chihli Clique leaders, Wu determined to schedule the caucus for September 8, and he arranged two attractive pieces of bait to lure a quorum of members to Peking in time for the meeting.[63] First, on August 24, he called a discussion meeting of the two houses and reported that discussion meetings would henceforth be held once a week and attendance at each meeting would be rewarded with a fee of 100 yuan.[64] Second, he scheduled a meeting of the House for September 7 to consider a bill amending the Parliamentary Organic Law to permit M.P.'s to serve not, as in the old law, three years for representatives and six for senators, but indefinitely until a new parliamentary election was held.[65] Senator Chang

registered in Shanghai, it is reasonable to conclude there was never a greater number of registrants. There were reports at times of as many as 500 or more M.P.'s being present in Shanghai, but presumably not all of them registered for salaries; see, e.g., *STSP* 1923.9.6.3; F.O. 228/3003, Despatch 157, Barton to Macleay, September 29, 1923.

61. In addition to Wu's change of tactics, another consequence of the unexpected delay in the election was a series of changes to enable the caretaker cabinet to function better over an extended period. Wellington Koo finally took office as foreign minister on July 23 (he had been appointed to the post by Chang Shao-tseng but had not taken office). Chang Hu was appointed minister of finance on August 14. Chang raised money to quiet the protests of unpaid government employees in Peking, including the garrison command officers and troops whose financial woes had played such a prominent role in driving Li Yuan-hung from Peking. On September 4, Li Ken-yuan and P'eng Yun-i of the Political Study faction were replaced as ministers of agriculture and commerce and of education by Yuan Nai-kuan and Huang Fu (who refused the post), and a vice minister of war was appointed acting minister of war to replace Chang Shao-tseng. See *PYCF*, 7:3; *STSP* 1923.7.19.2, 7.21.2, 7.24.2, 7.25.2, 7.27.2, 7.29.2, 7.30.2, 8.3.2, 8.4.2, 8.8.7, 8.15.2, 8.18.2, 8.19.2, 8.19.3, 8.22.2, 8.26.7, 8.30.2, 9.5.3, 9.11.2.

62. On August 25, the cabinet received cables from several senior Chinese ambassadors overseas urging consummation of the presidential election order in to avoid damage to China's international prestige. *STSP* 1923.8.27.2. It is tempting to speculate whether or not these cables, which apparently arrived simultaneously, were solicited by the cabinet.

63. *STSP* 1923.8.20.2, 8.21.2, 8.24.2. The quorum for the caucus would be a majority, i.e., 436 members. Of course, Wu also needed to obtain a quorum of 580 members for the election, which would presumably follow by a few days.

64. *STSP* 1923.8.25.3; Liu Ch'u-hsiang, *Kuei-hai cheng-pien*, pp. 145–46.

65. Specifically, the amendment recognized the three- and six-year terms as normal but added that "the office of Member . . . will be dissolved only after the completion of the next election, on the day before the new session opens." Needless to say, the effect of this amendment was to give M.P.'s indefinite tenure. Although the tenure situation of the old parliament was complicated because of its checkered history, most people seemed to believe

Lu-ch'üan was sent to Shanghai to urge M.P.'s there to make the trip to Peking, to cover the expense of which he was able to provide 400 yuan per man.[66] A Shanghai parliament counter offer of 150 yuan bonuses to members who were in Shanghai between August 31 and September 2 failed to prevent attendance at Peking meetings from climbing steadily upward.[67] On September 7, the House, for the first time since the June coup, had a quorum, and it passed the amendment to the Parliamentary Organic Law.[68] There were now rumored to be more than 500 delegates in Peking.[69]

September 8, the day set for the caucus, proved a disappointment. Only 424 M.P.'s attended, twelve short of the required 436. A second effort was scheduled for September 10, and on that day, after delaying the start of the meeting for an hour and a half, precisely 436 members were reported in attendance. The decision was made to hold the presidential election on September 12, one day before the caretaker cabinet's powers ran out. But five M.P.'s who had been listed as present protested that they had not in fact attended the meeting, and a member of the House Secretariat confirmed that he had been instructed to falsify the attendance records to bring the total from 431 to 436.[70] Nonetheless, the decision stood and the election preparations went forward.

Confident that the necessary 580 M.P.'s were in Peking and would not miss the opportunity to earn 5,000 yuan—the price set for each vote in the presidential election—Wu Ching-lien convened the September 12 election meeting. The police had ordered the city's merchants to hang congratulatory banners. Observers and guests gathered at the parliament building in a festive mood. But after twice delaying the opening of the meeting, Wu still lacked a quorum. Only 410 members had taken their seats. The meeting ended without electing a president.[71]

The failure of the September 12 election meeting doubtless owed something to continued jockeying within parliament over the terms of support, as con-

that the terms of the representatives and half the senators would end in October 1923. But under the new provisions, since new elections were not held, parliament continued to serve until it was dissolved in the aftermath of Feng Yü-hsiang's coup of October 1924. *STSP* 1923.9.8.2; Liu Ch'u-hsiang, *Kuei-hai cheng-pien*, pp. 150–56.

66. *STSP* 1923.8.30.2; Liu Ch'u-hsiang, *Kuei-hai cheng-pien*, pp. 151, 154.

67. *STSP* 1923.9.2.2. For climbing attendance rates at Constitutional Drafting Committee meetings, see *STSP* 1923.8.26.3, 8.29.7, 9.2.2, 9.5.3, 9.7.2.

68. *STSP* 1923.9.8.2; Liu Ch'u-hsiang, *Kuei-hai cheng-pien*, pp. 154–55. *STSP* says attendance was 308; Liu says 302. Only 298 were needed for a quorum of the House.

69. *STSP* 1923.9.6.3. Although only 437 attended the Constitutional Drafting Committee meeting of September 6, it was plausible that there were others in town who did not attend.

70. *STSP* 1923.9.9.2, 9.11.2, 9.12.2; Liu Ch'u-hsiang, *Kuei-hai cheng-pien*, pp. 159–66.

71. *STSP* 1923.9.13.2.

temporary observers speculated.[72] But a key background element was the continued vitality of the alternate parliament in Shanghai. The plan to set up a national government there seemed finally to be near fruition when Li Yuan-hung, after long delay, responded to the urgings of his supporters and on September 9 left Tientsin for Shanghai. Arriving on the 11th, he met with his supporters, and on the 12th he told reporters that, although he was not jealous of the position of president as such, it was necessary, in order to uphold the law, that he continue to serve until he was legally relieved of the post. That day, the Shanghai parliament decided to resume formal sessions on September 22.[73]

However, Li's scheme for a Shanghai government evaporated almost as soon as it was exposed to the open air. Lu Yung-hsiang of Chekiang and Ho Feng-lin of Shanghai had just signed a peace treaty with three other warlords on August 19, at the adamant behest of local gentry and merchant opinion, which committed them to avoid any political activities in Shanghai that might be controversial and cause war to break out. Although sympathetic to Li's anti-Chihli purposes, they could not allow his government to be established in Shanghai, and local public opinion also vociferously opposed the idea because of its potential dangers for local peace. By the end of September, Li's plan was effectively dead and on November 8 he left Shanghai for a long trip to Japan.[74]

The Shanghai parliament unraveled rapidly. From September 14 on, the House in Peking began to achieve a regular quorum.[75] Attendance at Constitutional Drafting Committee meetings hovered around 500.[76] On September 26, the Senate achieved its first quorum since June and passed the bill sent to it by the House extending M.P.'s term in office until the opening of the next session.[77] And on October 4, the Constitutional Drafting Committee had its first quorum since June, with a hefty attendance of 551, and passed some sections

72. E.g., *STSP* 1923.9.13.2; *Pei-ching pao* 1923.9.14 as quoted in Liu Ch'u-hsiang, *Kuei-hai cheng-pien*, p. 206.

73. Liu Ch'u-hsiang, *Kuei-hai cheng-pien,* pp. 166–71; *PYCF,* 7: 6–9. Li's timing in going south may have been influenced by the three-month deadline on service of caretaker cabinets. The September 22 meeting never occurred because there was no quorum of M.P.'s in Shanghai at that time. Yang Yu-chiung, *Li-fa shih*, p. 307.

74. Liu Ch'u-hsiang, *Kuei-hai cheng-pien*, pp. 170–71; *PYCF,* 7:9–10; F.O. 228/3003, Despatch 153, Barton to Macleay, September 16, 1923. Despite his deliberation before moving to Shanghai, Li was apparently misled by his advisors about the chances of success there.

75. *STSP* 1923.9.15.2.

76. *STSP* 1923.9.14.2, 9.19.2, 9.21.2, 9.23.2, 9.28.2, 9.30.3, 10.2.2, 10.3.2.

77. *STSP* 1923.9.27.2; Liu Ch'u-hsiang, *Kuei-hai cheng-pien*, pp. 155–56. On October 4, the amendment was promulgated by the cabinet. Some said the promulgation was a *quid pro quo* for the Ts'ao election; *STSP* 1923.10.4.2; Liu Ch'u-hsiang, *Kuei-hai cheng-pien*, p. 156. An order for the next election was also promulgated at the same time to mollify those who opposed parliament's self-serving self-extension, but the new elections were never held.

of the constitution dealing with local government.[78] This was the signal for the election to be held. It meant that negotiations with respect to the means of payment of the 5,000-yuan election fees had been settled; that agreement had been reached on the postelection distribution of sinecures, and that the date had been set for the completion of the constitution.[79] On October 5, parliament elected Ts'ao K'un president; the meeting was attended by 590 M.P.'s, of whom 480 cast votes for Ts'ao.[80] When the test came, the anti-Ts'ao holdouts still in Shanghai numbered only 275.[81]

The fact that election was taking place on October 5 was apparently not widely known in Peking. "Apart from the flags displayed under the directions of the police, there was an almost complete lack of any visible signs of public interest in the election," a diplomat reported.[82] On October 8, the Constitutional Drafting Committee completed the constitution, and on October 10, 1923, the day Ts'ao assumed office, the constitution was promulgated.[83]

Final Disillusionment

The Peking regime had at last discharged the solemn obligation set for it in 1912 by the Provisional Constitution: promulgation of a permanent constitution. The twists and turns of Peking politics had finally issued in the piece of paper so long regarded as a panacea for the republic's problems and for China's weakness. Now, as K'ang Yu-wei had dreamed in 1898, perhaps the nation would be strong, with the "rulers and the millions of their people united in a single body" under the constitution's sway.

But the consummation of the constitutionalist dream was also the moment of rude awakening. The bureaucrats, professionals, and intellectuals who a year earlier had allowed themselves to be caught up in the mood of national optimism could not now award their loyalty to a regime conceived in a bumbling *coup d'etat* and delivered in a flurry of blatant bribery. A photo of one M.P.'s bribery check of 5,000 yuan was published nationwide, and a shame list of M.P.'s accepting bribes was issued by parliamentarians in Shanghai. Denunciations of the "piggish" (*chu-tzu*) members came from the full range of political

78. *STSP* 1923.10.5.2. There had been forty-three meetings in a row without a quorum. "Sōtō senkyo to kenpō seitei," *Shina jōhō*, no. 4 (December 14, 1923), p. 22.

79. For these negotiations, see *STSP* 1923.9.15.2, 9.16.2, 9.17.2, 9.19.2, 9.20.2, 9.23.2, 9.27.2, 9.29.2; *PYCF*, 7: 12–13.

80. *STSP* 1923.10.6.2. Some sources give the attendance as 592 or 593.

81. They are listed in Liu Ch'u-hsiang, *Kuei-hai cheng-pien*, pp. 90–100. Another five M.P.'s must have died or resigned from parliament.

82. F.O. 371/9182, Despatch 586, Macleay to Curzon, October 17, 1923.

83. *STSP* 1923.10.9.2, 10.12.2; Yang Yu-chiung, *Li-fa shih*, pp. 310–11. Text of the new constitution in Ch'ien Tuan-sheng, *Government and Politics*, pp. 436–46.

and intellectual notables, non-Chihli warlords and provincial *fa-t'uan*. As for the rising political generation, the students, already denied a place in the constitutional order by government repression in the incident of May 4, 1919, had become increasingly politicized in the intervening years and now marked the promulgation of the constitution with another in a long series of demonstrations.[84]

The republic over which Ts'ao K'un presided, minus its constituency, was an empty shell. "Hereafter the only new hope was the Kuomintang,"[85] about to begin a reorganization leading to a Leninist organizational form, a mass base, a party army, and government based on mobilization and tutelage rather than constitutional republicanism.

Ts'ao had spent an estimated Mex. $13,560,000 to buy the presidency.[86] Although no doubt he enjoyed the pomp of the office, substantively the money was wasted. In the act of purchase, the presidency was devalued. Neither its prestige nor its powers served to awe Chihli's enemies. In Manchuria, Chang Tso-lin gathered his strength for a second clash with Wu P'ei-fu, and in October 1924 Chang's victory was assisted by the defection of Feng Yü-hsiang from Chihli's ranks. Tuan Ch'i-jui was called from retirement to head a new government. Finding the flag of "constitutional orthodoxy" too frayed to use, he declared the occasion a revolution, like that of 1911, and established a temporary Executive Government to await an entirely new constitution. But only those few directly involved could be absorbed in the idea of yet another constitution; to the rest of the nation, it was a charade. The constitution prepared under Tuan's regime was never promulgated, and when Tuan fell in April 1926, he was succeeded by a series of regency cabinets and then by Chang Tso-lin's Marshal's Government which, with little pretense to more than stopgap status, lasted until Peking's reunification with most of the rest of China under Kuomintang auspices in 1928. So far from realizing the resurgent hopes of 1922, the protracted factional struggles of 1922–23 merely marked the decisive stage in China's disillusionment with constitutional republicanism.

84. For reaction to the Ts'ao K'un election and constitution, see Liu Ch'u-hsiang, *Kuei-hai cheng-pien*, prefaces and pp. 218–68; *PYCF*, 7: 1, 15–16; Li Chien-niung, *Political History*, p. 435; "Chi Ts'ao K'un hui-hsuan an," *Chiang-su ko-ming po-wu-kuan yueh-k'an*, no. 13 (n.d.), 14 pp.

85. Li Chien-nung, *Political History*, p. 435.

86. "Chi Ts'ao K'un hui-hsuan," pp. 1–2; repeated in *PYCF*, 7:16.

VIII

CONCLUSION

This study approaches the early republic at several analytical levels. The first task is to decipher what was going on. This means, of course, learning who did what to whom, but the more challenging analytical aspect of the task is to understand the logic behind the complex political maneuvers thus discovered. To a considerable degree, the politicians' maneuvers become intelligible in the context of the constraints imposed by the dominant form of political organization—factions.

The model of factionalism developed in Chapter II defines a factional political system as one primarily organized by a kind of leader-centered, dyadically-structured, clientelism-based structure called a faction. The major Peking political units—the Tuan Ch'i-jui faction, the Chihli Clique, the Communications Clique, and so forth—appear to fit this definition, and the behavioral characteristics that the model describes for a system organized by such structures were likewise evidenced in the Peking political system.

One of the characteristics of a factional system is a code of civility, which limits the sanctions imposed on losers in a factional political conflict. The operation of this code is seen in the way Tuan Ch'i-jui and his followers were allowed to escape unharmed from Peking after the Anfu-Chihli war, and in the dignified departure of Hsu Shih-ch'ang from Peking after he was deposed as president. Even Li Yuan-hung, although forced from Peking and physically detained until he handed over the seals of office, was not harmed and lost no personal property in the course of the coup against him.

Another characteristic of a factional political system is that political initiatives are quite rare, and in fact, in the period covered by this study, their number was restricted to Tuan Ch'i-jui's attempt to win the presidency, Hsu Shih-ch'ang's peace initiative, the Chihli restoration of Li Yuan-hung, and Ts'ao K'un's assault on the presidency. The preference for secrecy in such initiatives,

221

noted by the model, is best illustrated by Hsu's protracted hatching of his peace plot but appears also in the other cases. Also as the model describes, the efforts of other factions to defeat such initiatives and protect their own power consumed most of the political energies available. The result, which is consistent with the model, was to block the emergence of a strong leader, such as Tuan, Hsu, or Li might otherwise have been.

The model requires that the factions operate within a broad ideological consensus, and this was provided by the faith in constitutionalism. But within the constitutionalist political elite, as the model prescribes, factional alliances were shifting and were not ideologically based. The Communications Clique cooperated first with Tuan, then with Hsu, then with Sun Yat-sen; at the end of the period, we find the Communications Clique opposing Ts'ao K'un in co-operation with their erstwhile enemy, Chang Tso-lin. The Research Clique supported Tuan Ch'i-jui in 1917, opposed him bitterly in 1919, cooperated again in 1925. Various factions of the Kuo-min tang denounced the northern war-lords in 1917–22 but worked closely with the Chihli Clique in 1922–24.

Decisions in the factional system were made by consensus—examples are the decisions to elect a new parliament in 1918, to elect Hsu Shih-ch'ang, to restore Li Yuan-hung to office. But, in the cycle identified in the model, decisions were followed by deterioration of the consensus in disputes over actions taken by the faction in power (here, opposition to Tuan's election as president in 1918, to Hsu's peace policy in 1919, and to Li's attempt to solidify his position as president in 1922–23). Each phase of deterioration ended in a crisis and test of strength (Tuan's unsuccessful efforts to persuade Ts'ao K'un to pursue war against the South at the second and third Tientsin conferences in 1917, the breakdown of the Shanghai peace conference followed by Hsu's inability to deal with the May Fourth Movement and the outeak of the Anfu-Chihli war, and the Chihli coup against Li Yuan-hung in 1923 followed by Ts'ao's bribery of parliament).

Factional politics, according to the model, are a politics of personality, characterized by rumor, character assasination, bribery, and deception. At the same time, in apparent contradiction, political struggle is couched in terms of abstract issues of ideology, honor, and face. The combination of high argument and low politics appeared frequently in our narrative, for example in connection with the fall of the "able men cabinet" and the tug of war over the votes of M.P.'s before the Ts'ao K'un election.

The statements the model makes about the size and shape of a factional system appear accurately to describe the Peking political arena in 1918–23. A factional arena is composed of a limited, fairly small number of factions, as was the case in Peking. Factional elites resist challenges to the legitimacy of the system; Peking factions opposed the intrusion into the system of such nonfactional political forces as the students of the May Fourth Movement and turned upon and ejected one of their own number, Li Yuan-hung, who stuck too literally to the written rules of the constitution when these conflicted with the unwritten rules of factionalism. Yet, constitutionalism as a basis of legitimacy was held inviolate by a few politicians—even until 1928—despite the fatal damage it incurred in the 1923 coup. The Peking government's failure to solve its financial problems or end the North-South split, much less to deal with warlordism or China's other fundamental ills, was characteristic of the immobilism affecting factional systems. As a result, although the system continued to replicate itself in Peking from one cycle of conflict to the next, it became increasingly isolated from the larger society, where political forces gathered to overthrow it.

The factionalism model, in short, makes political strategies intelligible and says something about the shape and evolution of the Peking political system. But to bring Peking politics into sharper focus, it is necessary to locate it in time and place. The empty category, "basis of legitimacy," has to be filled with the concept, "constitutionalism," and the attraction of this idea to political leaders must be explained. It is necessary to delineate the boundary between the constitutionalist political elite of bureaucrats, professionals, and politicians and the surrounding society, which was to nurture the forces challenging the Peking political system. We must be aware of a network of "connections" from which the clientelist ties making up factions were mobilized. The specific issues over which factional consensus was formed or crises occurred can be understood only in view of the institutional system of president, cabinet, and parliament, operating in a world of powerful militarists and foreign powers. In short, what can be understood in general terms in light of the factionalism model can be understood more concretely when the social, intellectual, and institutional context is sketched.

The political struggles described in chapters IV through VII were, however, no mechanistic combination of model and setting; they were contingent and unpredictable historical events, as the detailed narrative reveals. But, in the light of analysis, they should no longer seem baffling or incomprehensible. A meaningful language of political beliefs and strategies was being used.

Finally, it is possible to decipher the meaning of this era for China's political evolution. Constitutionalism was a modern, prestigious method of nation-building when China's leaders turned to it as a means of saving China in 1912. Theirs was a serious effort, one in a succession of serious but unsuccessful efforts for national self-strengthening. The failure of technological and educational reform as self-strengthening techniques had made necessary this more profound national transformation in search of wealth and power. The failure of constitutionalism would make deeper transformations necessary.

Those who led these later revolutions learned at least two things from the constitutionalist failure. First, it was not enough to transform the elite internally—its educational and professional composition and its political language—

while preserving its narrowness and estrangement from the masses. Forces traditionally excluded from legitimate politics—the students, the middle classes, the workers, and ultimately, although few people realized it in 1923, the peasants —were clamoring to be politically heard and no stable basis for politics could be found that did not include at least some of them. In this sense, the early republic was the last traditional Chinese polity—the last in which the legitimate political voice belonged to a narrowly circumscribed elite.

Second, the failure of the republic taught the need for a strong, unambiguous, single focus of loyalty. "Equality groups," in Lyon Sharman's phrase—non-hierarchical forms of organization, with ambiguous loci of power—did not work in early twentieth-century China. The politicians were uncomfortable in such settings and, when thrust into them, arranged themselves in the congenial form of factions, which provided some sense of hierarchy and stable affiliation. But there was still lacking, at the top, a supreme figure gripping the financial, military, personnel, and intelligence reins of power and buttressed by a legitimating ideology. In his absence, power was diffuse, not unitary; the struggle for it was expanded, not confined; and, with factions as the basis of political organization, the result was chaos. To counter factionalist tendencies, future political leaders would try to construct tightly hierarchical Leninist organizations, with the secret struggle for power sharply focused at the top.

But why, finally, did the republic fail? Without being able definitively to answer this larger question, we can summarize now what went most immediately awry. A small elite with a political culture framed largely in the traditional society knew just enough about constitutions to believe that they were easy to operate and efficacious in supplying stable government. The early republicans hoped to avoid conflict by gathering consensus around a constitutional process. But the process mandated by any republican constitution is precisely a process of conflict. Not unnautrally, practicing politicians fell back on the tools at hand—their subordinates, colleagues, schoolmates, and others tied to them by the hierarchical and personalistic values of their political culture. They formed factions, and consequently found themselves trapped in the frustrating and self-defeating political process we have described as factionalism. Long-term commitment to constitutionalism and to national wealth and power could not excuse them from the necessity of playing the immediate political game. As the factions kaleidoscopically turned against one another, no one could earn adequate power to carry out his ends. Power seemed tantalizingly near yet always evaporated when touched. While the mirage of power persisted, the politicians trapped in the system continued to play out their circular games, never stopping to realize that the system could neither settle into stability nor evolve into something new. Peking became increasingly divorced from China. It was the office of those excluded from the Peking political arena to recognize the necessity of rebuilding the political system on a new basis.

APPENDIX:

Profiles of Major Factions

This appendix profiles seven early republican factions or faction-based groupings whose members played prominent roles in the events of 1918–23. One purpose is to sketch *dramatis personae* and their relationships. A second is to illustrate the range of early republican factional formations by describing a military complex faction (the Chihli Clique), two bureaucratically-based civilian factions (the Communications Clique and New Communications Clique), a personal faction with its support structure (the Tuan Ch'i-jui faction and the Anfu Club), and three professional politicians' factions or factional alliances of varying degrees of structural stability (the Research Clique and the Political Study and I-yu groups). A third goal is to substantiate Chapter II's argument that connections influenced recruitment by pointing, where possible, to the recruitment-relevant connections within factions.

The profiles are far from complete, sketching only the portion of each faction that was active in the events under study and bringing factional histories no further through time than necessary to serve as background for the present study. The profiles are based mainly on biographical dictionaries and other secondary sources and will doubtless be improved upon when more research has been completed on specific individuals or factions. Meanwhile, one problem is that the best documented factions (in secondary sources) happen also to have been composed of bureaucrats and ex-bureaucrats (the Chihli, Communications, New Communications, Tuan Ch'i-jui, and, to some extent, Research groups); factions whose members were primarily professional politicians are harder to map because their members were less well-known. Thus, the apparently greater strength and clearer structure of ex-bureaucrats' factions may be to some extent an artifact of the data.

Biographical sources on members of the factions are usually cited only once, in the notes either to the appendix or to the text, wherever the person's background is most fully discussed or most relevant.

The figures illustrating the appendix are laid out to suggest the generational and "connections" structure of each faction. Lines between names, keyed with letters, indicate connections among faction members that seem to have played a role in their recruitment or in the subsequent operation of the faction (see Chapter II for a fuller discussion of connections). Further interpretation of the figures is provided in each factional profile.

The Tuan Ch'i-jui Faction and the Anfu Club

Tuan Ch'i-jui was a consummate politician who played a pivotal role in republican politics because of his broad range of contacts and connections with bureaucrats and politicians. Tuan graduated from the artillery course at the Peiyang Military Academy in 1887, and, after further study in Germany, he became commander of the artillery corps and superviser and chief lecturer at the artillery school at Hsiaochan, where Yuan Shih-k'ai was training his Newly-Founded Army.[1] Thanks to his important role at Hsiaochan, about half of the officers of the Newly-Founded Army, including many of the important North China militarists of the early republic, were his students.[2] Tuan had access to another large pool of political talent as a native of Hofei, Anhwei, a city whose sons displayed strong localistic identification and uncommon political skill (Li Hung-chang and many of his followers had been Hofei men). Although he was an army general, Tuan did not have a warlord-style political base in the direct command of troops or the control of territory.[3] His influence was based upon seniority, prestige, and skill, including skill in using an extensive network of connections, and particularly upon his large personal faction composed of politicians and military men of the highest caliber (see Figure 2). Tuan's personal faction should be distinguished, on the one hand, from the so-called Anhwei Clique, which may be defined as the set of militarists who fought on Tuan's side or supported him publicly in the Anfu-Chihli war of 1920, and, on the other, from the Anfu Club.[4]

1. Liu Feng-han, *Hsin-chien lu-chün* (Nankang, 1967), p. 113. The main source on Tuan's life is Wu T'ing-hsieh, *Ho-fei nien-p'u*. Also see Boorman and Howard, *Biographical Dictionary*, 3: 330–35.

2. *ATTA, chüan* 2, p. 7; *TTMJ*, 1: 29–31.

3. Tuan occasionally commanded forces, as in 1911 and 1917, but did not retain direct command after the end of hostilities. When he formed the War Participation (later Border Defense) Army in 1918–20, he delegated direct command of troops to Hsu Shu-cheng, while retaining overall charge of the headquarters. Tuan's ability to use these troops to his advantage thus depended on Hsu's loyalty to him.

4. In Chinese, there is a confusion of terminology. *Tuan-hsi* means Tuan's personal faction; *Wan-hsi* usually means the Anhwei military group (as in *Chih-Wan chan-cheng*); *Anfu-hsi* may refer to either of these or to the Anfu Club.

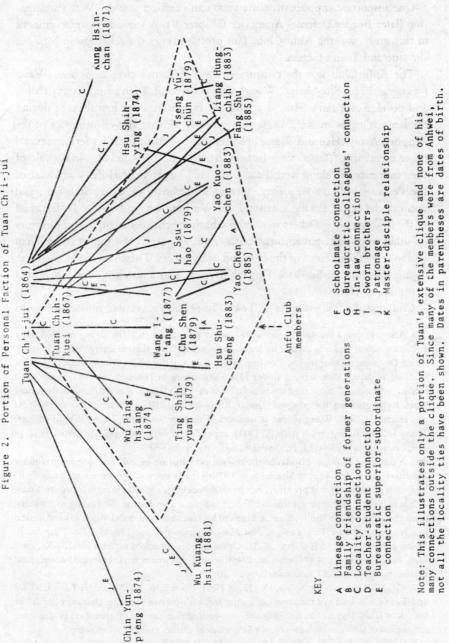

Figure 2. Portion of Personal Faction of Tuan Ch'i-jui

KEY

A Lineage connection
B Family friendship of former generations
C Locality connection
D Teacher-student connection
E Bureaucratic superior-subordinate
   connection

F Schoolmate connection
G Bureaucratic colleagues' connection
H In-law connection
I Sworn brothers
J Patronage
K Master-disciple relationship

Note: This illustrates only a portion of Tuan's extensive clique and none of his
many connections outside the clique. Since many of the members were from Anhwei,
not all the locality ties have been shown. Dates in parentheses are dates of birth.

One important support structure for Tuan's faction was the War Participation (later Border Defense) Army (see Chapter V). A second, more prominent in this study, was the Anfu Club. This profile stresses the relationship between the club and Tuan's faction.

The Anfu Club was the creature of two of Tuan's close associates, Wang I-t'ang and Hsu Shu-cheng. Wang[5] was a native of Tuan's home city, Hofei, and protégé of Tuan's. Hsu,[6] a young officer whom Tuan had selected during the late Ch'ing as an aide, was serving in early 1918 as vice-commander of the Fengtien Army. Hsu and Wang brought into the Anfu Club leadership several other members of Tuan's core faction. Among those invited to join because of their influence in Peking were Tuan Chih-kuei,[7] a native of Hofei, a graduate of the Peiyang Military Academy, former subordinate of Yuan Shih-k'ai, and commander of the Peking garrison; and Wu Ping-hsiang,[8] also of Hofei, chief of the Peking police. Others were men whom the club could support for cabinet or other important government posts, both to extend the influence of Tuan and to serve the interests of the club and its members. These included Chu Shen, Tseng Yü-chün, Li Ssu-hao, Ting Shih-yuan, Yao Kuo-chen, Yao Chen, and Liang Hung-chih.

Chu Shen,[9] a law graduate of Tokyo Imperial University, and according to

5. After earning a *chin-shih* degree at the age of twenty-six in 1904, Wang decided upon a military career and was invited by his co-provincial, Tuan, then in charge of the Peiyang Third Division, to visit him at Paoting. Wang rose rapidly under Tuan's patronage, first studying in Japan, then serving under Hsu Shih-ch'ang in Fengtien. In 1911, with Hsu's recommendation, Wang joined the personal staff of Yuan Shih-k'ai and subsequently served Yuan by organizing the progovernment Kung-ho tang (Republican party) in the first parliament. In 1916, Wang served as minister of the interior in the Tuan Ch'i-jui cabinet. Wang I-t'ang, *I-t'ang shih-ts'en* (n.p., 1941), appendix ("Nien-p'u"), p. 1b; *GJMK*, 1932, p. 219; Boorman and Howard, *Biographical Dictionary*, 3: 380–82.

6. A native of Kiangsu, Hsu failed the *chü-jen* examination in 1897 and decided to follow a military career. He went to Shantung in 1901 to try to get into the service of Yuan Shih-k'ai, then governor of that province, but he could not even get an appointment to see Yuan. While in Tsinan, he happened to meet Tuan Ch'i-jui in a restaurant. According to the story handed down in Hsu's family, Tuan, impressed by Hsu's toughness and vigor, invited him to join his personal staff. Hsu Tao-lin, *Hsu Shu-cheng nien-p'u*, pp. 139–45; Wu T'ing-hsieh, *Ho-fei nien-p'u*, p. 9; "SSG," pp. 30–31. Other sources consulted on Hsu include *Kuo-shih kuan kuan-k'an* 1, no. 4 (November 1948):86–88; Boorman and Howard, *Biographical Dictionary*, 2:143–46; *ATTA, chüan* 2, pp. 9–10.

7. *GJMK*, 1924, p. 609; "SSG," p. 32; *ATTA, chüan* 2, p. 12. Although Tuan Ch'i-jui and Tuan Chih-kuei had the same last name, and Ch'i-jui had the same character "chih" in his *tzu* as Chih-kuei had in his *ming-tzu*—suggesting that they were members of the same generation of the same lineage—none of my sources affirms a family relationship.

8. *GJMK*, 1924, p. 792; *GJMK*, 1932, pp. 116–17; *MJTC, chüan* 8, p. 152.

9. *GJMK*, 1932, pp. 150–51; *Who's Who*, p. 66; *ATTA, chüan* 2, pp. 10–11; *MJTC, chüan* 8, p. 32.

one source a relative of Hsu Shu-cheng, had served as an official on the Supreme Court and as minister of justice in Tuan Ch'i-jui's cabinet of March–August 1918. He joined the Anfu Club and with its backing was retained as minister of justice in the cabinets of Ch'ien Neng-hsun and Chin Yun-p'eng, serving also as acting minister of the interior from June to December 1919.

Tseng Yü-chün,[10] a Fukienese *chü-jen*, attracted the notice of Tuan Ch'i-jui in 1914 or 1915 and became one of Tuan's secretaries. Under Tuan's patronage, he served in such posts as chief cabinet secretary and director of the Peking-Hankow Railway. Tseng served in the Provisional National Council of 1917–18, which revised the parliamentary election laws. With Anfu Club backing, Tseng in 1919–20 served as acting minister and then minister of communications. He was in charge of the Liaison Department of the club Secretariat.

Li Ssu-hao[11] was the scion of a wealthy Ningpo merchant family who earned a *chin-shih* degree and pursued a career in the Ch'ing Board of Revenue (Ministry of Finance). Li's ability earned him the support of Tuan Ch'i-jui, and in 1917 Li became acting minister of finance, acting director-general of the Bank of China, and acting director-general of the Currency Reform Bureau. Having joined the Anfu Club, Li was vice-minister of finance in the Ch'ien Neng-hsun cabinet and minister of finance in the succeeding Chin Yun-p'eng cabinet.

Ting Shih-yuan[12] served as an officer under Tuan Ch'i-jui during the 1911 revolution. In 1916, he was brought from a provincial post to Peking and made head of the Peking-Suiyuan Railway. Having joined the Anfu Club, in late 1918 he was also given charge of the Peking-Hankow Railway (amalgamated with the Peking-Suiyuan Railway in 1919). Ting allegedly peculated huge sums from the two railways for the benefit of the Anfu Club and pro-Anfu militarists.[13] He also received appointment as comanager with Lu Tsung-yü of the government-owned Lungyen Iron Mining Company.[14]

Yao Kuo-chen,[15] a native of Anhwei and a graduate of Peking University, entered the Ministry of Communications shortly after the founding of the

10. *GJMK*, 1932, pp. 203–4; *Who's Who*, p. 236; *ATTA, chüan* 2, p. 10.

11. *GJMK*, 1932, pp. 376–77; *Who's Who*, p. 145; *ATTA, chüan* 2, p. 10; Ch'ang An, *Min-liu hou*, p. 9; Chia Shih-i, *Min-kuo ch'u-nien*, pp. 55–62. Chia considers Li one of the two most able ministers of finance in the republican period (p.83). While the warlords were deluging the government with demands for funds, Li published a budget that drew public attention to rocketing military expenses, meanwhile raising money through foreign loans to satisfy the warlords' demands and prevent the outbreak of civil war (p. 56).

12. *GJMK*, 1932, pp. 461–62; *ATTA, chüan* 2, p. 11.

13. Ch'ang An, *Min-liu hou*, pp. 53–55.

14. See *NCH* 1918.8.17.385.

15. *GJMK*, 1932, p. 349; *ATTA, chüan* 2, p. 18; *Who's Who*, p. 274; *Jimbutsu jihyō* 3, no. 5 (October 1925): 1–4.

republic. When in 1916 another Anhweinese and follower of Tuan, Hsu Shih-ying,[16] became minister of communications, Yao rose rapidly to director of the Bureau of Posts. Having joined the Anfu Club in 1918, Yao was promoted under Tseng Yü-chün to vice-minister of communications in 1919–20. In this post, Yao was allegedly in charge of allocating ministry funds for the support of the Anfu Club.

Yao's younger brother, Yao Chen,[17] a law graduate of Waseda University, served in the Board of Justice and as an official in the Supreme Court under the Ch'ing. In the republic, he continued as a staff member of the Supreme Court, joined the Anfu Club, and in 1918 became the head of the court—a position in which he would be able to protect any Anfu member who was charged with wrong-doing in an official capacity.

Liang Hung-chih[18] of Fukien was a graduate of Peking University who served in Tuan Ch'i-jui's personal secretariat. Under Tuan Chih-kuei, Liang became chief of the Secretariat of the Peking garrison command. He was appointed to a Senate seat to represent Tibet in 1918 and was appointed chief of the Senate Secretariat. Liang was a special cadre of the Correspondence Section, Secretarial Department, of the Anfu Club Secretariat.

By no means all the members of Tuan Ch'i-jui's core clique were associated with the Anfu Club. On the contrary, some of Tuan's most loyal and powerful followers seem to have regarded the club as a nuisance and a political liability. The club's struggles with Tuan's follower Chin Yun-p'eng (whose background is discussed in Chapter V) illustrate the tendency of republican factions toward vertical cleavage and internal rivalry. Another Tuan follower, Kung Hsin-chan, had serious clashes with the club while serving as minister of finance in March and April 1919.[19] Tuan's follower Fang Shu (profiled in Chapter IV) was sympathetic to the Anfu Club but not a member. One of Tuan's military associates, Wu Kuang-hsin (see Chapter V), had little to do with the club one way or another.

While the club's chief beneficiaries, in terms of office and influence, were those of Tuan's followers who belonged to it, the burden of parliamentary

16. Boorman and Howard, *Biographical Dictionary*, 2:140–43; *Saishin Shina yōjin*, pp. 43–44; HSC, p. 59; *Jimbutsu jihyō* 3, no. 1 (February 1925): 4–5.

17. GJMK, 1924, p. 581; GJMK, 1932, pp. 349–50; GJMK, 1937, p. 497; *Jimbutsu jihyō* 3, no. 3 (July 1925): 16–19; ATTA, *chüan* 2, p. 17.

18. GJMK, 1932, p. 410; ATTA, *chüan* 2, p. 18; Boorman and Howard, *Biographical Dictionary*, 2:351–53.

19. On Kung, see MJTC, *chüan* 2, p. 27; GJMK, 1924, p. 909; ATTA, *chüan* 2, p. 21; Chia Shih-i, *Min-kuo ch'u-nien*, pp. 83–86; TTMJ, 1:54–56. On his clash with the Anfu Club, see Nathan, "Factionalism in Early Republican China," pp. 314–25.

leadership was borne by a cadre of professional politicians recruited by Wang I-t'ang. Wang had become acquainted with most of these professionals during his service in the 1913–14 session of parliament. Typical members of this professional cadre were Hsieh Shu-ch'iang, Huang Yun-p'eng, Wu Tse-sheng, K'o-hsi-k'o-t'u, and K'ang Shih-to.

Hsieh Shu-ch'iang,[20] a member of the House from Kiangsu, had been a senator in the old parliament. He belonged to the Chin-pu tang in the 1913–14 parliament and the pro-Tuan Chung-ho Club in 1917. Hsieh was a cadre in the News Section of the Anfu Secretariat.

Huang Yun-p'eng[21] was a Szechwanese appointed to the Tibet House delegation in the Anfu parliament. He had studied in Japan, then was elected to the House of the old parliament to represent Szechwan. Like Hsieh, he belonged to the Chung-ho Club of 1917. In 1917–18, Huang was a member of the Provisional National Council, which rewrote the parliamentary election laws. When not serving in parliament, Huang worked as a banker and college teacher.

Wu Tse-sheng[22] and K'o-hsi-k'o-t'u (probably Keshigtu)[23] were influential Japanese-educated co-owners of a series of minor Peking newspapers. Wu was a Waseda University graduate; K'o-hsi-k'o-t'u (a Mongol) had attended Meiji University. Wu was appointed to parliament in 1913 to represent Mongolia, while K'o-hsi-k'o-t'u was appointed to represent Tibet. During the period between parliaments, they concentrated on their newspaper publishing and supported Yuan Shih-k'ai's campaign to become emperor. In 1918, both Wu and K'o-hsi-k'o-t'u were appointed to the Tibetan delegation in the House, where they served prominently as floor leaders for the Anfu Club. Wu was a cadre in the club's News Section, and K'o-hsi-k'o-t'u was a member of its Deliberative Assembly.

K'ang Shih-to,[24] a journalist, was elected to the House with Anfu support from the Metropolitan District. K'ang managed the Anfu Club's campaign in the parliamentary elections in Chihli, his native province. He was head of the Registry Section of the Anfu Club Secretarial Department.

Although the followers of Tuan and the political professionals recruited by Wang I-t'ang performed most of the leadership chores in the Anfu Club, two

20. "SSG," p. 2. On political parties mentioned here and in the following paragraphs, see Yang Yu-chiung, *Cheng-tang shih*, pp. 66–80, 89–98. Party affiliations of Hsieh and of many of the others described here are also listed in Hsieh Pin, *Cheng-tang shih*, Appendix 2.

21. *GJMK*, 1937, p. 173; "SSG," p. 2.

22. *GJMK*, 1932, pp. 7, 432; "SSG," pp. 3, 12–13.

23. *GJMK* 1937, p. 187; "SSG," pp. 3, 12–13. For the transliteration Keshigtu I am grateful to Professors Hyer and Jagchid of Brigham Young University.

24. *ATTA, chüan* 2, pp. 19–20; "SSG," p. 4.

other groups may be briefly mentioned as participating in the club leadership. In pursuance of Tuan Ch'i-jui's then current political alliance with the New Communications Clique (described below), the latter group's leaders—Ts'ao Ju-lin and Lu Tsung-yü—were brought into the club, made members of the Deliberative Assembly, given Anfu support for government posts, and worked for the club's welfare in their official positions. Also, the leaders of the major provincial delegations within the club—such as Kuang Yun-chin (Anhwei),[25] Liu En-ko (Fengtien),[26] Wang Yin-ch'uan (Honan),[27] and T'ien Ying-huang (Shansi)[28]—naturally played important leadership roles in the club, particularly in relaying club policy to the delegations and mustering support within the delegations for the policy. In contrast to the political journeymen recruited by Wang, they were well rooted in the local power structures of their home provinces and derived their leadership positions in the Anfu Club from this fact.[29]

The Chihli Clique

Like the Tuan Ch'i-jui faction, the Chihli Clique had its origins in Yuan Shih-k'ai's Newly-Founded Army. While Tuan headed the artillery school at Hsiab-chan, Feng Kuo-chang,[30] a Peiyang Military Academy graduate, ran the training office. (Yuan's third leading subordinate, Wang Shih-chen,[31] wielded some influence during the republic as a "Peiyang elder" but did not head a faction.) Feng lacked Tuan's talent for cultivating followers and inspiring loyalty: according to an obituary, his "relations with others were based on nothing more than mutual cooperation for mutual benefit, so there were very few who were personally loyal to Mr. Feng. His power was therefore far from comparable to that of Tuan Ch'i-jui in the solidity and depth of its foundation."[32] Nonetheless, as Governor of Kiangsu (1913–17) and as President of the republic (1917–18), Feng had military supporters in the Yangtze region and civilian aides in Peking; these came to be known as the Chihli Clique to distinguish them from Tuan's Anhwei or Anfu Clique with whom they were often at loggerheads.

25. "SSG," pp. 2–3.

26. GJMK, 1932, p. 477; "SSG," p. 4; Who's Who, p. 165; Satō, Minkoku, p. 370.

27. GJMK, 1932, p. 16; "SSG," pp. 1–2; Jimbutsu jihyō 3, no. 4 (September 1925): 5–8.

28. STSP 1918.11.12.2; "SSG," pp. 3–4; GJMK, 1932, p. 287.

29. See further Nathan, "Factionalism in Early Republican China," pp. 214–35, for a discussion of the makeup and leadership of each provincial delegation in the Anfu parliament

30. Boorman and Howard, Biographical Dictionary, 2:24–28; Liu Feng-han, Hsin-chien, pp. 114–15.

31. Boorman and Howard, Biographical Dictionary, 3:393–95; Liu Feng-han, Hsin-chien, p. 117.

32. STSP 1919.12.31.2.

Ts'ao K'un,[33] governor of Chihli and a former subordinate of Feng's at Hsiaochan, was popularly accounted among the members of Feng's Chihli Clique, but in fact he maintained good relations with both Feng and Tuan until Feng's death, and, as we have seen in Chapter V, broke with Tuan only in 1920. At this point, the name Chihli Clique came to be used to describe the military faction composed of Ts'ao and his followers (Figure 3). After defeating Tuan in 1920, the clique shared power in North China with Chang Tso-lin until 1922, when victory in the first Chihli-Fengtien war brought Ts'ao's faction to the height of its strength.

The Chihli Clique controlled most of North and Central China during 1922–24. Nineteen of the twenty-six former Peiyang divisions—North China's best troops—and sixteen of twenty-three mixed brigades were under Chihli Clique commanders.[34] At the time of the first Chihli-Fengtien war, the Chihli leaders disposed of an estimated 280,000 men, compared to about 170,000 available to Chang Tso-lin.[35] The most important Chihli forces were those of Wu P'ei-fu,[36] inspector general of Hunan and Hupei; Hsiao Yao-nan (Hupei);[37] Sun Ch'uan-fang (upper Yangtze);[38] and Ch'i Hsieh-yuan (Kiangsu).[39] However, the clique also commanded the loyalties of numerous smaller warlords, as well as the provisional allegiance of allied militarists such as Feng Yü-hsiang.[40] (Feng's treachery in 1924 helped to throw victory in the second Chihli-Fengtien war to Chang Tso-lin.) Wang Huai-ch'ing,[41] the Peking garrison commander who played an important role in the 1923 ouster of Li Yuan-hung, was an old Peiyang type who had picked the Chihli side in 1920 and so retained his Peking post.

The overall structure of the Chihli Clique has been described elsewhere.[42]

33. Boorman and Howard, *Biographical Dictionary*, 3:302–5; Liu Feng-han, *Hsin-chien*, pp. 115–16.

34. Wen Kung-chih, *Tsui-chin san-shih nien*, pien 2, pp. 14–18; cf. Wou, "Militarism," pp. 327–29.

35. *Nu-li chou-pao*, no. 2 (May 14, 1922), p. 3. But Wen Kung-chih, *Tsui-chin san-shih nien*, pien 2, p. 24, estimates Chihli strength at 250,000. For other estimates, see Wou, "Militarism," pp. 187–88.

36. Boorman and Howard, *Biographical Dictionary*, 3:444–50; Wou, "Militarism," *passim*.

37. *GJMK*, 1924, pp. 981–82; Boorman and Howard, *Biographical Dictionary*, 3: 446.

38. Boorman and Howard, *Biographical Dictionary*, 3:160–62; Wou, "Militarism," pp. 212–13.

39. Boorman and Howard, *Biographical Dictionary*, 1:297–99.

40. Boorman and Howard, *Biographical Dictionary*, 2:37–43; Wou, "Militarism," pp. 213–14; Sheridan, *Chinese Warlord*.

41. *GJMK*, 1932, p. 19; Wou, "Militarism," pp. 215–16.

42. Odoric Y. K. Wou, "A Chinese 'Warlord' Faction: The Chihli Clique, 1918–1924," 1 Andrew W. Cordier, ed., *The Dean's Papers, 1967*, Columbia Essays in International

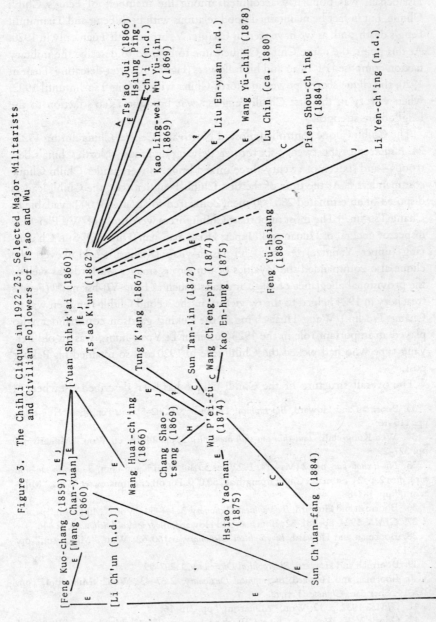

Figure 3. The Chihli Clique in 1922-23: Selected Major Militarists and Civilian Followers of Ts'ao and Wu

Selected additional connections not shown above:

C connections (Chihli) among Feng Kuo-chang, Ts'ao K'un, Ch'i Hsieh-yuan, Li Ch'un, Ts'ao Jui, Pien Shou-ch'ing, Wang Huai-ch'ing, Kao Ling-wei, Wu Yü-lin, Lu Chin, Liu Eh-yuan, Chang Shao-tseng.

F connections (Peiyang Military Academy) among Feng Kuo-chang, Ts'ao K'un, Wang Chan-yuan, Ch'i Hsieh-yuan, Li Ch'un, Wang Huai-ch'ing, Wang Ch'eng-pin, Wang Huai-ch'ing, Liu En-yuan, Wu P'ei-fu.

KEY

A Lineage connection
B Family friendship of former generations
C Locality connection
D Teacher-student connection
E Bureaucratic superior-subordinate connection
F Schoolmate connection
G Bureaucratic colleagues' connection
H In-law connection
I Sworn brothers
J Patronage
K Master-disciple relationship

Note: Bracketed names are those of deceased or factionally inactive predecessors.
Broken line indicates alliance. Dates in parentheses are dates of birth.

This profile focuses on an aspect of the faction that is especially germane to this study: the Ts'ao K'un/Wu P'ei-fu relationship and the strains introduced into it in 1922–23 by competition between the two men's political aides. For, like other warlords, Ts'ao and Wu were each served by a group of political agents and advisors who, among other tasks, represented their interests in the twists and turns of Peking politics.

Ts'ao's political advisors were split into two groups, one in Paoting at his headquarters, the other in Tientsin where his brother, Ts'ao Jui,[43] ex-civil governor of Chihli, lived. The Paoting group included[44] Kao Ling-wei,[45] an ex-bureaucrat who served in several cabinets as Ts'ao's representative; Wu Yü-lin,[46] a former military administrator who represented Ts'ao in the Chang Shao-tseng cabinet of 1923; Liu En-yuan,[47] a military officer who held various administrative posts under Ts'ao; Wang Yü-chih,[48] Ts'ao's long-time secretary; Hsiung Ping-ch'i,[49] Ts'ao's chief of staff; Lu Chin,[50] a staff officer of Ts'ao's; and Li Yen-ch'ing,[51] a notoriously corrupt young favorite of Ts'ao's. In Tientsin, besides his brother, Ts'ao was served by Pien Shou-ch'ing,[52] speaker of the provincial assembly, and others. The Tientsin group worked in close cooperation with Wang Ch'eng-pin,[53] the provincial governor and military affairs commissioner, whose headquarters were in Tientsin, and, at times, with Wu Ching-lien and other M.P.'s in Peking.

Affairs, vol. 3 (New York, 1968), pp. 255–71; expanded in Wou, "Militarism," chapters 4 and 5. Wou's analysis of the structural principles of Chinese military factions differs from that offered in Chapter II. He argues that such factions were perceived by their members as virtual clans and were organized and operated along clan-like lines. This is a suggestive analogy, but an adequate analysis should also illuminate the many differences in the political behavior of clans and military factions. Although in some respects analogous in gross structure to a clan, the Chihli Clique did not function like a clan and, in short, was not a clan.

43. GJMK, 1924, pp. 626–27; Boorman and Howard, Biographical Dictionary, 3:305. Ts'ao's other politically active brothers were Ts'ao Ying, a military commander, and Ts'ao Chün, a senator in the Anfu parliament. Boorman and Howard, Biographical Dictionary, 3: 305; STSP 1918.11.26.2; PYCF, 4: 108.

44. List based on Liu Ch'u-hsiang, Kuei-hai cheng-pien, p. 34; and PYCF, 6: 138; with a few additional names.

45. MJTC, chüan 1, p. 65; Chia Shih-i, Min-kuo ch'u-nien, p. 92; GJMK, 1924, p. 809; Who's Who, p. 120; Jimbutsu jihyō 2, no. 7 (November 1924): 4–5.

46. MJTC, chüan 8, p. 144; GJMK, 1924, p. 780.

47. GJMK, 1924, p. 378; GJMK, 1932, pp. 391–92; Chia Shih-i, Min-kuo ch'u-nien, pp. 89–90.

48. PYCF, 6: 184; GJMK, 1932, p. 15.

49. GJMK, 1932, p. 346.

50. GJMK, 1924, pp. 355–56; Jimbutsu jihyō 2, no. 7 (November 1924): 6–7. Both Hsiung and Lu were former subordinates of Feng Kuo-chang.

51. Li T'ai-fen, Kuo-min-chün shih-kao (Peiping, 1930), p. 119.

52. GJMK, 1932, p. 330.

53. GJMK, 1932, p. 29.

Wu P'ei-fu's aides, popularly called the "Loyang group" after Wu's head-quarters town, included[54] Sun Tan-lin,[55] Wu's co-provincial and secretary (later minister of interior); Kao En-hung,[56] also a co-provincial, an England-educated communications administrator and sometime minister of communications; Wu's secretarial and military staff; and his local government administrators.

Each set of advisors was anxious to advance the interests of its leader as it perceived them; the Loyang, Tientsin, and Paoting perspectives were not always the same. The decisive military strength of the clique was Wu P'ei-fu's, and it was under Wu's immediate command that the victories over Anfu and Fengtien had been won. Energetic, alert, and articulate, Wu won prestige by accompanying his victories with effective local rule and eloquent pleas for honest politics and obedience to the constitution.[57] Yet Ts'ao, the simple soldier, slow-moving and inarticulate, as Wu's commander reaped the rewards of his victories. After the Anfu-Chihli war, Ts'ao bowed to Chang Tso-lin's insistence that Wang Chan-yuan rather than Wu be made inspector general of Hunan and Hupei. After the Fengtien-Chihli war, the relative influence of Wu and Ts'ao in Peking remained to be tested.

The ploy of turning to Li Yuan-hung as a cat's paw to clear the stage of Hsu Shih-ch'ang and Sun Yat-sen had the stamp of Wu's mind on it rather than Ts'ao's.[58] The "restoration of constitutional orthodoxy" theme was consistent with Wu's public image. Wu's prestige shot up with soaring hopes for a successful reestablishment of constitutionalism. Some contemporaries even called the new government Wu-dominated and counted Ts'ao out of the picture. But Li's restoration also served Ts'ao's ends by opening a path to the presidency.

Wu's influence was clear in the composition of the W. W. Yen cabinet, which Li Yuan-hung appointed immediately upon taking office. Wu himself was appointed minister of war (but declined the post); Kao En-hung and the pro-Wu lawyer-politician Tung K'ang[59] were given the communications and

54. Some contemporary commentators erronously listed Western-oriented diplomats and lawyers like W. W. Yen, Wellington Koo, Wang Ch'ung-hui, and Lo Wen-kan with the Loyang group because Wu supported them for cabinet posts and they, in turn, shared the high hopes of many Westerners and Western-oriented Chinese that Wu would establish the republic on an Anglo-American-style footing.

55. *MJTC*, *chüan* 6, p. 63; *PYCF*, 6: 139.

56. *MJTC*, *chüan* 1, p. 75; *GJMK*, 1924, p. 805; *Who's Who*, p. 120; *PYCF*, 6:139; *Jimbutsu jihyō* 2, no. 6 (September 1924): 16–17.

57. E.g., cf. Rodney Gilbert, "Arms and Men in China," *Asia* 22, no. 9 (September 1922): 729; Perceval Landon, "China Threatened with Civil War," *Daily Telegraph*, March 22, 1924, clipped in F.O. 371/10243, F1177/19/10.

58. Cf. *Wu P'ei-fu hsien-sheng chi*, pp. 384–85; T'ao Chü-yin, *Wu P'ei-fu chuan*, pp. 78–80.

59. *GJMK*, 1932, p. 300; *Who's Who*, p. 239; Chia Shih-i, *Min-kuo ch'u-nien*, pp. 82–83; *PYCF*, 6:131.

finance posts. There was by contrast no immediate follower of Ts'ao K'un in the cabinet. Ts'ao Jui and Pien Shou-ch'ing found it unacceptable that while the fortunes of the Chihli Clique as a whole were on the rise, the Paoting and Tientsin branches were not profiting as much as Wu's Loyang branch. Using the financial problems of the government as a pretext, they launched a campaign to force the resignations of Tung and Kao. A troop mutiny in Paoting provided an opportunity to press the government urgently for funds. The staff of the Ministry of War, probably on Paoting's orders, demonstrated for the payment of back salaries and physically attacked Finance Minister Tung. Numerous rumors appeared in the press about Paoting's dissatisfaction with Tung and Kao. Stories also appeared suggesting that Wu, who was visiting Paoting, was being pressed by his mentor Ts'ao to reduce his involvement in Peking politics. After some weeks in Paoting, Wu announced that he was returning to Loyang and would henceforth remain aloof from civil politics. He was further reported as saying that he had no personal objection to the replacement of ministers Tung and Kao. Deprived of Wu's backing, and embarrassed by the attacks on their competence, Tung and Kao were obliged to offer their resignations.[60] Wu now sent his chief of staff, Li Cho-chang, to Paoting as an ambassador in order better to coordinate his future policies with those of Ts'ao K'un.[61]

Tensions emerged again over the issue of the "able men cabinet." The Chihli Clique as a whole opposed Li Yuan-hung's nominee for Prime Minister, T'ang Shao-i. Wu had coupled opposition to T'ang with support for Acting Prime Minister Wang Ch'ung-hui, calling upon Wang as a prestigious Western-trained lawyer and diplomat to form a nonparty cabinet.[62] The resulting "able men cabinet" was consistent with Wu's expressed beliefs in constitutional, liberal government. Furthermore, among its factionally aligned members, there were two (Kao En-hung and Sun Tan-lin) associated with Wu and only one (Kao Ling-wei) from Ts'ao's camp. A fourth, Chang Shao-tseng, while not tied exclusively to Wu, was related to him by marriage. The Lo Wen-kan incident, which soon broke out and toppled the cabinet, seems to have had the Tientsin group's support.[63] Wu Ching-lien and Chang Po-lieh, the immediate initiators, were allied to the Tientsin group; one source says that the assistant bank manager who brought Wu Ching-lien the check used to incriminate Lo was a relative of Pien Shou-ch'ing. In the immediate aftermath of the affair,

60. *STSP* 1922.6.25.2, 6.27.2, 6.29.2, 6.30.2, **7.2.2**, **7.6.2**, 7.8.2, 7.9.2, 7.14.2, 7.16.2, 7.17.2, 7.18.2, 7.19.2, 7.22.2, 7.25.2, 8.1.2. Kao's resignation was a symbolic one, from his concurrent post as acting minister of education; was this because he had been less frontally attacked than Tung.

61. *STSP* 1922.9.9.2.

62. *PYCF*, 6:173.

63. *Wu P'ei-fu hsien-sheng chi*, p. 385.

Wu P'ei-fu defended Lo while Ts'ao K'un attacked him. Wu, however, soon fell silent and allowed the cabinet to fall.[64] In the succeeding Chang Shao-tseng cabinet, Paoting was represented by Kao Ling-wei, Liu En-yuan, and Wu Yü-lin, while Loyang had no delegate.

Early in 1923, Ts'ao's agents began to push his presidential aspirations with increasing vigor (see Chapter VII). Wu repeatedly cautioned Ts'ao to move slowly and held himself aloof from the events in Peking. Although Wu may have been motivated in part by repugnance at the methods of Ts'ao's men, he was also concerned about the tactical prematurity of a grab for the presidency before the success of the military invasions of Kwangtung and Fukien.[65] Wu's defenders have tried to dissociate him from Ts'ao by pointing out that he refrained from attending Ts'ao's sixty-first birthday celebration and refused to send congratulations when Ts'ao assumed the presidency,[66] yet Wu continued to serve in his military posts under the Ts'ao presidential regime and never "turned his spear" against his master.

Ts'ao and Wu, in short, had many disagreements over both political values and tactics in 1922–23, which were often exacerbated by the advice and actions of their mutually jealous followers. But Wu always bowed to Ts'ao's decisions when these were finally reached, so that the "split" that contemporary authors kept expecting never came.

The Research Clique

The Research Clique (Figure 4) first began to take shape in the Chinese community in Japan in the first decade of the twentieth century, within the constitutionalist stream of which Liang Ch'i-ch'ao was the dominant figure. It later drew upon politicians who participated in the provincial and national assemblies of 1909 and 1910 and in the Hsien-yu hui (Constitutionalist friends club),[67] and finally emerged as a distinct political entity during the first session of parliament in 1913–14.

Liang,[68] a leader in the Hunan reform movement in the 1890s, fled to Japan after the Hundred Days of 1898. In Japan, he worked for constitutional democracy and established a school for Chinese students. Many Chinese students who were in Japan at the time (although not necessarily at his school) became

64. *STSP* 1922.11.24.2, 11.25.2, 11.26.2, 11.27.2; *PYCF*, 6:174–77; *Wu P'ei-fu hsiensheng chi*, p. 225.

65. Shen Yun-lung, *Li Yuan-hung*, p. 146; T'ao Chü-yin, *Wu P'ei-fu chuan*, p. 83.

66. *Wu P'ei-fu hsien-sheng chi*, pp. 225–27; also see *PYCF*, 6: 180.

67. Yang Yu-chiung, *Cheng-tang shih*, p. 46.

68. *GJMK*, 1932, pp. 409–10; Ting Wen-chiang, *Liang nien-p'u*; Boorman and Howard, *Biographical Dictionary*, 2:346–56.

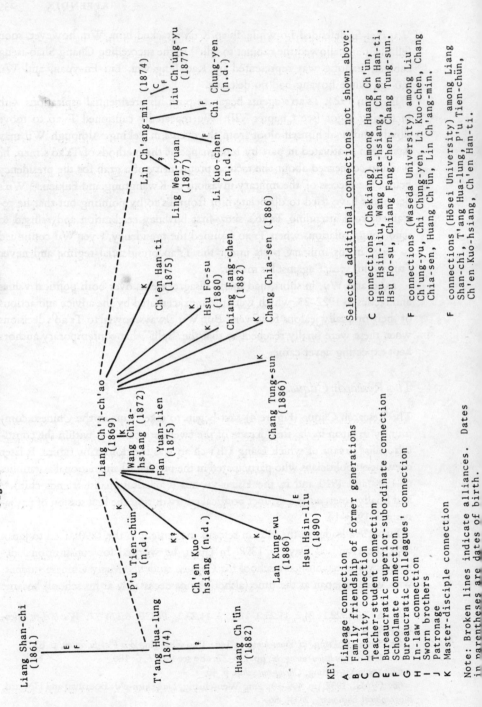

Figure 4. The Research Clique in Peking Politics

Liang Shan-chi (1861)

Liang Ch'i-ch'ao (1869)

T'ang Hua-lung (1874)

Huang Ch'ün (1882)

P'u Tien-chün (n.d.)

Ch'en Kuo-hsiang (n.d.)

Lan Kung-wu (1886)

Hsin Hsin-liu (1890)

Wang Chia-hsiang (1872)

Fan Yuan-lien (1875)

Chang Tung-sun (1886)

Ch'en Han-ti (1875)

Ling Wen-yuan (1877)

Hsu Fo-su (1880)

Chiang Fang-chen (1882)

Chang Chia-sen (1886)

Lin Ch'ang-min (1874)

Liu Ch'ung-yu (1877)

Chi Chung-yen (n.d.)

Li Kuo-chen (n.d.)

Selected additional connections not shown above:

C   connections (Chekiang) among Huang Ch'ün,
    Hsu Hsin-liu, Wang Chia-hsiang, Ch'en Han-ti,
    Hsu Fo-su, Chiang Fang-chen, Chang Tung-sun.

F   connections (Waseda University) among Liu
    Ch'ung-yu, Chi Chung-yen, Li Kuo-chen, Chang
    Chia-sen, Huang Ch'ün, Lin Ch'ang-min.

F   connections (Hōsei University) among Liang
    Shan-chi, T'ang Hua-lung, P'u Tien-chün,
    Ch'en Kuo-hsiang, Ch'en Han-ti.

KEY

A   Lineage connection
B   Family friendship of former generations
C   Locality connection
D   Teacher-student connection
E   Bureaucratic superior-subordinate connection
F   Schoolmate connection
G   Bureaucratic colleagues' connection
H   In-law connection
I   Sworn brothers
J   Patronage
K   Master-disciple connection

Note: Broken lines indicate alliances. Dates
in parentheses are dates of birth.

his disciples. These included Fan Yuan-lien,[69] who had been Liang's student in Hunan; Chang Chia-sen (Carsun Chang),[70] a Waseda student and later a writer on Liang's *Yung-yen pao*; Hsu Fo-su,[71] who joined Liang's reform movement while a student in Tokyo, and became co-editor with Liang of the *Hsin-min ts'ung-pao* before returning to China to work actively for constitutional reform; Lan Kung-wu,[72] who studied at Tokyo Imperial University and later served on *Yung-yen pao*; P'u Tien-chün,[73] who studied at Hōsei University, then returned to China where he was active in the constitutionalist movement; Wang Chia-hsiang,[74] who returned to China to work in the constitutionalist movement; Ch'en Kuo-hsiang[75] and Ch'en Han-ti,[76] two Hōsei University students; and, probably, Chang Tung-sun,[77] later a contributor to many of Liang's magazines. Interestingly, many of Liang's Tokyo followers, including Hsu Fo-su, Wang Chia-hsiang, Ch'en Han-ti, and Chang Tung-sun, were from Chekiang. Chiang Fang-chen,[78] another Chekiang student in Tokyo and manager of the Chekiang student association's *Che-chiang ch'ao* magazine, also became a Liang disciple at the time, later following a military career.

Others who had been influenced by Liang's thought joined his political following after he returned to China in 1911. Important among these new colleagues were two groups, one led by T'ang Hua-lung and the other by Lin Ch'ang-min.

T'ang Hua-lung[79] received his *chü-jen* degree in 1904, taught at Shansi University, then won his *chin-shih* and went to Japan, where he first met Liang. Graduating from Hōsei University in 1909, T'ang returned to Hupei and was elected to, and became Speaker of, the provincial assembly. In 1912, he became a member of the Provisional Senate in Nanking, where he and Lin Ch'ang-min

69. Boorman and Howard, *Biographical Dictionary*, 2:14–15; Hsien Pin, *Cheng-tang shih*, p. 81; *GJMK*, 1924, p. 59.

70. Boorman and Howard, *Biographical Dictionary*, 1:30–35; *GJMK*, 1937, p. 319; Yang Yu-chiung, *Cheng-tang shih*, p. 109.

71. *GJMK*, 1932, p. 170; "SSG," p. 22; Ting Wen-chiang, *Liang nien-p'u*, pp. 207–8.

72. *GJMK*, 1932, p. 369; "SSG," p. 23.

73. Yang Yu-chiung, *Cheng-tang shih*, pp. 46, 109, 123; *GJMK*, 1937, p. 473; Chang P'eng-yuan, *Li-hsien p'ai yü hsin-hai ko-ming* (Taipei, 1969), p. 298.

74. *MJTC*, chüan 3, p. 60; *GJMK*, 1932, p. 18; "SSG," pp. 21–22; *Who's Who*, p. 243; *Kuo-shih kuan kuan-k'an* 2, no. 1 (January 1949): 67–70.

75. "SSG," p. 22.

76. *GJMK*, 1937, p. 369; Hsieh Pin, *Cheng-tang shih*, p. 181.

77. Boorman and Howard, *Biographical Dictionary*, 1:129–33; *GJMK*, 1937, p. 344; Yang Yu-chiung, *Cheng-tang shih*, p. 109.

78. Boorman and Howard, *Biographical Dictonary*, 1: 312–17; *GJMK*, 1932, p. 179.

79. Boorman and Howard, *Biographical Dictionary*, 3: 230–32; *MJTC*, chüan 12, p. 64; *GJMK*, 1924, p. 106; Yang Yu-chiung, *Cheng-tang shih*, pp. 46, 60, 67, etc. On the Republican Construction Discussion Society, see Yang Yu-chiung, *Cheng-tang shih*, p. 53.

led in the establishment of the Republican Construction Discussion Society (*Kung-ho chien-she t'ao-lun hui*). Elected to the House, T'ang in 1912 participated in the formation of the Min-chu tang (Democratic party), a pro-Yuan Shih-k'ai party behind which Liang Ch'i-ch'ao also threw his weight. T'ang's group included Huang Ch'ün,[80] a Waseda graduate who was active in Hupei politics in 1911, joined the Min-chu tang in the 1913 parliament, and worked on Liang Ch'i-ch'ao's Shanghai newspaper, *Shih-shih hsin-pao*, in 1915; and Liang Shan-chi,[81] an older man (born 1861), a Hanlin compiler who studied at Hōsei University, later taught at Shansi University where he probably met T'ang, served as Speaker of the Shansi Provincial Assembly of 1909, and was elected to parliament in 1913.

Lin Ch'ang-min[82] met T'ang Hua-lung and other Chinese students in Japan, where Lin graduated from Waseda University. He returned to his native Fukien and served as secretary of the Fukien Provincial Assembly of 1909. As a member of the Nanking Provisional Senate, Lin was a leader with T'ang of the Republican Construction Discussion Society. Appointed to the 1913 House to represent Mongolia, he helped T'ang and Liang Ch'i-ch'ao found the Min-chu tang. Lin's followers included the lawyer, Liu Ch'ung-yu[83] (born 1877), a relative of Lin's and a Waseda graduate, who served in the late Ch'ing in the Fukien Provincial Assembly, in the Nanking Provisional Senate, and the 1913 House; Li Kuo-chen,[84] a Waseda graduate who was a member of the Nanking Provisional Senate and of the 1913 House; Chi Chung-yen,[85] another Waseda graduate who served in the 1909 Chihli Provincial Assembly, and the late Ch'ing National Assembly and was elected to the House in 1913 from Chihli;

80. *GJMK*, 1937, pp. 175–76. The attribution of Huang to T'ang's following is guesswork. I speculate that Huang's participation in the Hupei military government means that he followed T'ang there after meeting him in Japan. Huang was not a Hupei native.

81. "SSG," p. 26; Hashikawa Tokio, *Chūgoku bunkakai*, p. 519.

82. *GJMK*, 193, p. 418; "SSG," pp 23–24; *Jimbutsu jihyō* 3, no. 1 (February 1925): 1–3; Boorman and Howard, *Biographical Dictionary*, 2: 368–72. Lin's daughter married Liang Ch'i-ch'ao's son.

83. *GJMK*, 1937, p. 574; "SSG," p. 25; Yang Yu-chiung, *Cheng-tang shih*, p. 46. Liu's younger brother, Liu Ch'ung-chieh (born 1880), also a Waseda graduate, pursued a career in the Ministry of Foreign Affairs. In 1919 he accompanied Minister of Foreign Affairs Lu Cheng-hsiang to the Paris peace conference. The two traveled on the same boat as Liang Ch'i-ch'ao, who was going to observe the conference. At this period, the younger Liu was said by some to be Liang Ch'i-ch'ao's delegate overseas and was considered an extra-parliamentary member of the Lin Ch'ang-min section of the Research Clique. *GJMK*, 1937, p. 574; "SSG," pp. 25–26; *Who's Who*, p. 165; *STSP* 1918.12.25.2.

84. *GJMK*, 1937, p. 536; "SSG," pp. 26–27.

85. I have found no biographical data on Chi, despite his importance as an M.P., except that given by Chang P'eng-yuan, *Li-hsien p'ai*, p. 255; and the Parliament List. In attributing him to the Lin Ch'ang-min group, I am guessing on the basis of his being a Waseda graduate.

and, perhaps, Ling Wen–yuan,[86] who participated in the 1909 Kiangsu Provincial Assembly and in the Nanking Provisional Senate, and was elected to the House from Kiangsu in 1913.

Backed by T'ang, Lin, and their followers, Liang Ch'i-ch'ao threw his support behind Yuan Shih-k'ai's efforts to build a strong central government and a strong presidential role vis-à-vis parliament. Although Liang was not a member of parliament, many of his followers (P'u Tien-chün, Wang Chia-hsiang, Ch'en Kuo-hsiang, Lan Kung-wu) were in parliament and joined the Min-chu tang.[87] In the 1913–14 parliament, the Min-chu tang and two other parties amalgamated under Yuan Shih-k'ai's sponsorship to form the Chin-pu tang, in which Lin Ch'ang-min and T'ang Hua-lung were prominent leaders.[88] While the Chin-pu tang supported Yuan Shih-k'ai in parliament, Liang Ch'i-ch'ao served as minister of justice in the Hsiung Hsi-ling cabinet. The Research Clique and other elements of the Chin-pu tang did not break with Yuan until it was inescapably clear that he was attempting to overthrow the republic.[89]

With the restoration of parliament on August 1, 1916, parliamentary groupings went through further changes of name and membership, and the Research Clique emerged in a group called the Constitution Research Society.[90] In opposition to the Kuo-min tang position, the Constitution Research Society supported the Tuan Ch'i-jui government's policy of declaring war on Germany and Austria; in the Consfitutional Drafting Committee, the Research Clique battled the Kuo-min tang over the issue of local autonomy, taking the conservative position that the provincial government system should not be provided for in the constitution but should be enacted later by law.

After the dissolution of parliament in 1917, the Research Clique, instead of following the majority of parliament to Canton to join the constitution-protecting parliament, returned with Tuan Ch'i-jui to Peking and became a major element in his new cabinet. In the Tuan cabinet of July–November 1917, the Research Clique held three ministries particularly useful for the control of new

86. *GJMK*, 1932, p. 409; Hashikawa Tokio, *Chūgoku bunkakai*, p. 375; "SSG," p. 28. It is not clear from these sources whether Ling was more closely linked to T'ang Hua-lung or to Lin Ch'ang-min.

87. Yang Yu-chiung, *Cheng-tang shih*, p. 60. On the evolution of political groups from 1910 to 1914, see Li Chien-nung, *Cheng-chih shih*, 2: 362–72. The Min-chu tang also contained the Sun Hung-i group, but he broke away to found a rival organization in 1916.

88. On the Chin-pu tang, see Yang Yu-chiung, *Cheng-tang shih*, pp. 66–68. Membership information is in some cases based on the individual biographical data cited in preceding footnotes.

89. Li Chien-nung, *Cheng-chih shih*, 2: 410, 437, 438.

90. The name Research Clique came from the title of this organization. In fact, however, the Constitution Research Society numbered about 160 members of parliament, many of them only temporary supporters of the Research Clique. See Kokumin gikai, *Shina seitō no genjō*, pp. 5–7.

parliamentary elections, Finance (Liang Ch'i-ch'ao), Interior (T'ang-Hua lung), and Justice (Lin Ch'ang-min), as well as the Education Ministry (Fan Yuan-lien). Foreign Minister Wang Ta-hsieh[91] was also a Research Clique ally.

This cabinet marked the height of the Research Clique's influence. The clique had every prospect of doing well in new parliamentary elections. It was in this context that Liang Ch'i-ch'ao and T'ang Hua-lung argued for convening a new provisional national council to revise the election laws and elect a new parliament.[92] But before the parliamentary elections were carried out, the cabinet toppled, and no Research Clique members were included in the next cabinet. At the time of the 1918 elections, therefore, the Research Clique had no financial or governmental base from which to contest them and did very poorly. Liang Ch'i-ch'ao left China to travel in Europe and did not again participate in politics (he died in 1929); T'ang Hua-lung likewise left China to travel in Japan and America and was assassinated in September 1918, in Victoria, Canada; Ling Wen-yuan became a painter and professor of fine arts; Huang Ch'ün went into banking. Some of the other members practiced law or journalism. Of the original three leaders, only Lin Ch'ang-min remained in politics.

The few members of the Research Clique elected to the 1918 parliament worked with the anti-Anfu Club opposition and continued to be popularly known as the Research Clique. With the end of the Anfu parliament, they went their separate ways. In the restored old parliament of 1922–24, a number of former Research Clique members formed a small parliamentary group, which was again known by the Research Clique name.[93]

This profile has stressed the Research Clique's Peking political role, especially in parliament and the cabinet. As a great intellectual leader, however, Liang Ch'i-ch'ao enjoyed an influence and following far wider than that traced here. For example, among the figures usually classed as Liang's intimate disciples, and loosely referred to as Research Clique members, were the military man Chiang Fang-chen, the Shanghai banker Hsu Hsin-liu,[94] and the geologist Ting Wen-chiang.[95]

91. *MJTC*, *chüan* 10, p. 53; *GJMK*, 1924, p. 504; *GJMK*, 1932, pp. 41–42; Hsieh Pin, *Cheng-tang shih*, p. 181. During the Hsu Shih-ch'ang presidency, Wang was the head of the Foreign Affairs Commission, on which a number of Research Clique politicians held sinecures. This commission became a center of Research Clique anti-Anfu Club activity during the May Fourth Movement. See Chow, *May Fourth Movement*, p. 90.

92. *PYCF*, 4: 3–6.

93. Yang Yu-chiung, *Cheng-tang shih*, p. 123.

94. Boorman and Howard, *Biographical Dictionary*, 2:130–31; *GJMK*, 1932, p. 167; "SSG," p. 23; *Who's Who*, p. 94.

95. Boorman and Howard, *Biographical Dictionary*, 3:278–82; *MJTC*, *chüan* 4, p. 4; *Who's Who*, p. 23.

The Communications Clique

The Communications Clique's origins lay in the late Ch'ing Ministry of Posts and Communications (*Yu-ch'uan pu*, founded in 1906).[96] As resources were poured into it for constructing or redeeming railroads, extending the telegraph system, and founding the Bank of Communications, the ministry became an important locus of political and financial power and the object of a struggle between Yuan Shih-k'ai and Sheng Hsuan-huai.[97] Although he was forced into retirement in 1909, Yuan was the real victor in this struggle: from 1906 to 1911, crucial years of expanding activity in communications, followers of Yuan staffed the ministry and its agencies.

One of these followers was Liang Shih-i,[98] who from 1906 to 1911 held perhaps the most important post in the ministry, that of director-general of the Railway Bureau. During Yuan Shih-k'ai's presidency (1912–16), Liang held a number of powerful posts including that of Yuan's chief private secretary. U.S. Minister Paul Reinsch noted that Liang "was credited as being, next to Yuan Shih-k'ai, the ablest and most influential man in Peking." He described Liang as "highly educated according to Chinese literary standards[99] . . . [W]hile he has not studied Western science, he has a keen, incisive mind which enables him readily to understand Western conditions and methods. His outstanding quality is a faculty for organization. . . . Cantonese, short of stature and thickset, with a massive Napoleonic head, he speaks little, but his side remarks indicate that he is always ahead of the discussion, which is also shown by his searching questions. When directly questioned himself, he will always give a lucid and consecutive account of any matter."[100] Liang's political skill is suggested by a Japanese journalist's description of him as a tumbler-toy who could never be politically

96. This profile draws on, but at some points differs from, MacKinnon, "Liang Shih-i," pp. 581–602.

97. See, besides *ibid.*, Feuerwerker, *China's Early Industrialization*, pp. 73–82; Jerome Ch'en, *Yuan Shih-k'ai, 1859–1916: Brutus Assumes the Purple* (London, 1961), pp. 107–9.

98. The main source for the life of Liang Shih-i, and an important source for the study of many aspects of republican history, is *LSINP*. Also see Teng Chih-ch'eng, "P'ing Feng-kang chi-men ti-tzu pien 'San-shui Liang Yen-sun hsien-sheng nien-p'u'," *Yen-ching hsueh-pao*, no. 33 (December 1947), pp. 292–302; Tso Shun-sheng, "Liang Shih-i chih i-sheng (1869–1933)" in his *Wan-chu lou sui-pi* (Taipei, 1967), pp. 266–75; Chia Shih-i, *Min-kuo ch'u-nien*, pp. 31–40; Boorman and Howard, *Biographical Dictionary*, 2: 354–57.

99. Liang was in fact a *chin-shih* and Hanlin compiler and in 1903 had passed a special examination in economics with the highest mark. This earned him a reputation for brilliance and brought about his introduction by his fellow Cantonese, T'ang Shao-i, to Yuan Shih-k'ai.

100. Reinsch, *American Diplomat*, pp. 95–96.

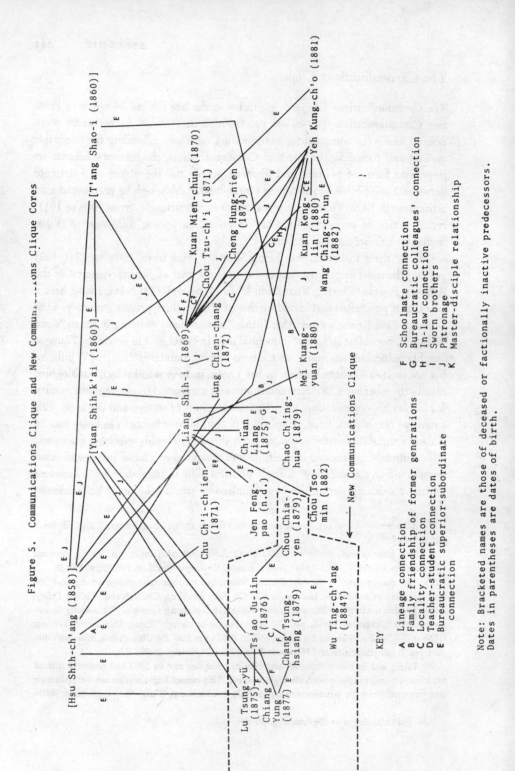

Figure 5. Communications Clique and New Communications Clique Cores

[Hsu Shih-ch'ang (1858)]

[T'ang Shao-i (1860)]

Kuan Mien-chün (1870)

Chou Tzu-ch'i (1871)

Cheng Hung-nien (1874)

Kuan Keng-lin (1880)

Yeh Kung-ch'o (1881)

Wang Ching-ch'un (1882)

[Yuan Shih-k'ai (1860)]

Liang Shih-i (1869)

Lung Chien-chang (1872)

Mei Kuang-yuan (1880)

Chu Ch'i-ch'ien (1871)

Ch'üan Liang (1875)

Chao Ch'ing-hua (1879)

Jen Feng-pao (n.d.)

Chou Chia-yen (1879)

Chou Tso-min (1882)

New Communications Clique

Lu Tsung-yü (1875)

Ts'ao Ju-lin (1876)

Chiang Yung (1877)

Chang Tsung-hsiang (1879)

Wu Ting-ch'ang (1884?)

KEY

A Lineage connection
B Family friendship of former generations
C Locality connection
D Teacher-student connection
E Bureaucratic superior-subordinate connection
F Schoolmate connection
G Bureaucratic colleagues' connection
H In-law connection
I Sworn brothers
J Patronage
K Master-disciple relationship

Note: Bracketed names are those of deceased or factionally inactive predecessors.
Dates in parentheses are dates of birth.

toppled;[101] his financial influence is suggested by the epithet applied by his contemporaries, "God of Wealth" (*Ts'ai-shen*).[102]

From 1906 to 1916, through his immediate followers, mostly Cantonese and their followers, Liang built a network of influence in the communications bureaucracy that did not disappear even when his core followers left their posts in the ministry. Liang's aides in the Communications Ministry included Yeh Kung-ch'o, Lung Chien-chang, Cheng Hung-nien, Kuan Keng-lin, Kuan Mien-chün, Wang Ching-ch'un, Mei Kuang-yuan, Ch'üan Liang, and Chao Ch'ing-hua.

Yeh Kung-ch'o[103] and Lung Chien-chang[104] were Cantonese who served under Liang in various posts concerned with management of the railways. Lung proved the less capable of the two. He broke with his mentor in 1915, opposing the imperial ambitions of Yuan Shih-k'ai, and, after a one-month appearance as minister of communications in 1917 he disappeared from the political scene. Yeh, however, was extremely capable. He served directly under Liang in the Railway Bureau, and even after he moved on to other posts, he retained influence with the railway managerial personnel[105] and served as chairman of the National Railways Association (*Ch'uan-kuo t'ieh-lu hsieh-hui*).[106] In the early republic, Yeh served as chief of the Railway Bureau, manager of the Bank of Communications, vice-minister of communications (1913–16, 1917–18), and minister of communications (1920–21, 1921–22, 1924–25).

Cheng Hung-nien,[107] another Cantonese, followed Yeh Kung-ch'o into the Ministry of Communications, and served as Yeh's aide throughout his political career. Cheng's posts included those of vice-minister of communications, vice-minister of finance in the Canton government (in both posts he served under

101. *Jimbutsu jihyō* 3, no. 1 (February 1925): 10.

102. This phrase was particularly suitable because the God of Wealth was considered capable of securing funds from all points of the compass and the center as well, i.e., from "the five routes" (*wu-lu*). Liang, in his early days at the Ministry of Posts and Communications, was in charge of the Inspectorate of the Five Railways (*Wu-lu t'i-t'iao ch'u*).

103. The major source for Yeh's life is Yü Ch'eng-chih, *Hsia-an hui-kao*. The whole third volume is taken up with Yeh's *nien-p'u*. Also see Boorman and Howard, *Biographical Dictionary*, 4: 31–33.

104. *MJTC*, *chüan* 2, p. 2; *GJMK*, 1924, p. 362; *GJMK*, 1932, p. 408; *HSC*, p. 57.

105. *ATTA*, *chüan* 2, p. 31.

106. This influential organization of high railway personnel, among other activities, carried on a successful struggle to prevent increased Western control over China's railways, thus preserving them under the political influence of the Communications Clique. See *LSI NP*, 2:11 ff.; Yü Ch'eng-chih, *Hsia-an hui-kao, nien-p'u*, pp. 53 and 76 ff., documents in F.O. 371/9189, 9190, 9191, 9192, and 9193 (file 22 of 1923); see also issues of *T'ieh-lu hsieh-hui hui-pao* for membership, budget, and activities of the association. Cf. Chapter III, note 6.

107. *GJMK*, 1932, p. 284; *Who's Who*, p. 39. Cheng wrote the preface to Yeh's collected writings and *nien-p'u* (Yü Ch'eng-chih, *Hsia-an hui-kao*).

Yeh), and, later, in Nanking, vice-minister of construction, vice-minister of industry, and secretary-general of the Administrative Yuan.

Kuan Keng-lin,[108] a Cantonese, entered the Board of Communications in 1907, shortly after Liang, and worked with Yeh Kung-ch'o in railway adminis-'tration.[109] Kuan was associated with Liang Shih-i in founding the National Railways Association. His career was spent mostly in the administration of railways and after the establishment of the Nanking government he served in the Ministry of Railways.

Kuan Mien-chün,[110] a relative and fellow-student of Liang Shih-i, came from the extreme eastern border of Kwangsi, near Liang's home town in Kwangtung, and made his early career under Liang in the Ministry of Communications. Kuan later filled several official posts in Kwangsi and served as Liang's messenger to Kwangsi warlord Lu Jung-t'ing in 1918 (see Chapter IV).

Wang Ching-ch'un[111] was a native of Chihli. Educated at Yale and at Illinois University, where he took a Ph.D. in railway administration, Wang entered the Ministry of Communications in railway work shortly after his return to China and served under Yeh Kung-ch'o. He followed Yeh to several assignments (for example, Yeh was chairman and Wang vice-chairman of the commission to unify the accounting and statistics of the railways),[112] and accompanied Yeh abroad in 1919 when the latter, temporarily excluded from the Ministry of Communications because of a clash with Ts'ao Ju-lin, was sent to inspect industrial affairs in Europe and America. Wang made his whole career in railway work.

Mei Kuang-yuan[113] was from Kiangsi. After some early service in the Board of Revenue, he became manager of the Nan-Hsun (Kiangsi provincial) Railway. In 1913, he was elected to the House, where he served as Liang Shih-i's lieutenant in organizing the Kung-min tang (Citizens' party) to support Yuan Shih-k'ai. Mei's original connection with the Communications Clique appears to have been an old family friendship between his family and that of Yeh Kung-ch'o. Yeh's father was a prefect (chih-fu) in Nanchang, Mei's home town, when Yeh and Mei were both in their early teens, and the two boys became friends.[114]

Ch'üan Liang,[115] after attending Tokyo Commercial College, joined the

108. GJMK, 1932, p. 71; "SSG," p. 9; Who's Who, p. 125.

109. See Yü Ch'eng-chih, Hsia-an hui-kao, nien-p'u, p. 10.

110. GJMK, 1932, p. 71; LSINP, 1: 18, 22, 33–34, 439.

111. GJMK, 1932, p. 21; "SSG," pp. 9–10; Who's Who, pp. 245–46; MJTC, chüan 3, p. 135.

112. On the valuable accomplishments of this commission, see The China Year Book 1926–7, p. 270.

113. GJMK, 1937, p. 449; "SSG," p. 6.

114. Yü Ch'eng-chih, Hsia-an hui-kao, nien-p'u, p. 4.

115. GJMK, 1932, p. 91; Who's Who, p. 69.

Ministry of Agriculture, Industry, and Commerce but was transferred to the Ministry of Posts and Communications, where, from the republic on, he made his career. He served as director-general of the Kirin-Huining Railway and managing director of the Kirin-Changchun Railway, and several times as vice-minister and acting minister of communications.

Chao Ch'ing-hua,[116] of Chekiang, attended telegraphy school in Canton and met Liang Shih-i when both were working under T'ang Shao-i. Chao's career took him to the management of several major railways and of the Shanghai branch of the Bank of Communications. He also served as an advisor to the Ministry of Communications, secretary to the cabinet, and foreign affairs counsellor to Chang Tso-lin.

This list does not exhaust the names of the many important railway personnel who started their careers under Liang and Yeh and remained loyal to their former supervisors.[117] Although many of these railway personnel were highly qualified professionals who avoided most political activity, the influence of the Communications Clique throughout the railway bureaucracy remained an important political resource. The technical qualifications of the personnel involved reinforced this influence, since they could not easily be replaced by unqualified political appointees of other factions or of local warlords.

A second important dimension of the Communications Clique's power was its influence in the world of banking. At the heart of this influence was Liang's control over the Bank of Communications, which had been opened on his initiative in 1908 to handle the finances of the railway, post, telegraph, and navigation administrations in the Ministry of Posts and Communications. As we have seen in Chapter III, Liang also founded many private banks, which, together with the Bank of Communications, enjoyed impressive influence in Chinese financial circles and considerable power over the Peking government. Liang staffed the Bank of Communications with his protégés, and those who proved themselves there were given major assignments in the private banks Liang controlled. Although such figures were loyal to Liang, their participation in politics was intermittent; the financial interests of the Communications Clique were as important as its political interests and as bankers these men had to be on good terms with politicians of various factions. Prominent examples were Chou Tso-min, Ch'ien Yung-ming, and Jen Feng-pao.

116. *GJMK*, 1937, p. 351; MacKinnon, "Liang Shih-i," p. 589.
117. A good example of the type is Liu Ching-shan (*Who's Who*, p. 165; *GJMK*, 1932, p. 394), whose career was heavily weighted on the technical side of railroad administration but who also handled the financing at one point for a newspaper that reflected the Communications Clique viewpoint, the English-language *Peking Daily News*. See F.O. 228/3553, Enclosure in Peking Despatch 470 of July 29, 1924; ms. of a memorandum on the press in China.

Chou Tso-min[118] joined the Bank of Communications in 1916, then became manager of the Kincheng Bank on its founding in 1917. During his distinguished banking career, Chou was a director of the Bank of China, the Bank of Communications, and the Pien-yeh (Frontier) Bank.[119]

Ch'ien Yung-ming[120] served as Shanghai branch manager of the Bank of Communications in 1914 and went on to hold many important banking and Chamber of Commerce posts, including directorships in the Hsin-hua Savings Bank, the banks of China and Communications, and the Kincheng and Ta–lu banks.

Jen Feng-pao[121] was a director of the Yien-yeh and Kincheng banks and the Exchange Bank of China. Jen was elected to the Senate in 1918.

While the foundations of the Communication Clique were thus laid in the late Ch'ing Railway Bureau and Bank of Communications, its membership as known in the republic was not completed until two senior figures—Chou Tzu-ch'i and Chu Ch'i-ch'ien—were recruited in the first years of the republic.

Chou Tzu-ch'i[122] was a Shantungese who was raised in Kwangtung. During the late Ch'ing, he served as consul in New York and San Francisco and in other posts in the Ministry of Foreign Affairs. Chou's career attracted the eye of Yuan Shih-k'ai, who appointed him vice-minister of finance in 1911. From 1912 to 1916, Chou served as civil governor of Shantung and several times as minister of finance and minister of communications. As an important supporter of Yuan Shih-k'ai, he became closely associated with Liang Shih-i and was one of Liang's major associates until Chou's death in 1923.

Chu Ch'i-ch'ien[123] served under Hsu Shih-ch'ang in Fengtien and became his adopted son. When Hsu was transferred from Fengtien to serve as minister of posts and communications, Chu came with him and became superintendant of the northern portion of the Tientsin-Pukow Railway.[124] In the early years of

118. GJMK, 1932, p. 157; Who's Who, p. 60; "SSG," p. 11; Boorman and Howard, Biographical Dictionary, 1: 427–29.

119. Banking directorships given here and below are based on biographical data plus 1924–25 lists given in Yin-hang yueh-k'an 4, no. 9 in GSK 1924.10.317–20, 346–55, and in SKJ, pp. 216–630, unless otherwise noted.

120. GJMK, 1932, p. 193; Boorman and Howard, Biographical Dictionary, 1:379–81. Some of these banking directorships were held in the 1940s: see Kagawa Shun'ichirō, Sensō, pp. 213, 225.

121. SKJ, p. 612–2 [sic]; Yang Yu-chiung, Cheng-tang shih, p. 108.

122. GJMK, 1924, p. 1036; "SSG," p. 8; ATTA, chüan 2, p. 28; Chia Shih-i, Min-kuo ch'u-nien, pp. 40–46; Boorman and Howard, Biographical Dictionary, 1: 429–31.

123. MJTC, chüan 8, p. 35; HSC, pp. 57–58; Who's Who, p. 62; GJMK, 1932, pp. 148–49; Hashikawa, Chūgoku bunkakai, p. 103.

124. The Tientsin-Pukow Railway was not directly under the control of Liang and Yeh at this time but was administered separately from the Railway Bureau. MacKinnon, "Liang Shih-i," p. 590, n. 44.

the republic, Chu, like Chou Tzu-ch'i, served in various ministerial posts and worked to promote Yuan Shih-k'ai's political ambitions. In his later years, Chu turned increasing attention to scholarly activities in the field of architecture.

The Communications Clique's most prominent members were actively associated with Yuan Shih-k'ai's attempt to make himself emperor.[125] After Yuan's death, the government issued a mandate for the arrest of eight monarchists allegedly responsible for Yuan's schemes, including Liang, Chou Tzu-ch'i, and Chu Ch'i-ch'ien, who had to flee Peking. But Liang continued to exert substantial influence behind the scenes. He appeared publicly in Tientsin and Peking and consulted with various political factions on financial matters.[126]

Yeh Kung-ch'o went to Nanking to serve as Feng Kuo-chang's secretary. When Chang Hsun's restoration attempt occurred, Liang instructed Yeh to arrange with the Bank of Communications for Mex. $2 million to be provided to Tuan Ch'i-jui to finance the expedition against Chang.[127] Not surprisingly, Feng and Tuan soon issued an order cancelling the proscription of Liang, Chu, and Chou.[128]

Liang moved with characteristic caution back toward the center of power. (Reinsch had noted that Liang was "always satisfied with the substance of power without its outward show.")[129] He worked quietly for the election of subordinates of his to the new parliament but avoided a large-scale campaign that might have aroused the jealousy of Wang I-t'ang and Hsu Shu-cheng.[130]

The New Communications Clique

The New Communications Clique has been diagrammed along with the old Communications Clique in Figure 5 in order to make clear the relationship between the two factions. While the leaders of both had been protégés of Yuan Shih-k'ai and Hsu Shih-ch'ang, the New Communications Clique was not, as is sometimes stated,[131] an offshoot or subset of the old Communications Clique.

125. The compilers of Liang's *nien-p'u* claim that he was not enthusiastic about Yuan's plans and was listed as a cosponsor of the pro-Yuan Ch'ou-an hui without his knowledge (*LSINP*, 1: 350). The more commonly accepted view of Liang as a willing activist in Yuan's cause is given by Huang I, *Yuan-shih tao-kuo chi* (Taipei, 1962), p. 25.

126. *HSC*, p. 57; *NCH* 1917.2.17.327.

127. *LSINP*, 1:374; Yü Ch'eng-chih, *Hsia-an hui-kao, nien-p'u*, p. 52. No mention is made of the sum having to be paid back.

128. *LSINP*, 1:402–3. The order was issued on February 4, 1918. The order for the arrest of the other alleged monarchists apparently still stood.

129. Reinsch, *American Diplomat*, p. 96.

130. "SSG," p. 7.

131. Yang Yu-chiung, *Cheng-tang shih*, p. 108, and Li Chien-nung, *Cheng-chih shih*, 2: 517, seem to make this error in their ambiguous descriptions of the origins of the New Communications Clique. Houn, *Central Government*, p. 143, makes the mistake explicitly.

It was a separate faction that tried to build influence in the same functional areas as the old Communications Clique, but it was much smaller, and, in part due to the blow dealt it by the May Fourth Movement, ultimately considerably less influential than the Communications Clique. Although often in competition, the two factions were not always at loggerheads. They sometimes cooperated when shared political or banking interests made cooperation profitable.[132]

The high point of New Communications Clique influence came in 1916–19, reflecting the use of the faction by Tuan Ch'i-jui to carry out a policy of close diplomatic ties with, and large loans from, Japan. The rise of the New Communications Clique at this time was also due in part to the relative eclipse of the Communications Clique because of the proscription of Liang, Chou, and Chu.

The New Communications Clique's leader, Ts'ao Ju-lin,[133] a Waseda University graduate, former foreign affairs official, and aide of Yuan Shih-k'ai, served as minister of communications during part of 1916 and from July 1917 to June 1919 (during that period he had a disagreement with Yeh Kung-ch'o, who was serving as vice-minister, and forced Yeh to resign),[134] and as acting minister of finance during most of 1918. Ts'ao's co-provincial and schoolmate, Chang Tsung-hsiang,[135] a graduate of Tokyo Imperial University and minister of justice during 1914–16, served as Chinese minister to Japan from 1916 to 1919 and helped to conclude the Nishihara Loans. Chiang Yung,[136] a Waseda graduate, served as vice minister of justice under Chang Tsung-hsiang, then followed Chang to Japan as supervisor of Chinese students there. A fourth major figure in the faction, Lu Tsung-yü,[137] also a Waseda graduate, served in the Senate; he played a role in the Nishihara Loans as a founder of the Exchange Bank of China, a Sino-Japanese joint venture, and was appointed to the financially influential post of director-general of the Currency Reform Bureau in 1918. In banking circles, associates of the New Communications Clique included Wu Ting-ch'ang,[138] who served as vice-minister of finance under Ts'ao Ju-lin in

132. E.g., see *STSP* 1919.1.25.2; *ATTA, chüan* 2, p. 15.

133. Boorman and Howard, *Biographical Dictionary*, 3: 299–302; *GJMK*, 1932, pp. 201–2; Chia Shih-i, *Min-kuo ch'u-nien*, pp. 74–78 and 99–111; *ATTA, chüan* 2, pp. 15–16; and Ts'ao Ju-lin, *I-sheng*.

134. For Ts'ao's version of this incident, see his *I-sheng*, p. 183. For the pro-Yeh account, see Yü Ch'eng-chih, *Hsia-an hui-kao, nien-p'u*, p. 61.

135. *MJTC, chüan* 1, p. 132; *ATTA, chüan* 2, p. 16; *GJMK*, 1932, p. 174; Boorman and Howard, *Biographical Dictionary*, 1: 127–29.

136. *MJTC, chüan* 10, p. 34; *Who's Who*, p. 48; *GJMK*, 1932, pp. 120–21; "SSG," pp. 17–18.

137. *GJMK*, 1932, p. 389; "SSG," p. 14; *HSC*, p. 62; *TTMJ*, 1: 53–54; *ATTA, chüan* 2, pp. 16–17; *Who's Who*, p. 181.

138. Boorman and Howard, *Biographical Dictionary*, 3: 452–53; *GJMK*, 1932, p. 114; "SSG," pp. 18–19; *Who's Who*, 1936, p. 265. Wu, however, was also on good terms with the Communications Clique.

1918 and subsequently as the director of a number of banks; and Chou Chia-yen,[139] a Tokyo Imperial University graduate who served as secretary to the Ministry of Finance under Ts'ao and later served on several bank boards.

The New Communications Clique was too small to seek influence through parliament. It did not contest the 1917 parliamentary election but threw its financial support to the Anfu Club.

The Political Study Group

The Political Study Group took firm shape in parliament in 1916 and persisted as an identifiable unit through parliament's final, 1922–24, session. It was not, properly speaking, a faction. Rather, the group's leadership core was the reflection in parliament of the alliance of several major factional leaders both within and outside the body (see Figure 6).[140] Additional M.P.'s attached themselves to the Political Study Group's successive organizational forms when its fortunes were on the rise and withdrew when they were waning.[141]

The roots of the Political Study Group lay in the Kuo-min tang of the first parliament. The Chin-pu tang and the Kuo-min tang were like the two waists of a double hourglass; nearly all the M.P.'s passed through one waist or the other, and once sorted the two categories seldom mixed again. There was a tendency for M.P.'s of a bureaucratic or constitutionalist background to pass through the Chin-pu tang and emerge eventually in the Research or Discussion cliques, the Anfu Club, or groups responsive to the Communications Clique. The Kuo-min tang, on the other hand, attracted a combination of former T'ung-meng hui members (themselves a mixture of professional revolutionaries, anti-Manchu students, and nationalistic military officers) and some members of the constitutionalist movement. Groups which emerged out of this stream included most prominently the "small Sun" (Sun Hung-i) and "large Sun" (Sun Yat-sen) factions and the Political Study and I-yu groups.[142]

In some cases, of course, such groups had gone into the hourglass waist already well established as factions—for example, the Sun Yat-sen faction or the Research Clique. Although this may well have been the case, too, with some of

139. *GJMK*, 1932, p. 155; "SSG," p. 18.

140. My list of Political Study Group members is based on Hsieh Pin, *Cheng-tang shih*, pp. 80–81 and appendices 2 and 8, plus scattered references in other sources when confirmed by biographical sources.

141. See, for example, the list in Hsieh Pin, *Cheng-tang shih*, Appendix 8, of the Political Study Group's officers in 1923. The majority of those on the list seem to have been short-term members.

142. See Hsieh Pin, *Cheng-tang shih*, Appendix 2. On the early Kuo-min tang, see George T. Yu, *Party Politics in Republican China: The Kuomintang, 1912–1924* (Berkeley, Calif., 1966), Chapter 4.

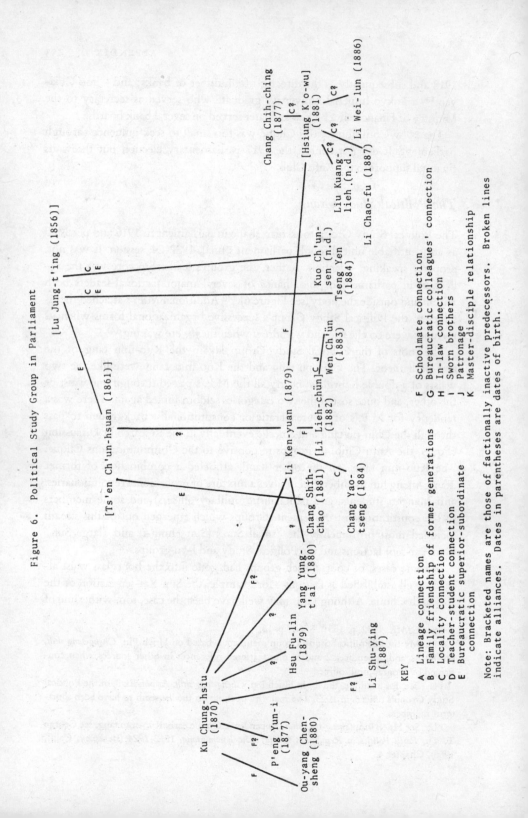

Figure 6. Political Study Group in Parliament

KEY

A Lineage connection
B Family friendship of former generations
C Locality connection
D Teacher-student connection
E Bureaucratic superior-subordinate
   connection
F Schoolmate connection
G Bureaucratic colleagues' connection
H In-law connection
I Sworn brothers
J Patronage
K Master-disciple relationship

Note: Bracketed names are those of factionally inactive predecessors. Broken lines
indicate alliances. Dates in parentheses are dates of birth.

the component factions of the Political Study Group, the secondary biographical data on its members is too slim to delineate these early associations. The major components of the Political Study Group emerge into clear focus only during the anti-Yuan Shih-k'ai struggles of 1913–16.

One segment of the the group coalesced around Ku Chung-hsiu and his anti-Yuan newspaper, *Chung-hua hsin-pao*, and magazine, *Cheng-i tsa-chih*, in Shanghai around 1915. Ku,[143] a Waseda graduate, was a constitutionalist and a member of the Chihli Provincial Assembly in the late Ch'ing. He joined the Kuo-min tang in 1912, was elected to parliament, and fled to Shanghai in 1913 when the Kuo-min tang was dissolved. In his anti-Yuan endeavors he was joined by several other former Kuo-min tang members, including Yang Yung-t'ai,[144] a former revolutionary journalist and senator; P'eng Yun-i,[145] a member of the House and future minister of education, and House members Hsu Fu-lin,[146] Ou-yang Chen-sheng,[147] and Li Shu-ying.[148] It is not clear whether any prior relationships influenced these associates to join Ku in Shanghai. It may be relevant that Ou-yang, Li, and P'eng were all, like Ku, Waseda graduates, and the others had also studied in Japan before the revolution.

A second component of the Political Study Group formed in approximately 1916 around Li Ken-yuan,[149] who as a Yunnanese military officer and T'ung-meng hui member had played an important role in Yunnan's 1911 revolution. Li was elected to the House as a Kuo-min tang member, and, when Yuan Shih-k'ai dissolved the Kuo-min tang, Li joined Ts'en Ch'un-hsuan in fomenting the second revolution. Again in 1916, Li and Ts'en cooperated in the fight against Yuan, when Ts'en headed the anti-Yuan military government at Chaoch'ing and Li served as a staff officer of the campaign. When parliament reconvened in 1916, Li was able to put together a group of M.P.'s representing connections and alliances constructed in the previous years. These included Chang Yao-tseng,[150] a co-provincial and like Li a former aide of Ts'en Ch'un-hsuan; Wen

143. *GJMK*, 1924, p. 831; *GJMK*, 1932, p. 135; Chün-tu Hsueh, *Huang Hsing and the Chinese Revolution* (Stanford, Calif., 1961), pp. 211–12, note 25; *Saishin Shina yōjin*, pp. 62–63.

144. Boorman and Howard, *Biographical Dictionary*, 4: 17–19; *GJMK*, 1932, p. 352.

145. *GJMK*, 1924, p. 70; *GJMK*, 1932, p. 334; Tahara Teijirō, *Shinmatsu minsho Chūgoku kanshin jimmeiroku* (Peking, 1918), pp. 562.

146. Tahara, *Shinmatsu*, pp. 317–18; *GJMK*, 1924, p. 952; *GJMK*, 1937, p. 238.

147. Tahara, *Shinmatsu*, pp. 713–14; *GJMK*, 1924, pp. 509–10; *GJMK*, 1937, p. 58.

148. *GJMK*, 1932, p. 377; "SSG," p. 49.

149. Boorman and Howard, *Biographical Dictionary*, 2: 305–7; *Saishin Shina yōjin*, p. 205.

150. *GJMK*, 1924, pp. 211–12; *MJTC*, *chüan* 5, p. 182; "SSG," p. 48; *GJMK*, 1932, p. 246. Chang doubtless knew Li from at least the first parliament, when Li was head of the Kuo-min tang's Yunnan branch and then head of the Kuo-min tang's M.P.'s Club in Peking. Chang was a Kuo-min tang member of parliament.

Ch'ün,[151] an aide of Li's former classmate and fellow T'ung-meng hui member, Li Lieh-chün;[152] Kuo Ch'un-sen[153] and Tseng Yen,[154] two Kwangsi M.P.'s who were aides of Kwangsi Tuchun Lu Jung-t'ing,[155] himself a former subordinate and now a political supporter of Ts'en Ch'un-hsuan; and Chang Shih-chao,[156] a Hunan senator who had worked closely with Ts'en in 1913 and 1916.

In addition to those already listed, a number of other important names were associated with the 1916–24 Political Study Group but it is not possible to delineate clearly their recruitment into or position in the group. There were a number of Szechwanese M.P.'s in the group leadership, most prominently including Li Chao-fu,[157] an old T'ung-meng hui member and later a lawyer; and Li Wei-lun,[158] Chang Chih-ching,[159] and Liu Kuang-lieh.[160] These men may have been political agents of Szechwanese warlord Hsiung K'o-wu,[161] who was a classmate of Li Ken-yuan and a sometime political ally of Ts'en Ch'un-hsuan. Other important Political Study Group leaders included T'ang 1,[162] Han Yü-chen,[163] Hsu Lan-shu,[164] and Ching Yao-yueh.[165]

On the basis of this grab-bag of alliances—and with the participation of the Ku Chung-hsiu group[166]—Li Ken-yuan was able to organize support in the

151. Tahara, *Shinmatsu*, p. 17; *GJMK*, 1924, pp. 748–49; *GJMK*, 1932, p. 328; *MJTC*, *chüan* 1, p. 124.

152. Boorman and Howard, *Biographical Dictionary*, 2: 312–16.

153. *GJMK*, 1924, p. 717; *NPIHWH*, p. 107.

154. Tahara, *Shinmatsu*, p. 553; *NPIHWH*, p. 107; *GJMK*, 1924, p. 635. Both Kuo and Tseng were members of the southern delegation to the 1919 Shanghai peace conference.

155. Boorman and Howard, *Biographical Dictionary*, 2: 447–49.

156. Boorman and Howard, *Biographical Dictionary*, 1:105–9. Although Chang was probably a Political Study Group member in 1916, he was decreasingly active in parliamentary politics thereafter and was not subsequently an important member of the group.

157. Chou K'ai-ch'ing, *Min-kuo Ssu-ch'uan jen-wu chuan-chi* (Taipei, 1966), pp. 120–21; *GJMK*, 1937, p. 548.

158. *GJMK*, 1937, p. 527; Tahara, *Shinmatsu*, p. 153.

159. *GJMK*, 1924, p. 154; Tahara, *Shinmatsu*, p. 436.

160. *GJMK*, 1924, p. 388; *NPIHWH*, p. 107.

161. Boorman and Howard, *Biographical Dictionary*, 2: 110–12.

162. *GJMK*, 1924, pp. 108–9; *GJMK*, 1932, pp. 296–97; *Jimbutsu jihyō* 3, no. 1 (February 1925): 21–22; Tahara, *Shinmatsu*, p. 569.

163. *GJMK*, 1924, p. 554; Tahara, *Shinmatsu*, p. 743.

164. *GJMK*, 1937, p. 239; Tahara, *Shinmatsu*, pp. 322–23.

165. *GJMK*, 1937, p. 118.

166. The basis of the alliance between the Ku and Li groups is unclear. Both, of course, had been active against Yuan Shih-k'ai. Furthermore, Li in 1913 or 1914 enrolled in Ku's alma mater, Waseda University. There was also a bond between Li and Yang Yung-t'ai. Yang had been the head of China branch of the Ou-shih yen-chiu hui (European affairs study association, a group organized by Li in Tokyo in 1914, sometimes considered the forerunner of the Political Study Group) and is said to have become a "close political

1916 parliament for Ts'en Ch'un-hsuan for the vice-presidency. When Feng Kuo-chang was elected instead, Li's group split from the larger alliance of ex-Kuo-min tang M.P.'s to which it had adhered and formed the separate Political Study Association, which managed to win a number of cabinet and vice-ministerial posts in 1916–17.[167] Although Li resigned from parliament in 1917, the Political Study Group remained viable because of the continued existence of the outside alliances on which it was based. Thus, in the constitution-protecting parliament, the Political Study Group cooperated with Ts'en Ch'un-hsuan and Lu Jung-t'ing in countering the influence of Sun Yat-sen and his followers. When parliament was restored in Peking, the Political Study politicians threw in their lot with Li Yuan-hung. When Li fled from Peking, Li Ken-yuan, T'ang I, and other Political Study politicians led the effort to establish a government under Li in Shanghai. With the failure of this effort, the Political Study Group as a coherent unit seems to have ceased action. The name, however, persisted and was loosely applied by political journalists during the Nanking decade to Yang Yung-t'ai (then a high-ranking aide of Chiang Kai-shek) and his allies, and after Yang's death in 1935, to Chang Ch'ün and his associates. The loose journalistic use of the name should not conceal the fact that in each of its three[168] incarnations the Political Study Group was a different set of men with a different factional structure.[169]

The I-yu She

Like the Political Study group, the parliamentary I-yu she emerged out of the 1912–13 Kuo-min tang, taking clear shape for the first time in the 1916–17 parliament. It was a complex and only moderately stable alliance of several factions, some based within and some based outside parliament (see Figure 7). The group split severely over the election of Ts'ao K'un and disappeared as a distinct political force in 1923. As with other parliamentary groups, the I-yu group's membership expanded and contracted with its fortunes; here we describe only the core leadership.[170]

associate" of Li during their joint service in the Chaoch'ing military government (Boorman and Howard, *Biographical Dictionary*, 4: 18).

167. Chang Yao-tseng, minister of justice; Ku Chung-hsiu, minister of agriculture and commerce; Wen Ch'ün, vice-minister of agriculture and commerce.

168. Or four, if one counts the totally unrelated Cheng-hsueh hui of the late Ch'ing National Assembly. See Chang Yü-fa, *Ch'ing-chi ti li-hsien t'uan-t'i* (Taipei, 1971), p. 494.

169. See Boorman and Howard, *Biographical Dictionary*, biographies of Yang Yung-t'ai, 4: 17–19; Chang Ch'ün, 1: 47–52. Also see Han Ssu, *K'an! Cheng-hsueh hsi* ([Hongkong?]), 1947), *passim*.

170. The list of I-yu she members upon which the following sketch is based comes from Hsieh Pin, *Cheng-tang shih*, pp. 81–82, 92, 98; *STSP* 1922.7.11.2; and Yu, *Party Politics*,

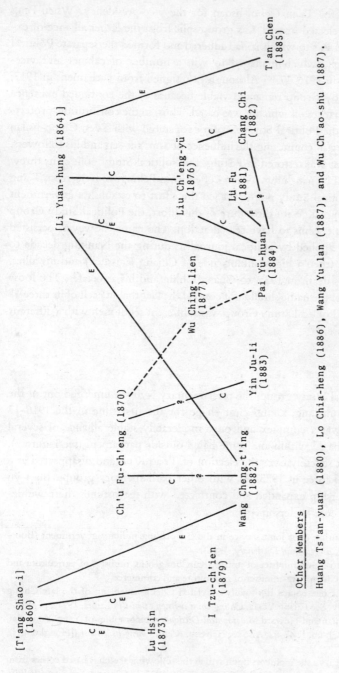

Figure 7. I-yu she Leadership in Parliament

Other Members

Huang Ts'an-yuan (1880), Lo Chia-heng (1886), Wang Yu-lan (1887), and Wu Ch'ao-shu (1887).

KEY

A Lineage connection
B Family friendship of former generations
C Locality connection
D Teacher-student connection
E Bureaucratic superior-subordinate
   connection

F Schoolmate connection
G Bureaucratic colleagues' connection
H In-law connection
J Sworn brothers
J Patronage
K Master-disciple relationship

Note: Bracketed names are those of factionally inactive predecessors. Broken lines
indicate alliances. Dates in parentheses are dates of birth.

The central figure of the I-yu group was Wu Ching-lien,[171] a politically skillful, Japanese-educated member of the House from Fengtien. No revolutionary background is revealed in the slim sources on Wu's life; rather, he appears to have been an influential member of the local gentry, interested in education, who was elected speaker of the late Ch'ing Fengtien Provincial Assembly and backed Fengtien's accession to the 1911 revolution in order to avoid local disorder. In the provisional Senate of 1911–12, Wu was a leader of the T'ung-i kung-ho tang (United republican party), and he participated in the negotiations merging his party with the T'ung-meng hui and other parties to form the Kuo-min tang in 1912. In 1913, he was elected to the House of Representatives. There, he played the role of a political entrepreneur, bringing together a number of disparate groups to form what emerged in 1916 and survived until 1922 as the I-yu she.

The first group centered on Pai Yü-huan, a member of the House from Hupei.[172] Pai, together with Liu Ch'eng-yü (also Hupei, Senate)[173] and T'an Chen (Hunan, House),[174] had been active revolutionaries in student days in Tokyo (Pai and T'an were founding members of the T'ung-meng hui), and in 1911 had all returned to Hupei and served in the Hupei revolutionary government under the nominal leadership of Li Yuan-hung. Pai, we may speculate, was also the recruiter into the I-yu group of Lü Fu,[175] a member of the House from Chihli who had attended the same university (Meiji University), and of Chang Chi,[176] a well-known T'ung-meng hui activist who, like Pai, had political ties with Huang Hsing. The Pai group was to split with Wu Ching-lien in 1923 over the issue of Ts'ao K'un's election.[177]

---

p. 144. The outline history of the group's parliamentary career, except as otherwise noted, comes from Hsieh Pin, *Cheng-tang shih*, passim.

171. *GJMK*, 1932, p. 108; Satō, *Minkoku*, p. 101; Yu, *Party Politics*, pp. 97 and 101; P'eng-yuan Chang, "The Constitutionalists," p. 179; *Who's Who*, p. 261.

172. *GJMK*, 1924, p. 51; K. S. Liew, *Struggle for Democracy: Sung Chiao-jen and the 1911 Chinese Revolution* (Berkeley, Calif., 1971), pp. 48, 64, 72; Tahara, *Shinmatsu*, p. 75.

173. *GJMK*, 1924, p. 367; *GJMK*, 1932, p. 401; *GJMK*, 1937, p. 575; Yu, *Party Politics*, pp. 35, 40, 74–75; "SSG," p. 50; Harold Z. Schiffrin, *Sun Yat-sen and the Origins of the Chinese Revolution* (Berkeley, Calif., 1968), pp. 260, 276, 330, 342.

174. Boorman and Howard, *Biographical Dictionary*, 3:210–13; *Saishin Shina yōjin*, p. 114; *GJMK*, 1932, p. 215.

175. *GJMK*, 1924, p. 18; *GJMK*, 1932, p. 423; Tahara, *Shinmatsu*, p. 207.

176. Boorman and Howard, *Biographical Dictionary*, 1: 15–20; *GJMK*, 1932, pp. 230–31; Chün-tu Hsueh, *Huang Hsing*, pp. 40, 183. The Huang Hsing relationship is not shown in Figure 6, but Chang Chi was one of Huang's closest colleagues from 1904 until Huang's death in 1916. Pai's relationship with Huang is conjectural, based on his having been present at a meeting in 1905 with Huang, Chang Chi, and others to meet with Sun Yat-sen prior to the founding of the T'ung-meng hui (Liew, *Struggle*, p. 48).

177. Liu, *Kuei-hai cheng-pien*, p. 75.

A second group that joined the I-yu she was a segment of the Chekiang provincial parliamentary delegation led by Ch'u Fu-ch'eng,[178] a Japan-educated revolutionary and member of the late Ch'ing Chekiang Provincial Assembly. Two other Chekiang M.P.'s who are listed as I-yu members may have been recruited into the group through Ch'u: Wang Cheng-t'ing[179] (later minister of foreign affairs in the nationalist government) and Yin Ju-li.[180] Like the Pai group, the Chekiang group split with Wu Ching-lien in 1923, supporting Li Yuan-hung while Wu supported Ts'ao K'un.[181]

A third component of the I-yu leadership—known to have been active only in 1922-23—consisted of two followers of T'ang Shao-i, Lu Hsin[182] and I Tz'u-ch'ien,[183] both Kwangtungese and both business partners of T'ang's. In 1922, Wu Ching-lien energetically supported Li Yuan-hung's effort to appoint T'ang as prime minister, and Lu Hsin was named minister of agriculture and commerce in the 1922 T'ang cabinet but like his mentor did not take office.

A number of other M.P.'s were listed as part of the I-yu leadership at one time or another, but their relationship to one another, to outside forces, and to Wu Ching-lien is not clear. These included Wu Ch'ao-shu (C. C. Wu),[184] Wang Yu-lan,[185] Lo Chia-heng,[186] and Huang Ts'an-yuan,[187] to mention only those who were relatively well known.

The severe splits in the I-yu group during the Ts'ao K'un election left only Wu Ching-lien and I Tzu-ch'ien of the original leadership active in Peking after Ts'ao's election. But Wu recruited fresh allies, including Chi Chung-yen of the Research Clique and Lo Chi-han,[188] a Hupei M.P. Wu's new group, the Min-hsien t'ung-chih hui (Association of comrades for a people's constitution), continued to be active, under Lo's direction, even after Wu had to flee from

178. GJMK, 1932, p. 221; MJTC, chüan 12, p. 50; GJMK, 1924, p. 121; Mary Backus Rankin, "The Revolutionary Movement in Chekiang: A Study in the Tenacity of Tradition," in Mary Clabaugh Wright, ed., China in Revolution: The First Phase, 1900-1913 (New Haven, Conn., 1968), p. 359, note 97. That Ch'u was the head of a group of Chekiang M.P.'s within the I-yu group is specifically stated by Hsieh Pin, Cheng-tang shih, p. 114.

179. Boorman and Howard, Biographical Dictionary, 3: 362-64; "SSG," p. 40; GJMK, 1932, pp. 31-32.

180. GJMK, 1924, pp. 9-10; GJMK, 1932, pp. 3-4.

181. Liu, Kuei-hai cheng-pien, p. 75.

182. MJTC, chüan 7, p. 27; PYCF, 6:153; STSP 1922.7.11.2; Tahara, Shinmatsu, pp. 730-31.

183. Satō, Minkoku, p. 144; Tahara, Shinmatsu, pp. 258-59; GJMK, 1937, p. 10; STSP 1922.7.11.2.

184. Boorman and Howard, Biographical Dictionary, 3: 412-15.

185. Tahara, Shinmatsu, p. 33; GJMK, 1937, p. 49.

186. GJMK, 1924, p. 672; GJMK, 1932, p. 364; GJMK, 1937, p. 519.

187. Tahara, Shinmatsu, pp. 539-40; GJMK, 1924, p. 712.

188. Tahara, Shinmatsu, pp. 739-40.

Peking because of a clash with the government.[189] But the Feng Yü-hsiang coup of 1924, which brought an end to the life of the old parliament, also caused Wu Ching-lien's retirement from his remarkable career of political juggling.

189. Hsieh Pin, *Cheng-tang shih*, pp. 118–19, 123–24.

BIBLIOGRAPHY OF WORKS CITED

Aglen, Sir Francis. "China and the Special Tariff Conference." *Nineteenth Century*, August 1925. Reprint. *British Chamber of Commerce Journal*, n.d., pp. 376–79. Clipping in F.O. 371/10937, F49 190/10, p. 378.

Anderson, James N. "Buy-and-Sell and Economic Personalism: Foundations for Philippine Entrepreneurship." *Asian Survey* 9, no. 9 (September 1969): pp. 641–68.

Bailey, F. G. "Parapolitical Systems." In Marc J. Swartz, ed., *Local-Level Politics: Social and Cultural Perspectives*. Chicago: Aldine Publishing Co., 1968.

Baltimore News. January 16, 1928.

Barnes, J. A. "Networks and Political Process." In Marc J. Swartz, ed., *Local-Level Politics: Social and Cultural Perspectives*. Chicago: Aldine Publishing Co., 1968.

Bau, Joshua Mingchien. *Modern Democracy in China*. Shanghai; Commercial Press, 1923.

Bavelas, Alex. "Communications Patterns in Task-Oriented Groups." In Daniel Lerner and Harold D. Lasswell, eds., *The Policy Sciences.* Stanford, Calif.: Stanford University Press, 1951.

Bergère, Marie-Claire. "The Role of the Bourgeoisie." In Mary Clabaugh Wright, ed., *China in Revolution: The First Phase, 1900–1913*. New Haven, Conn.: Yale University Press, 1968.

Blau, Peter M. *Exchange and Power in Social Life*. New York: John Wiley and Sons, 1964.

Boorman, Howard L., and Howard, Richard C., ed. *Biographical Dictionary of Republican China*. 4 vols. New York: Columbia University Press, 1967, 1968, 1970, 1971.

Britton, Roswell S. *The Chinese Periodical Press, 1800–1912*. 1933. Reprint. Taipei: Ch'eng-wen Publishing Co., 1966.

Burgess, John Stewart. *The Guilds of Peking*. 1928. Reprint. Taipei: Ch'eng-wen Publishing Co., 1966.

Cameron, Meribeth E. *The Reform Movement in China, 1898–1912*. 1931. Reprint. New York: Octagon Books, 1963.

Chang Hao. *Liang Ch'i-ch'ao and Intellectual Transition in China, 1890–1907*. Cambridge, Mass.: Harvard University Press, 1971.

Chang P'eng-yuan 張朋園. "Ch'ing-chi tzu-i-chü i-yuan ti hsuan-chü chi ch'i ch'u-shen chih fen-hsi" 清季諮議局議員的選舉及其出身之分析 [China's first election of provincial assemblies in 1909 and the analysis of the background of the members]. *Ssu yü yen* 思與言 [Thought and word] 5, no. 6 (March 1968): 1435–45.

———. "The Constitutionalists." In Mary Clabaugh Wright, ed., *China in Revolution: The First Phase, 1900–1913*. New Haven, Conn.: Yale University Press, 1968.

———. *Li-hsien p'ai yü hsin-hai ko-ming* 立憲派與辛亥革命 [The constitutionalists and the 1911 revolution]. Taipei: Chung-kuo hsueh-shu chu-tso chiang-chu wei-yuan hui 中國學術著作獎助委員會, 1969.

——— and Shen Huai-yü 沈懷玉. "Min-kuo chih-kuan nien-piao ch'u-kao" 民國職官年表初稿 [Tables of central and provincial government officials, Republic of China, 1912–16 (Preliminary)]. *Chin-tai shih yen-chiu so chi-k'an* 近代史研究所集刊 [Bulletin of the Institute of Modern History, Academia Sinica] 3, Part 2 (December 1972), separately paginated, pp. 1–122.

Chang Ping-lin 章炳麟. *T'ai-yen hsien-sheng tzu-ting nien-p'u* 太炎先生自定年譜 [An autobiographical chronology of the life of Chang Ping-lin]. 1957. Reprint. Hongkong: Lung-men shu-tien 龍門書店, 1965.

[Chang] Tzu-sheng [張]梓生. "Feng-Chih chan-cheng chi-shih" 奉直戰爭紀事 [Record of the Fengtien-Chihli war]. *Tung-fang tsa-chih* 20, no. 8 (April 25, 1922): 59–88.

———. "Li Yuan-hung fu-chih chi" 黎元洪復職記 [Record of Li Yuan-hung's return to office]. *Tung-fang tsa-chih* 19, no. 12 (June 25, 1922): 53–81.

Chang Yü-fa 張玉法. *Ch'ing-chi ti li-hsien t'uan-t'i* 清季的立憲團體 [Constitutionalist groups of the Ch'ing]. Taipei, Chung-yang yen-chiu yuan chin-tai shih yen-chiu so 中央研究院近代史研究所, 1971.

Ch'ang An 暢盦 (probably pseud.). *Min-liu hou chih ts'ai-cheng yü chün-fa* 民六後之財政與軍閥 [Finance and the warlords since 1917]. Peking: n. p., [1922?]. Seen at the Tōyō Bunko.

Ch'en Ch'eng-tse 陳承澤. "Fa-t'ung wen-t'i ti yen-cheng chieh-shih" 法統問題的嚴正解釋 [A rigorous analysis of the question of legal orthodoxy]. *Tung-fang tsa-chih* 19, no. 15 (August 10, 1922): 123–30.

Ch'en Hsi-chang 陳錫璋. *Pei-yang ts'ang-sang shih-hua* 北洋滄桑史話 [History of the disorders of the Peiyang period]. 2 vols. Tainan: Ch'en Hsi-chang, 1967.

Ch'en, Jerome. *Yuan Shih-k'ai, 1859–1916: Brutus Assumes the Purple*. London: George Allen and Unwin, 1961.

Cheng-fu kung-pao 政府公報 [Government gazette]. Peking, daily, 1918–23.

Cheng, Sih-gung. *Modern China: A Political Study*. Oxford: The Clarendon Press, 1919.

Chi Ping-feng 元冰峯. *Ch'ing-mo ko-ming yü chün-hsien ti lun-cheng* 清末革命與君憲的論爭 [The controversies between revolutionists and constitutionalists in the late Ch'ing period]. Nankang: Chung-yang yen-chiu yuan chin-tai shih yen-chiu so, 1966.

"Chi Ts'ao K'un hui-hsuan an" 紀曹琨賄選案 [Record of the case of election by bribery of Ts'ao K'un]. *Chiang-su ko-ming po-wu-kuan yueh-k'an* 江蘇革命博物館月刊 [Monthly of the Kiangsu museum of the revolution], no. 13 (n.d.), bound as a separate booklet, 14 pp. Seen at the Kuomintang Party History Archives in Taichung.

Chia Shih-i 賈士毅. *Min-kuo ch'u-nien ti chi-jen ts'ai-cheng tsung-chang* 民國初年的幾任財政總長 [Several finance ministers of the early republic]. Taipei: Chuan-chi wen-hsueh ch'u-pan she 傳記文學出版社, 1967.

———. *Min-kuo ts'ai-cheng shih* 民國財政史 [History of finance during the republic]. *Cheng-pien* 正編 [original edition], 2 vols.; *hsu-pien* 續編 [supplemental edition], 3 vols. 1917 and 1932–34. Reprint. Taipei: Commercial Press, 1962. *Pien* (parts) are separately paginated.

Chiang Ch'i-chou 姜啓周. "Wo-kuo chün-fei tsai ts'ai-cheng shang chih ti-wei" 我國軍費在財政上之地位 [The place of military expenditures in our country's finances], *Yin-hang yueh-k'an* 銀行月刊 [Bankers' monthly] 4, no. 7 (July 1924). In Hatano Ken'ichi, comp., *Gendai Shina no kiroku* (q. v.), 1924. 10.20–56.

Chiang Yü-sheng 姜玉笙. "Hu-fa cheng-yen (hsuan-lu)" 护法靜言 (选条) [Arguments for constitution-protection (selection)]. Reprinted in *l-chiu-i-chiu nien Nan-Pei i-ho tzu-liao* 一九一九年南北議和資料 [Materials on the 1919 North-South peace conference], special issue no. 1 of *Chin-tai shih tzu-liao* 近代史資料 [Modern history materials] (1962) pp. 358–75.

Ch'ien Tuan-sheng. *The Government and Politics of China, 1912–1949*. 1950. Reprint. Paperback ed. Stanford, Calif.: Stanford University Press, 1970.

Chih-Feng ta-chan shih 直奉大戰史 [History of the great Chihli-Fengtien war]. [Shanghai]: Ching-chih t'u-shu kuan 競智圖書館, 1922. Seen at the Kuomintang archives in Taiwan.

Chih-yuan lu 職員錄 [Record of officials]. Peking. quarterly, 1918–23. Each issue consists of several *ts'e* (Chinese-style bound volumes).

"Chihō seikyō (ichi)" 地方政況 (一) [Local political situations, part 1]. *Shina jōhō* 支那情報 [China Intelligence] (Gaimushō 外務省, Tokyo), no. 9 (April 16, 1924), entire issue.

Chin, Robert and Ai-li S. *Psychological Research in Communist China: 1949–1966*. Cambridge, Mass.: M.I.T. Press, 1969.

The China Year Book. H.G.W. Woodhead, ed. Volumes for 1915 through 1926–27. London: George Routledge and Sons, 1916–21; Tientsin: Tientsin Press, 1921–28.

"China's Internal Loans." *Bulletin of the Government Bureau of Economic Information* 2, no. 19 (June 17, 1922), 14 pp. A copy was found in F.O. 371/9200 at the Public Record Office, London.

The Chinese Social and Political Science Review. Peking: Chinese Social and Political Science Association, quarterly, 1916–26.

Ching-shih shui-wu yueh-k'an 京師稅務月刊 [Peking taxation affairs monthly] no. 1 (n.d.). Seen at the Tōyō Bunko.

Ching-tu shih-cheng hui-lan 京都市政彙覽 [Overview of Peking city government]. Ching-tu shih-cheng kung-so 京都市政公所, ed. Peking: Ching-hua yin-shu chü 京華印書局, 1919. Seen at the East Asian Library, Columbia University.

"Chō Shō-sō naikaku to sōtō kaisen mondai" 張紹曾內閣と總統改選問題 [The Chang Shao-tseng cabinet and the problem of electing a new president]. *Shina jōhō*, no. 3 (June 20, 1923), entire issue.

Chou K'ai-ch'ing 周開慶. *Min-kuo Ssu-ch'uan jen-wu chuan-chi* 民國四川人物傳記 [Biographies of personalities of republican Szechwan]. Taipei: Commercial Press, 1966.

Chow Tse-tsung. *The May Fourth Movement: Intellectual Revolution in Modern China*. 1960. Paperback ed. Stanford, Calif.: Stanford University Press, 1967.

Chu Ch'i-ch'ien 朱啓鈐, comp. *Nan-Pei i-ho wen-hsien* 南北議和文献 [Documents on the North-South peace conference]. Reprinted in *I-chiu-i-chiu nien Nan-Pei i-ho tzu-liao*, special issue no. 1 of *Chin-tai shih tzu-liao* (1962), pp. 35–286. Abbreviated *NPIHWH*.

Close, Upton (pseud. of Josef Washington Hall). "Closeups of China's 'Money Josses.' " *China Review* 2, no. 4 (April 1922): 198–204.

——— *In the Land of the Laughing Buddha: The Adventures of an American Barbarian in China*. New York: G. P. Putnam's Sons, 1924.

Cohen, Paul A. "Wang T'ao's Perspective on a Changing World." In Albert Feuerwerker, Rhoads Murphey, and Mary C. Wright, eds., *Approaches to Modern Chinese History*. Berkeley and Los Angeles: University of California Press, 1967.

Collins, Barry E. and Raven, Bertram H. "Group Structure: Attraction, Coalitions, Communications, and Power." In Gardner Lindzey and Elliot Aronson, eds., *The Handbook of Social Psychology*, vol. 4. 2d ed. Reading, Mass.: Addison-Wesley, 1969.

Coser, Lewis A. *The Functions of Social Conflict*. Paperback ed. New York: Free Press, 1964.

[Dazai Matsusaburō (sometimes given as Shōzaburō) 太宰松三郎]. *Chūka minkoku daijūnenshi* 中華民國第十年史 [History of the Chinese republic in 1921]. Dairen: Minami Manshū tetsudō kabushiki kaisha 南滿州鐵道株式會社, 1922.

———. *Chūka minkoku daijūichinenshi* 中華民國第十一年史 [History of the Chinese republic in 1922]. Dairen: Minami Manshū tetsudō kabushiki kaisha, 1923.

DeGlopper, Donald R. "Doing Business in Lukang." In W. E. Willmott, ed., *Economic Organization in Chinese Society*. Stanford, Calif.: Stanford University Press, 1972.

Dibble, Vernon K. "The Organization of Traditional Authority: English County Government, 1558 to 1640." In James G. March, ed., *Handbook of Organizations*. Chicago: Rand McNally, 1965.

Dix, Robert H. *Colombia: The Political Dimensions of Change*. New Haven, Conn.: Yale University Press, 1967.

"Document of the Central Committee of the Chinese Communist Party, *Chung-fa* (1972) No. 12." *Issues and Studies* 8, no. 12 (September 1972): 64–71.

Eastman, Lloyd E. "China's Abortive Revolution: China under Nationalist Rule, 1927–1937." Manuscript of a forthcoming book, n.d.

Eckstein, Harry. *Division and Cohesion in a Democracy: A Study of Norway*. Princeton, N.J.: Princeton University Press, 1966.

———. "Introduction: Constitutional Engineering and the Problem of Viable Representative Government." In Harry Eckstein and David E. Apter, eds., *Comparative Politics: A Reader*. New York: Free Press, 1963.

———. "A Perspective on Comparative Politics, Past and Present." In Harry Eckstein and David E. Apter, eds., *Comparative Politics: A Reader*. New York: Free Press, 1963.

Etzioni, Amitai. *Modern Organizations*. Englewood Cliffs, N.J.: Prentice-Hall, 1964.

Fairbank, John King. *Trade and Diplomacy on the China Coast: The Opening of the Treaty Ports, 1822–1852*. 1954. Reprint. Paperback ed. Stanford, Calif.: Stanford University Press, 1966.

Fairbank, John K., Edwin O. Reischauer, and Albert M. Craig, *East Asia: The Modern Transformation*. Boston: Houghton Mifflin Co., 1965.

Fei Chueh-t'ien 費覺天. "Chung-kuo cheng-chih pu-neng shang cheng-kuei ti chen-yin chi chin-hou ying-tsou ti tao-lu "中國政治不能上正軌底眞因及今後應走的道路 [The real reason why China's government cannot get on the right track and the road it should take from now on]. *Tung-fang tsa-chih* 19, no. 11 (June 10, 1922): 7–18.

Fei Hsing-chien 費行簡 (pseud. Wo-chiu chung-tzu 沃丘仲子; sometimes listed as Fei Ching-chung 敬仲). *Hsu Shih-ch'ang* 徐世昌 [A biography of Hsu Shih-ch'ang]. 1918. Reprint. Taipei: Wen-hai 文海, 1967. Abbreviated *HSC*.

———. *Tang-tai ming-jen hsiao-chuan* 當代名人小傳 [Brief biographies of famous men of today]. 2 vols. Shanghai: Ch'ung-wen shu-chü 崇文書局, 1919. Abbreviated *TTMJ*.

Feng Han-chi. *The Chinese Kinship System*. Cambridge, Mass.: Harvard University Press, 1948.

Fervin, A. W. *Chinese Currency and Finance*. Washington, D. C.: U.S. Government Printing Office, 1919.

Feuerwerker, Albert. *China's Early Industrialization: Sheng Hsuan-huai (1844–1916) and Mandarin Enterprise*. Cambridge, Mass.: Harvard University Press, 1958.

Fincher, John. "Political Provincialism and the National Revolution." In Mary Clabaugh Wright, ed., *China in Revolution: The First Phase, 1900–1913*. New Haven, Conn.: Yale University Press, 1968.

Folsom, Kenneth E. *Friends, Guests, and Colleagues: The Mu-fu System in the Late Ch'ing Period*. Berkeley and Los Angeles: University of California Press, 1968.

Foster, George M. "The Dyadic Contract: A Model for the Social Structure of a Mexican Peasant Village." In Jack M. Potter, May N. Diaz, and George M. Foster, eds., *Peasant Society: A Reader*. Boston: Little, Brown, 1967.

Freedman, Maurice. *Chinese Lineage and Society: Fukien and Kwangtung*. London: Athlone Press, 1966.

Friedrich, Carl J. "Constitutions and Constitutionalism." In David L. Sills. ed., *International Encyclopedia of the Social Sciences*, vol. 3. New York: Macmillan and Free Press, 1968.

Gaimushō jōhōbu 外務省情報部 (Intelligence section of the Japanese Ministry of Foreign Affairs). *Gendai Shina jimmeikan* 現代支那人名鑑 [Biographical dictionary of contemporary Chinese]. Tokyo, 1924 and 1928 editions. The 1932 edition was published under the title *Gendai Chūka minkoku Manshūkoku jimmeikan* 現代中華民國滿洲國人名鑑 [Biographical dictionary of contemporary Republic of China and Manchukuo] and the 1937 edition as *Gendai Chūka minkoku Manshūteikoku jimmeikan* 帝. Each edition is different. Abbreviated *GJMK*, 1924; *GJMK*, 1928; etc.

Gallin, Bernard. "Political Factionalism and its Impact on Chinese Village School Organization in Taiwan." In Marc J. Swartz, ed., *Local-Level Politics: Social and Cultural Perspectives*. Chicago: Aldine Publishing Co., 1968.

Gasster, Michael. *Chinese Intellectuals and the Revolution of 1911: The Birth of Modern Chinese Radicalism*. Seattle: University of Washington Press, 1969.

Geertz, Clifford. "Ideology as a Cultural System." In David E. Apter, ed., *Ideology and Discontent*. New York: Free Press, 1964.

Gilbert, Rodney. "Arms and Men in China." *Asia* 22, no. 9 (September 1922): 725–31, 752–54.

Gillin, Donald G. *Warlord: Yen Hsi-shan in Shansi Province, 1911–1949*. Princeton, N.J.: Princeton University Press, 1967.

Goodnow, Frank J. *Principles of Constitutional Government*. New York: Harper and Row, 1916.

————. "Actual Workings of the Chinese Republic." Newspaper clipping dated New York, December 14, 1914, from an unknown newspaper, Goodnow collection, The Johns Hopkins University. Shown to me by Professor Y. C. Wang.

Great Britain. Foreign Office Archives. Housed in the Public Records Office, London. Series F.O. 317 and F.O. 228, 1916–28.

A Guide to the Press of Asia. 2d edition. London: Great Britain, Foreign Office, 1925, vol. 3, *China*.

Hakuun-sō shujin 白雲莊主人 [Master of the white-cloud villa]. *Chō Saku-rin* 張作霖 [Chang Tso-lin]. Tokyo: Shōwa shuppansha 昭和出版社, 1928.

Hamilton, Walton H. "Constitutionalism." In Edwin R. A. Seligman, ed., *Encyclopedia of the Social Sciences*, vol. 4. New York: Macmillan, 1931.

Han Ssu 翰斯. *K'an! Cheng-hsueh hsi* 看！政學系 [Look! The political study clique]. [Hongkong?]: Hua-nan ch'u-pan she 華南出版社, 1947.

Hashikawa Tokio 橋川時雄. *Chūgoku bunkakai jimbutsu sōkan* 中國文化界人物總鑑 [Biographical dictionary of cultural personalities of China]. Peking: Chūka hōrei hen'inkan 中華法令編印館, 1940.

Hatano Ken'ichi 波多野乾一, comp. *Gendai Shina no kiroku* 現代支那之記錄 [Records of contemporary China]. [Peking]: Enjinsha 燕塵社, monthly, 1924–26. Abbreviated *GSK*. In the example "*Ching pao* 1924.10.12 in *GSK* 1924.10.226–27," the source cited is the *Ching pao* issue of October 12, 1924, as reprinted in *Gendai Shina no kiroku* of October 1924, pp. 226–27.

———. *Gendai Shina* 現代支那 [Contemporary China]. Tokyo: Shina mondai sha 支那問題社, 1921.

Hawgood, John A. *Modern Constitutions Since 1787*. London: Macmillan, 1939.

Ho, Ping-ti. *The Ladder of Success in Imperial China: Aspects of Social Mobility, 1368–1911*. 1962. Reprint. Paperback ed. New York: John Wiley and Sons, 1964.

Hobbes, Thomas. *Leviathan, Or the Matter, Forme and Power of a Commonwealth, Ecclesiastical and Civil*, edited by Michael Oakeshott. New York: Collier, 1962.

Hollnsteiner, Mary R. "Social Structure and Power in a Philippine Municipality." In Jack M. Potter, May N. Diaz, and George M. Foster, eds., *Peasant Society: A Reader*. Boston: Little, Brown, 1967.

Houn, Franklin W. *Central Government of China, 1912–1928: An Institutional Study*. Madison: University of Wisconsin Press, 1957.

Howard, Richard C. "The Concept of Parliamentary Government in 19th Century China: A Preliminary Survey." Paper read at University Seminar on Modern East Asia—China and Japan, January 9, 1963, at Columbia University, New York City.

Hsieh Pin 謝彬, *Min-kuo cheng-tang shih* 民國政黨史 [A history of political parties in the republic]. 1925. Reprint. Taipei, Wen-hsing, 1962.

Hsu Shih-ch'ang ch'üan-chuan 徐世昌全傳 [Complete biography of Hsu Shih-ch'ang]. [Shanghai?]: Ching-chih t'u-shu kuan, 1922.

Hsu Tao-lin 徐道鄰. *Hsu Shu-cheng hsien-sheng wen-chi nien-p'u ho-k'an* 徐樹錚先生文集年譜合刊 [Selected writings and chronological biography of Mr. Hsu Shu-cheng, published together]. Taipei: Commercial Press, 1962.

Hsueh, Chün-tu. *Huang Hsing and the Chinese Revolution*. Stanford, Calif.: Stanford University Press, 1961.

Huang I 黃毅. *Yuan-shih tao-kuo chi* 袁氏盜國記 [How Yuan (Shih-k'ai) plundered the nation]. 1916. Reprint. Taipei, Wen-hsing, 1962.

Ichiko, Chūzō. "The Role of the Gentry: An Hypothesis." In Mary Clabaugh Wright, ed., *China in Revolution: The First Phase, 1900–1913*. New Haven, Conn.: Yale University Press, 1968.

Iriye, Akira. *After Imperialism: The Search for a New Order in the Far East, 1921–1931*. Cambridge, Mass.: Harvard University Press, 1965.

Jackson, Karl D. "Communication and National Integration in Sundanese Villages: Implications for Communications Strategy." Paper prepared for Indonesia Seminar, March 30–April 1, 1972, of Southeast Asia Development Advisory Group, New York City.

Jimbutsu jihyō 人物時評 [Biographical sketches of currently prominent persons]. [Peking], Enjinsha, monthly. The Tōyō Bunko has an incomplete set running from 2, no. 5 (August 1924) to 4, no. 2 (November 1926). *Jimbutsu jihyō* was published together with *Shina Shokuin hyō* (q.v.). The editors were Hatano Ken'ichi (through April 1925) and Satome Hajime 里見甫 thereafter.

Juan Hsiang 阮湘, *et al. Ti-i-hui Chung-kuo nien-chien* 第一回中國年鑑 [The China yearbook—number one]. Shanghai: Commercial Press, 1924.

Kagawa Shun'ichirō 香川峻一郎. *Sensō shihon ron* 錢莊資本論 [On (Chinese) money shop capital]. Tokyo: Jitsugyō no Nihonsha 實業之日本社, 1948.

Kaji Ryūichi 嘉治隆一. "Shina ni okeru shimbun hattatsu shōshi" 支那に於ける新聞發達小史 [A short history of the development of newspapers in China], *Keizai shiryō* 經濟資料 13, no. 3 (March 20, 1927), entire issue.

Kann, E. "Chinese Government Loans." In *The China Year Book 1934*, edited by H.G.W. Woodhead. Shanghai: The North-China Daily News and Herald, [1934].

Kao Yin-tsu 高蔭祖. *Chung-hua min-kuo ta-shih chi* 中華民國大事記 [Chronology of major events in the history of the Chinese Republic]. Taipei: Shih-chieh she 世界社, 1957.

Klein, Donald W. and Anne B. Clark. *Biographic Dictionary of Chinese Communism, 1921–1965.* 2 vols. Cambridge, Mass.: Harvard University Press, 1971.

Ko Kung-chen 戈公振. *Chung-kuo pao-hsueh shih* 中國報學史 [A history of journalism in China]. 1927. Reprint. Taipei: Hsueh-sheng shu-chü 學生書局, 1964.

Ko-ming wen-hsien 革命文獻 [Archives of the revolution], vols. 10, 41. Taichung: Chung-kuo kuo-min tang chung-yang wei-yuan hui tang-shih shih-liao pien-tsuan wei-yuan hui 中國國民黨中央委員會黨史史料編纂委員會, 1955, 1967.

Kōjima Shōtarō 小島昌太郎. *Shina saikin daiji nempyō* 支那最近大事年表 [A chronology of major recent events in China]. Tokyo: Yūhikaku 有斐閣, 1942.

Kokumin gikai 國民義會 [*sic*]. *Shina seitō no genjō* 支那政黨の現狀 [The present state of China's political parties]. N.p., n.d. [1917?], 22 pp. Appears to be a reprint of the last part of Inoue Ichiō 井上一葉. "Shina seitōshi" 支那政黨史 [History of China's political parties]. *Shina kenkyū shiryō* 支那研究資料 [China research materials] 1, no. 2 (May 5, 1917): 1–71. Both are in the Tōyō Bunko.

Ku Hsiu-sun 古薛孫. *Chia-tzu nei-luan shih-mo chi-shih* 甲子內亂始末紀實 [Record of the whole story of the disorders of 1924]. Tientsin: Chung-hua shu-chü 中華書局, 1924.

Ku Tun-jou 顧敦鍒. *Chung-kuo i-hui shih* 中國議會史 [A hsitory of the Chinese parliament]. 1931. Rev. ed. Taichung: Tung-hai ta-hsueh 東海大學, 1962.

Kuo-fu nien-p'u 國父年譜 [Chronological biography of Sun Yat-sen]. Chung-kuo kuo-min tang chung-yang tang-shih. shih-liao pien-tsuan wei-yuan hui, comp. 2 vols. Taipei: Chung-hua min-kuo ko-chieh chi-nien kuo-fu pai-nien yen-ch'en ch'ou-pei wei-yuan hui 中華民國各界紀念國父百年誕辰籌備委員會, 1965.

Kuo-shih kuan kuan-k'an 國史館館刊 [Journal of the bureau of national history]. (Nanking) December 1947–January 1949. Reprint. Hongkong: Lung-men shu-tien, n.d.

Kwok, D. W. Y. *Scientism in Chinese Thought, 1900–1950.* New Haven, Conn.: Yale University Press, 1965.

Lai-chiang cho-wu 淶江濁物 (pseud.). *An-fu ta-tsui an* 安福大罪案 [An indictment of the big crimes of the Anfu clique]. 8 separately paginated *chüan* in 2 vols. Peking, Hsin-shih pien-chi she 信史編輯社, 1920. Most of the text is reprinted in *Chin-tai shih tzu-liao*, no. 2 (1962), pp. 11–103; the original was seen at the Kuomintang Party History Archives, Taichung. Abbreviated *ATTA*.

Lai Ch'ün-li 賴群力 (probably pseud.), comp. "I-ho wen-hsien chi-ts'en" 議和文獻輯存 [Collected documents of the peace conference]. *I-chiu-i-chiu nien Nan-Pei i-ho tzu-liao*, special issue no. 1 of *Chin-tai shih tzu-liao* (1962), pp. 287–318.

Landé, Carl. H. "Networks and Groups in Southeast Asia: Some Observations on the Group Theory of Politics." *American Political Science Review* 67, no. 1 (March 1973): 103–27.

Lee, Robert H. G. *The Manchurian Frontier in Ch'ing History.* Cambridge, Mass.: Harvard University Press, 1970.

Legg, Keith R. *Politics in Modern Greece.* Stanford, Calif.: Stanford University Press, 1969.

Legge, James. *The Chinese Classics: With a Translation, Critical and Exegetical Notes, Prolegomena, and Copious Indexes.* 7 vols. London: Trübner and Co., 1861.

Leites, Nathan. *On the Game of Politics in France.* Stanford, Calif.: Stanford University Press, 1959.

Leong Sow-theng. "China and Soviet Russia: Their Diplomatic Relations, 1917–1924." Unpublished manuscript, Canberra, 1972.

Levenson, Joseph R. *Liang Ch'i-ch'ao and the Mind of Modern China.* Cambridge, Mass.: Harvard University Press, 1953.

Li Chien-nung 李劍農. *Chung-kuo chin-pai nien cheng-chih shih* 中國近百年政治史 [A political history of the last century in China]. 2 vols. 1947. Reprint. Taipei: Commercial Press, 1959.

———. *The Political History of China, 1840–1928.* Translated by Ssu-yu Teng and Jeremy Ingalls. Princeton, N.J.: D. Van Nostrand Co., 1956. This translation of the preceding entry has been cited in preference to the original except where my translation differs from it.

Li T'ai-fen 李泰棻. *Kuo-min-chün shih-kao* 國民軍史稿 [Draft history of the Kuominchün]. Peiping: n.p., 1930.

Li T'ing-yü 李廷玉, comp. "Li T'ing-yü so-ts'en tien-kao" 李廷玉所存电稿 [Telegrams preserved by Li T'ing-yü]. *I-chiu-i-chiu nien Nan-Pei i-ho tzu-liao,* special issue no. 1 of *Chih-tai shih tzu-liao* (1962), pp. 1–34.

Li Yun-han 李雲漢. *T'sung jung-kung tao ch'ing-tang* 從容共到清黨 [From admission of the Communists to the purge]. 2 vols. Taipei: Chung-kuo hsueh-shu chu-tso chiang-chu wei-yuan hui, 1966.

Liew, K. S. *Struggle for Democracy: Sung Chiao-jen and the 1911 Chinese Revolution.* Berkeley and Los Angeles: University of California Press, 1971.

Linden, Allen Barnard. "Politics and Higher Education in China: The Kuomintang and the University Community, 1927–1937." Ph.D. dissertation, Columbia University, 1969.

Liu Ch'u-hsiang 劉楚湘. *Kuei-hai cheng-pien chi-lueh* 癸亥政變紀略 [Record of the 1924 coup]. 1924. Reprint. Taipei: Wen-hai, 1967.

Liu Feng-han 劉鳳翰. *Hsin-chien lu-chün* 新建陸軍 [The Newly-Founded Army]. Nankang: Chung-yang yen-chiu yuan chin-tai shih yen-chiu so, 1967.

Liu Shou-lin 劉壽林. *Hsin-hai i-hou shih-ch'i nien chih-kuan nien-piao* 辛亥以後十七年職官年表 [Tables by year of officials, 1911–28]. 1966. Reprint. n.p., n.d. [Kyoto? 1974?].

Lo Kuang 羅光. *Lu Cheng-hsiang chuan* 陸徵祥傳 [A biography of Lu Cheng-hsiang]. 1948. Reprint. Taipei: Commercial Press, 1967.

Lo Wen-kan 羅文幹. *Yü-chung jen yü* 獄中人語 [Words from prison]. 1924? Reprint. Taipei: Wen-hai, [1967?].

Loewenstein, Karl. "Reflections on the Value of Constitutions in Our Revolutionary Age." In Harry Eckstein and David E. Apter, eds., *Comparative Politics: A Reader.* New York: Free Press, 1963.

MacKinnon, Stephen R. "Liang Shih-i and the Communications Clique," *Journal of Asian Studies* 29, no. 3 (May 1970): 581–602.

———. "The Peiyang Army, Yüan Shih-k'ai, and the Origins of Modern Chinese Warlordism," *Journal of Asian Studies* 32, no. 3 (May 1973): 405–23.

"Mandate on the Organization of the Ta-yuan-shuai Government, June 18th 1927." *Public Documents Supplement of the Chinese Social and Political Science Review* 11, no. 1 (January 1927): 133–34.

Mayer, Adrian C. "The Significance of Quasi-Groups in the Study of Complex Societies." In Michael Banton, ed., *The Social Anthropology of Complex Societies.* London: Tavistock Publications, 1966.

Metzger, Thomas A. *The Internal Organization of Ch'ing Bureaucracy: Legal, Normative, and Communication Aspects.* Cambridge, Mass.: Harvard University Press, 1973.

Mintz, Sidney W. "Pratik: Haitian Personal Economic Relationships." In Jack M. Potter, May N. Diaz, and George M. Foster, eds., *Peasant Society: A Reader*. Boston: Little, Brown. 1967.

Munro, Donald J. "The Malleability of Man in Chinese Marxism." *China Quarterly*, no. 48 (October–December 1971), pp. 609–40.

Nan-hai yin-tzu 南海胤子 (pseud.). *An-fu huo-kuo chi* 安福禍國記 [How the Anfu clique brought disaster on the country]. 3 vols. n.p., 1920. The copy seen at the Kuomintang Party History Archives in Taichung lacked the third volume. Abbreviated *AHKC*.

Nathan, Andrew James. "Factionalism in Early Republican China: The Politics of the Peking Government, 1918–1920." Ph.D. dissertation, Harvard University, 1970.

———. "A Factionalism Model for CCP Politics." *China Quarterly*, no. 53 (January–March 1973), pp. 34–66.

Nicholas, Ralph W. "Factions: A Comparative Analysis." In Michael Banton, ed., *Political Systems and the Distribution of Power*. London: Tavistock Publications, 1965.

Nihon gaikō bunsho 日本外交文書 [Documents on Japanese foreign policy], 1918, vol. 2, part 1. Tokyo: Gaimushō, 1969.

Nivison, David S. "The Problem of 'Knowledge' and 'Action' in Chinese Thought since Wang Yang-ming." In Arthur F. Wright, ed., *Studies in Chinese Thought*. 1953. Reprint. Chicago: University of Chicago Press, Phoenix Books, 1967.

The North-China Herald and Supreme Court and Consular Gazette. Shanghai, weekly, 1916–28. Abbreviated *NCH*. References in notes are to year, month, day, and page, respectively.

Nu-li chou-pao 努力週報 [The endeavor]. Peking, weekly, May 7, 1922–December 1, 1923.

Palmer, R. R. *The Age of the Democratic Revolution, a Political History of Europe and America: The Challenge*. Princeton, N.J.: Princeton University Press, 1959.

Parliament List. I compiled a list of the members of all early republican parliaments and arranged it so as to show the parliamentary career of each member, as well as membership in the late Ch'ing provincial and national assemblies, in the Peking Provisional National Council of 1912, and in the Government Council of 1914–16. Membership or nonmembership in the Anfu Club was indicated for the 1918–20 parliament. The list is cited as a source of biographical information and of some tables in this book. The sources for the list, each cited in full elsewhere in this bibliography, are:

    Chang P'eng-yuan, *Li-hsien p'ai yü hsin-hai ko-ming*, pp. 247–320.

    Juan Hsiang, *et al.*, *Ti-i-hui Chung-kuo nien-chien*, pp. 159–63.

    Ku Tun-jou, *Chung-kuo i-hui shih*, pp. 288–310.

    Nan-hai yin-tzu, *An-fu huo-kuo chi*, 1:55–64.

The lists of M.P.'s in Liu Shou-lin, *Hsin-hai i-hou shih-ch'i nien chih-kuan nien-piao*, which became available after the completion of this book (see Chapter III, note 29), cover the same ground and appear to be more authoritative.

Parsons, Talcott, *The Social System*. New York: Free Press, 1951.

Payne, James L. *Patterns of Conflict in Colombia*. New Haven, Conn.: Yale University Press, 1968.

Pei-ching kuan-liao tsui-e shih 北京官僚罪惡史 [History of the crimes of Peking officialdom]. 10 vols.? [Peking?]: Cheng-ch'ün she 正群社, 1922. I have seen only vol. 1, which is at the Kuomintang Party History Archives, Taichung.

Powell, John Duncan. "Peasant Society and Clientelist Politics." *American Political Science Review* 64, no. 2 (June 1970): 411–25.

Pugach, Noel. "Embarrassed Monarchist: Frank J. Goodnow and Constitutional Development in China, 1913–1915." *Pacific Historical Review* 42, no. 4 (November 1973): 499–517.

Pye, Lucian W. *The Spirit of Chinese Politics: A Psychocultural Study of the Authority Crisis in Political Development*. Cambridge, Mass.: M.I.T. Press, 1968.

————. *Warlord Politics: Conflict and Coalition in the Modernization of Republican China*. New York: Praeger Publishers, 1971.

Rankin, Mary Backus. "The Revolutionary Movement in Chekiang: A Study in the Tenacity of Tradition." In Mary Clabaugh Wright, ed., *China in Revolution: The First Phase, 1900–1913*. New Haven, Conn.: Yale University Press, 1968.

Reinsch, Paul S. *An American Diplomat in China*. 1922. Reprint. Taipei: Ch'eng-wen Publishing Co., 1967.

Riggs, Fred. W. *Thailand: The Modernization of a Bureaucratic Polity*. Honolulu: East-West Center Press, 1966.

Riker, William H. *The Theory of Political Coalitions*. New Haven, Conn.: Yale University Press, 1962.

Rousseau, Jean-Jacques. *The Social Contract, or Principles of Political Right*. In Frederick Watkins, trans. and ed., *Rousseau: Political Writings*. Edinburgh: Thomas Nelson and Sons, 1953.

Sahlins, Marshall D. "On the Sociology of Primitive Exchange." In Michael Banton, ed., *The Relevance of Models for Social Anthropology*. London: Tavistock, 1965.

Saishin Shina yōin den 最新支那要人傳 [Latest biographies of important Chinese]. Osaka: Asahi shimbunsha 朝日新聞社, 1941.

Sanetō Keishū 實藤惠秀. *Chūgokujin Nihon ryūgakushi* 中国人日本留学史 [A History of Chinese students in Japan]. Tokyo: Kuroshio shuppan くろしお出版, 1960.

Satō Saburō 佐藤三郎, ed. *Minkoku no seika* 民國之精華 [Biographies of members of the upper and lower houses in China]. 1916. Reprint. Taipei: Wen-hai, [1967?].

Schiffrin, Harold Z. *Sun Yat-sen and the Origins of the Chinese Revolution*. Berkeley and Los Angeles: University of California Press, 1968.

Schurmann, Franz. *Ideology and Organization in Communist China*. Berkeley and Los Angeles: University of California Press, 1966.

Schwartz, Benjamin I. *Chinese Communism and the Rise of Mao*. Cambridge, Mass.: Harvard University Press, 1952.

————. "On Attitudes Toward Law in China." Reprinted in Jerome Alan Cohen, *The Criminal Process in the People's Republic of China, 1949–1963: An Introduction*. Cambridge, Mass.: Harvard University Press, 1968.

————. "The Reign of Virtue: Some Broad Perspectives on Leader and Party in the Cultural Revolution." In John Wilson Lewis, ed., *Party Leadership and Revolutionary Power in China*. Cambridge, England: Cambridge University Press, 1970.

Scott, James C. *Comparative Political Corruption*. Englewood Cliffs, N.J.: Prentice-Hall, 1972.

————. "Corruption, Machine Politics, and Political Change." *American Political Science Review* 63, no. 4 (December 1969): 1142–58.

————. "Patron-Client Politics and Political Change in Southeast Asia." *American Political Science Review* 66, no. 1 (March 1972): 91–113.

Selle, Earl Albert. *Donald of China*. New York: Harper and Row, 1948.

Shan-hou hui-i kung-pao 善後會議公報 [Reconstruction Conference gazette]. Peking, 1925–26. Seen at East Asian Library, Columbia University.

Sharman, Lyon. *Sun Yat-sen: His Life and Its Meaning; A Critical Biography*. 1934. Paperback ed. Stanford, Calif.: Stanford University Press, 1968.

Shen Yun-lung 沈雲龍, *Li Yuan-hung p'ing-chuan* 黎元洪評傳 [Critical biography of Li Yuan-hung]. Nankang: Chung-yang yen-chiu yuan chin-tai shih yen-chiu so, 1963.

———. Interview, Nankang, Taiwan, February 19, 1968.

Sheridan, James E. *Chinese Warlord: The Career of Feng Yü-hsiang.* 1966. Paperback ed. Stanford, Calif.: Stanford University Press, 1970.

Shina kin'yū jijō 支那金融事情 [The financial situation in China]. [Tokyo]: Gaimushō tsū-shōkyoku dainika 通商局第二課 (Foreign Ministry, office of trade, second section), March 1925. Marked "secret." Seen at the Tōyō Bunko. Abbreviated *SKJ.*

"Shina ni okeru shimbun hattatsu shikō" 支那に於ける新聞發達史稿 [Draft history of the development of newspapers in China]. *Pekin Mantetsu geppō* 北京滿鐵月報 [South Manchurian Railway Peking monthly] 1, no. 3 (July 15, 1924), appendix (41 pp.).

Shina shokuin hyō 支那職員表 [Who's who of the Chinese government service, central and provincial]. [Peking], Enjinsha. Monthly; the Tōyō Bunko has an incomplete set running from 11, no 5 (August 1924) to 4, no. 2 (November 1926). The editors were Hatano Ken'ichi (through April 1925) and Satome Hajime thereafter.

Shun-t'ien shih-pao 順天時報 [Peking news]. Peking, daily, 1918–23. Abbreviated *STSP.* References in notes are to year, month, day, and page, respectively.

Siegel, Bernard J. and Alan R. Beals. "Pervasive Factionalism." *American Anthropologist* 62, no. 3 (June 1960): 394–417.

Silin, Robert Henry. "Management in Large-Scale Taiwanese Industrial Enterprises." Ph.D. dissertation, Harvard University, 1970.

———. "Marketing and Credit in a Hong Kong Wholesale Market." In W.E. Willmott, ed., *Economic Organization in Chinese Society.* Stanford, Calif.: Stanford University Press, 1972.

Simmel, George. *Conflict and The Web of Group-Affiliations.* Translated by Kurt H. Wolff and Reinhard Bendix. New York: Free Press, 1955.

Snow, Edgar. *Red Star Over China.* 1938. Reprint. New York: Grove Press, 1961.

Solomon, Richard H. *Mao's Revolution and the Chinese Political Culture.* Berkeley and Los Angeles: University of California Press, 1971.

Somit, Albert and Joseph Tanenhaus. *The Development of American Political Science: From Burgess to Behavioralism.* Boston: Allyn and Bacon, 1967.

"Sōtō senkyo to kenpō seitei" 總統選舉ト憲法制定 [Election of the president and completion of the constitution]. *Shina jōhō,* no. 4 (December 14, 1923), 30 pp.

Spiro, Melford E. "Factionalism and Politics in Village Burma." In Marc J. Swarz, ed., *Local-Level Politics: Social and Cultural Perspectives.* Chicago: Aldine Publishing Co., 1968.

Strong, C. F. *A History of Modern Political Constitutions.* 1963. Reprint. New York: Capricorn Books, 1964.

Sun Yao 孫曜, comp. *Chung-hua min-kuo shih-liao* 中華民國史料 [Historical materials of the Chinese Republic]. 1930. Reprint. Taipei: Wen-hai, [1967]. The reprint has consecutive pagination, unlike the first edition; reference in these notes is to the reprint edition.

Ta yin-chü-shih 大隱居士 (pseud.). *Cheng-wen chi-yao* 政聞紀要 [Jottings on politics]. In *I-chiu-i-chiu nien Nan-Pei i-ho tzu-liao,* special issue no. 1 of *Chin-tai shih tzu-liao* (1962), pp. 376–494. Abbreviated *CWCY.*

Tahara Teijirō 田原禎次郎. *Shinmatsu minsho Chūgoku kanshin jimmeiroku* 清末民初中國官紳人名錄 [Biographical dictionary of Chinese gentry and officials of the late Ch'ing and early republic]. Peking: Chūgoku kenkyūkai 中國研究會, 1918. Reprint. [Taipei]: n.p., n.d.

Tamagna, Frank M. *Banking and Finance in China.* New York: Institute of Pacific Relations, 1942.

T'ang Chi-yao 唐繼堯 [A biography of T'ang Chi-yao]. 1925. Reprint. Taipei: Wen-hai, 1967.

T'ao Chü-yin 陶菊隐. *Pei-yang chün-fa t'ung-chih shih-ch'i shih-hua* 北洋軍閥統治時期史話 [History of the period of the rule of the Peiyang militarists]. 7 vols. Peking: San-lien shu-tien 三联书店, 1957–59. Abbreviated *PYCF.*

———. *Wu P'ei-fu chuan* 吳佩孚傳 (A biography of Wu P'ei-fu). 1941. Reprint. Taipei, Chung-hua shu-chü 中華書局, 1963. First published as *Wu P'ei-fu chiang-chün chuan* 將軍傳 [A biography of General Wu P'ei-fu]. The reprint edition does not identify the author.

Teng Chih-ch'eng 鄧之誠. "P'ing Feng-kang chi-men ti-tzu pien 'San-shui Liang Yen-sun hsien-sheng nien-p'u' " 評鳳岡及門弟子編「三水梁燕孫先生年譜」[A critique of "A chrono-logical biography of the life of Mr. Liang Yen-sun (Shih-i) of San-shui *hsien*" by the disciples of Feng-kang (academy)]. *Yen-ching hsueh-pao* 燕京學報 [Yenching journal of Chinese studies], no. 33 (December 1947), pp. 292–302.

Teng Ssu-yü and John K. Fairbank. *China's Response to the West: A Documentary Survey, 1839–1923.* Cambridge, Mass.: Harvard University Press, 1961.

T'ieh-lu hsieh-hui hui-pao 鐵路協會會報 [Chinese railway association maganize]. Peking, 1917–18. Seen at the Tōyō Bunko.

Tien, Hung-mao. *Government and Politics in Kuomintang China, 1927–1937.* Stanford, Calif.: Stanford University Press, 1972.

Ting, Leonard G. "Chinese Modern Banks and the Finance of Government and Industry." *Nankai Social and Economic Quarterly* 8, no. 3 (October 1935): 578–616.

Ting Wen-chiang 丁文江. *Liang Jen-kung hsien-sheng nien-p'u ch'ang-pien ch'u-kao* 梁任公先生年譜長編初稿 [Preliminary draft of a composite chronological biography of Mr. Liang Ch'i-chao]. 2 vols. Taipei: Shih-chieh shu-chü, 1962.

Tokō Fumio 都甲文雄. "Shina seitō no genkyō" 支那政黨の現況 [The present lineup of political parties in China]. *Chōsa shiryō* 調査資料 [Investigation materials], no. 10 (June 28, 1919), pp. 95–143. Abbreviated "SSG."

Tolchin, Martin and Susan. *To The Victor . . . Political Patronage from the Clubhouse to the White House.* New York: Vintage, 1972.

Ts'ai Tung-fan 蔡東藩. *Min-kuo t'ung-su yen-i* 民國通俗演義 [Popular romance of the republic]. 8 vols. Shanghai: Hui-wen t'ang hsin-chi shu-chü 會文堂新記書局, 1936.

Tsao, Y. S. [Ts'ao Yun-hsiang]. "The Cause of Democracy in China." *The Chinese Social and Political Science Review* 10, no. 1 (January 1926): 62–91.

Ts'ao Ju-lin 曹汝霖. *I-sheng chih-hui i* 一生之回憶 [Reminiscences of a lifetime]. Hongkong: Ch'un-ch'iu tsa-chih she 春秋雜誌社, 1966.

Ts'en Ch'un-hsuan 岑春煊. *Le-chai man-pi* 樂齋漫筆 [Leisurely jottings from a pleasant study]. 1945. Reprint. Taipei, Wen-hsing, 1962.

Ts'en Hsueh-lü 岑學呂. *San-shui Liang Yen-sun hsien-sheng nien-p'u* 三水梁燕孫先生年譜 [A chronological biography of the life of Mr. Liang Yen-sun (Shih-i) of San-shui *hsien*]. 2 vols. 1936. Reprint. Taipei: Wen-hsing. 1962. The original edition identifies the author only as Feng-kang chi-men ti-tzu 鳳岡及門弟子 (disciples of Feng-kang [academy]). Abbreviated *LSINP.*

Tso Shun-sheng 左舜生. "Liang Shih-i chih i-sheng (1869–1933)" 梁士詒之一生 (1869–1933) [The life of Liang Shih-i, 1869–1933]. In his *Wan-chu lou sui-pi* 萬竹樓隨筆 [Sketches written in the chamber of ten thousand bamboo]. 1953. Reprint. Taipei: Wen-hai, 1967.

Tsou Lu 鄒魯. *Hui-ku lu* 回顧錄 [Reminiscences]. 1946. Reprint. 2 vols. Taipei: Tu-li ch'u-pan she 獨立出版社, 1951.

Ts'ung Yen 宗淹. "Ch'ung-kao chiu kuo-hui i-yuan" 忠告舊國會議員 [A warning to the members of the old parliament]. *Nu-li chou-pao*, no. 9 (July 2, 1922), p. 3.

Tung-fang tsa-chih 東方雜誌 [Eastern miscellany]. Shanghai, twice monthly, 1918–23.

T'ung-chi yueh-k'an 統計月刊 [Statistical monthly]. Peking: Kuo-wu yuan t'ung-chi chü 國務院統計局 [Cabinet statistical bureau]. 1918–1923. Seen at the Tōyō Bunko.

Udaka Yasushi 宇高寧. *Genkō Shina gyōsei* 現行支那行政 [Current Chinese administration]. Shanghai: Fuzanbō 富山房. 1926.

Waley, Arthur. *Three Ways of Thought in Ancient China.* 1939. Paperback ed. New York, Doubleday, n.d.

Wang Ching-lien 王景濂 and T'ang Nai-p'ei 唐乃霈. *Chung-hua min-kuo fa-t'ung ti-shan shih* 中華民國法統遞嬗史 [A history of the changes in the constitutional order of the Chinese republic]. [Shanghai?]: Min-shih she 民視社, 1922. In East Asian Library, Columbia University.

Wang I-t'ang 王揖唐. *I-t'ang shih-ts'en* 逸塘詩存 [Poems of Wang I-t'ang]. N.p, 1941. Seen at the Tōyō Bunko.

Wang Shih-chieh 王世杰 and Ch'ien Tuan-sheng 錢端升. *Pi-chiao hsien-fa* 比較憲法 [Comparative constitutions]. 2 vols. Shanghai: Commercial Press, 1938.

Wang, Y. C. *Chinese Intellectuals and the West, 1872–1949.* Chapel Hill: University of North Carolina Press, 1966.

Weber, Max. *The Religion of China: Confucianism and Taoism.* Translated and edited by Hans H. Gerth. Glencoe, Ill.: Free Press, 1951.

———. "Politics as a Vocation." In *From Max Weber: Essays in Sociology,* translated and edited by H. H. Gerth and C. Wright Mills. 1946. Paperback ed. New York: Galaxy Press, 1958.

———. *The Theory of Social and Economic Organization.* Translated by A. M. Henderson and Talcott Parsons. New York: Free Press, 1964.

Weiner, Myron. *Party Building in a New Nation: The Indian National Congress.* Chicago: University of Chicago Press, 1967.

———. *Party Politics in India: The Development of a Multi-Party System.* Princeton, N.J.: Princeton University Press, 1957.

Wen Kung-chih 文公直. *Tsui-chin san-shih nien Chung-kuo chün-shih shih* 最近三十年中國軍事史 [A history of military affairs in China in the last thirty years]. 3 separately paginated *pien* in 2 vols. 1930. Reprint. Taipei: Wen-hsing, 1962.

Who's Who in China: Biographies of Chinese Leaders. 3d and 5th eds. Shanghai: The China Weekly Review, 1925 and 1936. 5th ed. reprinted [Hongkong, Lungmen, 1968?]. The 1925 3d ed. is cited in full in the notes, while the 1936 5th ed. is abbreviated *Who's Who.*

Whyte, William Foote. *Street Corner Society: The Social Structure of an Italian Slum.* Enl. ed. Chicago: University of Chicago Press, 1955.

Wilbur, C. Martin. "Military Separatism and the Process of Reunification under the Ntionalist Regime, 1922–1937." In Ping-ti Ho and Tang Tsou, eds., *China in Crisis.* Chicago: University of Chicago Press, 1968. Vol. 1, *China's Heritage and the Communist Political System,* book 1.

Williams, Philip M. *Crisis and Compromise: Politics in the Fourth Republic.* Paperback ed. Garden City, N.Y.: Doubleday and Company, 1966. Originally published as *Politics in Postwar France.* London: Longmans Green and Co., 1954.

Willoughby, W. W. *Constitutional Government in China: Present Conditions and Prospects.* Washington, D. C.: Carnegie Endowment for International Peace, 1922.

Wolin, Sheldon S. *Politics and Vision: Continuity and Innovation in Western Political Thought*. Boston: Little, Brown, 1960.

Wou, Odoric Y. K. "A Chinese 'Warlord' Faction: The Chihli Clique, 1918–1924." in Andrew W. Cordier, ed., *The Dean's Papers, 1967*. Columbia Essays in International Affairs, vol. 3. New York: Columbia University Press, 1968.

———. "Militarism in Modern China as Exemplified in the Career of Wu P'ei-fu, 1916–1928." Ph.D. dissertation, Columbia University, 1970.

Wright, Mary Clabaugh. *The Last Stand of Chinese Conservatism: The T'ung-Chih Restoration, 1862–1874*. 2d printing, with additional notes, 1962. Paperback ed. New York: Atheneum, 1966.

Wright, Stanley F. *China's Customs Revenue Since the Revolution of 1911*. 3d ed., revised and enlarged. Shanghai: The Maritime Customs, 1935.

———. *The Collection and Disposal of the Maritime and Native Customs Revenue Since the Revolution of 1911, With an Account of the Loan Services Administered by the Inspector General of Customs*. 1927. 2d ed., revised and enlarged. Taipei: Ch'eng-wen Publishing Co., 1966.

Wu Hsiang-hsiang 吳相湘. "Ts'en Ch'un-hsuan" 岑春煊 [(A biography of) Ts'en Ch'un-hsuan]. In Ts'en Ch'un-hsuan, *Le-chai man-pi* (q. v.), appendix.

Wu P'ei-fu hsien-sheng chi 吳佩孚先生集 [Collected works of Wu P'ei-fu]. Taipei: Wu P'ei-fu hsien-sheng chi pien-chi wei-yuan hui 吳佩孚先生集編輯委員會, 1960.

Wu T'ing-hsieh 吳廷燮. *Ho-fei chih-cheng nien-p'u* 合肥執政年譜 [A chronological biography of Chief Executive Tuan Ch'i-jui of Hofei *hsien*]. 1938. Reprint. Taipei: Wen-hsing, 1962.

Yang Chia-lo 楊家駱. *Min-kuo ming-jen t'u-chien* 民國名人圖鑑 [Illustrated biographies of famous men of the republic]. 12 separately paginated *chüan* in 2 vols. Nanking: Chung-kuo tzu-tien kuan 中國辭典館, 1937. Abbreviated *MJTC*.

Yang Hsien-chün 楊先鈞. "Ti-kuo chu-i ching-chi ch'in-lueh hsia chih Chung-kuo" 帝國主義經濟侵略下之中國 [China under the economic invasion of imperialism], parts 5 and 6. *Shang-hai tsung shang-hui yueh-pao* 上海總商會月報 [Journal of the General Chamber of Commerce, Shanghai] 7, no. 9 (September 1927), 12 pp.

Yang Ju-mei 楊汝梅. *Min-kuo ts'ai-cheng lun* 民國財政論 [On the finances of the republic]. Shanghai: Commercial Press, 1927.

———. "P'ing-lun min-kuo i-lai chih ts'ai-cheng ta-shih" 評論民國以來之財政大事 [A critical discussion of major financial events since the founding of the republic]. *Yin-hang chou-pao*, no. 404. In Hatano Ken'ichi, comp., *Gendai Shina no kiroku* (January 1925), pp. 49–65.

Yang Lien-sheng. "The Concept of *Pao* as a Basis for Social Relations in China." In John K. Fairbank, ed., *Chinese Thought and Institutions*. Chicago: University of Chicago Press, 1957.

Yang Yu-chiung 楊幼炯. *Chin-tai Chung-kuo li-fa shih* 近代中國立法史 [Legislative history of modern China]. 1930. Rev. ed. Taipei: Commercial Press, 1966.

———. *Chung-kuo cheng-tang shih* 中國政黨史 [A history of political parties in China]. 1930. Reprint. Taipei, Commercial Press, 1966.

Yen, W. W. [Yen Hui-ch'ing]. "An Autobiography." Unpublished manuscript, kindly made available to me by Dr. Yen's daughter, Mrs. Ping-sheng Chin.

Yu, George T. *Party Politics in Republican China: The Kuomintang, 1912–1924*. Berkeley and Los Angeles: University of California Press, 1966.

Yu-ming 郁明 (pseud.). *Chang Tso-lin wai-chuan* 張作霖外傳 [An unauthorized biography of Chang Tso-lin]. 2 of a projected 3 vols. Hongkong: Yü-yu ch'u-pan she 宇宙出版社, 1967.

Yü Ch'eng-chih 俞誠之. *Hsia-an hui-kao (fu nien-p'u)* 退菴彙稿(附年譜) [Collected public papers of Yeh Kung-ch'o, with a chronological biography of his life]. 3 vols. 1946. Reprint. Taipei: Wen-hai, [1967?]. The pagination of the *nien-p'u* referred to in the footnotes is the pagination of the old edition, which is carried over, together with a new pagination, in the reprint edition.

Yun Tai-ying 惲代英. "Chung-kuo ts'ai-cheng chuang-k'uang shu-p'ing" 中國財政狀況述評 [Description and criticism of China's financial condition]. *Hsin chin-she* 新建設 [New construction magazine] 1, no. 6 (May 20, 1924): 118–40.

GLOSSARY

Place names, well-known persons and institutions, and obvious terms are not included.

An-fu chü-le-pu 安福俱樂部
An-fu hsi 安福系

Chan-hou ching-chi tiao-ch'a wei-yuan hui 戰後經濟調查委員會
Chang Chi 張繼
Chang Chia-sen 張嘉森
Chang Chien 張謇
Chang Chih-chang 張熾章
Chang Chih-ching 張知鏡
Chang Chih-pen 張知本
Chang Chih-t'an 張志潭
Chang Ching-yao 張敬堯
Chang Ch'ün 張羣
Chang Hsueh-liang 張學良
Chang Hsun 張勳
Chang Hu 張弧
Chang Huai-chih 張懷芝
Chang I-lin 張一麐
Chang Ju-chün 張汝鈞
Chang Jui-ch'i 張瑞璣
Chang Kia-ngau (Chang Chiao-ao) 張嘉璈
Chang Kuang-chien 張廣建
Chang Kung-chen 張拱宸
Chang Kuo-kan 張國淦
Chang Lu-ch'üan 張魯泉
Chang Ping-lin 張炳麟
Chang Po-lieh 張伯烈
Chang Shao-tseng 張紹曾
Chang Shih-chao 章士釗

Chang Tso-lin 張作霖
Chang Tsung-hsiang 張宗祥
Chang Tung-sun 張東蓀
Chang Yao-tseng 張耀曾
Chang Ying-hua 張英華
ch'ang-jen kan-shih 常任幹事
ch'ang-kuan 常關
Chao Ch'ing-hua 趙慶華
Chao Erh-hsun 趙爾巽
Chao Hsi-en 趙錫恩
Chao-hsin (treasury notes) 昭信
Chao Ping-lin 趙炳麟
chao-tai so 招待所
Chao T'i 趙倜
Che-chiang ch'ao 浙江潮
Che-chiang chün-wu shan-hou tu-pan 浙江軍務善後督辦
Ch'en Chen-hsien 陳振先
Ch'en Chieh 陳介
Ch'en Chin-t'ao 陳錦濤
Ch'en Chiung-ming 陳烱明
Ch'en Han-ti 陳漢第
Ch'en Kuang-yuan 陳光遠
Ch'en Kuo-hsiang 陳國祥
Ch'en Lu 陳籙
Ch'en Ming-chien 陳銘鑑
Ch'en pao 晨報
Ch'en Shu-fan 陳樹藩
Ch'en Tu-hsiu 陳獨秀
Cheng-chih shan-hou t'ao-lun hui 政治善

後討論會
Cheng-hsueh hui 政學會
Cheng Hung-nien 鄭洪年
Cheng-i tsa-chih 正誼雜誌
cheng-shih 正式
cheng-wu hui-i 政務會議
Cheng-wu yen-chiu hui 政務研究會
Ch'eng K'o 程克
Ch'eng Pi-kuang 程璧光
Chi Chung-yen 籍忠寅
chi-i 籍誼
chi-kang 紀綱
chi-kang pu-su 紀綱不肅
Chi-wei chü-le-pu 己未俱樂部
ch'i 期
Ch'i-hao chü-le-pu 七號俱樂部
Ch'i Hsieh-yuan 齊燮元
Chiang Fang-chen 蔣方震
Chiang Han 江瀚
Chiang Shao-chieh 江紹杰
Chiang T'ien-to 江天鐸
Chiang Yung 江庸
Chiao-chi k'o 交際課
Ch'iao-yuan 僑園
chieh-pai hsiung-ti kuan-hsi 結拜兄弟關係
chien-jen 薦任
chien-tu 監督
ch'ien-chuang 錢莊
Ch'ien Neng-hsun 錢能訓
Ch'ien Yung-ming 錢永銘
chih-fu 知府
Chih-Wan chan-cheng 直皖戰爭
chih-yuan 職員
Chin-pu tang 進步黨
chin-t'ieh 津貼
Chin Yun-p'eng 靳雲鵬
Chin Yung-yen 金永炎
ch'in-ch'i kuan-hsi 親戚關係
ch'in-shu kuan-hsi 親屬關係
Chinda 珍田
Ching-chi tiao-ch'a chü 經濟調查局
ching-lueh-shih 經略使
Ching pao 京報
Ching Yao-yueh 景耀月
Chou Chia-yen 周家彥
Chou T'ing-li 周廷勱
Chou Tso-min 周作民
Chou Tzu-ch'i 周自齊

Ch'ou-an hui 籌安會
ch'ou-pei ch'u 籌備處
ch'ou-pei yuan 籌備員
Chu Chao-hsing 朱兆莘
Chu Ch'i-ch'ien 朱啓鈐
Chu Shen 朱深
chu-tzu 猪子
Ch'u Fu-ch'eng 褚輔成
Ch'u Yü-p'u 褚玉璞
chü-le-pu 俱樂部
Ch'ü T'ung-feng 曲同豐
Ch'ü Ying-kuang 屈映光
chuan-jen kan-shih 專任幹事
Ch'uan-kuo shang-yeh (bank) 全國商業
Ch'uan-kuo t'ieh-lu hsieh-hui 全國鐵路協會
Ch'uan-yeh (bank) 勸業
Ch'üan Liang 權量
Chuang Yun-kuan 莊蘊寬
Chung-ho chü-le-pu 中和俱樂部
Chung-hua ch'u-hsu yin-hang 中華儲蓄銀行
Chung-hua hsin-pao 中華新報
Chung-hua min-kuo cheng-fu tsu-chih ta-kang 中華民國政府組織大綱
Chung-hua min-kuo lin-shih cheng-fu chih 中華民國臨時政府制
Chung-hua p'ing-min she 中華平民社
Chung-kuo shih-yeh (bank) 中國實業
chung-yang chuan-k'uan 中央專款
chung-yang hsuan-chü hui 中央選舉會
Chung-yang hsueh-hui 中央學會
Ch'ung-wen men shui 崇文門稅

Fa-chih chü 法制局
Fa-kuan hsun-lien so 法官訓練所
fa-lü shang 法律上
fa-lü wen-t'i 法律問題
fa-t'uan 法團
fa-t'ung 法統
Fa-t'ung wei-ch'ih hui 法統維持會
Fan Chih-huan 范治煥
fan-hsing 反省
Fan Yuan-lien 范源濂
Fang Shu 方樞
fei-tu ts'ai-ping 廢督裁兵
Feng Chia-sui 馮家遂
Feng Ho-chien, (i.e., Feng Kuo-chang) 馮河間
Feng Keng-kuang 馮耿光

Feng Kuo-chang 馮國璋
Feng-sheng (clique) 豐盛
Feng Yü-hsiang 馮玉祥
fu 府
Fu-ch'ien (industrial bonds) 富籤
Fu Liang-tso 傅良佐
Fu Ting-i 符定一
Fu Tseng-hsiang 傅增湘

Gotō 後藤

Ha Han-chang 哈漢章
Han Yü-chen 韓玉辰
hao-jen nei-ko 好人內閣
Hara Kei 原敬
Hayashi 林
Ho Feng-lin 何豐林
Ho-p'ing ch'i-ch'eng hui 和平期成會
ho-p'ing hui-i 和平會議
Ho-p'ing ts'u-ch'eng hui 和平促成會
Ho-p'ing ts'u-chin hui 和平促進會
ho-p'ing t'ung-i 和平統一
Ho-p'ing t'ung-i hui 和平統一會
Ho Te-lin 賀德霖
Ho Wen 何雯
hsi 系
Hsi-pei ch'ou-pien shih 西北籌邊使
Hsi-pei pien-fang chün 西北邊防軍
Hsia Shou-k'ang 夏壽康
Hsiao-ch'uan (i.e., T'ang Shao-i) 少川
Hsiao Yao-nan 蕭耀南
Hsieh Shu-ch'iang 解樹強
Hsieh Yuan-han 謝遠涵
Hsien-cheng t'ao-lun hui 憲政討論會
hsien-fa t'ao-lun hui 憲法討論會
Hsien-fa yen-chiu hui 憲法研究會
hsien-hsien hou-hsuan 先憲後選
Hsien-yu hui 憲友會
Hsin chiao-t'ung hsi 新交通系
Hsin-hsin kuo-hui 新新國會
Hsin-hua (savings bank) 新華
Hsin-min ts'ung-pao 新民叢報
Hsin-wen pao 新聞報
hsiu-ting fa-lü kuan 修定法律館
Hsiung Hsi-ling 熊希齡
Hsiung K'o-wu 熊克武
Hsiung Ping-ch'i 熊炳琦
Hsu Chi-yü 徐繼畬

Hsu Fo-su 徐佛蘇
Hsu Fu-lin 徐傅霖
Hsu, George (Hsu Ch'ien) 徐謙
Hsu Hsin-liu 徐新六
Hsu Lan-shu 徐蘭墅
Hsu Shih-ch'ang 徐世昌
Hsu Shih-i 徐世一
Hsu Shih-ying 許世英
Hsu Shu-cheng 徐樹錚
Hsu Tung-hai (i.e., Hsu Shih-ch'ang) 徐東海
hsuan-cheng shu 選證書
hsuan-chü fa 選舉法
Hsueh Chih-heng 薛之珩
Hsueh Tu-pi 薛篤弼
hu-fa 護法
Hu Han-min 胡漢民
Hu-pei hui-kuan 湖北會館
Hu Shih 胡適
Hua-ch'iao hsuan-chü hui 華僑選舉會
Hua-hsing hui 華興會
Hua-wei yin-hang 華威銀行
Huang Ch'ün 黃羣
Huang Fu 黃郛
Huang Hsing 黃興
Huang Ts'an-yuan 黃贊元
Huang Yen-p'ei 黃炎培
Huang Yun-p'eng 黃雲鵬
hui 會
hui-ch'i 會期
Hung-hsien 洪憲

I-shih pao 益世報
I Tz'u-ch'ien 易次乾
I-yu she 益友社
I-yuan fa 議院法
I-yuan hui 議員會

Jao Ming-luan 饒鳴鑾
Jen Feng-pao 任鳳苞
Jen K'o-ch'eng 任可澄

K'ang Shih-to 康士鐸
K'ang Yu-wei 康有爲
Kao En-hung 高恩洪
Kao Ling-wei 高凌霨
Kincheng [Chin-ch'eng] (bank) 金城
ko fa-t'uan 各法團
ko hsuan-chü ch'ü hsuan-chü jen 各選舉區選

舉人
ko hsuan-chü hui hsuan-chü jen 各選舉會選
舉人
k'o (department) 課
k'o-chang (section head) 科長
K'o-hsi-k'o-t'u 克希克圖
Koo, Wellington (Ku Wei-chün) 顧維鈞
ku (section) 股
Ku Chung-hsiu 谷鐘秀
ku-wen 顧問
K'uai-chi k'o 會計課
kuan-hsi 關係
Kuan Keng-lin 關賡麟
Kuan Mien-chün 關冕鈞
Kuang Yun-chin 光雲錦
Kung-ho chien-she t'ao-lun hui 共和建設討論
會
Kung-ho tang 共和黨
Kung Hsin-chan 龔心湛
kung-kuan 共管
Kung-min tang 公民黨
kung-tien 公電
Kung-yen pao 公言報
Kuo Ch'un-sen 郭椿森
Kuo-hui fei-ch'ang hui-i 國會非常會議
Kuo Jen-chang 郭人漳
Kuo-k'u cheng-ch'üan 國庫證券
kuo-min ching-chi hsieh-chin hui 國民經濟協
進會
Kuo-min hui-i 國民會議
Kuo-min ta-hui 國民大會
Kuo-min tang 國民黨
kuo-shih hui-i 國是會議
"Kuo-shih hui-i lun" 國是會議論
Kuo-shih pao 國是報
Kuo Sung-ling 郭松齡
Kuo Tse-yun 郭則澐
Kuo T'ung 郭同

la-shang kuan-hsi 拉上關係
Lan Kung-wu 藍公武
Leng Yü-ch'iu 冷雨秋
li (rules of conduct) 禮
li (distance) 里
Li Chao-fu 李肇甫
Li Chi-chen 李繼楨
Li Cho-chang 李倬章
Li Ch'un 李純

Li Hou-chi 李厚基
Li Huang-p'i (i.e., Li Yuan-hung) 黎黃陂
Li Hung-chang 李鴻章
Li Ken-yuan 李根源
Li Kuo-chen 李國珍
Li Lieh-chün 李烈鈞
Li Sheng-to 李盛鐸
Li Shih-wei 李士偉
Li Shu-ying 李述膺
Li Ssu-hao 李思浩
Li Ting-hsin 李鼎新
Li Tsung-jen 李宗仁
Li Wei-lun 李爲綸
Li Yen-ch'ing 李彥青
Li Yuan-hung 黎元洪
Liang Ch'i-ch'ao 梁啓超
Liang Ch'i-hsun 梁啓勳
liang-hui tzu-hsing chieh-chueh 兩會自行解決
Liang Hung-chih 梁鴻志
Liang Shan-chi 梁善濟
Liang Shih-i 梁士詒
liang-Sun-p'ai 兩孫派
Liangshi Yi (see Liang Shih-i)
liao-shu kuan-hsi 僚屬關係
Lin Ch'ang-min 林長民
Lin Pao-i 林葆懌
Lin Shao-fei 林紹斐
lin-shih hui-i 臨時會議
Lin-shih ts'an-i yuan 臨時參議院
Lin-shih yueh-fa 臨時約法
Ling Wen-yuan 凌文淵
Liu Ch'eng-yü 劉成禺
Liu Ching-shan 劉景山
Liu Ch'ung-chieh 劉崇傑
Liu Ch'ung-yu 劉崇佑
Liu En-ko 劉恩格
Liu En-yüan 劉恩源
Liu Hsien-shih 劉顯世
Liu Kuan-hsiung 劉冠雄
Liu Kuang-lieh 劉光烈
Liu Kuei-i 劉揆一
Lo Chi-han 駱繼漢
Lo Chia-heng 羅家衡
Lo Hung-nien 羅鴻年
Lo Wen-kan 羅文幹
Lu Cheng-hsiang 陸徵祥
Lu Chin 陸錦
Lu Hsin 盧信

Lu Jung-t'ing 陸榮廷
Lu Tsung-yü 陸宗輿
Lu Yung-hsiang 盧永祥
Lü Chün 呂均
Lü Fu 呂復
lü-shih hui 律師會
Lung Chi-kuang 龍濟光
Lung Chien-chang 龍建章
Lung-yen (iron mining company) 龍煙

Mei Kuang-yuan 梅光遠
men-hsia 門下
men-sheng 門生
men ti-tzu 門弟子
Meng En-yuan 孟恩遠
Meng-Tsang (bank) 蒙藏
Meng-Tsang yuan 蒙藏院
Miao Chia-shou 繆嘉壽
Min-chu tang 民主黨
Min-hsien t'ung-chih hui 民憲同志會
min-pa fen-tzu 民八份子
Mo Jung-hsin 莫榮新

Nan-Hsun (railway) 南潯
Nei-kuo kung-chai chü 內國公債局
"ni P'u-sa" 泥菩薩
'Ni Ssu-ch'ung 倪嗣冲
Nishihara 西原
Niu Yung-chien 鈕永建
Nung-kung (bank) 農工
Nung-shang (bank) 農商

Ou-shih yen-chiu hui 歐事研究會
Ou-yang Chen-sheng 歐陽振聲

Pai Yü-huan 白逾桓
p'ai 派
P'an Fu 潘復
Pao Kuei-ch'ing 鮑貴卿
Pei-ching kuo-min ts'ai-ping ts'u-chin
  hui 北京國民裁兵促進會
Peiyang 北洋
Peiyang pao-shang (bank) 北洋保商
Pen-pu kan-shih pu hsi-tse 本部幹事部細則
P'eng Yun-i 彭允彝
Pi-chih chü 幣制局
Pi Kuei-fang 畢桂芳
Pien Shou-ch'ing 邊守靖

Pien-yeh (bank) 邊業
Pien Yin-ch'ang 卞蔭昌
P'ing-i hui 評議會
P'u Tien-chün 蒲殿俊
P'u-i 溥儀

Sa Chen-ping 薩鎮冰
san-chiao t'ung-meng 三角同盟
Shan-hou ch'ou-pei ch'u 善後籌備處
Shan-hou hui-i 善後會議
shang cheng kuei-tao 上正軌道
Shang pao 商報
shang-p'u tu-pan 商埠督辦
shang-wu hui 商務會
Shen-chi yuan 審計院
Shen Hung-ying 沈鴻英
Shen pao 申報
sheng-chang 省長
Sheng Hsuan-huai 盛宣懷
shih-chiao kuan-hsi 世交關係
shih-i kuan-hsi 世誼關係
shih-sheng kuan-hsi 師生關係
Shih-shih hsin-pao 時事新報
shih-shih shang 實事上
shih-shih wen-t'i 實事問題
Shih Yü 施愚
shu 署
Shu-wu k'o 庶務課
ssu-chang 司長
suan-chang feng-ch'ao 算帳風潮
Sun Ch'uan-fang 孫傳芳
Sun Chung 孫鐘
Sun Hung-i 孫洪伊
Sun Jun-yü 孫潤宇
Sun Pao-ch'i 孫寶琦
Sun Tan-lin 孫丹林
Sze, Alfred Sao-ke (Shih Chao-chi) 施肇基

Ta-Ch'ing (dollar) 大清
Ta li-t'ang 大禮堂
Ta-li yuan 大理院
Ta-lu (bank) 大陸
Ta tsung-t'ung hsuan-chü fa 大總統選舉法
tai 代
T'an Chen 覃振
t'an-hua hui 談話會
T'an Jui-lin 譚瑞霖
T'an Li-sun 談荔孫

T'an Yen-k'ai 譚延闓
tang 黨
T'ang Chi-yao 唐繼堯
T'ang Chi-yü 唐繼虞
T'ang Erh-ho 湯爾和
T'ang Hua-lung 湯化龍
T'ang I 湯猗
T'ang Shao-i 唐紹儀
tao-te 道德
T'ao Li 陶立
T'ao-lun hsi 討論系
T'ao-lun hui 討論會
T'ao Pao-chin 陶保晉
T'ao-yuan 陶園
t'e-pieh hsing-cheng ch'ü 特別行政區
Terauchi 寺內
T'ien Chung-yü 田中玉
T'ien Wen-lieh 田文烈
T'ien Ying-huang 田應璜
Ting-kuo chün 定國軍
Ting Shih-to 丁世鐸
Ting Shih-yuan 丁士源
Ting Wen-chiang 丁文江
Ts'ai-cheng t'ao-lun wei-huan hui 財政討論委員會
Ts'ai Ch'eng-hsun 蔡成勳
ts'ai-kuan 裁官
Ts'ai-shen 財神
Ts'ai Yuan-p'ei 蔡元培
Ts'an-chan t'ung-chih she 參戰同志社
Ts'ao Chün 曹鈞
Ts'ao Ju-lin 曹汝霖
Ts'ao Jui 曹銳
Ts'ao K'un 曹錕
Ts'ao Ying 曹鍈
Ts'ao Yun-hsiang 曹雲祥
Ts'en Ch'un-hsuan 岑春煊
Tseng Kuo-fan 曾國藩
Tseng Yen 曾彥
Tseng Yü-chün 曾毓雋
Tso Tsung-t'ang 左宗棠
Tsu-chih fa 組織法
Tu Hsi-kuei 杜錫珪
Tuan Ch'i-jui 段祺瑞
Tuan Chih-kuei 段芝貴
Tuan Ho-fei (i.e., Tuan Ch'i-jui) 段合肥
Tuan-hsi 段系
tuli 督理

Tung K'ang 薰康
Tung-lu (bank) 東陸
t'ung-hsiang kuan-hsi 同鄉關係
t'ung-hsin ch'u 通信處
t'ung-hsueh kuan-hsi 同學關係
t'ung-i 統一
T'ung-i kung-ho tang 統一共和黨
T'ung-i tang 統一黨
t'ung-kao 通告
t'ung-liao kuan-hsi 同僚關係
T'ung-meng hui 同盟會
t'ung-shih hsia-yeh 同時下野
t'ung-tien 通電
tupan 督辦
tutu 都督
tzu 字
tz'u-ling 此令

Uchida 內田

Wai-Meng shih-i tu-pan 外蒙事誼督辦
Wan-hsi 皖系
Wang Chan-yuan 王占元
Wang Cheng-t'ing (C. T. Wang) 王正廷
Wang Ch'eng-pin 王承斌
Wang Chia-hsiang 王家襄
Wang Chih-lung 王郅隆
Wang Ching-ch'un 王景春
Wang Ch'ung-hui 王寵惠
Wang Huai-ch'ing 王懷慶
Wang I-shu 汪詒書
Wang I-t'ang 王揖唐
Wang Jen-wen 王人文
Wang K'o-min 王克敏
Wang Nai-pin 王迺斌
Wang Po-ch'ün 王伯群
Wang Shih-chen 王士珍
Wang Shu-nan 王樹枏
Wang Ta-hsieh 汪大燮
Wang Wen-hua 王文華
Wang Wen-pao 王文豹
Wang Yin-ch'uan 王印川
Wang Yu-lan 王有蘭
Wang Yu-ling 王有齡
Wang Yü-chih 王毓芝
Wen Ch'ün 文羣
Wen Tsung-yao 溫宗堯
Wen-tu k'o 文牘課

"Wo-men ti cheng-chih chu-chang" 我們的政治主張

Wu Ch'ao-shu (C.C. Wu) 伍朝樞

wu cheng-fu chuang-t'ai 無政府狀態

Wu Chi-sun 吳笈孫

Wu Ching-lien 吳景濂

Wu Kuang-hsin 吳光新

wu-li t'ung-i 武力統一

Wu-lu t'i-t'iao ch'u 五路提調處

Wu-ming (i.e., Lu Jung-t'ing) 武鳴

Wu P'ei-fu 吳佩孚

Wu Ping-hsiang 吳炳湘

wu-tang chu-i 無黨主義

Wu Ting-ch'ang 吳鼎昌

Wu T'ing-fang 伍廷芳

Wu Tse-sheng 烏澤生 (sometimes given as 聲)

Wu-tsu ho-p'ing hui 五族和平會

Wu-tsu shang-yeh yin-hang 五族商業銀行

Wu Tsung-lien 吳宗濂

Wu-wu t'ung-pao she 戊午同袍社

Wu Yü-lin 吳毓麟

ya-shui 牙稅

Ya-yuan 雅園

Yang Shan-te 楊善德

Yang Tseng-hsin 楊增新

Yang Yung-t'ai 楊永泰

Yao Chen 姚震

Yao Kuo-chen 姚國楨

Yeh Chü 葉舉

Yeh Kung-ch'o 葉恭綽

yen-ch'i shui 驗契稅

Yen-chiu hsi 研究系

yen-chiu p'ai-chao shui 烟酒牌照稅

yen-chiu shui 烟酒稅

Yen Hsi-shan 閻錫山

yen-hui 延會

Yen, W. W. (Yen Hui-ch'ing) 顏惠慶

Yien-yeh [Yen-yeh] (bank) 鹽業

yin-ch'in kuan-hsi 姻親關係

yin-hang kung-hui 銀行公會

yin-hao 銀號

yin-hua shui 印花稅

Yin Ju-li 殷汝驪

Yoshizawa 芳澤

Yu-ch'uan pu 郵傳部

yu-i 友誼

Yu-i k'o 游藝課

Yu Ts'ung-lung 由宗龍

yü-lun 輿論

Yü Pao-hsien 于寶軒

Yü Yu-jen 于右任

Yuan Hsiang-ch'eng (i.e., Yuan Shih-k'ai) 袁項城

yuan-lao 元老

Yuan Nai-kuan 袁乃寬

Yuan Shih-k'ai 袁世凱

Yung-yen pao 庸言報

INDEX

Able men cabinet, xvi, 193–204 *passim*, 222, 238–239

Accounts controversy (1918), 98n

Administration, central government, 14, 20, 32, 58, 108, 110, 140, 147, 155, 176; factions in ministries, 46; weakness and resources of, 59–64; roles of ministries, 66–69; political level in, 72–73, 191–192; section head level in, 73, 73n; financing of, 74–75, 79–80, 206, 207, 207n. *See also* Bureaucracy; Finance; Presidency; Prime ministership; specific ministries and bureaus

Administrative Court, 16

Aglen, Sir Francis, 75, 78, 88–90 *passim*, 206

Alliance, as a kind of political behavior, 35, 36, 39–42, 45, 47, 51, 55–58, 69, 92, 111–112, 113, 118–119, 120, 130, 136n, 147, 151n, 160n, 164, 167, 168–169, 174, 175, 191, 222, 225, 232, 253–261 *passim*

Altai, 164

American revolution, 1, 19

Anfu-Chihli war (1920), xvi, 3, 5, 165n, 166n, 176, 181n, 182, 205n, 221–222, 226, 237

Anfu Clique, 18, 107n, 117, 147n, 160, 232. *See also* Anfu Club; Tuan Ch'i-jui faction

Anfu Club, 16, 69, 97n, 115, 140, 164, 166n, 173–175, 213, 225, 226–232, 244, 244n, 253; in parliamentary elections, 97–98; strength in parliament, by province, 101–103; strength in parliament, overall, 103, 106n, 119–120; organization of, 106–110; role in 1918 presidential election, 117–123; and Ch'ien Neng-hsun cabinet, 141–142, 144–145; and peace talks, 146–148, 154, 155–157; and May Fourth Movement, 160–163; struggle with Chin Yun-p'eng in 1919–1920, 167–172

An-fu hu-t'ung, 106, 107, 107n

Anfu parliament. *See* Parliament

Anhwei, 52, 94, 101, 102–103, 107n, 108, 110, 118, 139, 140n, 144, 147, 148, 156, 157, 183n, 191, 211, 226, 227, 228, 229, 232

Anhwei Clique, 58, 226, 232

Anhwei military group, 226n

Arnhold Bros. and Co., Ltd., 197n

Audit Bureau, 136

Australia, 75n

Austria, 136, 196, 197, 243

Austrian Loans, 196–197, 199, 200

Authoritarianism, 1, 22, 26

Authority: justification of, 23; understanding of, 27; dependency on, 27n; not basis of factions, 32–34; of the father, 51; of provincial regimes, 99–100; of central government, 100, 125, 162n; alleged abuse of, 142

Banditry, 9, 44, 57, 60, 63n, 151, 151n, 206, 214, 214n

Bank of China, 84, 85, 137, 166n, 229, 250

Bankers' associations, 13–14, 88, 89n

Bank of Communications, 84, 85, 86–87, 119n, 166n, 245, 249–250, 251

Bank of Communications faction, 85n

Banks and banking, 9, 13, 16, 32, 44, 46, 53, 58, 71, 74, 137, 138, 147, 148, 155, 231, 244, 252–253; unit of account, xiii; foreign banks and customs revenue, 61, 83; charters, 68, 84–85; directors, 68, 86–87, 119n; new-style banks and government finance, 74–90, 192–193, 195, 206, 210; foreign banks in China, 83, 143n; joint Sino-foreign banks, 83n; Communications Clique role in, 86–88, 118, 118n–119n, 166, 249–250. *See also* Currency; Customs

Banque Industrielle de Chine, 81

Barker, Major Augustine, 197n

Bavelas, Alex, 34n

285